35-

Pound/Lewis

E. POUND

A N N O
XVII
VIA MARSALA 12-5

RAPALLO

Waal

My instink IZ/ you let thet portraT ALONE. Az Jim Whistler
said abaht shootink the artisk.

If you must diddle an MONKEY with problumbs you take a GNU
canvasss or paper and you do a ABstrakk dEEsign about

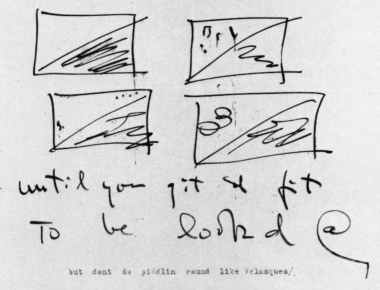

until you git it fit
To be lookd @

but dont do piddlin round like Velasques/.

three hosses hooves whaaar one orter be/ and Messin up
the paint in that thaaar north west corner.

yrz. EZ.

THE CORRESPONDENCE OF EZRA POUND

Pound/Lewis

The Letters of Ezra Pound
and Wyndham Lewis

EDITED BY TIMOTHY MATERER

A NEW DIRECTIONS BOOK

Manufactured in the United States of America
First published clothbound in 1985
Published simultaneously in Canada by Penguin Books Canada Limited

Library of Congress Cataloging in Publication Data
Pound, Ezra, 1885–1972
    Pound/Lewis, the correspondence of Ezra Pound and Wyndham Lewis.
(A New Directions Book)
    Bibliography: p. 307
    Includes index.
    1. Pound, Ezra, 1885–1972—Correspondence.   2. Lewis, Wyndham, 1882–1957—Correspondence.   3. Poets, American—20th century—Correspondence.   4. Authors, English—20th century—Correspondence.   5. Artists—Great Britain—Correspondence.
I. Materer, Timothy, 1940–   . II. Title.
PS3531.082Z488   1985   811'.52 [B]   85–3007
ISBN 0-8112-0932-6
New Directions Books are published for James Laughlin
by New Directions Publishing Corporation,
80 Eighth Avenue, New York 10011

Contents

Notes on the Editing

Edith Hamilton once told Ezra Pound of "a great Confucian scholar, such a scholar that he wrote a letter, and there was only one man in all China who could understand it. . . . That is aristocratic, like you, Mr. Pound." I have often thought of these words while editing this volume, and also of Pound's reply: "It is democratic as long as it provides that any one may have the opportunity to learn enough to read that letter." *Pound/Lewis* tries to provide this democratic opportunity, but the difficulties are considerable. One of the chief ones is that Pound from the late thirties on refers familiarly to events and personalities that are so private or obscure that even his correspondents do not recognize them. Close friends such as William Carlos Williams, T. S. Eliot, Ford Madox Ford, and Lewis himself all complained of the obscurity of his references. I have dealt with this problem in three ways. Brief identifications and clarifications are made in brackets in the text of the letters; endnotes provide more detailed information when necessary; and information on many references (chiefly to people) which may or may not interest the reader appear in the glossorial Index. Readers may decide for themselves if they wish to turn to the Index for a brief identification of someone's importance to Ezra Pound or Wyndham Lewis. I have tried to provide the essential information a reader needs to grasp the substance of these letters. Further information is available in the books and articles listed in the Bibliography.

An indication of the form and number of pages of each letter appears at the beginning of each letter. For example, TL indicates an unsigned typed letter and TLS a typed letter signed by the author. Other abbreviations used are: ALS—autograph letter signed; TNS—typed note signed; TCS—typed card signed; AN—autograph note; ANS—autograph note signed; PC—post card. "Pmk" indicates the postmark for the letter.

Only a facsimile edition, which would have to be enormously large, could show the vivid way Pound composed his letters to strike both the eye and the ear. However, we have tried at least to suggest the way Pound placed the words on the page through the following devices. Headings of both the Pound and Lewis letters reproduce as nearly as possible the form and placement of the original. Brief descriptions of the letterheads are given when significant, and supplied places and dates appear in brackets. Salutations reproduce the placement and punctuation of the original. In the body of the letter, indentations have been standardized in a relative fashion to conform as closely as possible to Pound's and Lewis's practice. When a new paragraph begins without indentation, an extra line space is inserted after the last line of the preceding paragraph.

Spelling and idiosyncratic orthography are reproduced as in the originals except for trivial spelling errors (such as Pound's "hypocricy" for *hypocrisy* and Lewis's "seige" for *siege*) and transpositions such as "hte" for *the. Sic* is used in a few cases where confusion might otherwise result. Pound's and Lewis's spelling of proper names was often an indication of how well they knew or how much they disliked certain people. Names are therefore given as Pound and Lewis spelled them with the correct spellings in brackets. Capitalizations appear as in the originals. Pound's eccentric punctuation is also followed, with the exception of the extra spacing which he sometimes put before and after quotation marks and before periods. Significant holograph and typed insertions are placed in angle brackets. Conjectural readings are followed by bracketed question marks. Foreign words or phrases are translated within brackets only when the reader may not otherwise understand that the word or phrase is foreign. Cross-outs are restored as editorial insertions when significant by enclosing the material in brackets and identifying it with the designation *"crossout."* Ellipses are reproduced as in the originals. There are no editorial ellipses because every letter in this collection is reproduced in its entirety.

In the closings and signatures, all indentations are standardized to conform as closely as possible to the original. Signatures are located in relation to the closing in approximation of Pound's and Lewis's usage. Line spacing of closings has also been standardized. Closing signatures and dates (if given at the end of the letter) are reproduced as in the original.

With one exception, Pound's letters to Lewis are in the Wyndham Lewis Collection of the Olin Library, Cornell University. The exception is Letter 231, which is in the Agnes Bedford Collection at Simon Fraser University. This letter or note was included in a letter to Agnes Bedford, and I believe it should be considered a letter to Lewis. (Many of Pound's letters to Bedford contain material that Pound wished her to show to Lewis.) Most of Lewis's letters to Pound are in the Pound Archive of the Collection of American Literature, Beinecke Rare Book and Manuscript Library, Yale University. There are ten letters of Lewis to Pound in the Ezra Pound Collection at the Lilly Library, Indiana University: 111, 188, 194, 196, 198, 201, 205, 226, 228, 233. One letter (186) is from the Ezra Pound Collection at the Humanities Research Center, University of Texas. One letter (126) and two drafts for letters (203, 213) are from the Wyndham Lewis Collection at Cornell, and a carbon of a letter at Cornell is used for Letter 242.

Most of the letters here are published for the first time. Ten to Lewis were published in *The Letters of Ezra Pound, 1907–1941,* ed. D. D. Paige. Following the numerical order of Paige's edition, they correspond to the following letters in the present volume: Nos. 24, 41, 43, 50, 85, 99, 106, 108, 117, 180. Twenty-three letters of Lewis (many of them based on the carbons which were the only copies then available) were published in *The Letters of Wyndham Lewis,* ed. W. K. Rose. They correspond to the following letters in this collection: 2, 11, 34, 55, 56, 81, 89, 91, 96, 100, 126, 186, 188, 190, 194, 196, 198, 205, 213, 226, 239, 242, 245.

Every scholarly book is a collaboration to some degree, but a collection of letters by two writers of this century is happily a collaboration with the writers' friends and acquaintances as well as with other scholars in the field. (The virtues of this edition are mostly theirs and the editorial faults entirely mine.) My thanks go first to Omar Pound and Mary de Rachewiltz, who both read the complete manuscript and suggested revisions that I could have received from no one else. I am equally indebted to Donald Gallup, without whom I could not have surmounted (and I hope that I have) the difficulty of transcribing Lewis's letters. Alan Munton was unfailingly perceptive in helping me through the mysteries of Lewis's handwriting and in understanding his references. Any student of Pound's works is indebted to the author of *The Life of Ezra Pound,* Noel Stock; and he was always ready to answer my questions or to point to further sources to explore. I also relied upon W. K. Rose's edition of *The Letters of Wyndham Lewis,* Jeffrey Meyers's *The Enemy: A Biography of Wyndham Lewis,* and three valuable bibliographies: Donald Gallup's *Ezra Pound: A Bibliography;* Omar Pound's and Philip Grover's *Wyndham Lewis: A Descriptive Bibliography;* and Bradford Morrow's and Bernard Lafourcade's *A Bibliography of the Writings of Wyndham Lewis.* Walter Michel's *Wyndham Lewis: Paintings and Drawings* was also essential. Michel's reference numbers for the art works by Lewis mentioned in this volume are found in the glossorial Index under "Lewis, Wyndham. Paintings and Drawings." Reproductions of most of the works cited are in Michel's book.

I thank the following for assisting me to use the resources of their libraries: Donald Eddy, librarian, and Lucy Burgess of the Olin Library, Cornell University; David Schoonover, curator of the American Literature Collection, Bienecke Rare Book and Manuscript Library, Yale University;

Ellen S. Dunlap, research librarian, Humanities Research Center, University of Texas; Saundra Taylor, curator of manuscripts, and Virginia Lowell Mauck of the Lilly Library, University of Indiana; and Percilla Groves, Special Collections, Simon Fraser University Library. I am grateful as well to my colleagues at the University of Missouri–Columbia, who patiently squinted at photocopies, listened to peculiar questions and often gave invaluable answers: M. Bonner Mitchell, Tom Quirk, Russ Meyer, Howard Hinkel, Bob Sattelmeyer, and Mary Lago. Clair Willcox has given me expert help in creating the Index and Bibliography. Helga Meyer typed the manuscript with great care, and Marilynn Keil painstakingly typed the revisions. I would also like to thank Victor Cassidy, Walter Michel, William French, Massimo Bacigalupo, Carroll F. Terrell, and James Laughlin for valuable assistance. Special thanks are due my wife Barbara for making our many hours of proofreading a pleasant time. Research for this book was funded in part by the American Council of Learned Societies and the Research Council of the Graduate School, University of Missouri–Columbia.

For their generous support of Lewis studies, I am grateful to the Wyndham Lewis Trust: J. W. Dolman, C. J. Fox, and O. S. Pound.

"great Confucian scholar": This anecdote is found in Eustace Mullins, *This Difficult Individual, Ezra Pound,* pp. 307–9.

Introduction
Doppelgänger: Ezra Pound in His Letters

If a personal letter is an attempt "to give back a reflection of the other person," as Virginia Woolf thought, the letters of Ezra Pound are not "personal" in any usual sense. He is utterly unlike such famous letter writers of English literature as Lord Byron and D. H. Lawrence, who are rich in anecdotes and observations about everyday life. Not even James Joyce's letters are so limited to the world of writing and publishing. As a correspondent Pound is what Wyndham Lewis called him, a "Rock Drill," blasting away tirelessly to move someone to some good action for the republic of letters. The letters Pound himself includes in his *Cantos,* from the ones found in Sigismondo Malatesta's postbag to those written by John Adams, usually concern practical rather than personal matters. Lewis scarcely exaggerated when he said that Pound's letters "can be of no interest to anyone but a writer. It is a craftsman speaking throughout about his craft, and the single-minded concentration is magnificent." It is magnificent because his involvement in the life of literature, unlike Joyce's, is impersonal; he is as unselfishly interested in furthering the careers of other writers as he is in furthering his own. He felt that any number of writers, from Iris Barry to T. S. Eliot, needed "Uncle Ez" to look after them. Many letters in this collection demonstrate his generosity; for instance his self-effacement when he recommended Lewis to the Guggenheim Foundation in 1925 without a thought of applying for a fellowship himself is characteristic.

His self-effacement, however, is matched by a paradoxical self-assertion that could be annoying as well as "magnificent." The assumption behind almost any letter by Ezra Pound is that the fate of culture, and not just literary culture, depends on his actions; and this assumption could be disturbing if his current plan was to set up an embarrassing charitable fund, as he wished to do for Eliot, or an impractical publicity scheme, as he often tried to do for Wyndham Lewis. Lewis was profoundly troubled by the contradictory quality of Pound's character and considered the problem in both his essays and his fiction. In his review of Pound's *Selected Letters,* he wrote that the "tone of the letters almost from the beginning is authoritarian, not to say pontificatory," and he thought it seemed a "rather strange tone for the author of *Cathay,"* who was the most restrained and sensitive of lyricists. He attributes this disjunction to Pound's Americanism: "If we remember that the voice of the Bull Moose president resounded in his young days, it is perhaps less to be wondered at that Ezra himself should have wished to wield the 'Big Stick.'" Lewis sees Pound as a man, inherently gentle and impersonal, who strains to take on a persona which is antithetical to his true nature. This characterization of Pound might surprise many of the poet's readers, but we need to explore Lewis's view of Pound in order to understand the tone of their correspondence.

As the author of *Personae,* the title of his collected shorter poems as well as a volume of 1909, Pound adopted the personae of the great creative spirits of the past. He did so for the same reason that W. B. Yeats put on his masks. Yeats considered himself at heart a dreamy, lyric poet, but he could put on the mask of the public figure and play the role convincingly. In "Ego Dominus Tuus," Yeats writes that the result of the "modern hope" of finding the self is that

> We have lit upon the gentle, sensitive mind
> And lost the old nonchalance of the hand. . . .

Yeats's spokesman proposes to lose the "timid, entangled" self by adopting a persona which, even though it is his "double," shall "prove of all imaginable things/The most unlike, being my anti-self. . . ." Pound wanted to transcend his limitations in this way, but the strain on his personality was greater than it was for Yeats because Pound took his roles more seriously. He wore his masks with little of Yeats's self-awareness and irony.

Yet his ability to take on a variety of roles was even greater than Yeats's. As Lewis wrote of Pound, *"By himself* he would seem to have neither any convictions nor eyes in his head. . . . Yet when he can get into the skin of somebody else, of power and renown, a Propertius or an Arnaut Daniel, he becomes a lion or a lynx on the spot." When Lewis painted Pound's portrait in 1919, he portrayed him as a larger-than-life figure in a Renaissance pose and not as a contemporary. Pound's character is like that of the poet as John Keats describes it: "he has no Identity—he is continually . . . filling some other body." Pound could have shared Keats's confusion at times about whether he was speaking from his own self or "from some character in whose soul I now live." Pound writes in the early poem "Histrion":

> Thus am I Dante for a space and am
> One François Villon, ballad-lord and thief

> Or am such holy ones I may not write,
> Lest blasphemy be writ against my name. . . .

In a poem called "On His Own Face in a Glass," he says that the "ribald company" and "saintly host" he sees within the mirror give him no sense of his own self. Pound related his technique as a lyric poet to this concern with the self in his "Vorticism" essay of 1914: "In the 'search for oneself,' in the search for 'sincere self-expression,' one gropes, one finds some seeming verity. One says 'I am' this, that, or the other, and with the words scarcely uttered one ceases to be that thing. I began this search for the real in a book called *Personae,* casting off, as it were, complete masks of the self in each poem."

To the Villon and Dante of "Histrion," one could thus add the whole cast of *Personae,* including Cino, Piere Vidal, Paracelsus (one of the "holy ones"), and of course Sextus Propertius and Hugh Selwyn Mauberley. Mauberley, however, is unusual among Pound's personae because he is a modern figure and a minor poet. Pound wanted to bury and not revive Mauberley, just as he said that the Mauberley persona wanted to "bury" Ezra Pound and get "rid of all his troublesome energies." The character of Mauberley reveals the danger of assuming multiple personae. Mauberley suffers from the fracturing of his ego and becomes

> A consciousness disjunct,
> Being but this overblotted
> Series
> Of intermittences. . . .

To avoid Mauberley's fate, Pound wanted to unify his sensibility through creating a long poem—an epic and not a series of lyrics. He envied the achievement of *The Waste Land* and admitted to Eliot his concern that he was not creating an original work himself but instead was "always exuding my deformative secretions in my own stuff, and never getting an outline. I go into nacre and objet d'art." With James Joyce he was even more self-questioning and wrote to him of his concern that he was "perhaps better at digging up corpses of let us say Li Po, or more lately Sextus Propertius, than in preserving this bitched mess of modernity." By creating a long poem he would no longer drift like Mauberley but master events and achieve a "hard outline." In the original Canto I, in which he addresses his poetic model Robert Browning, Pound writes that he has more difficulty in putting his life into a poem than Browning had in *Sordello:*

> You had one whole man?
> And I have many fragments, less worth? Less worth?

> Ah, had you quite my age, quite such a beastly
>   and cantankerous age?
> You had some basis, had some set belief.

To write an epic that would speak for the modern age may seem an unlikely ambition for a man who is so unsure of the character of his age and
his identity within it. Nevertheless, the very analysis Pound gives to this
problem shows that he is preparing to overcome it, if only by the sheer
assertion of his will. He was determined to impose order on both his
poetic and political concerns and to fashion out of his personae a poetic
character capable of unifying his experience.

Charles Olson appreciated the dimensions as well as the dangers of
Pound's ambition when he described his elimination of historical time in
the *Cantos:* "He has driven through it so sharply by the beak of his ego,
that, he has turned time into what we must now have, space & its live air."
All of Pound's personae and characters, from Li Po to Jefferson and
Mussolini are contemporary with him; and Pound assumes, according to
Olson, that he can "outtalk them all." Pound makes them all his contemporaries through "his ego: his single emotion breaks all down to his equals
or inferiors (so far as I can see only two, possibly, are admitted, by him,
to be his betters—Confucius, & Dante.)" Olson praises Pound's attempt
to escape his historical limits, but the younger poet seeks an alternative to
the "ego-position" because this position allows the poet to speak only for
himself and so without epic authority. He argues that Pound's protest
against the tyranny of modern civilization is merely bohemian or aesthetic
because it is so personal or, at most, a protest merely on behalf of the
artist.

To both Charles Olson and Wyndham Lewis, the result of Pound's assertion of his ego was the "tragic fracture," as Lewis called it, of his personality. W. B. Yeats had predicted in a general way the direction Pound's
personae were taking him. In his inventory of human types in *A Vision,*
Yeats described Pound as a man of Phase 12, who enjoys "immense
energy" and creativity. If the man of this phase chooses the wrong mask,
however, he is driven "into all sorts of temporary ambitions, opposed to
his nature [which] he defends by some kind of superficial intellectual action, the pamphlet, the violent speech. . . . He spends his life in oscilla-
tion between the violent assertion of some commonplace pose, and a dog-
matism which means nothing apart from the circumstance that created it."
Pound's economic pamphlets, his support of Mussolini, and his radio
speeches during World War II brought him to St. Elizabeths Hospital in

Washington, D.C., when he was judged mentally unfit to stand trial for treason. After meeting Pound at St. Elizabeths in 1946, Charles Olson wrote: "In Pound I am confronted by the tragic Double of our day. He is the demonstration of our duality. In language and form he is as forward, as much the revolutionist as Lenin. But in social, economic and political action he is as retrogressive as the Czar." The conception of the double also came to Lewis, who expressed his feelings about Pound's development in his "Doppelgänger: A Story" of 1954.

Although the satire in "Doppelgänger" is mild, especially by Lewis's standards, Lewis is so fearful of seeming unfair to his old friend that he begins the story with a fictional preface in which the author of "Doppelgänger" tells his editor that he does not wish to "debunk" Pound, or as he is called in the story, Thaddeus Trunk. The preface concludes:

> The shallow or the inexperienced might absolutely misunderstand this story. Let me add, therefore, that Trunk is a very majestic Word-Man, a great poet. . . . And he is a man who has so perfect a devotion to litera-ture, that you will never hear from him a valuation which is tainted with the personal. His creative work . . . benefits by the same detachment. Any mistakes of judgement he may have made derive merely from the occasional frailty of his reason.

This "frailty" leads Trunk to take on the persona of a rugged, outspoken Yankee to impress the disciples who surround him at his mountain-top cabin, as the group Pound called *les jeunes* surrounded him at St. Eliza-beths. Solitude is required to create great art, Lewis writes, but Thaddeus Trunk "was almost submerged, spiritually, by a horde of anonymous be-ings. Yes, through his childish mania for publicity, poor Trunk brought a multitude up onto the mountains, polluting the air; and he may be regarded as a victim of the Public." To impress his public he distorts his character:

> He had always the itch to offer advice, to tell others what to do with their lives, to teach them how to Write, to teach them how to Read. He realized that this could not be done, unless it were done comically. And so, puffing a little through his moustache, and frowning portentously, he would say, "Listen to what your old bourgeois Papa tells yew!" or something of that kind.

One of Trunk's visitors introduces himself as a near relation, although the exact relationship is never clear, and tension between them quickly de-velops as the "Stranger" shows that he knows more than Trunk about everything from Catullus to Chinese characters. Soon the Stranger is writ-ing improved versions of the poems Trunk himself is trying to write. As

the Stranger proves himself calm and rational where Trunk is emotional
and overexcited, the story begins to resemble Edgar Allan Poe's "William
Wilson," where Wilson's double is his moral superior. But the conclusion
of Lewis's story is not so violent as Poe's. The final break between the
poet and the Stranger is over Trunk's wife Stella, who is clearly modeled
on Dorothy Pound. Lewis had been Dorothy's friend since 1912, when
they both painted in the abstract "Vorticist" style, and the story expresses
his concern for her suffering during Pound's imprisonment. When Stella
sees that the Stranger is everything "Uncle Thad" is minus the egotistic
posturing, she leaves him on his mountain top with his immature followers
and returns to civilization with the Stranger. Trunk's pose had been held
so long that it became part of him, "like the extraordinary grimaces some
men affect, until, two-thirds of the way through life, the face integrally includes the grimace." Only a "shell" of Thaddeus Trunk is left on the
crowded mountain top.

Lewis's sense that the "real" Pound is a man of "natural detachment"
would no doubt have seemed mistaken to many of Pound's friends. William
Carlos Williams, for example, saw no dramatic break in Pound's character
but rather a development in which, as he wrote in 1939, his "youthful
faults are creeping up on him fast." But there's no question here of achiev-
ing an accurate picture of Pound. He himself wrote of human identity as
"shifting changes,/ A broken bundle of mirrors. . . ." Lewis gives us
only a partial reflection of Pound as the "other person," but their correspondence shows how he arrived at this impression.

Pound's early letters to Lewis show him in what Lewis believes to
be his natural role of a man with quiet and scholarly tastes. He is the
man revealed in the 1918 collection *Pavannes and Divisions,* the translator
of the dialogues of Fontenelle, and satirist of the poem in couplets
"L'Homme Moyen Sensuel." Pound and Lewis first met in a group of
scholars and artists who lunched at the Vienna Café near the British Museum, and later they would meet at Ford Madox Ford's South Lodge. They
grew closer when they founded the movement called "Vorticism" and col-
laborated on its journal, *BLAST.* Their earliest letters concern contributions to *BLAST* from such artists as T. S. Eliot and the sculptor Henri
Gaudier-Brzeska. *BLAST,* however, ran only for two issues before the far
greater explosion of World War I ended its avant-garde career. The combative Lewis enlisted as soon as he recovered from a long illness in 1915,
and Pound generously offered to look after Lewis's affairs when he left
London. Lewis soon regretted enlisting without waiting for an officer's
commission. Once he started training as a bombardier, or gunner, he

chafed under his superiors and felt they were holding him back from a commission. When he complained bitterly, Pound replied with practical advice that shows how well he understood Lewis's irascible character: "I can but ask you to contemplate the position as deeply as you are able, and that without passion, and from all points of view. [. . .] For the rest, dont be more irritating to your unfortunate 'superior' officers than you find absolutely necessary to your peace of mind, or at least try not to be." (Letter 41.)

In addition to using the few influential contacts he still had to help Lewis get a military commission, Pound was selling Lewis's paintings and trying to find a publisher for his novel, *Tarr*. He had sold Lewis's "Timon of Athens" drawings to John Quinn and hoped he would buy Lewis's large canvas "Kermesse" once he got used to Lewis's semi-abstract style. Lewis was sincerely grateful, but his pay as an enlisted man was so low that he often pestered Pound about the Quinn money. Pound replied with firmness and good humor: "My position is a little embarrassing as I have constantly to approach you in the paternal, admonitory, cautionary, epicierish blood-guttily INartistic angle." (Letter 49.)

In these early letters we see how Ernest Hemingway could describe Pound as "a sort of saint." This is the period in which Pound is attempting to get not only Lewis's but James Joyce's first novel published, selling both Lewis's and Gaudier-Brzeska's art works to John Quinn, launching T. S. Eliot in his literary career, as well as writing his own great poems *Homage to Sextus Propertius* and *Hugh Selwyn Mauberley*. A concern for the public good rather than personal gain runs throughout his correspondence. In a letter of 1922 to Lewis, in which he describes the Bel Esprit plan which was to give Eliot and other writers enough money to write without financial pressures, Pound frankly told Lewis that he was not a likely candidate for the scheme: "Certainly can't start on you – as you have to the public eye had nothing but leisure for years – nothing to prevent or to have prevented your doing any damn thing you liked – save yr. habit of fuss & of having a private life & allowing it to intrude on yr. attention." (Letter 108.) Pound was again perceptive about Lewis, whose obsessive secrecy and tangled personal relationships immensely complicated his career. Yet Pound's suggestion that one's private life can "intrude," as if it were a dubious luxury, is extremely revealing. Only Pound's exalted sense of the artist's role in society could account for this statement. He also scolded Harriet Monroe for having a private life when she was considering closing down *Poetry* magazine rather than have it continue without her. The letter opens with typical abruptness and frankness: "Dear Harriet: The intelligence of the nation more important than the comfort or life of any one individual or the bodily life of a whole generation." As a "responsible intellect," Pound objects to her plan to abandon *Poetry* out of personal motives: "merely because you have a sister in Cheefoo or because there are a few of your friends it would be pleasanter to feed or spare than to shoot."

Pound was undoubtedly right about *Poetry,* and his argument reveals the seriousness of a great artist. He also appealed to William Carlos Williams to rise above the merely personal when Williams was offended by some criticism Pound made of him. He told Williams that his reaction was unworthy of him and typical only of a lesser writer such as Skipwith Cannéll: "But really this 'old friend' hurt feeling business is too Skipwith-cannéllish, it is *peu vous.* I demand of you more robustezza." The dislike of the personal is of course behind his theory that poetry presents "equations for the emotions" and is not merely personal. In 1933 he refused William Rose Benèt's request to contribute to an anthology in which the poets comment on their own work, which Pound dismissed as "god damn'd sob stuff, personal touch, absolutely, absolutely anything, to shield yr. booblik from fact, what is printed on page." These opinions fed his anti-psychological bias, whether against Freud and Jung or self-conscious writers such as Proust and Virginia Woolf. He wrote to Lewis of the "Viennese sewage" which was "in fact hoax for paralyzing the will of the victim, like the wopse or whatsodam that lays egg in caterpillar, thru providing MEAT fer its progeny." (Letter 224.) His de-emphasis of psychological reality corresponded to an overvaluation of economic reality. He scorned "people fussing with in'nards which are merely the result of economic pressure" and dismissed "Hamlet's melancholy" as "the problem of the renaissance dyspeptic." The irony of Pound's mental breakdown is that he steadily underrated the importance of the merely psychological.

The "tragic fracture" of Pound's character was for Lewis a sudden eruption of "molten material." Although this opinion no doubt overdramatizes the change that took place, the nearly hysterical tone of Pound's letters in 1936 gives some evidence for it. In December 1936, Pound sent Lewis a manifesto in the style of the 1914 *BLAST* which he wanted Lewis and others to sign and Eliot to publish in the *Criterion. BLAST* had urged the Vorticists to "Kill John BULL with Art," but Pound would no longer confine his aggressiveness to art. The letter's opening sentence refers to pictures of Prime Minister Stanley Baldwin in the newspapers: "Waaal ole SawBUKK: When a furriner looks at Baldwin's MOOG in dh' wypers he SEES why you orter KILL J. BULL. [. . . The enclosed] refers to a Blast

by the undersigned/ intended as opining GUN IF the very reverend episcopal ELYot [T. S. Eliot] will print it. I trust it will (IF it passes the edtr/
the 'ed=eater, the deaditor) do more good than harm or at any rate cheer
the worthy and infastidiate the opposers of light." (Letter 160.) The hard-
ening of Pound's attitudes is seen in the phrase "opposers of light" for
those who merely disagree with his economic ideas, and later passages in
the letter reveal an ominous enthusiasm for Italy's invasion of Abyssinia.
When Lewis refused to join him in any of his economic schemes, Pound
was not offended but kept bombarding him with letters that became in-
creasingly violent and anti-Semitic. To Lewis it seemed that the Pound he
once knew had departed as finally as the Stranger leaves Thaddeus Trunk
in "Doppelgänger."

To say that Pound lost the practical sense that made him the great leader
of the revolution in modern poetry does not mean that he also lost his
generosity and unselfishness. Nor did the humiliation of arrest and imprisonment after World War II alter his convictions or break his spirit.
The accusation of treason made against him was the greatest threat to his
identity imaginable. As a prisoner in St. Elizabeths Hospital for the criminally insane, he referred to himself as "the anonymous" (Letter 204) because he was without legal rights. He faced these conditions with the old
assertiveness. His drive and goodwill were still intact, though often in mis-
directed forms. His energy was poured into disseminating economic rather
than literary innovations through such publications as *Current, Strike,* and
Four Pages rather than *The Egoist* and *The Little Review.* He wanted to
draw Lewis into his campaigns by publishing extracts from Lewis's works
in the Square Dollar pamphlet series that two of his economic disciples
were publishing. A passage from a letter of 1951, in which Pound urges
Lewis to contribute to the series, shows that Pound's charm and goodwill
had not diminished. The passage also demonstrates, through its concluding
pun, that Pound's verbal play was still brilliant: "The Sq/$ pair are ready
to be of USE. it dont mean much spondooliks, but it does mean 10%
royalty AND personal distribution to the best grade of peruzer. [. . .]
Curiosity, damBit, KU-RI-osity / as to source of lies / of slanders/ W.L.
has occasionally stimulated thought / let him steer the good guys onto
CURiosity. Hownd-dawgz on trail." (Letter 221.) Lewis complained that
in the letters from St. Elizabeths Pound's "egotism forbids him to examine,
much less accept, other's mentality. He is a pigheaded dominy, but a
benevolent one." The benevolence can even be detected behind the violence of his opinions. For he was convinced that mankind was inherently
good—he scorned "the original sin racket" in Canto 97—and that it was

only economic and political systems that corrupted humanity. When Pound can free his mind from his economic obsessions, he recovers his artistic power. One sees this recovery not only in passages throughout the *Rock-Drill* and *Thrones* Cantos but also in some at least of his late letters. In one of the last letters he wrote to Lewis, Pound meditates on Plotinus's distinction of *Eidos* (form) and *Eikon* (likeness), which he relates to the issues raised in the Imagist program of 1913. The poetic theory he discussed with Lewis a half-century earlier was still a rich source of contemplation. Letter 251 concludes:

> easy enough to sink into clichés re/ Plato's ideas etc.
> however, shapes there before you can think
> and the similitudes imitated.
>   basta.
>   saluti   EZ

The contrast between the contemplative poet and the economic pundit returns us to the sense that Lewis and Olson had of Pound's doubleness. Their concept of the double does not "explain" Pound's development but rather expresses their shock and concern with the drastic consequences of Pound's fate. However, the insight behind their idea is that Pound projected on the world an aggressive persona which, like the doubles in a Dostoevsky or E. T. A. Hoffman tale, eventually dominates the original self. Pound himself grasped the relevance of this theme to his own career. Olson records that while at St. Elizabeths Pound brooded on Henry James's story of a double, "The Jolly Corner." Like T. S. Eliot, Pound was fascinated by this tale in which an American expatriate speculates on what he might have been like had he never left America. Its theme of a split between power and refinement is prophetic of Pound's career.

The protagonist of "The Jolly Corner," Spencer Brydon, leaves America as a young man and returns thirty years later. To the Americans he now meets, he seems to have led a "selfish frivolous scandalous life" in Europe. His clairvoyant lady friend is not so critical, but tells him that had he stayed in America "you'd have had power." He traded power for sensitivity and culture, but also perhaps for over-refinement and decadence. Although he eventually wins his lady, Spencer Brydon is essentially one of James's sensitive gentlemen, such as John Marcher or Lambert Strether, from whom the character type of Pound's Hugh Selwyn Mauberley descends. Brydon has the Mauberley-like fear that he has "drifted precipitate" by living a life without outward accomplishments. He feels that he will meet his double, the man he might have been if he had not left America, in his empty family home. When he finally meets his ghostly double at dawn, he feels in this hard, elegant figure with its mutilated hand a force "evil, odious, blatant, vulgar." Yet when the spectre advances "as for aggression," he also feels a "roused passion of a life larger than his own, a rage of personality before which his own collapsed. . . ." Brydon learns that the vulgar and evil qualities of the double are nevertheless integral to "a life larger than his own," and here James's theme is relevant to the case of Ezra Pound.

Pound wanted and did not achieve political power, but he did acquire the power indicated by the double's "rage of personality." Could Pound have written the *Cantos* without this "roused passion"? He needed it to support his poetic career as surely as he needed the historical and economic sections of the *Cantos* as background for its great lyric and elegiac passages. There was no middle ground, as there was for Henry James, between passionate but violent achievement and a humane but ineffectual sensitivity. He became a man with the "roused passion" that sustained one of the great achievements of modern poetry. But James's vision of the aggressive double, with its wounded appearance, suggests the immense personal cost for Pound of this assertion of self.

Notes

"other person": The Letters of Virginia Woolf, IV: 1929–31, ed. Nigel Nicolson, p. 98.

"single-minded concentration": Wyndham Lewis, "The Rock Drill," in *Ezra Pound: Perspectives*, p. 201.

" 'Big Stick' ": Ibid., p. 200.

"old nonchalance": W. B. Yeats, "Ego Dominus Tuus," *The Collected Poems,* pp. 157–59.

"on the spot": Lewis, *Time and Western Man,* p. 86.

"I now live": Selected Letters of John Keats, ed. Robert Pack, pp. 113–14.

"against my name": Ezra Pound, "Histrion," *Collected Early Poems of Ezra Pound,* p. 71.

his own self: "On His Own Face in a Glass," *Ibid.,* pp. 34–35.

"complete masks of the self": Pound, "Vorticism," in *Gaudier-Brzeska: A Memoir,* p. 85.

"troublesome energies": Quoted in K. K. Ruthven, ed., *A Guide to Ezra Pound's Personae,* p. 126.

"intermittences": Pound, *Hugh Selwyn Mauberley,* in *Persona: Collected Shorter Poems,* p. 203.

"objet d'art": Selected Letters of Ezra Pound, ed. D. D. Paige, p. 48.

"mess of modernity": Pound/Joyce, ed. Forrest Read, p. 48.

"set belief": Pound, "Three Cantos," *Poetry* 10 (June 1917): 115.

"live air": Charles Olson, *Selected Writings,* ed. Robert Creeley, p. 82.

"Confucius, & Dante": Ibid., pp. 81–82.

"tragic fracture": Lewis uses the phrase in his new novel *Self Condemned* (p. 402) to describe René Harding, whose character is based in part on Pound's.

"circumstance that created it": W. B. Yeats, *A Vision,* p. 128. According to Richard Ellmann in Chapter IV of *Eminent Domain,* Yeats later moved (and demoted) Pound to Phase 23.

"as the Czar": Charles Olson and Ezra Pound: *An Encounter at St. Elizabeths,* ed. Catherine Seelye, p. 53.

"frailty of his reason": Lewis, "Doppelgänger: A Story," in *Unlucky for Pringle: Unpublished and Other Stories,* eds. C. J. Fox and Robert T. Chapman, p. 207. "Thaddeus" was the first name of Pound's paternal grandfather.

"something of that kind": Ibid., p. 299.

"includes the grimace": Ibid., p. 211.

"youthful faults": The Selected Letters of William Carlos Williams, ed. John C. Thirlwall, p. 182.

"bundle of mirrors": Pound, "Near Perigord," *Personae: Collected Shorter Poems,* p. 157.

"sort of saint": Ernest Hemingway, *A Moveable Feast,* p. 108.

"than to shoot": Selected Letters of Ezra Pound, p. 237.

"robustezza": Ibid., p. 124.

"on page": Ibid., p. 224.

"renaissance dyspeptic": Ibid., p. 252; *ABC of Economics,* p. 18.

"benevolent one": The Letters of Wyndham Lewis, ed. W. K. Rose, p. 462.

"rage of personality": Henry James, "The Jolly Corner," in *Henry James: Selected Fiction,* pp. 576–77.

Part I
Blasting
1914-1917

Mr Lewis had been to Spain
       Mr Binyon's young prodigies
pronounced the word: Penthesilea
          There were mysterious figures
that emerged from recondite recesses
       and ate at the WIENER CAFÉ. . . .

               Canto LXXX/ p. 506

Ezra Pound met Wyndham Lewis in 1909 during what he called the "British Museum era," a golden though rather stuffy age when scholars, artists, and museum officials would meet beneath the glass ceiling of the Vienna Café on New Oxford Street. As he recalls in *The Pisan Cantos,* Pound met Lewis through Laurence Binyon, an Orientalist and keeper of prints and drawings at the museum as well as a poet and translator:

> So it is to Mr. Binyon that I owe, initially,
> Mr Lewis, Mr P. Wyndham Lewis. His bull-dog, me,
>   as it were against old Sturge M's bull-dog. . . . (Canto 80, p. 507)

Like Binyon, T. Sturge Moore the poet and artist was of a generation earlier than Pound's and Lewis's. Neither of these Edwardian poets needed or deserved "bull-dogs" to defend or advance their work. The image more accurately reflects the lifelong loyalty and respect the younger men felt for the older. Both Binyon and Sturge Moore stood for creativity polished by learning and seemed to represent a time when talent had ample time to ripen. Pound associated the phrase "Slowness is beauty" (Canto 87, p. 572) with Binyon, and in a letter to Sturge Moore in 1941 Lewis re-called "the last days of the Victorian world of artificial peacefulness . . . when you used to sit on one side of your work-table and I on the other, and we would talk with trees and creepers of the placid Hampstead domesticity beyond the windows. . . ."

In 1909 Pound was twenty-four and had been in England only a year; Lewis was twenty-seven and though his first six years were spent in America, he was educated in England at Rugby and the Slade School of Art in London, where he was a brilliant but undisciplined scholarship student. After leaving the Slade in 1901, he traveled widely and studied art in Munich and Paris. In 1909 he had just returned from a long residence in Paris and was still (as he later called himself) an "idle student," although in that year he had published three stories in Ford Madox Ford's *English Review* and had many works in manuscript. As his letters to Sturge Moore show, he was then laboriously writing and rewriting an autobiographical novel about his life in the Paris art world. Sturge Moore encouraged

Lewis's efforts, but it is significant that it was only through Pound that the novel *Tarr* was finally published in 1918. Despite his youth and newness to the literary scene, Pound could energize London's artistic life more effectively than could the Englishmen themselves. Indeed it was Pound's energy and youth that made him, as Lewis remembers, suspect to the Vienna Café group:

> The British in question were not of the impressionable kind—hated above
> all things being impressed and people who wished to impress them. I may add
> that they also disapproved of Americans. . . . As to learning, those
> possessing it usually did nothing with it, and he showed them its uses (how-
> ever faulty his own may have been). But Pound arrived as an unassimilable
> and aggressive stranger: with his Imagism he became aesthetically a
> troublesome rebel.

As Pound's Imagism was bringing British poetry into the modern world, Lewis was taking charge of the modern movement in painting. From 1911–12 he belonged to the Camden Town Group, which had advanced as a movement only as far as French Impressionism. In 1912 he exhibited in Roger Fry's Second Post-Impressionist Exhibition and joined Fry's Omega Workshops in July 1913. But the Omega style, as represented by the paintings of Duncan Grant and Fry himself, seemed timidly representational and dominated by French standards. After a quarrel with Fry, Lewis broke from the group along with the painters Edward Wadsworth, Frederick Etchells, and Cuthbert Hamilton. In a public letter they denounced the Omega's "Prettiness, with its mid-Victorian languish of the neck . . . despite the Post-What-Not fashionableness of its draperies." These four artists were the nucleus of the Rebel Art Centre, which was established by Lewis with Kate Lechmere's financial backing in March 1914. They were joined by the painters William Roberts, Jessica Dismorr, and Helen Saunders and the London-based French sculptor Henri Gaudier-Brzeska.

Lewis founded the journal *BLAST* to attack the decaying aesthetic ideas left over from the Victorian age. Dependence on nature imagery and mimetic form were to be replaced with mechanistic and urban scenes and a move, still rather tentative, to abstract form. The prospectus of the Rebel Art Centre announced that it would "by public discussion, lectures and gatherings of people, familiarize those who are interested with the ideas of the great modern revolution." Pound assumed responsibility for the literary rebellion and proved his genius as, in Lewis's phrase, "poet and impresario" by naming the movement "Vorticism." Although Lewis used the Vortex motif in his nearly abstract series of drawings, *Timon of Athens,* it was Pound who saw that the term "Vorticism" would help to distinguish the British movement from the closely-related ones of Italian Futurism and French Cubism. Pound provided Imagist, or rather Vorticist, poems—the image as a force rather than a picture—and threw himself into propagandizing the revolution. The first letter from Pound to Lewis that we have is a brief one that encloses a list of over seventy names of people on several continents who should receive the Rebel Prospectus, and the other early letters concern contributions from such Pound discoveries as T. S. Eliot.

Lewis's and Pound's work for the Rebel Centre transformed their relationship. At the Vienna Café, the aggressive American poet had seemed to Lewis a "bombastic galleon," but as Lewis learned more about this pirate craft, he said he "discovered beneath its skull and cross-bones . . . a heart of gold." Pound's kindness was drawn upon when World War I drastically altered Lewis's comfortable life. As if to prove Pound's claim that artists were the "antennae of the race," the blast of war soon followed the Vorticist revolution. *Blast,* no. 2, long delayed because of Lewis's health, was already a war number. An era was over before it was well started. The Vienna Café was closed because it was staffed by German nationals. Thus Pound in Canto 80:

> And also near the museum they served it mit Schlag
>   in those days (pre 1914)
>   the loss of that café
>   meant the end of a B. M. era
>   (British Museum era)

(p. 506)

Lewis's illness in 1915 may have saved his life because it delayed his early enlistment and service at the front. When he did enlist in March 1916, Pound became his agent and general adviser. He arranged for *Tarr* to be serialized and then published, helped to catalog Lewis's paintings and drawings and then sold many of them to John Quinn, made plans for a new issue of *BLAST,* and did what he could to help Lewis obtain an officer's commission. All this went on as he was helping to "modernize" W. B. Yeats while staying with him at Coleman's Hatch in Sussex, trying to publish James Joyce's first novel *A Portrait of the Artist,* and acting as executor for Henri Gaudier-Brzeska, who had died fighting in France even before his prose "Vortex" and photographs of his sculptures could appear in the 1915 *BLAST*. In these early letters we see Pound as Lewis described him in *BLAST*: "Demon pantechnicon driver, busy with removal of old world into new quarters." As we will see in one of the last letters in this collection (Letter 250), Pound remembered an early letter from Lewis (now missing) which asked for " 'something nasty for *BLAST*.' " In the following letters, however, *BLAST*, no. 1 (June 1914) is already in proof and plans are being made for the second number of July 1915.

"Hampstead domesticity": The Letters of Wyndham Lewis, ed. W. K. Rose, p. 292.
"troublesome rebel": Lewis, "Ezra Pound," in *Ezra Pound: A Collection of Essays*, ed. Peter Russell, p. 259.
"Post-What-Not fashionableness": The Letters of Wyndham Lewis, ed. Rose, p. 49.
"great modern revolution": Quoted in Walter Michel, *Wyndham Lewis: Paintings and Drawings*, p. 68.
"heart of gold": Lewis, *Blasting and Bombardiering*, p. 278.
"new quarters": BLAST, no. 2 (July 1915): 82.

1. TLS–4.

STONE COTTAGE . . COLEMAN'S HATCH . . . SUSSEX

Dear Lewis

Please send proofs of my stuff direct to above address. Send me three or four sets of proofs s.v.p. if you can get 'em.

Please have copies of prospectus of the Rebel Centre sent to the following . . . dont bother about sending the school circular.

⟨N.B.—youd better keep this list of addresses permanently.⟩

ALSO please send ME a few more copies.
Keep the above list for reference. I should send announcements of BLAST

and of the lectures to the above tho' obviously some of 'em are only good
for Blast.   some are local press.

Hah.   thats some typing.

Yrs ever

E. Pound

30–4–'14

Rebel Centre: With the financial backing of Kate Lechmere, Lewis founded the
Rebel Art Centre in March 1914 and published a *Prospectus: The Rebel Art
Centre,* which announced that the center would further the revolution in modern art. Another circular, *Prospectus: The Rebel Art Centre: The Art School,*
announced plans to open a school of drawing, painting, and applied art, but
the centre lasted only four months and the art school never opened.

list of addresses: The names on Pound's list are: Mrs. Adams, Madame Italico
Brass, Milton Bronner, Miss Phyllis Bottome, L. C. Bromley, Robert Bridges,
Mrs. Brunton, Miss Natalie Barney, H. M. Barzun, Mrs. Benson, Miss Ella
Coltman, Antonio Cippico, R. B. Cunninghame Graham, Mrs. Caird, Mrs.
Clifford, Mrs. Dilke, Henri de Regnier, Sir A. Dean Paul, H. Dolmetsch,
Miss Darragh, Mrs. Deyer Edwards, Mrs. Foster, Mrs. Fowler, W. L.
George, K. M. Ghose, E. Gosse, C. Grinnell, Arthur Gray, E. Heron-Allen,
Miss A. H. Hudson, Mrs. W. P. Henderson, Mrs. Herbert, Rex Henderson,
Maurice Hewlett, Gilbert Hirsch, P. J. Jouve, Edgar Jepsom, James Joyce,
Alfred Kreymborg, Basil King, W. G. Lawrence, D. H. Lawrence, W. J.
Long, E. Legouis, Miss A. Lowell, Walter Lippmann, W. Lewis, Dr. Hector
Munro, Mrs. Meynell, Alexandre Mercereau, Mrs. McMillan, Mrs. Patmore,
Mrs. Prothero, Mrs. Rawlinson, Frank Rummel, De Forest Snively, G. M.
Smith, R. A. Scott-James, C. W. Stork, Cornelius Weygandt, Mrs. Silk,
Jas. W. Smith, Mrs. Sargant, Madame Sartoris, Miss Netta Syrett, Miss
Hyde-Lees, A. Thorold, Allen Upward, Charles Vildrac, Mrs. Woods, Robert
Gilbert Welsh, Charles D. Wadsworth, G. C. Woodward, Mrs. L. C. Wilcox,
Mrs. Shakespear.

2. ALS–2. [January 1915].

18 Fitzroy Street

Fitzroy Square, W.C.

Dear Pound.   Many thanks for your excellent piece on Binyon & the Sea
Serpent.

I think by the way of <u>Blessing</u> the Vienna Café.

Can you give me Coburn's address. Arbuthnot has a malicious photograph

of me in an article in Leaders of <u>Modern Movements</u>. There I figure with
Poynter, Sargent, Jacob [Epstein] & John. Poynter, they say, is the leader
of a "movement that is almost extinct." It is full of wit. But for Arbuthnot's behaviour I know no parallel in the history of art. I must at once see
Coburn. I feel Arbuthnot must be fought against.

Eliot has sent me Bullshit & the Ballad for Big Louise. They are excellent bits of scholarly ribaldry. I am longing to print them in <u>Blast</u>; but
stick to my naif determination to have no "Words Ending in -Uck, -Unt
and -Ugger."

I am doing a power of painting. If I get my head blown off when I
am pottering about Flanders, I shall have left something.

I have a piece of news. The excellent Mrs. Turner is going to take a
large studio or hall near Park Lane and there house my squadron of paintings, until after the war a large building is constructed for them in the rear
of her own house. She will pay the rent, furnish it & I suppose supply a
page boy or secretary: also a stage for Theatrical Performances, Lectures
etc: En voila une bonne nouvelle!

I hear that your article on the Vortex came out sooner than was expected. Wadsworth is giving it me tomorrow—I have not seen it yet. Any
thing to be Blessed or Blasted where you are (except Yeates [Yeats].)?

Blast should be under way this week. I will notify you of the start.
My compliments to Mrs. Pound. I hope she is drawing. My respects to
your host.

Yrs

Wyndham   Lewis

Binyon: Pound's "Chronicles," *BLAST*, no. 2 (1915): 85–86 commented on
 Laurence Binyon's introduction to Oriental art, *The Flight of the Dragon*
 (1911).

Blessing: *BLAST* "blessed" the allies and "blasted" the enemies of modern art,
 but the Vienna Café was not in fact blessed.

Modern Movements: In "Leaders of Modern Movements in British Art," Hugh
 Stokes wrote that Lewis's influence would not "survive the martial tone of the
 present crisis." *The Ladies' Field* (9 January 1915): 281.

Bullshit & The Ballad for Big Louise: These poems did not appear in *BLAST*,
 and Eliot never published them.

Mrs. Turner: She had bought and commissioned works from Lewis, but their
 relationship ended before Lewis left for France. See glossarial Index.

article on the Vortex: Pound's "Affirmations . . . II. Vorticism," *New Age* 16
 (14 January 1915): 277–78; Reprinted in *Ezra Pound and the Visual Arts*,
 ed. Zinnes, pp. 5–10.

3. TLS–1. [January 1915].

Stone Cottage, Coleman's Hatch, Sussex

Dear Lewis

Convey my approbations to Mrs. Turner. Coburn's address is 9 Lower Mall, Hammersmith, just a little way beyond the bridge.

I dare say Eliot will consent to leaving blanks for the offending words.

I am getting a certain amount of vorticism into all the New Age articles. the one entitled "Vorticism" is about the weakest. (I hope)

Yeats says there is no one for you to work on here except the Vicar (pace, enough vicars, with Pennyfeather)

D. sends her respects. She has done one design, snow.

Salutations to the brethren

yours.
E Pound

New Age articles: Pound wrote a series of seven articles on modern art and society for the *New Age* between 5 January 1915 and 25 February 1915. "Vorticism" (14 January 1915) is the second in the series. See *Ezra Pound and the Visual Arts,* ed. Zinnes, pp. 5–28.
snow: Dorothy Shakespear's "Snow-Scene" appeared in *BLAST,* no. 2, p. 35.
brethren: Pound jokingly alludes to the Pre-Raphaelite Brotherhood of the 1850's, with whom the Vorticists should not be confused. Pound recorded such a confusion in Canto 80 (p. 504) in describing the old gentleman who
"said to Yeats at a vorticist picture show:
"You also of the brotherhood?"
Pennefeather: Edward Pennyfeather; see glossarial Index and Letter 4.

4. ALS–1. [Spring 1915].

18. Fitzroy Street.
Fitzroy Square.
W.C.

Dear Pound. I read through yesterday the items you left with me. I like the poems immensely. I had not had time before to read them properly. The two small papers many thanks for, as well. I wish I could patch up a truce between you and that pale Galilian. But I suppose it is out of the question so long as Pennyfeather's Bells annoy you.

I hope you & Mrs. Pound will be able to come round on Saturday.

Yrs
Wyndham Lewis

———————

pale Galilian: Algernon Charles Swinburne's epithet for Christ in his "Hymn to Proserpine" is the "pale Galilean." Pound's *BLAST* poems do not seem anti-Christian, but Lewis knew that Pound regarded the ringing of the bells at St. Mary Abbots near Pound's Kensington flat a symptom of Christian decadence. The Vicar of St. Mary Abbots, Edward Pennefeather, was "blasted" in both numbers of *BLAST*.

5. ALS–1. On stationery imprinted: 169 Sloane Street. S.W.1.

Sat

1

June [1915]

Dear W.L.

I seem to spit blood every time I venture out after sunset.

If I don't get rid of this god damned cold altogether in a few days praps we might lunch instead of dining unless that busts up yr. day too much.

yrs
E.P.

am having telegram sent you re. this evening.

6. TLS–1. [before July 1915]. Letter encloses a note from Miss Dora Marsden.

5 Holland Place Chambers
Kensington. W.

Dear Lewis

    I've sent off the advertisements simply giving the address "BLAST", Newman St. W.C.

    The postman will bring letters if asked, at least they do here for me. Still it would be better to have the exact number of the house.

    Miss Marsden, as per enclosed wants "official confirmation" that THE EGOIST will get a page ad. in BLAST. You needn't really worry about its being the back page, I suppose. Anyhow here's her scribble.

    Please answer to Miss Dora Marsden   The Hay, Hatfield Rd. Ainsdale. Southport.

yrs
E Pound

page ad.: Miss Dora Marsden and Lewis exchanged advertisements for their journals.

7. ALS–2. [before July 1915]. On stationery embossed: 5, Holland Place Chambers, Kensington. W.

Dear Lewis

    Is monday at 6 p.m. any good? both today & tomorrow are full up.

    No. you took the Brzx [Henri Gaudier-Brzeska] <u>mss.</u> you put it in the right hand pocket of your coat & departed.

    Probably <u>the other</u> coat . . . any how put your hand in yr. rt. hand outside coat pocket on chance.

yrs
E Pound

Brzx. mss.: The sculptor's "Vortex (written from the Trenches)" appeared in *BLAST,* no. 2. (1915): 33–34; Reprinted in Pound, *Gaudier-Brzeska: A Memoir,* pp. 27–30. The manuscript of this essay, with corrections in Lewis's hand, is in the Firestone Library, Princeton University.

8. ALS–3. [before July 1915]. On stationery embossed: 5, Holland Place Chambers, Kensington. W.

Dear Lewis

It is the expression of an idealist who would like to contribute to the contents of BLAST but is probably unfitted for such an action. of course despised & rejected.

The enclosed (in print) almost too expressive. but shd. be kept in nat[io]n[a]l archives. as food for the adolescent flame.

yrs
E Pound

enclosed: Missing from letter—evidently a submission for *BLAST*.

9. ALS–3. [before July 1915]. On stationery embossed: 5, Holland Place Chambers, Kensington. W.

Sunday p.m.

Cher L.

My invaluable helpmeet [Dorothy Pound] suggests that the Thursday dinners [to discuss *BLAST*] would maintain an higher intellectual altitude if there were a complete & uncontaminated absence of women. She offers to contribute her own absence to that total & desirable effect.

Offer duly accepted.

yrs
E.P.

10. ALS–4. [before July 1915]. On stationery embossed: 5, Holland Place Chambers, Kensington. W.

Dear Lewis.

With regard to future potentialities I think that this thing of Eliot's would probably be more advantageous than anything of Rodker's admitting that it is a bit archaic = still as the mouthpiece of intelligence, one had better be the mouthpiece of Eliot than of Rodker. I have not seen Eliot since this A.M. so if you want to use this Portrait you'll have to get his permission. =or I will have to.

=Any how we can discuss the matter on Tuesday.

yrs
E.P.

Portrait: Eliot's "Portrait of a Lady" did not appear in *BLAST*, but his "Preludes" and "Rhapsody on a Windy Night" did in *BLAST,* no. 2 (1915): 48–51.

11. ALS–1. [before July 1915].

18. Fitzroy Street.
Fitzroy Square. W.C.

Dear Pound.   Sorry about Coburn hitch. Isn't he going to do it? —If he is, when do you think it will be?

I am sending you tomorrow a copy of Timon for Quinn.

Thank you for Elliot [Eliot] poem. It is very respectable intelligent verse, as you say, & I found Rodker a most poisonous little bugger on Saturday, repellently hoarse (this may be a form of jealousy) & with abominable teeth, not to mention his manners. I am sure you cant say anything too bad about him. He told me he had written a lot of filthy sexual verse, which, if he sends it, I shall hang in the W.C. He described it as Verlainesque, damn his dirty little eyes. Well, well.

Sturge Moore turned up, & we had Bomberg to entertain us, on Saturday.

Is Mrs. Pound still busy in the Vortex?

Blast will not be delayed many hours now.

Yrs   W Lewis

Timon: Lewis's *Timon of Athens* (1913). These illustrations for Shakespeare's play were highly praised after six of the sixteen drawings were shown at Roger Fry's Second Post-Impressionist Exhibition, October–December 1912.

Introduction to Letter 12.

After convincing John Quinn that the patron of an original artist was as "creative" as the artist, Pound was full of creative plans to spend Quinn's money. He not only sold Vorticist artworks to Quinn, including hundreds of pounds' worth of Lewis's paintings and drawings, but he also persuaded him to finance a Vorticist exhibition in America, which after many delays took place in January 1917 at New York's Penguin Club. Pound abandoned plans for an American number of *BLAST* but convinced Quinn to back *The Little Review*. Quinn's money was a godsend to Lewis during the war years. He wrote to Quinn in January 1917: "Let me say how much I appreciate your action in buying my drawings, and all the kindness and interest you have shown in my work and my friends'. You may believe also that this is quite genuine, and that, apart from pleasant financial results, I see what it means for a man to be angel enough to find himself invariably on the side of the angels." He tactfully kept Quinn aware of his financial problems and later in 1917 confided in Quinn enough to tell him he had two illegitimate children to support. Quinn was unfailingly generous even when he did not like some of Lewis's work.

"side of the angels": The Letters of Wyndham Lewis, ed. W. K. Rose, p. 86.

12. ALS–1. [August 1915]. On stationery embossed: 5, Holland Park Chambers, Kensington. W.

Dear Lewis:

I have succeeded in borrowing £ 20 & can let you have £ 5 of it, if that's any use to you.

But I shall have to repay myself out of the very first cash that comes from Quinn, whether it is £ 10 or £ 40, for Blast or pictures or whatever. —as I owe more than £ 20 elsewhere already & have very little onrush of funds in sight.

yrs.   E.P.

13. TLS–4. [October? 1915]. On stationery embossed: 5, Holland Place Chambers, Kensington. W.

Monday

Dear Lewis

I have not answered your note until now as I thought Quinn's letter would come this A.M.

However no american mail has yet come in.

I don't think there's any use sending off anything until I do hear from Q. as he may want the whole 40 drawings sent over for the show & then the lot can go together and it won't accelerate the cheque to send anything now. I will of course write (or? telegraph) the instant Q.'s cash comes.

I can't offer you an advance on it for my gross income has averaged just 2 guineas 4d per month for the past three months and I'm in about as bad a hole as you are.

How long do you want me to hold back Joyce's novel from Lane? Have you fixed up your affair with him?

Speriamo.
E.P.

Lane: Pound was trying to place both Lewis's *Tarr* and Joyce's *A Portrait of an Artist as a Young Man* and did not want simultaneously to send the manuscripts to the same publisher.

14. ALS–1. [Pmk: London, 12 October 1915].

18. Fitzroy Street.
Fitzroy Square, W.C.
=

My dear Pound.   Your letter just received. =

There is no hurry for a week or so. If in the course of the next 2 weeks nothing turns up, or if Q[uinn]. writes with nothing decisive as to a New York show, then I should like you to send off the goods already acquired. But I naturally surrender to your judgement in that matter, it being your affair, in any case. I should not intervene with any suggestion, even were I not hard up. = As to an advance from you, I never wanted that, although I appreciate your reference to it.

15

I shall have my book finished this week. But you make me feel very guilty in telling me that my harmless little observation has held back another person's work. Perhaps you want me to? I thought you said that in any event you would not be taking it round just yet.

My compliments to your wife. I trust you are flourishing. I hear Corria [?] is doing dials.

Yours   Wyndham Lewis

P.S. Come & see your old friend sometime.

another person's work: Joyce's *Portrait,* which Pound did not want to send to the publisher John Lane while he was considering Lewis's *Tarr.*

15. ALS–2. [December 1915].

18. Fitzroy St.
Fitzroy Sq. W.C.

Dear Pound.   A thousand thanks for your action with Quinn, & for the advance (£ 10) sent me by Miss S[aunders].

I will despatch the things tomorrow. Today up to 8 I was working at the Restaurant room. = I have not yet heard from Laurie. I will let you know the result of that affair as soon as it is settled one way or the other.

=

Try if you can, in due course, to get Quinn to acquire a painting, since his cable is so large. In the deepest confidence the following: = I owe my landlord £ 7.10, Leveridge £ 10, £ 4 to a furniture man, £ 1 for frames at the shop of my Percy Street landlord, and £ 10 of other desultory debts. = I am in arrear at least £ 25 with the upkeep of my son and heir etc: I reckoned on getting £ 50 for my book, £ 10 for a cover etc: and there was the £ 30 from Quinn. This would have left a little margin for my pocket. But if I get a commission, I shall need any margin I can scrape together & as an officer shall get no money for my kids. As a private, it would only be a few shillings. And for the rest of this war there will be no more accretions from the works of my pen or brush. = I can manage alright, I expect, whatever happens. But keep the line clear to Quinn for a masterpiece for some time or other. = As Miss S. told me you said to her, I daresay this is not the moment. = I dont care a tinker's curse, naturally, if my neighbour knows I am hard up (and they might guess it, in any case, in these times.) But I think we should not let it be known that the Vortex is bankrupt, except such as Quinn, who naturally must know if they are to be of use.

Well, a happy Christmas! = Thanks to your activity in my behalf this week of festival is not so cloudy as I had feared it would be.

I may send you a section or two of that Novel [*Tarr*] along. Read it in an incredulous and argumentative voice, full of mat [*sic*] harsh emphasis, if you do read it.

Yrs

Wyndham Lewis.

Restaurant room: Lewis was painting abstract decorations for the Eiffel Tower Restaurant, assisted by the Vorticist painter Helen Saunders, who also helped him with his literary and artistic arrangements throughout the war.

Laurie: Lewis had sent *Tarr* to the publisher Werner Laurie.

Leveridge: Leveridge and Co., the printer of *BLAST*.

16. ALS–1. [December 1915].

18. Fitzroy St:

Fitzroy Sq.

W.C.

Dear Pound.   Here are the 2 Blast drawings for Quinn, neatly though not expensively mounted.

Tomorrow I will send round the 2 drawings from the Doré Gallery. If you like momentarily to withhold the news of that purchase from our friends, I will still say nothing about it. = You will be doing me a considerable favour in getting them despatched to America soon. I will help you pack them if you like.

Yrs.   W   Lewis

17. TLS–1. [December 1915].

Stone Cottage   Colemans Hatch   Sussex

Cher W.L.

Enclosed arrives.

Has Miss W[eaver]. agreed to publish the ⟨your⟩ novel in book form at once IF Joyce's finds a publisher?

At any rate, supposing Laurie chucks it. This seems to be a definite offer, including £50 down, a possibility of publication in volume form at the end of a year (by her) or at the end of the war, or failing that the years leisure to find another publisher in.

This seems to me better than the uncertainty of my magazine, and the very probable delay. ANYTHING may happen before next autumn, and I dont suppose I'd get started before then, not actual publication, I mean.

I proposed that if they do an abbreviation, they should start off with a special number consisting of only the weekly notes, and a big gob of the novel. This she seems disposed to do. . . I gather.

It isn't as if we wouldn't both of us have more copy by autumn, IF I do get underweigh.

                              yrs.   E.P.

Enclosed: Missing from letter—probably an offer from Harriet Weaver to serialize *Tarr* in *The Egoist*.
my magazine: John Quinn had offered to arrange the financing for a magazine that Pound would edit.

18. TLS–1. [December 1915].

Stone Cottage, Coleman's Hatch, Sussex

Dear Lewis

I have written to Quinn, to say that THIS IS the time to buy a big picture or a collection of drawings by Mr W.L.

I have also sent a suave and incomprehensible reply to Johnnie's enclosed outbust. God damn the fucking lot of 'em, readers, hog washers, etc.

18

If Laurie rejects, you are to write to Miss H.S. Weaver 74 Gloucester Place, W. and make an appointment.

I suggest that you call and read her the opening of the novel. I think you can have something at once and the rest of £50 as soon as I get back to London to arrange matters. The publication would begin on Feb 1st.

It will be horrible to split up the novel into such minute scraps, but still (if she passes it at all, and she's not a damn fool utterly) you would get the £50 now and have the chance of getting another wad years hence when you publish in a volume.

Gawd save all pore sailors on a night like this.

your hell blastally
E.P.

enclosed outbust: Probably a reference to John Lane, with whom Pound quarreled when he refused to publish Lewis's *Tarr* because it was "too strong a book." See *The Letters of Wyndham Lewis,* ed. W. K. Rose, p. 74.

19. ALS–2. [Pmk: London, 27 December 1915].

18.Fitzroy St.
Fitzroy Sq.

Dear Pound.

I enclose Laurie's letter. We need not go further, I think. I seem to have written a very good book.

Thank you for letter, advice as regards Miss Weaver, and your action in the Quinn quarter. = Lane's letter was a tribute to the indecorum of your "outburst" in the direction of his reader. I hope it will ⟨not⟩ have for result an alienation between you and that important Publisher. It is unlikely, however. To trounce his readers every six months or so would be a good thing, and probably in no way interfere, once he had got used to it, with the even tenour of your relations with him personally. "Pound is a queer fellow. He always spanks my readers" he would say to himself. = There is nothing else. I am going to move into cheaper quarters, & within 1 month either enlist in some regiment I should wish to get a commission in, or join an O[fficer's]. T[raining]. C[amp]. I will let you know what Miss Weaver has to say.   yrs. = W Lewis =

P.S. The report of Laurie's reader said that my book dealt entirely with Germans, and English people who were not much better. He found it extremely "clever". I am sure every Publisher's reader in London would find it wonderfully 'clever', Blast their dingy brains! = But the "Futurist" pictures Mr. Lewis delighted in painting, were found in this book in great profusion. Here followed quotations. = The report was a long and gloomy statement of antipathy.

W.L.

Laurie's letter: Lewis enclosed the formal letter of rejection the publisher Werner Laurie sent him concerning *Tarr.* Laurie offered to let Lewis see the reader's report, which he evidently did.

20. ALS–2. [December 1915].

Stone Cottage
Coleman's Hatch
Sussex

Dear Lewis.
      Here is the remaining £15 of Quinn's.

I have paid his cheque into my wife's account so there'll be enough there tomorrow to meet this cheque of hers.

I think this is the quickest way to get the cash to you.

Hang Laurie. =
                  yours E.P.

21. ALS–2.

18. Fitzroy Street
Fitzroy Square.
W.C.

Friday. Dec. 31ˢᵗ· [1915].

Dear Pound. I have seen Miss Weaver. She appears to think that the book is too long to serialize, although she says they want a serial. As to the possibility of bringing it out in volume form at once, that is reserved for Joyce's book [*A Portrait of the Artist*]; so presumably Laurie has been guilty of a double mistake.

I have also read the first chapter of my book to Goldring. But I am afraid he is no good: he does not seem even able to get tick with his printer.

I saw Miss Weaver at 11 yesterday morning at Oakley House. I read her the first 4 pages, and then left off, as I was sure she would not like it, and we were in an empty room under depressing conditions. = I did not leave the MSS. with her: I thought I must make some further move with it. I cannot unfortunately afford to fold up my standards now, to unfurl them again on some brighter day in King Ferdinand's words. = I am afraid I may have bungled the Weaver business.

Many thanks for the cheque £15. You have taken out of Quinn's cheque the £5 for the Blasts? Did he say nothing of interest in his letter? = If your Review is coming into being, you might, as you have said once or twice, find a little corner where my big book could creep.=

I may see you on your return from your holiday.

Yrs   Wyndham Lewis

serial: An abridged version of *Tarr* was serialized in *The Egoist* in nineteen installments from April 1916 to November 1917.
your Review: See note on "my magazine," Letter 17.

22. TLS–2.

Jan 1. 1916

Dear Lewis

Heard from Miss Weaver yesterday. yours this a.m.
If that ass Laurie rejects Joyce, I see only one way left.

You might prepare a "serial version", i.e. an abbreviation of Tarr, for the Egoist, with the understanding that they print the whole novel at the end of the year, paying you £50 at once.

Whether They would give you another wad on publication in volume, I dont know . . It is only a scheme to get you £50 at once, and depends on whether that is all important.

///////

I have had no letter from Quinn, only cables, brief cables.

I am sorry there was only £15 left. I did not however subtract the Blasts £5. The cheque was £30. £10 covered my wife's cheque of the other day, and £5 the £5 I lent you months ago, writing at the time that it was part on a sum advanced to me, and that I should have to grab it absolutely from the first instalment from Quinn, for whatever reason it came.

Even if I stay down here two months I shall hardly get square,

and the Egoist £50 depends on my raising £20 of it to lend them, on six months credit.

Q.'s £30 covers

Blast	£5
Ink drawing of Kermess	£5
Two coloured drawings	£20

I hope you have sent them off, as they should help my letter to Quinn advising him to take the big Kermess at once.

Q's cheque was cabled by him via some bank. No whisper of "my" review.

Oh well, its a world, bigod its a planet, a dewey satalite [sic].

Lane has sent me proofs of the "Gaudier", so my epistles haven't completely interrupted his processes.

yours

E. P.

Stone Cottage
  Colemans Hatch
    Sussex

"my" review: See note to Letter 23.
"Gaudier": John Lane published Pound's Gaudier-Brzeska: A Memoir in 1916.

23. TLS–1. [January 1916].

Stone Cottage   Colemans Hatch   Sussex

Dear W.L

    Cable from Quinn saying he still hopes to get cash for the Magazine.

    I should probably have to rush off to New York. Heaven only knows when I should be able to pay for mss.

He still says he is going to write presently.

For God's sake dont stop trying to place the novel on the strength of this faint rainbow.

Still IF   IF   IF   IF   IF   it comes off, I should probably be able to manage so[me] sort of advance.

yours

E. P.

Magazine: On 1 January 1916, Quinn cabled that if he succeeded in financing the review they were planning, Pound would have to come to America to start it.

24. TLS–1. [February 1916]. On stationery embossed: 5, Holland Place Chambers, Kensington. W.

Place Chambers, Kensington. W.

Dear Lewis

    I have cabled to Quinn, written to Miss Weaver, and had up Pinker's [a literary agent] office on the phone. They say he wont be back today (I phoned at 2.15, it is now 2.25). His secretary says Joyce's mss. is now at Werner Lauries. I dont think that matters, but . . . . , no. I dont think it matters save V[iolet Hunt]'s pull will be strengthened or weakened according as W.L. likes or dislikes the Joyce.

yrs.

E.P.

Perhaps old Stg. Moore could do something with the Royal Lit. Fund.

V[iolet Hunt]'s pull: Violet Hunt had persuaded Laurie to read Joyce's novel.
Stg. Moore: Pound thought that the Royal Literary Fund might provide money
   to publish *Tarr.* T. Sturge Moore had already told Lewis, however, that he had
   not published enough yet to apply to the fund.

25. TLS–1. [March 1916]. [5, Holland Place Chambers, Kensington. W.].

Dear Lewis
            Long letter from Q[uinn]. he evidently intends to take Kermess
etc.
            Have you sent the drawings? If not wait till I get back.
            Have you hysterical need of any more cash at once? or will you wait
till it can be managed by letter.
            Personally I think it would be well to get the stuff ready for ship-
ment. However if you are bleeding at the pores I am told to cable for
what you need in advance.
            Would rather wait till I see you. Shall be chez moi Tuesday morning.
At 5 H[olland].P[ark].C[hambers].

                              yrs
                              E.P.

Kermess: Quinn agreed to buy Lewis's paintings *Kermesse* and *Plan of War* for
   £100.

26. ALS–1. [Pmk: London, 6 March 1916].

                              18. Fitzroy St.
                                 Fitzroy Sq.

Dear Pound.   Quinn is concentrated virtue: he obviously works like an
ox, and in narrow breathing-spaces despatches cheques to the ends of the
Earth in exchange for pictures. How different to the palaver and idleness
of our despicable amateurs! = Passons. = Many thanks for your happy
initiative in the matter. It is a very great service you have rendered me
at this time.

As to the cabling of the money, there is no need for that haste except in one event. Should you suspect your great country of being on the eve of war with England, then it would be well to have it cabled. = Is there a likelihood of that? The newspapers seem to indicate political restlessness. = Or can it be Germany that it thinks of choosing? It's perplexing. You are the best judge in matters of welt-politik.

I shall be here at 3.15 tomorrow (Monday) & hope to see you then. =

Yrs

Wyndham Lewis

---

27. ALS–3. [March 1916]. [5, Holland Park Chambers, Kensington. W.].

Friday

Dear Lewis

I am still glued to this mattress & shall not get to see the "Kermess" this P.M. =

I find it is not paralysis but sciatica = depression of last saturday logically explained.

I have had another note from yet another am. pub. = i.e. american publisher wanting mss. of a book. contents unspecified.

I hope you will leave the drawings with Miss S[aunders]. or somewhere available for if I get a chance to do a book on you & them, I shall certainly do that much to "keep the 'ome fires burning" =

Of course these publishers feelers are usually no good, but as this is the 2nd in a weeks time, I think my market must be bullish. =

What the hell I shall say in the book gawd only knows but it should count as "affichage" or theatrical "printing" =

Also the N. Y. show must come off sometime before doomsday. — good luck.

yrs
E P.

am. pub.: Probably the American publisher John Marshall. See note on *"This Generation,"* Letter 38.

28. TLS–2. [March 1916]. On stationery embossed: 5, Holland Place

Chambers, Kensington. W.

Dear Lewis

I am afraid I was rather inconsiderate an hour ago, in asking Miss S[aunders]. to tell you to come out, if you could, some morning to catalogue the drawings. Also to set prices. as you are bound to be busy.

I think I have now got them in my head. At least I have named 'em so that I can distinguish them. I dont know whether you have named 'em or not.

What is the price of the small blue drawing, like a sea in storm. White figure, in posture as if hands tied high above head, other figure as if floating in swish of sea? [Two sketches by Pound]

I have just writ to Q[uinn]. to say that I have GOT to do a book on you or on "Vorticists" consisting mostly of you. And that I hope he can get the reproductions made in N.Y.

For this I must have some way of keeping track of the drawings I want used to illustrate it. I dont know whether to scribble my titles on the back of the mounts, or whether you have arranged the numbers you were talking about yesterday. I dont want to "impose" titles, where you've got better ones of your own. It will be easier to talk about particular drawings to Q. if they have names.

I dont know whether you were thinking of a uniform £10. That would certainly be wrong. The dancing "Joyeuse" and "Cholly" have £10 difference between 'em

Yours

E.P.

Introduction to Letter 29.

From March 1916 until he left for France in May 1917, Lewis was training in a series of army camps. He regretted enlisting without an officer's commission and chaffed under the routine of training as a gunner at artillery camps in Dover, Weymouth, Horsham, and Lydd. His position improved only slightly when he became a bombardier and, as a non-commissioned officer, began training recruits at Menstham Camp in Dorset. He considered the firing of howitzers an appropriate occupation for the editor of *BLAST,* but his combative nature led to tensions with his superiors. Pound replied to Lewis's complaints with good advice and much practical help.

29. ALS–2. [Pmk: Dover, 25 March 1916].

Dover.

Dear Pound. I have no complete address for the moment. = I shall probably be here for 2 or 3 weeks. I am gunner Lewis: a so far hungry and bored gunner. Food is obviously difficult to obtain in the army. I am now in the town looking for a square meal. I send you this word hurriedly to put you au courant of the drawing-muddle.

I intended asking you (I intended visiting you for that purpose) to keep all my mounted drawings for a short time. Out of those the ones you chose for Q[uinn]. could have been sent off by Miss S[aunders]. =As it is I had not time (naturally) this morning to get more than the smaller ones sent off to you.

Will you keep these till I turn up with the rest? Will you keep the rest in a neat packet for a few weeks? When I come (some time next week I hope,) I can price, name & number the lot: decide which should cross to New York, & in short put everything ship-shape.

Miss S. is sending off the first packet. As soon as all the drawings are together we can send off the 5 new ones.

My appetite as I write this tells me that before very long Q.'s money should come, especially as my physical exertions will gradually increase until presumably I shall have to perform the work of 4 cart-horses. All my companions are cart-horses. I am glad of this. But even pretending to be a cart-horse will require food.

Still, you have written. There is nothing more to be done for the moment. Only in a week or two, if Q. is quiescent, be a dear & jog his memory.

I shall write you again monday, with an address, & more as regards Kermesse. Now must eat.

Yrs   W   Lewis

30. ALS–1. [Pmk: Dover, 27 March 1916].

Address.

Gunner W. Lewis.

Depot 1. R.G.A.

Hut 20.

Fort Burgoyne.

Dover.

Dear Pound.   The above is what I have come to. = I have been put in siege section, that is Mobile section, & shall probably in 3 weeks go to the Howitzers at Sheereness or somewhere further away: Hull, per-haps: — I hope. I must not worry these good people for a little time about leave. But before I leave here I shall be able to get a day or two's leave to see Dentist, & in that time can put finishing touches to Kermesse, with military celerity, & get the drawings sorted out.

Should anything of moment happen, let me know.

Yrs ever W Lewis.

Sheereness: possibly Sheerness on the Kentish coast.

31. ALS–2. [Pmk: Dover, 29 March 1916].

Gunner W. Lewis,

Depot. 1. R.G.A.

Hut 20. Fort Burgoyne.

Dover

Dear [*crossout:* Pound] Poet. Many thanks for letter, and news.

London, County and Westminster Bank, 106. Finchley Road. N.W. is my bank. It is into that Bank I should be obliged if you would pay any cheque coming for me.

I find squad-drill a gentle and underrated amusement. I quite look forward to it now. I shall shift from here in 3 or 4 weeks. I hope to Hull: but it may be Leith, Weymouth or elsewhere. = Woolwich is only for the heavy guns, and the siege ones, I am sorry to say. Our hut is on the top of Dover Cliff. When it blows the music at night is antediluvian.

I shall try & get up for my teeth in a week or two, when I could see you if you were then in town.

Miss S[aunders]'s address is 4. Phéné Street. Chelsea S.W. You should not always lose it. It is an address to remember. = She was ill, by the way, when I last saw her & I have not heard from her. Hope there is nothing wrong.

Your limerick is all right. = My hut is much more comparable to a Canadian trappers shack than to the torrid rigours of Kut, however: except that the food is nothing like so good, I expect. = Bless Quinn.

Yours ever. Wyndham Lewis

limerick: Missing from letter.

32. ALS–1. [April 1916]. [Dover].

Dear Pound. Thank you for letter and its various announcements. I have not time at this moment to comment on Quinn contents: except as usual, to bless Quinn. (I think if I were a poet like you, I would write a poem to Quinn. But perhaps you have.)

I am being shifted out from here with the draught on Saturday to Weymouth I believe. Then [?] after that will be France in a couple of months, I expect, perhaps sooner. So do not address me here. I will send you my new address.

I will write you more about drawings in a day or two. Remember me to Mrs. Pound.

Yrs   W.L.

33. ALS–1. [Pmk: Weymouth, 9 April 1916].

Weymouth.

Dear Pound. Here I am at the other side of England. But I believe it is only for a few days. = I will give you a more permanent address as soon as I have one. = I write this from a Y.M.C.A. hut: a man is making a shit of himself on a piano. I am surrounded by tame Australians:

(there are only 5 tame ones in camp: all the rest are wild, pacing up and down the town, flouting officers & the police.)

I found myself among Duchesses again today for a moment at Waterloo, where I eat six pieces of bread and treacle with great relish at a charity Bar. The Duchesses were very treacly too. = I much prefer meeting them under those conditions.

As soon as I get to the Battery I will write you.

P.S. The man at the piano has become less of a bugger. = But I must tell you some day about the Sailors at Dover.

Yours ever   W Lewis

Sailors at Dover: Lewis tells of getting drunk with mandolin-playing soldiers in Part II, Chapter VII of *Blasting and Bombardiering.*

34. ALS–2. [Pmk: Weymouth, 12 April 1916]. On stationery imprinted: The Salvation Army. Recreation and Reading Room for His Majesty's Troops.

Gunner W. Lewis.
71050. Hut. 61.
R.G.A. Westham Training Unit.
Weymouth. = Dorset.

Dear Pound. I have got shifted in here, and lost my leave. Heaven knows when I shall get any leave now. They wont let me go to town about my teeth: and if I get a week-end, it will only be noon Saturday to midnight Sunday. Then I shall have to wait 20 weeks before getting any more leave: or rather, as most likely we shall [be] off with a Siege Battery in a couple of months, my next leave after my first leave (supposing I get that) will be my two days before going Abroad. = These are new War office regulations, applying to all Camps and people, & it is difficult to get round them.

This being so, what is to be done about the pictures? = We will suppose I induce the Sergeant-Major to let me up next week-end (a Sunday rather.) = That will leave no time except to move from my flat. Now, the Kermesse is in its primitive state: as it stands it was praised by Roger Fry in the Nation, John wrote "thanking me" for it etc: But even for a Wall painting it is too uncouth and its unfinished state would not recommend it to the very discriminating, with which ideal audience we must always suppose we are dealing.

Now, the problem as regards the Quinn money appears to me as simple as A. B. C. ==You hold a number of my drawings. –Eventually (as soon as I get up to town) you will, if you accept the responsibility & are willing to store them, hold all that I have completed and arranged with a view to immediate exhibition.

You also could have within your grasp the Kermesse as it is. Should I come through the War safe & sound, I can, and undoubtedly shall, paint a hundred Kermesses, finishing Quinns to begin with. Quinn does not mind waiting 12 months before entering into possession of an important picture, I imagine, if he has guarantees. Well then, should all go well, Quinn has nothing to fear: I will do him another Kermesse, & throw it in, to celebrate Peace. (This is without prejudice.)

On the other hand, should I get killed or smashed up so that I cant paint any more Kermesses, he can have 1. The Kermesse as it is: = or 2. As many more drawings as would, by their combined price, cover the money he had paid out. = The drawings are good ones: you could recommend this without qualms of conscience.

My provisions with reference to any accident to myself in this way are aimed at putting into the hands of my mother any pence that could be scraped together to help with the education of the children. Therefore when I say I intend to put good prices on the drawings you must not accuse me of fancy-pricing my things. = I have always priced my drawings & things remarkably low. But I know that little lot of drawings will bear looking into & count for something in what is being done nowadays. And if they sell at all they can sell well: (this excepting those already reserved for Quinn.)

Please digest this letter, the facts contained therein, & their reference to the £70 you hold for Kermesse. I may add I have about £1 in my Bank, & I find soldiering costs about 30/– a week, with occasional additional sums for odds & ends. = It will be cheaper a little later on. It is cheaper already. ≡ I have been put into an N.C.O. class, & have an Examination in a month for my stripe. = I shall be here 1 month, I expect. = I have seen the Colonel, who was very amiable and discussed the Indépendants etc. & and I may get a commission. That would mean 6 weeks or 2 months at Cadet School I expect. But the liklihood of the commission I shall know about later. ≡ Do not under any circumstances speak to Masterman, by the way. ≡ How are you getting on?

Yours ever, W   Lewis.

Roger Fry: In his review of the AAA exhibition, Roger Fry wrote (*The Nation* [20 July 1912]: 583–84) that only Lewis with "Kermesse" has "risen to the occasion."

education of the children: Lewis's two illegitimate children were being cared for by his mother.

N.C.O. class: Non-commissioned officer class.

Indépendants: Lewis apparently discussed the annual exhibition of "Independent" artists in London with Colonel Inglis.

Masterman: Pound was going to ask C. F. G. Masterman, Director of Wellington House (Propaganda Department), to help Lewis obtain a commission.

35. ALS–1. [Pmk: Weymouth, 26 April 1916].

> Bdr. W. Lewis.
> 71050.
> Hut 61.
> R.G.A. Westham Training Unit.
> Weymouth= Dorset.

Dear Pound.   Will you render me the following service: will you send me two £1 notes; I enclose a cheque for two pounds. There is money in the bank.

I should [be] extremely obliged if you could send it back fairly swiftly. Miss S[aunders]. is away, or I should not have to trouble you.

The Invasion they are hourly expecting causes us some discomfort. I have to hurry back to camp. = Did Miss S. give you my novel: if so, you did not mind?

Yrs   Wyndham Lewis

36. ALS–4. [April 1916]. On stationery embossed: 5, Holland Place Chambers, Kensington. W.

Cher W. L.

Here is the 2 £ in cash.

Sheldon's cart took off the Vort. show yesterday = I've a receipt labled simply "pictures". I suppose I am now at liberty to send you the enclosed.

as per previous cheque	5
" " " "	5
rent of 18 Fitzroy	
paid to Miss S[aunders].	3
enclosed	57
	£70

for which please send receipt for J[ohn]. Q[uinn].

I'm not very keen on spending Q's money on The Egoist. Shall I try to get it shifted & bring out another number of Blast — possibly an American number — with Q's assistance.

---

to have some thing new for the N.Y. show

---

possibly to reduce Leveridge's claims.

---

you must get Lane to take his usual batch [of *BLAST*] if I tackle Q. for some "starter".

=

R.S.V.P. immediate if the scheme pleases you

I am to jaw with Egoistes on Saturday.

yrs
E.P.

no. Miss S. did not give me the novel.

Sheldon's cart: Sheldon's Art Gallery shipped the Vorticist show to New York.
Leveridge's claims: Leveridge and Co. was the printer for *BLAST* under an arrangement in which Lewis, not the publisher John Lane, would bear the printing costs.
Egoistes: Probably Harriet Shaw Weaver and Dora Marsden.

37. ALS–2.

Weymouth.

April 29th. 1916.

Dear Pound.   Excuse delay in answering your letter. = I have made various efforts to get out. But we have for 2 or 3 days now been confined to Camp. They seem to be expecting some attempt to land somewhere. The result is much inconvenience to all the people quartered here. = This morning I was told of a hole in the hedge, & I shall risk being met & take this to the letter-box.

===

Thank you very much for the cheque for £57, which with the £3. you paid to Miss S[aunders]. for rent Fitzroy St. & the £10. you advanced me when I was up in Town, makes the £70 of Quinn's cheque on account £120.

===

I think your idea of transferring Quinn's literary money to the launching of a fresh number of Blast, which you could call an American Number, is an excellent notion. = You would have to conduct it, largely, I expect. = I personally should be very pleased to see Blast do another lap. Some of the New York Show works might embellish it. = Henceforth I shall have some little time to do a drawing or two & a little writing.

Let me know any details about your scheme of common-interest. = What exactly would be your idea of the Publication? = Your long poem ["L'Homme Moyen Sensuel"?] would be used? Would Eliot be able to contribute? etc: 1 Coloured reproduction?

The Colonel is waiting with anxiety to see what I am going to do with the Red Barracks, the Fort, & other things under his care!

My compliments to Mrs. Pound.

Yours ever

W Lewis.

Red Barracks: Lewis was apparently doing sketches of the camp.

38. TLS–2.

Respected artist, author and bombadier:

Available funds (10/) shipped last evening on receipt of your ukase. Enclosed please find balance due (£2/10). The corruption of his majesty's forces by capital is heart-rending. I trust you are not being a pigeon.

The goods seem to have arrived at Sheldons, I have had a sort of list from them.

1.

Agenda: Can you send me a simple receipt for Q[uinn]'s £70. not a statement embedded in a letter, as I desire to forward said receipt to said J. Q. in order to lead him to think that I have delivered the cash and not swallowed it or spent it on women myself.

2.

As I have made overtures to Q. re/ BLAST, can you tell me definitely (d-e-f-i-n-i-t-e-l-y) how many copies Lane will take and what he will pay for them, so that I may know where I am at if I attempt to swing the thing, and how much leeway I have, and how much I am to edit it etc.

Did I say that an American publisher is doing (at least so I read the letter) a book by me called "This Generation" dealing with contemporary events in the woild-uv-letturs, with passing reference of about 3500 words on vorticism. including my original essays on you and Edward [Wadsworth].

The Times Lit Sup has two columns (minus 3 inches) on the "Gaudier-Brzeska", saying that the critics should be more grateful to vorticists etc. I will send it on when I get a copy. The atheistical vicar [Rev. Arthur Galton] writes to my mother in law that the Times appears to understand "neither Brzx., Pound nor himself". Which statement seems fairly accurate, but the tone of the review is what is called "respectful" (i.e. anxious not to appear too damd a fool)

yrs
E.P.

3/5/'16 [3 May 1916]

address   5

five
Holland Place Chambers

35

ukase: Lewis had cabled his need for money for military supplies.

"This Generation": John Marshall was negotiating for the book, but it never appeared. See Donald Gallup, *Ezra Pound, A Bibliography,* p. 447.

essays on you and Edward: "Wyndham Lewis," *Egoist* 1 (15 June 1914): 233–34; "Edward Wadsworth, Vorticist. An Authorised Appreciation," *Egoist* 1 (15 August 1914): 306–7.

Times Lit Sup: "The New Sculpture," *The Times Literary Supplement,* no. 745 (27 April 1916): 199.

atheistical vicar: Rev. Arthur Galton, a friend of Olivia and Dorothy Shakespear, who published essays on controversial religious subjects.

39. ALS–2. [Pmk: Weymouth, 16 May 1916]. A section of the second page has been cut away, obscuring the two words completely bracketed below.

Weymouth.

Tuesday.

My dear Pound.   I should have written some time ago, in answer to your last letter. But many boring events have intervened, & deprived me of the necessary time etc:

I am here for another 4 or 5 weeks. I have, as usual, found an enemy. For Christ's sake always blast Captain Ninn [Lewis's Instructor of Gunnery] whenever you are 'blasting'. He has nearly been my undoing. But I also have found a friend, I think, in the Adjutant of the Portland Garrison. He told me this morning that he took fancies to people; & incidentally did me an extremely good turn. Therefore, always have the Adjutant of the Portland defences in your prayers.

I will write you on other matters this morning. = Do [what] is best as regards Q[uinn]. & New York Blast. Try to have a [third] number. You would have to organise it, though.

Yrs ever W. Lewis.

40. ALS–3.

Weymouth

B^dr. W. Lewis

71050.

Hut 78.

R.G.A. Westham Training Unit.

Weymouth.

Dorset.

June 22./16

Dear Pound. I dont know if I wrote you from East Weare? I am back here now, anyway. = I will at once inform you as to how my personal affairs (commission etc.) stand. I think it unlikely that I shall ever be recommended for a commission from this place. I have been put into another N[on] C[ommissioned] O[fficer] Class, & commanded to excel. Nns. Ninn, the I.G. — Instructor of Gunnery, Examiner etc. on whom my fate depends, is beyond a doubt determined that no commissions should come out of this command. Since he had to work for 20 years for his commission and support the insolence of office, other [?] jealousies etc. of the military state during half a lifetime, he is resolved that no one else shall find an emergency short-cut by way of him. Two men [?] wrote the colonel the other day asking for his recommendation. They had left here 2 or 3 weeks, & a month ago got better marks than I did for instance. = The Colonel took the letter to Ninn who immediately vetoed it.

Now, Ninn, when he returns from Portland, will regard my turning up again in the class as a challenge. He will say visibly with his eyes, broken nose, & teeth: "Ah, there you are again? Well, have another try if you like. You are quite welcome to have another try. As many as you like." I shall be snubbed, harried, & worn down, & at the end of 4 or 5 weeks, have 50% jury marks knocked off for "delivery" or some elusive thing. In the last exam I am convinced that my more positive marks were even tampered with. Knowing all this, I volunteered for the Siege Battery that they have just formed. But the S[ergeant]. M[ajor]. told me that there was no room, & told me to stop where I was. I have a great deal of dung to swallow just at present, & have a most 'morne' and vexatious existence. = Supposing I join a siege, the moment I am away from here, pull any string you can catch hold of, & see if an Artillery Cadet School can be managed: = as I think I told you, I met "Quix" of the Evening News, when I was up in town. He was at the Royal Artillery School at St. Johns Wood, had joined after me, & never dreamed of going through ranks. But I am afraid that "the Ranks" are a trap. I regret my attestation—and many things.

Should I stop here, & things not go well (as they wont) perhaps
something could be done by my appealing to some Power or other. = But
there is just a vague chance that the Adjutant may recommend me. I will
see first what happens a little. But this is the last lap, & I am accumulating
a sinister report. The longer I stop here, the more justification Ninn will
seemingly have for denying me either merit or industry in my new occupation. = The Adjutant is half-cracked & very unreliable, although still
well-disposed. = The Colonel a week ago sent for me on the field, to ask
me what "Imagisme" was. With my rifle at the slope I explained as best I
could. But the Colonel said that I would never make him understand such
things, & carrying my right hand smartly across the body, I placed it,
palm downwards on the small of the butt: then cutting it smartly to the
side, took a step to the rear, & turning rapidly about, moved back to continue the instruction of my squad.

So much for the military outlook. How are other things going on? Has
Quinn got the stuff? What does he say about it? May I hope for any more
money soon? Out of any further money I get I shall not have to pay out a
large sum, as I did this time, for relatives. Also I have had to pay heavily
for help here, & so far it has not done me much good.

I never see the Egoist, but hear through Miss S[aunders]. that Miss
W[eaver].'s corrections [of the serialized version of *Tarr*] are alright. But
she points out to me that the German is unworthy and wrongly spelt,
capitals in wrong place etc: = I wonder if that could be rectified, & how?
Miss Shepler [Schepeler] & Miss S. could go through it together, or you
may have some German friend who would serve.

I hear that Edward [Wadsworth] has departed. How are you getting
on? Have you written anything new lately? I suppose the book on your
contemporaries ["This Generation"] is not yet out. = General news of
any sort? =

Yrs   Wyndham Lewis.

Edward: The Vorticist painter Edward Wadsworth served in the Royal Naval
   Volunteer Reserve in the Mediterranean in 1915–17.

5 Holland Park Chambers.
Kensington. W.

Dear Lewis. Judging the matter from the depths of my moderately comfortable arm chair, with the products of your brush, pen and the reproductory processes of the late publisher M. Goschen before me—or from free seats at the opera—I can not see that the future of the arts deamns [sic] that you should be covered with military distinctions. It is equally obvious that you should not be allowed to spill your gore in heathen and furrin places.

I can only counsel you to endure your present ills with equanimity and not to be too ready to see malice where mayhap none is intended. Nothing exists without efficient cause. I can but ask you to contemplate the position as deeply as you are able, and that without passion, and from all points of view.

I should suggest that you spend your spare time with a note book, preparing future compositions. If you like I will send a copy of Cathay so that the colonel may be able to understand what is imagisme.

You didn't send me your address so I couldn't forward the Egoists, which I send herewith.

Ed. Wad[sworth]. went off yesterday for Lemnos. Dont think my opening paragraphs unfeeling. I only ask you to consider all possible interpretations of fact before you rush to an emotive conclusion. I trust you will not think the remarks imply a personal bias on my part, but take them rather as a point of view which may be held by persons other than the writer.

I appear to be the only person of interest left in the world of art, London. I have had a fine row over "Lustra", as both Mathews and the printer decline to go on with it on grounds of indecorum. I am getting 300 copies printed almost unabridged at Mathews expense and he is to print the rest castrato. I have placed a Jap book with MacMillan, which is a peg up for me. The enclosed circular, with the young damsel squirming neath the jujube tree, is for your comfort. It will fill you, in the midst of your afflictions, with a sense of your own dignity, and show how badly you are needed here as a police force. However it is supposed to net me £20 which I bloody well need.

Met that pig Martin Secker at the U.S. consulate. by accident. He gave me a taxi ride and a good cigarette. He said he would be very glad to consider Tarr if I could get him a loan of the mss. Publication after the war.

Pinker also wanted to know if he might be allowed to vend the mss. As he has been no use re/Joyce's stuff, and I have done all the work, I dont see that there is much use dealing with him. A. P. Watt [the literary agent] fixed me up with MacMillan in about a week. I dont know whether Tarr is in his line.

I have not heard from Quinn, re/ receipt of pictures. He didn't seem keen on paying for Blast. He said he put up as much as I thought he ought to, but I did not feel it would be wise to press the matter. I should want £100 to lubricate it.

I have now £25 of his which I have asked permission to pay over to you.

For the rest, dont be more irritating to your unfortunate "superior" officers than you find absolutely necessary to your peace of mind, or at least try not to be.

And dont get wroth with the Egoist for cutting the novel. The sooner they get through serializing it the better, for then we can get it published decently in vol. form.

And do try to penetrate the meaning of some of this note.

Yours ever,
E.Pound

24/6/16.

M. Goschen: Max Goschen was the printer of Lewis's *Timon of Athens* portfolio (1913).

free seats at the opera: Pound was music critic of the *New Age,* 1917–21.

efficient cause: Pound has attributed this expression at different times to both Aristotle and St. Thomas Aquinas.

enclosed circular: Missing from letter.

Jap book: Pound refers to *'Noh' or Accomplishment* (1916).

Introduction to Letter 42.

By June 1916, Lewis had almost despaired of being recommended for the Cadet Artillery School at Exeter. Pound was a loyal but also realistic friend during this time. He used what contacts he still had among the rich and powerful on Lewis's behalf, but the irony of the situation was that Pound's very association with Lewis and Vorticism limited his influence. Pound learned a bitter lesson about the way the established powers worked in 1914 when the editor of the venerable *Quarterly Review* wrote to him: "I do not think I can open the columns of the Q. R. . . . to any one associated publicly with such a publication as *Blast*. It stamps a man too disadvantageously." Lewis should have learned the same lesson when he was displayed at fashionable parties as the leader of the latest avant-garde movement. He met Prime Minister Asquith, for example, at Lady Ottoline Morrell's and Lady Cunard's, and was invited to lunch with the prime minister at Downing Street. Yet none of the people he met in the drawing rooms of Mayfair and Waterloo Place, as he recalled in 1937, bought a single one of his paintings.

In addition to working for Lewis's commission, Pound was publicizing Lewis's art in *The Egoist* and dealing with the complications arising from the New York Vorticist Show. Quinn planned the show for the Montross Gallery in the spring of 1916, but shipping delays and confusion over the ownership of Gaudier-Brzeska's works delayed arrival of the works until June. By then the Montross Gallery had cancelled their offer to hold the show, and John Quinn was stuck with the shipping bills. Quinn took full responsibility for the cancellation and even turned down an offer by the American artist Arthur B. Davies to pay half the show's cost. His annoyance over these difficulties was increased by his dislike of much of the show's content, including Lewis's paintings. Quinn suspected that he had relied too much on Pound's enthusiasm.

After this low point in June, Lewis's fortunes soon turned up. Quinn arranged for the Vorticist Show at the Penguin Club, and Lewis was finally accepted as an officer candidate near the end of 1916. The new arrangements for a show were due in part to Pound's continued success in educating John Quinn. Quinn's taste in modern art was formed by the Impressionists, and he disliked the subdued colors, especially the drab reds, of Lewis's work. Lewis's use of pigment was in fact a reaction to what he considered the merely decorative use of color and lack of form in the Impressionist school. Pound shrewdly explained this to Quinn by praising Lewis's "fundamental realism" in his attempt "to show the beauty of the colour one actually sees in a modern brick, iron, sooty, rail-road-yarded smoked modern city. . . . All this as distinct from the pretty brightness of Picabia or 1910 Paris." Quinn was eventually won over and became a still more generous supporter of Lewis. Even the delay in getting his commission was to Lewis's advantage, for it kept him out of the line of fire for many extra months.

"too disadvantageously": The Prothéro letter is quoted in Noel Stock, *The Life of Ezra Pound,* p. 162.

one of his paintings: See *Blasting and Bombardiering,* p. 51.

"1910 Paris": Pound to Quinn, 13 July 1916 (John Quinn Memorial Collection: New York Public Library).

42. ALS—4.

Weymouth.

Sunday. June 25th/16.

Dear Pound.   Thank you for your letter. I have penetrated your meaning perfectly & think your advice very good. Only I fear that this time I am not imagining malice. =Ninn gave a very damaging report of my doings at E. Weare, which astonished me very much, & grieved the Adjutant. There was no justification for that report. I dont see how I can expect anything but a similar hostility in the future. And all I am worrying about is that any position in 4 or 5 weeks, if I fail in this new examination, will be worse than it is now as regards the recommendation for the Cadet School. I might have to go to France as reinforcements almost at once; & once there I should never get any commission. Besides, I dont want to go there just yet. I shall have to go there quite soon enough. I want to go there as an officer; & as the war is evidently going on for another year or so, in 4 or 5 or even 6 months time would suit me excellently. Apart from the question of France, if you knew exactly how it was in the Ranks— the many reasons why it is desirable to be an officer—you would understand my being anxious to change my state.

Anyhow, I am in for this bloody course again now, I suppose. If I withdraw brusquely I should put the Adjutant's back up, & do myself no good. But I have a bad time in front of me: there is not much hope for a satisfactory result from the Examination.

= I have just written a more or less pot-boiling article on a military subject; I should like at once to get it into some paper. Would Watt the agent be any good for that. I think the Daily Mail would be the best place for it to appear. = Its appearance might help me here.

If you ask Matthews [*sic*] to send a copy of Cathay to Colonel Inglis.

O. C. Portland Defences.
Red Barracks.
Weymouth.
Dorset.

it might be a good thing, & save me some definitions so far too much in the air. I should have something to talk to my O[fficer] C[ommanding] about, & my commission might ripen in your bed of Chinese interpretations.

Write me, if you have time, about the Daily Mail article, giving me your advice.

If you have time & are that way, I wish you would keep your eyes on that book of mine that Goschen took & paid for, & which was his (in MSS. still) behind the book-shop in Coptic Street. Our Wild Body it was called: I may have spoken [to] you about it.

By all means let us have a show in London in the Autumn: there are plenty of drawings.

Is the £25 mine soon, at once, or when Q[uinn]. answers? = I am curious to hear what he thinks of the works sent, especially Kermesse. =

Do you know, does your wife know, Pat a Beckett? There is a man here called Captain Pat Abeckett (or à Beckett) who is the sort of character who might be useful to me. He has been on stage, & is somewhat a nut. I will copy out my address again:

Bdr. W. Lewis.
71050.
Hut 78.
R.G.A. Training Unit.
Westham.
Weymouth.

Yours ever   Wyndham Lewis

pot-boiling article: In *Blasting and Bombardiering,* p. 102, Lewis writes: "The 'Bull-gun', an article which I wrote at the time, speaks of 'the romance of the big guns, which has boomed loud for over a century.' " It was never published. A draft of this article is in the Wyndham Lewis collection in the Olin Library, Cornell University.

somewhat a nut: Lewis uses the word "nut" in the sense of a smartly-dressed or stylish person.

43. TLS–2.

28-6-'16.

5 Holland Park Chambers,
Holland Park.

Dear Lewis: I still rather doubt whether you have got to the bottom of
my beastly letter. The information I received, or the assurances were very
definite and at the same time very general. They are hardly repeatable,
and as they tacitly forbade me to make any further more meticulous enquiry.

Their substance was very much what I have already conveyed to
you . . . but in a sort of categorical and imperial tone.

That is to say "The gods grant your prayers to the letter, neither
more nor less, . Cease from troubling the gods."

I will have a copy of "Cathay" transmitted. I think I perhaps sympa-
thize more with your desire for advancement than the tone of my last
note might seem to show. I will wait for a fitting moment. Balfour between
the second and third acts did not seem to me to present a favourable
target. It is not his dept. and he would have been distinctly annoyed, He
considered that Shelley's best work was done in his youth etc.

Your Colonel seems more contemporary in his interests. Besides you
see more of him.

I dont believe A.P. Watt would be any use re/ an article for the
Dily Mile [*Daily Mail*]. The last link with Goshen is either "joined up"
or evading the military. God knows I dont know how to go at a thing of
this sort, (article into D. Mail) I have never been able to get printed in
any english paper save the New Age and Egoist, and the more august
reviews.

The £25 malheureusement is not yours till Q[uinn]. instructs me
to pay it you. which wont be till he gets my letter saying I have recovered
it for him.

We know not any à Beckett, but D[orothy]. thinks she may have a
cousin who does. She has never met the cousin.

I am bubbling at my Jap plays for Mac.M[illan]. If Q. is successful
in N.Y. in placing various things, I may get started on the brochure concerning your glory. De Bosschere is very much impressed with "Timon",
says "we have nothing like it in Paris". Not exactly news. ma che.

Yrs.
E.P.

Balfour: Arthur Balfour, the former prime minister, was at this time the British
foreign secretary.

44. ALS–1. [Pmk: Weymouth, 8 July 1916]. On a letter card.

Weymouth.

Saturday   July 8th

Dear Pound.   The S[ergeant].M[ajor]. has just told me that I am for
medical inspection tomorrow for Service Overseas: & that I shall either
join one of the Siege Batteries at present partially formed in the camp, or
be sent to Boxhill. The last draught that went to Boxhill was sent to
France within a week, without their six days leave. I expect I could manage, however, to get the leave. = When I returned last week the Adjutant
saw me, said that he had not good reports of me, & that I should have
"another show." I was to have had a "special course [?]" in the Camp,
& be attached to the Training Unit. But I suppose that since then the
official dung in this camp has again, with great esprit de corps, reported
darkly on me. =

It is just as well, on the whole. I could not have stood the present
state of affairs much longer. France will be decidedly better than that. I
shall take care not to mention the word "commission" when I get there:
else I feel I should certainly be a dead man.

I have been treated here with the most absolute & unwavering unfair-
ness: but I dont think it is a personal matter. I think any one who had
been fool enough to enlist would have, in varying degree, the same difficulties. = I might now be shifted from here, then, at any moment. But
this will be my address probably for a few days. Will let you know how
things turn out.

Yrs W. L.

45. ALS–1. [Pmk: Weymouth, 13 July 1916]. In pencil on a letter card.

Weymouth.

Dear Pound: I have just heard that I am posted to 183 Siege. So that
has settled that matter. I shall not be recommended from this place. = But
in all probability I shall be 6 weeks at Aldershot, & it will be a fresh
start. —Or I hope it will. —I can then work for the Cadetship. Meantime, I shall be here another 10 days or 2 weeks, I expect.
=

Try if you can manage it to solve temporarily my financial situation, as
you have often before. Oh bless Quinn,   oh Bless Pound!

Yrs   W.L.

46. TLS–2. [July 1916]. On stationery embossed: 5, Holland Place Chambers, Kensington. W.

Dear Bomb. W.L.

Quinn has spent £65 on getting the vort[icist]. show to N. Y., to be exact 324 dollars and 58 cents. He now contemplates the cost of frames etc.

I enclose a page of his epistle, which please return. Don't worry about the "Neighing" it is safe here. I dont know why Sheldon should have assumed that they had sent it to N. Y.

Your photo. shows the influence of the Y.M.C.A. in a highly "striking" degree. Excellent young man, virtuous, gentle, sweet in disposition, deferential etc. etc.

No one has the least sympathy with your present troubles. I jawed to the charming wife of your supposed friend B[onham].C[arter]. for a quarter of an hour the other day. "What! GARRISON artillery'"!!, my dear, safe as a church,".

Four brothers in much more uncomfortable position, just as clever, well no, two of 'em just ordinary and two really talented. AND Orpen in the ranks.

"Anybody who gets through this war without mutilation, etc. etc." "
"If he's any good, he'll get recommended for promotion anyhow, etc."

No, mon ami, you have not, in the past, ingratiated yourself with certain people, and you have left your stuff in a filthy and dusty pile on the floor of your studio so that apart from the humble writer of this epistle and yourself and perhaps a few stray hetairae [sic] there is no one in this island who knows who and what you are, etc. etc. and etc.

Despite the sunday-school face on your last DEEliscious fotograft. Corpo di Bacco. Cocco di Fucco etc.

Also one of her brothers did get into "Information" and it bored him so that he got out again at the end of a week and went back to killin' and murther.

Also BLAST is better known than Timon and some of your hitherto invisible masterwork, such as drawings (OF a frightful obscenity), and it isn't everyone that likes Blast.

The P[rime].M[inister]. dont for one. Though attempts have been made with some success to convert him to milder phases (or persona).

I really dont see anything for it except for you to be quiet, sober and industrious, (bloody and god damd industrious), and I doubt if that will do any good. I should give up "costly" mechanations [sic].

Yes, I have reminded J[ohn] Q[uinn], twice or thrice. etc. I trust the Secker affair comes to something.

Votre bien devoué

E.

photo: This could be the photograph that appears in *Blasting and Bombardiering* facing p. 32.

Orpen: William Orpen, a traditional painter who was "blasted" in the 1915 *BLAST*.

47. AL–4. [Pmk: Weymouth, 16 July 1916].

My dear Pound.   Thank you for letter, & good news on postcard as regards Secker.

I have just received a note from Secker saying he wishes to negotiate for the publishing of Tarr next year.

I am enclosing the sheet of Quinn's epistle that you forwarded. Now that of course is very bad news. It's unfortunate that the whole lot of my things did not arrive at once. Also that he was in doubt as to authorship. = Naturally, some home product has to be supported. Is Davies really as good as can be found? From the reproductions I have seen he appears only a fashionable & not very interesting phenomenon. As to "the French", of course they have arrived in New York in great force; all the experts whom Quinn allows himself to be guided by would be of that camp, Pasquin [Pascin] or others. = The fact, however, as regards myself is Q. unfortunately is not touché. Well, he will be in the end. Meantime, I need money to an uncomfortable degree. You can say to him from me, if you care, that as the goods have not given satisfaction in proportion to his hopes, that something could be knocked off the sum originally agreed upon, if I could have the money soon. I must just now get in something, if there is still a 'must' for such a held-up & fettered individual as myself. You can tell him that Red is not a predilection of the English, but a quite wilful, a perhaps unpleasant, invention of my own. The stupidity of our countrymen is, it is true, most crudely displayed in red pillar boxes, soldiers' vermilion coats, and the cold bright dashes of colour females choose. Greenery-yallery are, however, the National Art-colours of England.

As to Ministerial circles: I believe you are always thinking about some drastic means of securing my safety: but I feel that however desirable that may be, it is quite impossible to compass it. Secondly, I think that, confused with this larger and vaguer claim for me, the simple request for a cadetship might, some day, stand a chance. I must here claim as well, without any pretention to being a "brave", that a disinclination to go into the firing line is not very great with me. I contemplate going to France with perfect equanimity, although, you may believe me, I think very seldom about it. My strivings have not had for their object an avoidance of this inevitable development of my present activities, but only to secure myself favourable conditions. In the end it will worry me a certain amount to think I am so utterly wasting my time. ⟨As an officer I might be able to count on a few steady hours a week in which I could write or draw.⟩ = As to the R[oyal]. G[arrison]. A[rtillery]. being as "safe as a church," churches in France are the most notoriously unsafe buildings tc be found. The R.G.A. is much safer than any church. To resume: you need not worry about death & mutilation. But about the Ranks, c'est autre chose. Orpen has not been in the Ranks probably even as long as myself; & he probably derives sentimental satisfactions from his rough life that I scorn to find. Also, there are differences. I have had, you can again believe me, a particularly disagreeable time. I dont mind the roughness of the life physically. Most of that I enjoy.

The Siege (183) is so far a pleasant enough little battery. The Sergeant in charge told me that I did better on the field than any corporal present. I have got a slight promotion, 4 1/2d a day more. = But there are no officers as yet! —except one lifeless individual.

===

I have adopted the Roman Catholic category in my siege battery. This will eliminate one of the chief nuisances of life in the Army, those dreadful English churches. I can think of nothing on earth as imbecile & despicable as the music & words of those hymns. = The Mass is a function I shall not object to.

====

I expect after that letter of Quinn's you feel that you have sold him something that he will regret having bought. Under the circumstances, the Vorticist show will do me little good; if its promoter is "not hit" himself, it is unlikely that other people will be. The Quinn news is the worst

I have heard for some time. But it cant be helped. Until I can get back
to life again, & continue & intensify my deployment, things must remain so.

> My address is   Hut 44.
> 183. Siege Battery.
> Westham Camp.
> Weymouth.

48. ALS–3.

> Hut 44.
> 183. Seige Battery. R.G.A.
> Westham Camp.
> July 17/16.

Dear Pound.   As I consume sufficient excretion here, why not a little
more? Not but what I am sure that your hand would never offer me that
sustenance (it is sustaining, of course.) But still, to talk about money
except from some secure elevation, transfers me to a boggy plane. = Descend with me, Poet, to my miniature personal, military hell for a second.
= If Quinn's consent to your transference of some funds you have of his
to me (that you spoke to me of) does not arrive in a week or so, I shall
be penniless. On Wednesday a pound or so well-spent would really (no
machinations) have a certain magic. If you could advance me (without
entering into unnecessary details) £5 at once things may take a turn
decidedly for the better.

Another painful fact = as regards Quinn, he will, to judge from the
fragment of his letter that I read, be of no use to me in a big way for
some time. I should need to deploy myself more,—have five books behind me, the recognition of Paris, another fuller & better Timon etc. etc.
before I could approach him again. —So, as far as I am concerned, it is
only a matter of getting such funds as would last me till I got to France &
the Secker arrangement or some other came along.

As to your feeling in the matter, do not let a shadow of doubt enter
your mind that you have made anything but a very satisfactory arrangement for Quinn. = Quinn himself will tell you so some day. You have
enabled me by your services in the direction of Quinn, (& now it looks as

though you had won me Secker) to pass my days bearably while 'doing time.' Dont think I am ungrateful: or that I would send an appeal if I were not cornered. Secondly, you have seen for yourself that I am anything but worldly, and not able, in nine cases out of ten, to do any good for myself in the subterranean galleries of our Aristocratic Golcondas, or amongst the peevish streams of remoter Klondykes. I am an 'enfant de la Nature,' that is why you believe in me, of course. = Well, to you I can speak with the certainty of a steady understanding. Can you see any way out of my present impasse? If I could tell you everything you would know how I require some funds. But dont do anything to prejudice your hold over Quinn & I quite see, since you have shown me his words, that it is more difficult to speak of helping me now, by expeditious payments, that he may possibly be grudging.

Yrs.   W. Lewis.

49. TLS–3. On stationery embossed: 5, Holland Place Chambers, Kensington. W.

Dear Lewis

Enclosed please find etc. £5/. BUTT the B-loody trouble is, that I dont like to fork out more of Q[uinn]'s funds than I can in case of EEEEmergency cover. AND in this the third year of the BBBBBloody and Ensanguined WARRRR that sum is not egregious BUTTT on the kawntrary. AND there are in my relations with Q. various sources of possible irritation, the female relict of Brzeska being enough to exhaust various funds of patience, etc.

I don't think in the end you need to be too despondent about Q. I think he intends taking rather more than £120 worth of things but he hasnt come to any definite conclusion. I dont think he is at present wild about the Kermess. Neither can you count on his keeping a few things hung up before him, as I have done, until they sink in and illuminate the spectatorial mind.

Obviously he has had the "Timon" portfolio for a long time without getting an exhuberant or at least articulate enthusiasm from it.

ALSO there are other artists at hand, HIS hand, ALSO I doubt if the child of nature naturalness will go very far with him. He makes all he spends. My position is a little embarrassing as I have constantly to approach you in the paternal, admonitory, cautionary, epicierish bloodguttily INartistic angle. I add to the £5/, 7/6 which I owe you (or Leveridge) for two copies of Blast sold to an Amurkn artist. (No I. @ 5/ and No. 2. @ 2/6) My own life has been always(?, yes unfortunately, or frequently) an model of order and frugality, with a few exceptions, and it has damaged my temper to a degree, to several degrees. ⟨I do not advise such a course for anyone else, let alone an artist.⟩ DAMN it all, I DID begin my attack on Mrs. B[onham].C[arter]. with a "cadetship", and it was at a time when my hostess expected me to be doing something else. (And the result was as I wrote.)

I do not see any way out of your impasse. Nor of several of my own either. However nil desesperandum [*sic*], Invicta, tabernis, putae, scortae, prostitutae, saltantes, ver, vinum, vimmen, nec inutilis sepultis, (all except the last).

Can you suggest any bloody way to keep MY income wholly from disappearing, from innocuous desuetude, from what G.R.S. Mead calls the eternal mystery of non-being?????

IF Quinn succeeds with MacMillan in America for me, then part of the job may be a book on you with illustrations, ALL of which will take time. Probably there'd be no advance payment. I have an order from the MacM. here for a book on Jap plays, no advance payment, either, but the thin end of the eternal wedge which seems never to have anything else but a thin edge.

I have not seen the empress [probably Mrs. Bonham-Carter] for some time. Life, in the language of our respected fellow citizen Mr Flanniggan, ...!!!!!!!!'

etc. etc. and etc. let us consider the lily. It has roots, tenacious of the ground, wherethrough it deriveth its sustenance, but we, we have no roots, neither Fundy nor Idaho give us gold. This is a very great evil and an exceeding carelessness in the Cosmos.

If, for instance, any plan occurs to me, I shall, need I say, act. Ma che Krisstto.

⟨Even pampered producers the Dulacs are "feeling the pinch" as the "Sidelights from Germany" put it. How then shall particles hostile to the current ???? shall end by quoting the late Mr Swinburne. If I dont stop first.⟩

Yrs ever

E.P.

relict of Brzeska: When Henri Gaudier-Brzeska died in the war in 1915, the woman he had lived with, Sophie Brzeska, had possession of most of Gaudier's works but no clear legal ownership of them. This uncertainty complicated Pound's efforts to sell some of Gaudier's works to John Quinn.

Fundy nor Idaho: Pound and Lewis were born, respectively, in Hailey, Idaho and the Bay of Fundy, Amherst, Nova Scotia (on the Lewis family yacht).

50. TLS–2. [July 1916]. [5, Holland Place Chambers, Kensington. W.].

Dear Lewis

Quinn has sent the other £25, which I will forward to you as soon as I hear that the address on this envelope is still the right one.

He now says he "agrees with what" I say about Lewis. He expects to make an offer for certain other works "ten or twelve" or "possibly 15." That is rather indefinite and I doubt if you could sue legally if he changed his mind. HOWEVER!!!!. Davies seems to be friendly. He offered to pay half the freight when Montrose refused. Quinn naturally wouldn't let Davies do it. Still it shows a sporting mind on the, or in the[,] skull of Davies. Q. thinks, or thought, in a former note that Davies might buy something.

The £25 which I now have for you, finishes up the £120 of the agreement with Q. for the Kermoos [*Kermesse*] etc.

I have just returned from a dam'd week by the seawaves. Eliot present. Eliot in local society. Fry, Canon [Gilbert Cannan], Lowes Dickenson [Dickinson], Hope Johnson [Hope-Johnston]. (None of whom I met). Had the ineffable pleasure of watching Fry's sylph-like and lardlike length bobbing around in the muddy water off the pier.

Met Hueffer's brother-in-law [David Soskice] on the plaisaunce. He said a shell had burst near our friend and that he had had a nervous breakdown and was for the present safe in a field hospital. Ford's brother Oliver is in the trenches. (These small bits of news will doubtless cheer and enlighten you. Thank God I have got back to the court-suburb.)

ED Wad has arrived in Mudros. He has written me an epistle which I will forward to you if you have not received one of your own.

P.S. Eliot, after mature deliberation, has discovered that Fry is "an ass". Eliot has walked into his landlady's bed room, "quite by mistake", said he was looking for his wife. Landlady unconvinced. Wife believes in the innocence of his intentions. Landlady sympathetic with wife. Landlady spent Sunday placing flowers on her mother's grave. Landlady (in parenthesis) unmarried but under fifty.

Oh yes, called at Leicester gallery day before I went toward seawaves. Phi[l]lips away ill, so accomplished nothing.

yrs
E.P.

Montrose: The Montross (not Montrose) Gallery canceled their offer to hold a Vorticist exhibition in New York.

shell had burst: In July 1916 Ford Madox Ford was attached to an infantry brigade that fought in the battle of the Somme. See Arthur Mizener, *The Saddest Story,* pp. 291–94.

51. ALS–2.

Weymouth.
Hut 44.
183. Siege Batt.
R.G.A.
Westham Camp.
July 23. 1916.

Dear Pound: Many thanks for the two cheques: first the one for £5.7.6 and secondly that for £20.0.0; £25 that is off amount of my sales to Quinn, 7/6 for 3 copies of Blast. ≡ That is very cheering news you send me from Q. I suppose I owe that in part to my fellow-artist, Davies. Davies has evidently given a "good report!" I feel I have been promoted, & may get a little more pay. But I am not of course unduly sanguine.

I got the Catalogue you sent me. I was struck by a certain disparity between the proud calm words of the Preface upholding divorce from representation and associated ideas, & the probable character of the works. Or rather once more I notice that a promoter of those very sound ideas is apt to choose work of any artist to be shown of a sort that the Public will "understand." The consequent self-flattery on the part of the citizen will put him in a good temper. = I feel that in Blast, to begin with, we were a trifle too conscientious.

=   =   =

I have just been inoculated, & expect in an hour or so that the beastly stuff will begin to work. I was complimented on my drill the other day by the Adjutant: also, following an appearance of my photograph in Mirror, one of the authorities in the Camp remarked that Bdr. Lewis was drilling better than he had ever heard him before. But I shall undoubtedly, & despite this, remain a Bombardier to the end of the chapter.

No news from Secker yet. I wrote 4 or 5 days ago. = Tell me any further news of Quinn.

Yours ever   Wyndham Lewis.

Catalogue: The catalog was of an exhibition entitled, "Philadelphia's First Exhibition of Advanced Modern Art, May 17th to June 15th, 1916," written by Morton L. Schamberg.

Mirror: A photograph of Lewis appeared in the London *Daily Mirror* for 18 July 1916 (p. 10) in a column that reported: "Mr. Lewis is about to publish a series of articles showing how a Vorticist views military life."

52. ANS–1. [Pmk: Weymouth, 5 August 1916].

> 183.Siege Battery.
> Lydd.   Kent.
> Aug: 1916.

Dear Pound.   Thank you for cheque of Quinn's, for £25, received today, on account of sum agreed on for purchase of paintings & drawings. Is that the lot?—I have lost count.

Yours ever   Wyndham Lewis.

53. TLS–1. [August 1916]. On stationery embossed: 5, Holland Place Chambers, Kensington. W.

Dear Lewis

No news. The Eddie-Marsh-Asquith-Beerbohm-Trees section of society does not favour an advance in thought. The opera season ends this week. Wrote a long letter on vort[icism]. to a western american paper, to keep the jaw from dying out. Printers slower than ever.

Can you, by the way, send me a regular receipt for Q[uinn]'s £25. I want it to send on to him. I cant very well send your letter.

I will try to see Phillips of the Leicester Gallery re a show of drawings sometime soon. I met him a few weeks ago and he seemed to be vacillating about "what effect the war....etc.". ? new art coming in? I told him NEW art was coming in. Dead would be buried etc. (It's not particularly true, but then .....). Anyhow I dont think one can expect much of him, but will have a try.

yrs. E.P.

54. ACS–1. [Pmk: Lydd, 20 August 1916].

Herewith a picture of a stubborn looking object, sufficiently stupid, sullen and phallic?   W.L.

picture: The postcard shows a crew of soldiers moving a heavy gun.

55. ALS–2. [Pmk: Lydd, 20 August 1916].

Bdr. W. Lewis. 71050.
Hut 60. = Wood Town. =
(C. Sub-Section.)
183 Siege Battery.
Lydd.
Kent.

Dear Pound. My stay at Horsham was short. I had a day in town, & visited you. But you were away. I shall be up again before long, I hope. In any case we get our 6 days Overseas leave here. = We stop here 3 or 4 weeks, going through a firing course. I may add that occasionally first blood is drawn at this so called "live" camp. But it is chiefly signallers that are killed.

Your letter was forwarded me from Westham. I delayed acknowledging it till I got here, & had an address. = I was very glad to hear that Quinn now has matured his judgement; and that there are prospects of a further sale over there. I hope we may arrange for a small show in London this autumn: but England is a bloody and abominable place to be anything but a fool in.

I am progressing favourably in my military exercises, I think. I might even put in successfully for a commission. But we have no commanding officer as yet: & it would be no good applying to the beshitten suet-faced little microbic Sub. who is at present in his place.

We are attached to the F. Brigade, which is in Egypt. So I expect the Balkans or Asia Minor is where we shall eventually find ourselves.

I am writing a book called "The Bombardier:" only in my head, of course. = I have received a letter from my naval colleague [Edward Wadsworth] at Mudros, who is surrounded by warships & volcanoes, he tells me. Such propinquity, and the seclusion of his island office, should in the end produce a furtive woodcut or two, printed in romantic reds.

Are you being very active? = Will you send the Quinn cheque to above address (rather unwieldly, I am afraid) in a registered letter?

Thank you for news—Hueffer's shell shock etc. Do you ever hear of Mrs. Turner?

Yours ever   Wyndham Lewis.

56. ALS–1. [Pmk: Lydd, 23 August 1916].

> Bdr. W. Lewis. 71050.
> Hut 60. Wood Town.
> 183. Siege Battery.
> C. Sub Section.
> > Lydd.
> > > Kent.

Dear Pound.   Many thanks for cheque. Am sending with this an isolated acknowledgement.

Give Quinn time, & he is alright. The slow-starters are not the worst in the long run, etc. The news generally is very good; and I am particularly glad that Bobby [Roberts] is going to get something. I hope the show will be a success. Edward [Wadsworth]'s peasant-mania about pence has no doubt not been seen as a charming, almost graceful, weakness, but as a stunted and disagreeable sign.

Bobby is jogging round France with an ammunition column, leading a pleasant caravan-like life. = I will send you his address tomorrow, & Etchells' if I can find it.

Yours ever   Wyndham Lewis.

Bobby: Roberts was included in the Vorticist show in New York.

57. TLS–1. On stationery embossed: 5, Holland Place Chambers, Kensington. W.

26–8–'16

Dear W.L.

Q[uinn]. is evidently warming up. He has sent another £10 for Etchells and also £10 for an Ed. Wad[sworth]. drawing. Though he expresses a preference for the works of il capo riconociuto W. L.

Would you mind signing & dating the receipt here adjoined. Q. has expressed himself on artistic vagueness .... quite incidentally .... but I think there will be no harm in using this form in stead of the more breezy one you sent me.

I haven't yet Etchells or Bobby's [Roberts] addresses, though Mrs Fan[ny] Wad[sworth] has given me a more modern domicile of Etchells than the one I had. Q. evidently isn't going to waste the £60 he spent on freight, and certainly isn't going to have anything like so large a freight bill for the return trip.

yours   E.P.

Introduction to Letter 58.

Lewis finally achieved his ambition to be trained as an officer in September 1916 when the colonel at his gunnery camp recommended him for a commission. As the following letter shows, Pound and his other friends continued to help by signing the necessary recommendation forms. Lewis went to the training school at Exeter, where he was taught to ride a horse, and then to the Trowbridge Cadet School, where he received his officer's "pip." When he sailed for France, he was a subaltern in a siege battery. No letters to Pound survive from this training period, if indeed Lewis had the leisure for such correspondence at this time. (He told John Quinn that he had "ten hours of lectures and notes" per day.) His last letter to Pound before he left for France concerns one of Lewis's best stories, "Cantleman's Spring-Mate," which describes the last few weeks in England of a soldier who is about to be shipped to France. Although Lewis "expurgated" the text of this story, its sexual frankness provoked the U.S. Post Office to suppress the October 1917 issue of *The Little Review*. Lewis's farewell to Pound manages to express Lewis's excitement at going into action at the same time it shows his awareness of how popular sentiment has romanticized the "adventure" of war.

"ten hours of lectures": The Letters of Wyndham Lewis, ed. W. K. Rose, p. 86.

58. ACS. [Pmk: Kensington, 7 September 1916]. On stationery embossed: 5, Holland Place Chambers. Kensington. W.

WHAT D̲o̲ you want done with the blue form which you sent to V[iolet]. H[unt]. instead of wherever she expected you to send it. Met her gesticulating on a corner & trying to catch a bus. = She has not left me his address. Who else is to sign it?

yrs   E.

WHY hadn't you been to Binyon???

blue form: This apparently was an application for a commission that C. F. G. Masterman, Violet Hunt, and Laurence Binyon were to sign. See *The Letters of Wyndham Lewis,* ed. W. K. Rose, pp. 84–85.
his address: Laurence Binyon's.

59. ALS–2.

22/5/17.
Cosham.

Dear Pound.   I couldn't manage to get round on Saturday morning. Subsequent visits did not find you at home. Tant pis. But there was not much to settle. = I am sending you tomorrow MSS. of second story: and Cantelman's Spring Mate, expurgated, is arriving if it has not already by Miss S[aunders].'s fair hands.

Our advance party sails this afternoon, and we are standing by. Two days should see us pushing forward on what the Daily Mail, Sphere, Morning Post and John Bull describe as the Great Adventure. = We are not taking our guns out: we dont know if we are going as reinforcement to sadly depleted Trench Mortars, taking over German guns or what. This is of course unsatisfactory.

I am writing all necessary letters, for once. Au revoir. À bientôt!

Yrs   W.L.

Cantelman: Lewis spelled the name of his character as "Cantelman" as well as "Cantleman" before he settled on "Cantleman."

Part II
Bombardiering
1917-1919

And Wyndham Lewis went to it,
With a heavy bit of artillery,
      and the airmen came by with a mitrailleuse,
And cleaned out most of his company,
      and a shell lit on his tin hut,
While he was out in the privvy,
      and he was all there was left of that outfit

Canto XVI/pp. 71–72

Bombardiering   1917–1919

Ezra Pound described Wyndham Lewis as a "man at war" in June 1914, two months before World War I began and almost two years before Lewis left for the front lines in France. As the Vorticist artists responded to the spirit of violent change that preceded the war, Pound claimed that their generation would "sweep out the past century as surely as Attila swept across Europe." The Vorticists supported revolutionary change, at least in theory, even if it were violent. In a list of "Blesses," *BLAST* praised representatives of the same disruptive movements that George Danger-field credits with destroying the Liberal establishment in England before the war: the Labour movement, the Ulster rebels, and the Suffragettes. The only form of violent protest the Vorticists disapproved was the destruction of works of art by the Suffragettes. *BLAST* praises their movement but warns: "leave Art alone, brave comrades!"

Pound celebrated the power of artists, "the antennae of the race," to anticipate the currents of change in society. Lewis, on the other hand, wrote in 1937 that he found it

> somewhat depressing to consider how as an artist one is always holding the mirror up to politics without knowing it. My picture called "The Plan of War" [BLAST, no. 1] painted six months before the Great War "broke out," as we say, depresses me. . . . With me war and art have been mixed up from the start.

In *Rude Assignment* (1950), Lewis shows how far back this mixture of war and art goes in his life. He recalls that as a child of eight he stitched together his own war epics, which he describes as "no stupider than the Volsungensaga but in range even narrower, being confined altogether to war, instead of practically altogether to war." His first drawings were of primitive Redskins and palefaces as illustrations for his stories:

> I was a denizen of the "Leatherstocking" world. I started life at eight as a war-chronicler therefore. It never ceases for me to be unpleasant that the tiny mind of a little animal like myself at eight and earlier should be filled by its elders with such pasteboard violence, initiating it into this old game of murder. Born into a military aristocracy life begins full of excited little bangs and falsetto war-cries.

Although scarcely one of the military "aristocracy," Lewis's father was trained at West Point and served in the Civil War as a captain in Sheridan's Cavalry. This military heritage was still a force in Lewis's life when he attended Rugby and attempted unsuccessfully to transfer to the army class, but he had no doubt rejected it by the time he started at the Slade School of Art in 1898. In a manuscript of 1914, his autobiographical protagonist "Cantleman" is astonished when a friend claims that a European war is imminent: "What was war? He had no idea. . . . His father had been a soldier. That was a reason to misunderstand war, or think little about: what his father had done he would not do."

We never learn why Cantleman reacts so decidedly against his father, but we know that Lewis himself disapproved of his father and perhaps even felt betrayed by him. Charles Edward Lewis married an English-woman, Anne Stuart, and then lived on both sides of the Atlantic until Percy Wyndham was ten, when they separated and Anne Lewis and her son settled in England. Charles Lewis supported his son erratically. Lewis wrote to his mother in 1907: "I suppose, as you say, it's difficult to extract money—even one's due, from our fellow beings especially at Christmas time. —I didn't certainly think that the Parent over the Water would respond to my amiable letter: he's an old rip." His feelings about his father surface in his autobiographical first novel *Tarr*. One of the novel's characters, Kreisler, is supported as an art student in Paris by his father. When his father cuts off his allowance and marries Kreisler's own fiancée, the artist begins a desperate series of actions that finally leads to his suicide. It is also significant that a character in Lewis's play *The Ideal Giant* (1917) asserts her identity by murdering her father. This deed inspires the Lewis figure in the play, who so far has merely theorized about the relationship of thought to action, to defend the murderess from the detective who attempts to seize her. These works were being written as Charles Lewis's support of his son dwindled to nothing. As late as 1937, Lewis said he felt "cheated of my patrimony."

Yet Lewis's paternal heritage as well as his service in World War I shaped his personality throughout his life. John Rothenstein wrote of Lewis as he was in the thirties: "War played, I think, a considerable part in his imaginative life: he occasionally used military terms to describe his own operations, offensive or defensive, and he alluded more than once to his belonging by birth 'to a military caste.'" Lewis's attitude toward his father eventually mellowed, and in 1940 he began but never finished edit-ing selections from his father's war memoirs, wishing to preserve the memory of "this one-time captain in Sheridan's Cavalry—this fox-hunting, brigantine-owning, essay-writing *bum* . . . this odd-man-out in a society of go-getters." Lewis characterizes his father as a political näif. Charles Edward Lewis left West Point in 1862 prepared to fight on the side of his friends at the academy, who were Southerners. This decision horrified his family back in upstate New York, and they soon convinced him that he should fight on the Northern side. Lewis sees this vacillation as typical of his father:

> That he had any understanding, however rudimentary, of the true back-grounds of this great Civil disturbance, there is no evidence. To learn for instance that it was a war made by an industrial community upon an agri-cultural community . . . or anything abstractly political of that nature, would have surprised and abashed him very greatly I am sure. He might never have fought at all, for either side, had any notions of that sort been introduced into his already confused head.

Lewis's own father is the first of the political "simpletons" that Lewis scorned throughout his life.

The son, however, was as much a "simpleton" as his father. When Lewis reflected on a photograph of himself in uniform, he compared the soldier to the child who wrote and illustrated war chronicles:

> I see the same self that was responsible for the booklets: but this time he is not a child, he is in uniform among belted, pouched, tin-hatted, fellow-soldiers of world war I. I perceive a sort of repetition—it is the same pattern, only the bangs and cries of battle had become real, for the figure in the photograph, not academic.—And I am ashamed to say that even then I still saw these things as a child does.

Lewis admits elsewhere in *Rude Assignment* that he tends to exaggerate the naiveté of his early attitudes, and I believe that is the case here. No one, of course, could have foreseen how disastrous the first modern war would prove to be.

A conviction about his pre-war naiveté was in any event a cherished part of his personal myth, and he liked to compare his inexperienced opinions to what he assumed was the wisdom of older friends such as T. Sturge Moore and Ford Madox Ford. Ford is the model for the friend who predicts the war in the "Cantleman" fragment in which the protago-nist reacts against his father's military career. The fictionalized scene is not so amusing as the actual one as remembered by Lewis in *Blasting and Bombardiering*. In August 1914 Lewis was staying with Pound, Ford and Violet Hunt at the countryhouse of Mrs. Turner—the novelist Mary Borden, who was one of Lewis's patrons. The Berwickshire setting was a strangely quiet one in which to hear of the outbreak of war, and Ford himself felt that this weekend was a "charmed occasion, a last, magical Edwardian pause before the crash of the war." Lewis agreed with his hostess when she told Ford:

> "There won't be any war, Ford. Not here. England won't go into war."
> Ford thrust his mouth out, fish-fashion, as if about to gasp for breath. He goggled his eyes and waggled one eyelid about. He just moved his lips a little and we heard him say, in a breathless sotto voce—
> "England will."
> "England will! But Ford," said Mrs. Turner, "England has a Liberal Government. A Liberal Government cannot declare war."
> "Of course it can't," I said, frowning at Ford. "Liberal governments can't go to war. That would not be liberal. That would be conservative."
> Ford sneered very faintly and inoffensively: he was sneering at the British Government, rather than at us. He was being the omniscient, bored, and sleepy Ford, sunk in his tank of sloth. From his prolonged siesta he was staring out at us all with his fish-blue eyes—kind, wise, but bored. Or some such idea. His mask was only just touched with derision at our childishness.

About this talk of "liberal" and "conservative" Lewis said "he knew as little as the peacocks at the zoo." The "blasting" of England was such fun for the Vorticists because they felt secure themselves: "Life was one big bloodless brawl, prior to the Great Bloodletting."

However naive or inexperienced Lewis may have been, he was not emotionally unprepared for the war. The fiction he wrote before he fought in France shows how far he was from conventional sentiments and expectations about the war. Lewis's fellow Vorticist Henri Gaudier-Brzeska, an avowed anarchist, praised the war as a "great remedy." Lewis expresses his more realistic view of the war in his story "The French Poodle" (1916), when a character contradicts H. G. Wells's famous description of the war: " 'This "great war" is the beginning of a period, far from being a war-that-will-end-war, take my word for it.' " Lewis's protagonist in "The French Poodle" is so shocked by the way war reduces men to a level below animals that he severs relations with those closest to him and transfers his affection to a dog, preferring to man's barbarity the "sanity of direct animal processes." Lewis traces the development of the gunner's "sullen neurasthenia" into a psychotic state in which he kills his dog rather than leave it among men. He wishes for death himself, in part because he has shot his dog, and is killed as soon as he returns to the front. This sympathetic study of the impact of war on a sensitive mind resembles "The King of the Trenches" (1916), in which another shell-shocked veteran is described. However, he never published this later story. Like Yeats in writing of Wilfred Owen, Lewis could not consider "passive suffering" a worthy response to the war. He felt a more aggressive and sardonic reaction was needed to the spectacle of mass slaughter. He attempts this harsher reaction in the same issue of *The Egoist* in which "The French Poodle" appears. In a brief vignette entitled "A Young Soldier," Lewis contrasts a soldier who is childlishly excited about going to war with a soldier who "was a born warrior, meant to kill other men as much as a woman is meant to bear children." Lewis develops this idea by stating that the processes of both birth and death share the violence of a world in which only the strongest survive. In departing from the sympathetic tone of "The French Poodle," Lewis adopts a cynical one that seems as much a pose or mask as the attitudes that he ridicules in "The Young Soldier." Yet the piece is a genuine attempt to find a response adequate to the fact of war and, for the soldier, the nearness of death.

One can sense in the tone of this work the intellectual and personal crisis Lewis was undergoing at this time. He was enlisting for a war without idealistic motives, and he was leaving behind family responsibilities that he would neither entirely accept nor reject. Lewis had an illegitimate son and daughter (born in 1911 and 1913) by Olive Johnson, whom he had met in 1909. Lewis's mother was taking care of the children at this time, and Lewis supported them as well as he could; but his enlistment would drastically limit that support. (Thus Pound reluctantly but faithfully agreed to keep an eye on Lewis's children as well as his books and paintings.) This was not the only complication caused by Lewis's prewar bohemian life (Olive Johnson moved in the circles surrounding the painters Augustus John and Walter Sickert). For periods in 1914 and 1915, a venereal infection flared up and made Lewis seriously ill. These pressures upon Lewis find an outlet in his story "Cantleman's Spring-Mate," in which the disconcerting savagery of the tone is barely but brilliantly controlled by the force of Lewis's style.

"Cantleman's Spring-Mate" was finished and sent to Pound for *The Little Review* in May 1917. The Cantleman of the story is in Lewis's situation of waiting in a camp to be shipped off to fight in France. Cantleman like Lewis is thinking of what experience lies ahead: "In a week he was leaving for the Front, for the first time. So his thoughts and sensations all had, as a philosophic background, the prospect of death. . . . He was pretty miserable at the thought, in a deliberate, unemotional way." Cantleman's meditations have for background the beauty of an English spring which he is unable to appreciate:

Cantleman walked in the strenuous fields, steam rising from them as though
from an exertion, dissecting the daisies specked in the small wood, the
primroses on the banks, the marshy lakes, and all God's creatures. The heat
of a heavy premature Summer was cooking the little narrow belt of earth-
air, causing everything innocently to burst its skin, bask abjectly and
profoundly.

The "dissecting" Cantleman does is mental rather than physical, though
the momentary image of the soldier picking apart flowers is appropriate;
his analysis of the spring mating season links, in the manner of "The
Young Soldier," mating with death: "The only jarring note in this vast
mutual admiration society was the fact that many of its members showed
their fondness for their neighbour in an embarrassing way: that is they
killed and ate them." Nature is at war also, or so it seems to Cantleman's
imagination: "He saw everywhere the gun-pits and the 'nests of death'.
Each puff of green leaves he knew was in some way as harmful as the
burst of a shell."

Cantleman attempts to dissociate himself from the natural and un-
natural mechanisms of death. He has a Nietzschean dream of a "new
human chemistry," but concludes that "he must repudiate the human entirely, if that were to be brought off." He is therefore disturbed that he is
attracted to a spring-mate of his own, a woman he has met on his walks
to town. He admits that he must give in to the "humiliating gnawing and
yearning in his blood," but justifies this surrender by resolving not to
romanticize the relationship. When he seduces her it is consciously a
mating and not a love affair. Cantleman imagines that he has outwitted
nature even after he has arrived in France and the woman writes to say
that she is pregnant. He ignores her letters and does not reflect that his
part in her life might be "supremely unimportant" to her. For nature has
betrayed Cantleman by inducing him to bring another being into the
world through his spring-mate. But nature betrays Cantleman through
the war still more. A description of the animal world, in which only the
fittest survive, opens the story; it concludes by describing Cantleman
fighting in the violent world of man at war, in which brute force and
cunning prevail no less than they do in the animal world. Although
Cantleman feels that he is defying nature by destroying its prime product,
man, he is really furthering nature's scheme:

And when he beat a German's brains out, it was with the same impartial
malignity that he had displayed in the English night with his Spring-mate.
Only he considered there too that he was in some way outwitting Nature; he

had no adequate realization of the extent to which, evidently, the death of
a Hun was to the advantage of the animal world.

Cantleman is merely carrying on the evolutionary struggle. The Nietzschean moral is that "Hatred, delight in mischief, rapacity and ambition . . . belong to the marvellous economy of the conservation of the
race. . . ." Whether seducing his mate or killing a Hun, Cantleman is furthering nature's schemes. There are no exceptions; defiance is impossible.

The story of Cantleman resembles the plot of Lewis's prewar novel,
Tarr, in which Tarr proclaims the artist a "new sort of person" who rises
above merely human frailties. Yet the comedy of Tarr's story is that he
spends his time, not creating works of art, but extricating himself from one
mistress and acquiring another. The greater power of the Cantleman story
derives from the bitterly ironic perspective it takes of the war, and it is
this perspective that sustains Lewis in his letters to Pound during the war.

Lewis's eagerness for new experience and what he once called the
"courage of one's sensations" account for the literary power of his war
letters. He ridiculed what *The Daily Mail* called the "great adventure" of
the war, but was not indifferent to what adventure there was. He wrote to
Pound in 1917: "=I want to be in another battle or two, & get as much
experience as I can. . . . I am glad I am here, and this experience is
valuable. Unless I get knocked out, I don't intend to abridge it." (Letter 67.) Lewis recorded these "valuable" experiences with the impersonal,
understated style that was not only natural to him, as one sees from the
early short stories of *The Wild Body,* but also appropriate to the experience of war. After writing of shell craters "big enough to put a horse
and cart in," for example, Lewis describes his encampment with the
traditional litotes of war literature: "It is a bad spot." He never lets his
experience overwhelm him. As Marshall McLuhan claims of Lewis's style:
"The artist's personality at hostile grip with the environment is dramati-
cally offered not for its pathos or anguish or as a moral evaluation, but as
a means of clairvoyance." This comment on the "dramatic" power of
Lewis's prose is especially relevant to these letters written in the hostile
environment of war.

Lewis's "clairvoyance," even in the sense of prophetic vision, is evident
throughout his wartime writings. In the "War Number" of *BLAST*
(1915), he wrote with Orwellian perception when he said that "Perpetual
War may well be our next civilization." He envisioned a civilization in
which "in-fighting has been established everywhere, with hosts of spies
and endless national confusions" and frontiers which are "miles of wire

and steel mazes, and entanglements crackling with electricity." Despite his pessimistic awareness, he volunteered for the army as early as his health allowed and asserted in *BLAST* "the absolute necessity to resist and definitely end this absurd aggression from the centre of Europe." Nor does his cynicism or "clairvoyance" rule out, as McLuhan suggests, a moral evaluation of his experience. His Nietzschean mask helps him to remain calm and impersonal, but these letters show that he cannot wear it indefinitely. In both his war stories and his letters, his disgust at the wartime waste of human resources—at what he calls the "despicable inhuman swindle"—accounts for the passion of his vision. The war showed him that the energy the Vorticists believed would create a new culture was instead directed into mass destruction. His anger at this per-verted development is intensely if not conventionally moral. Even before he experienced the front lines, he wrote in the wartime *BLAST* as a moral-ist as well as an artist:

> There is a tragedy of decay and death at the end of all human lives. It is all a matter of adjustment of tragedy: a matter almost of Taste—where to place the Tragedy, like where to place a blackness in a picture. But this is perhaps rather consolation than anything else. And it would be no con-solation for the people this War will have crushed with grief.

"swept across Europe": Ezra Pound, "Wyndham Lewis," *The Egoist* 1 (15 June 1914): 233–34.

George Dangerfield: The Strange Death of Liberal England. The representatives blessed are Sir Edward Carson, leader of the Ulster rebels; Robert Applegarth, a trade unionist; and Lillie Lenton, a suffragette who burned down the tea pavillion in Kew Gardens. See Appendix B of William C. Wees, *Vorticism and the English Avant-Garde.*

"war and art": Wyndham Lewis, *Blasting and Bombardiering,* p. 4.

"falsetto war-cries": Lewis, *Rude Assignment,* p. 110.

"what his father had done": Lewis, "The County House Party," in *Unlucky for Pringle, Unpublished and Other Stories,* eds. C. J. Fox and Robert T. Chap-man, p. 47.

"old rip": The Letters of Wyndham Lewis, ed. W. K. Rose, p. 33.

"cheated of my patrimony": Lewis, *Blasting and Bombardiering,* p. 211.

" 'military caste' ": John Rothenstein, *Brave Day, Hideous Night: Autobiography, 1939–1965,* p. 42.

"confused head": Lewis, "The Do-Nothing Mode," *Agenda* 7–8 (Autumn/ Winter, 1969): 217, 221.

"as a child does": Lewis, *Rude Assignment,* p. 110.

"crash of the war": Arthur Mizener, *The Saddest Story: A Biography of Ford Madox Ford*, p. 248.

"Great Bloodletting": Lewis, *Blasting and Bombardiering*, pp. 62–63.

"war-that-will-end-war": Lewis, "The French Poodle, in *Unlucky for Pringle: Unpublished and Other Stories*, eds. C. J. Fox and Robert T. Chapman, p. 56.

"The King of the Trenches": "The King of the Trenches" and "The War Baby" are included in *Unlucky for Pringle: Unpublished and Other Stories*.

bear children: "A Young Soldier," *The Egoist* 3 (March 1916): 46.

"abjectly and profoundly": Lewis, "Cantleman's Spring-Mate," *The Little Review* 4 (October 1917): 8. A later version of the story is reprinted in *Unlucky for Pringle: Unpublished and Other Stories*, pp. 77–84.

"killed and ate them": Ibid., p. 8.

"burst of a shell": Ibid., pp. 12–13.

"animal world": Ibid., p. 14.

conservation of the race: Friedrich Nietzsche, *Joyful Wisdom,* trans. Thomas Common, pp. 31–32.

"means of clairvoyance": Marshall McLuhan, "Lewis's Prose Style," in *Wyndham Lewis: A Revaluation,* ed. Jeffrey Meyers, p. 67.

"next civilization": BLAST, no. 2 (July 1915): 11.

"crackling with electricity": Ibid., p. 13.

"centre of Europe": Ibid., p. 6.

"crushed with grief": Ibid., p. 14.

60. ALS–1. [Pmk: Army P.O. 1, 27 May 1917].

Dear Pound.   We are here at base for a few days. We dont know when or where we are going yet, or with what guns.—We are leading a pleasant life in tents. As soon as we move up to the Line I will let you know. But for present my address will be 2/$^{Lt.}$ P. Wyndham Lewis. 330. Siege Battery R.G.A. B.E.F. France. I am afraid before leaving I was compelled to shed a good number of letters, instructions etc. I hope you got the MSS. all right?

Yrs.   W.L.

61. TLS–1. On stationery embossed: 5, Holland Place Chambers, Kensington. W. ⟨8.⟩

Cher Veend'am:

Wrote you this a.m. anent other matters. Have just sold "Sanctity" for £12 (as marked on your list) money to be paid at the end of July. (purchaser being the one who was considering the head of the "very interesting infant" ["Baby's Head"]. Option of changing for "Standing Figure" at same price, if they change their mind.

Also rec'd offer of £7 for fishermen ["Dieppe Fishermen"], priced @ £9. money payable in July. ⟨Will you direct me re/ this latter.⟩

Yrs.

E.P.

30–5–'17.

62. ALS–1. [France].

2/6/17 [2 June 1917].

Dear Pound. £12 for Sanctity, & £7 also acceptable for "Fishermen". I have not so far received your A.M. letter. = We are not having the guns we expected. We are going up the line at any moment now on some unknown (& almost certainly far less agreeable) gun. Will let you know as soon as I move. I hope your letter wont go astray. But we probably shall not be off until tomorrow. = I have bought a lot of stupid French books, C. Lewis Phillipe's [Charles-Louis Philippe's] letters, André Gide etc.

Have seen many of Quinn's countrymen, with flag unfurled. The French are looking forward to fleecing them. The only French officer I have talked to made the following remark "If this is a war, that's allright. But if it is a joke, it is a damned bad one!"=I had some difficulty in convincing him that the second hypothesis was inadmissable. = "English Humour", you see, again; and the suspicions that that tradition breeds in the mind of the Foreigner!

Yours ever, P Wyndham Lewis. 330 Siege Battery. R.G.A. B.E.F. France.

" *'English Humour'* ": Lewis wrote in *BLAST*, no. 1, p. 17: "BLAST HUMOUR Quack ENGLISH drug for stupidity and sleepiness."

63. ALS–2.

Dear Pound.   I am here (in firing line) since yesterday. Battery split up, & I have come as reinforcements. = My address is now 224. Siege Battery. R.G.A. = B[ritish]. E[xpeditionary]. F[orce]. = France. Whizzing, banging, swishing and thudding completely surround me, and I almost jog up & down on my camp bed as though I were riding in a country wagon or a dilapidated taxi. = I am, in short, my dear colleague, in the midst of an unusually noisy battle. If you glance again at the third line of my letter you will notice that the Germans are making a similar din a mile or so away! Where this unfortunate conflict is occuring I can give you no information. I have not got your second letter (the one you said you had written me at same time as note.) I expect it will turn up soon. = I wrote Quinn 2 weeks ago on eve of my departure. Letters take about 3 days I believe to reach this spot from London.

Yrs.   W.L.

third line of my letter: The third line reads: "I have come as reinforcements," but it seems no more shaky or illegible than other lines in the letter.

64. ALS–2. [France].

8/6/17 [8 June 1917].

My dear Pound.   I have had a day or two full of incident and movement. = The night before last I was gassed in my sleep (lethal shells): the sentry did not apparently know that I was sleeping in dugout, and omitted to wake me. However, by about eleven I had recovered from that, and proceeded to an O[bservation].P[ost]. on the top of a hill. From there I saw an immense and smoky struggle for a village: saw tanks advancing, cavalry etc.: tanks hit, air fights—panorama of war, in fact. Then in afternoon I returned to my Battery, and in late afternoon walked up with my Battery commander to the line gained a few hours before: through the desolation of the Bosche concrete dugouts in a wilderness of charred spikes that was formerly a wood, everything not trenches [was] pits and gashes: dead Germans lying about like bloody waxworks: and up to present line which was too confused to be present. We passed through a field Battery that was being shelled, though quiescent itself, and there I came nearest to a black shell-burst: about twenty yards, twice. They were coming over every few seconds. I picked up a copy of Voss's Gazette in the German lines, & have been applying my German dictionary to it. = So I covered a good deal of ground yesterday along roads to the O.P., across country to the front line, and saw a lot of War. I have been particularly lucky in dropping into the midst of a very big attack. The attack has been especially successful, and today is like a quiet day in the country; no row, fine sun, the map-room; waiting for an aeroplane to come along & signal she is ready: a half hour's shooting, more calm etc. etc. – I hope: For I want to sleep tonight. = I still have not got your letter sent me at the Base. But I expect in a day or two it will arrive. Tell Miss S[aunders]., if you see her, to send me a copy (type-written or otherwise) of the first 8 pages (the doubtful pages) of the Soldier of Humour. I should probably have time to put that right. — My compliments to Mrs. Pound.   Yrs

W.L.

P.S. Do not print Soldier of Humour until I have made that alteration. = As to photographs: that funny one with my legs apart mustnt be reproduced, since the paper will come to England. The second batch I had printed is not bad (or some of those will probably do). Get Miss S. to procure two or three (I will send her money). Her address is the same.

W.L.

immense and smoky struggle: Lewis is describing the British attack on the Messines Ridge near the Belgian border on 7 June 1917.

Soldier of Humour: Lewis published "A Soldier of Humour. Part I." in *The Little Review* 4 (December 1917): 32–46, and "Part II" in *The Little Review* 4 (January 1918): 35–51.

As to photographs: Lewis may refer to the photograph by Alvin Langdon Coburn which is the frontispiece to *Wyndham Lewis, Paintings and Drawings,* ed. Michel.

65. ALS–3. [France].

My dear Pound. I have just got your second letter (of May 30th.) At
the same time I received a letter from another quarter describing your
latest choreographic exploits in Maida Vale. The One Step, as I understand it, is just the same as the Fox Trot, only it is twice as quick. It also,
requiring more acrobatic skill, is less adapted for luxurious degustation
of your mate. – A double-twinkle is a thing that should immediately be
learnt. – I know no official wriggle: you can make them up as you go
along. = That "alert" photo is napoo. There are others, that I trust you
have by now, more fit for international, rather than purely national, consumption. = I have got the first pages of the "Soldier of Humour", which
I will overhaul & return. (You see the date at the head of the letter).

This morning is peaceful: the enemy is now much farther away, and
we are temporarily derelict among 12″ railway mountings, horse lines:
minor Headquarters are even moving up among us. I expect we shall have
to go pretty soon. Yesterday once more I took my way to the forward
intelligence O. P. We were shelled out of it yesterday morning, the side
of the dugout being disorganized by an 8″ shell. = Imagine a stretch of
land one mile in depth sloping up from the old German first-line to the
top of a ridge, & stretching to right & left as far as you can see. It looks
very large, never-ending and empty. There are only occasional little groups
of men round a bomb-dump, or building a light railway: two men pushing a small truck on which a man is being brought back, lying on his
stomach, his head hanging over the side. The edge of the ridge is where
you are bound for, at the corner of a demolished wood. The place is
either loathesomely hot, or chilly according to the time of day at which
you cross it. It is a reddish colour, and all pits, ditches & chasms, & black
stakes, several hundred, here & there, marking the map-position of a
wood. Shells never seem to do more than shave the trees down to these
ultimate black stakes, except in the few cases when they tear them up, or
a mine swallows them.

The moment you get in this stretch of land you feel the change from
the positions you have come from. A watchfulness, fatigue and silence
penetrates everything in it. You meet a small party of infantry slowly
going up or coming back. Their faces are all dull, their eyes turned in-
wards in sallow thought or savage resignation; you would say revulsed, if
it were not too definite a word. There is no regular system of communication trenches yet; this is the bad tract, the narrow and terrible
wilderness. As a matter of fact it only becomes clearly unsafe as you

approach the ridge. You get nearer to the shell bursts on the crest, until
the nearest black cloud is only a hundred yards away, on the road at the
skyline. Perhaps to your right, half way up, there has been heavy shelling,
but not near enough to require craft, & the noise is inconsiderable. There
are shrapnel bursts overhead almost continually, but for some reason
absurdly high and ineffective. = As to the ridge: I have been three times.
Yesterday as we got within a hundred yards of the road there was suddenly a swooping whistle: my commanding officer shouted down: we
crouched in a shell-hole, and a 5.9 burst about 15 or 20 yards away,
between us & the wood—about 3 shell holes away, you could say, they
were so regular thereabouts. Another came over about 15 yards nearer
the wood, & at the third, actually in the wood, we concluded it was the
wood corner they were after, & proceeded. The road at the top runs along
the front of the wood for about 100 yds; the O.P. on the edge of the
wood, being about 40 yds from where we struck the road. This road for
its own sake is being shelled constantly, & because the Bosche imagines
that there are machine gun emplacements at farther end. He also imagines
that the wood is bristling with batteries; & is fatuous enough, in addition,
to believe that his beautiful concrete dugouts are being used by our men.
(You notice how guarded my language is.) As we reached this road,
four black bursts came in succession halfway down the short stretch we
could see. Straight for those bursts we made: but I shall not repeat that
often. Nothing else came over as it happened. But as soon as we had
reached the handsomely concreted German dugout, three 5.9's dropped
just outside the door. This goes on the whole while up there. = Shall I
or shall I not ask to go up there again tomorrow? There is nothing there
you cannot imagine: but it has the unexpected quality of reality. Also the
imagined thing and the felt are in two different categories. This category
has its points. I will write you further on the subject of War. Do not expect my compositions to be well-worded, as letters (my letters) are only
meant to be chat and slop. —Remember me to Mrs Pound.

                                                          Yrs

                                                          W.L.

letter from another quarter: From Augustus John.
"alert" photo: See note, "As to photographs," Letter 64.

66. ALS–1. [France].

18/6/17

My dear Pound.   When that money for drawings comes along, will you pay it into Barclay & Co's, my account, 1. Pall Mall East. Also when Quinn sends, if he sends directly to you, will you pay it into that account? = I will send you an amended Soldier of Humour tomorrow, or as soon as I get a registered envelope.

My latest experience is being nearly blown out of bed by a large shell. It occurred at 2.30 this morning. It rained earth & stones on my roof, but fortunately was some yards away. The conscientious enemy is almost [?] certain to repeat his work this morning. We have been taking the magnetic bearing of the line of the shell-craters, and meditating on his possible intentions. But his overnight proceedings admitted of several interpretations. Anyhow he has pitted our position with holes big enough to bury a horse in. He has had aeroplanes over photographing them this morning. = Two of his planes were brought down together yesterday near us. = I am under the impression that he uses his guns more flexibly than we do: more as a man does a rifle, & less as a large fixed machine. He also is much more difficult to follow in his timing:—for we cannot be difficult at all! On the other hand we send over about ten to his one. = What is going on in connection with Jacob [Epstein]? There are references to his "case" in the letters I get. His apple-cart, from what I can gather, seems to have been slightly tilted to one side. I hope some of the fruit of his deplorable activities has been upset on the ground? = How is the Little Review going? Thank you for Egoist.   Yrs.   W.L.

Epstein: The controversy surrounding a temporary exemption from military service granted to the sculptor was in the newspapers in June 1914. In a fragment of a letter, Pound apparently sent Lewis a newspaper clipping concerning the Epstein case: "His pretty face will cheer you to vicarious slaughter. It is possible that the war will not reform Sargent or Augustus [John]." This fragment may also contain a reference to the "Imaginary Letters" (originally titled "Letters from Petrograd"): "your fuckin' Rooshuns are doing 'em selves proud—nebulous combustion in nine futile & different directions."

67. ALS–3. [France].

19/6/17.

Dear Pound. Have you any news of Quinn? The German is becoming very active at night. The Battery was not shelled last night, but he nagged and plodded away all round us. At daybreak I was woken by the most infernal din: all the Archies and Lewis guns in the neighbourhood were clapping and popping away. I put my head out of my dugout, and was shocked and flabbergasted to find the atmosphere whistling with machine-gun bullets. = I withdrew, put on my tin-hat, and, recovered from my amazement, once more protruded my person from my minuscule fortress, & looked towards the clouds. Imagine my indignation and interest on finding two of the abominable enemy flying at an insolently low altitude, and pooping off in all directions. No sign of a British plane anywhere. There were such crowds of archies firing at the two Bosches that they seemed partially embedded in an archipelago of tiny clouds, repeated little points of light showing where they flew, like a warship signalling at night. This continued for fully a quarter of an hour, when three or four English planes hove in sight, and Heine pushed off. (Heine is a good new name for the stinking foe.)

I am so far, you will be glad to hear, well. The perpetual opening and shutting, slamming and slapping of doors that goes on here, the ceaseless rush of outgoing shells, and fatigued complaint, or surprised whistle, of incoming ones; the panics on either side, when a British or Bosche rifle goes off by accident, and an S.O.S. lights up the whole front, makes sleep probably thinner and less nourishing: canned food may bring pimples: but it will be a few years yet before I am reduced to suing for peace. = Meantime, life is not as simple as it looks, even here. I visited my old Battery yesterday, which has reformed. It is doing fatigues at present, pending the arrival of guns. But there seems a chance of it being revived entirely as a Battery. In that case I should have to return. = I left my old colleagues yesterday with a feeling of the acutest depression. There are only three of them there: the Brummagem Jew, crossed with a cape Dutchwoman, the Bank clerk from Lewisham, and the hysterical and stunted little north-country lawyer (the board-school master is not yet back.) Well, I said to myself, Na: I refuse any longer to make part of that surely unexampledly dreary circle. On the other hand, what am I to do? If I ask for a transfer, I should be asked my reasons for wanting one. I should probably be posted to the most disagreeable corner of the earth they could find for me (& they have resources in that way): fastidiousness, I imagine, would not appeal to the authorities. My present Battery is just what I should have chosen: but they have one officer too many, & that is myself: and the Major, who 'phoned up the Group Headquarters, was told I was merely attached and not posted. But I am to stop with 224. unless they move out of the Group. Now, if I were once more sent back to my old Battery, within 6 weeks, or 1 month I would apply for a transfer to the Intelligence, & there you might aid me. When you get that S.O.S. (which if I go back to the old Battery would probably be in 2 months time, as I shall stop here a week or two longer,) you must roll your sleeves up, & work for me for a few hours hard. But I daresay that there would be no difficulty of an insurmountable sort. My Major O[fficer]. C[ommanding]. has said to me twice now: "You know, you are a bloody fool. With your knowledge of languages etc. you are a B[loody]. F[ool]. to be sitting on your Bo-hind in this Mess. You could be making a pound a day, and have a red tab on your coat." = I explained to him as best I could that I was not such an imbecile as I looked, & that that matter had received my best attention. = I want to be in another battle or two, & get as much experience as I can, so that if necessary my knowledge of languages would be reinforced with knowledge of gunnery, & war conditions. In any case, I am glad I am here, and this experience is valuable. Unless I get knocked out, I dont intend to abridge it. If I could stop in this Battery, I would go on with them for four months, or apply for a job where my special aptitudes would give me an advantage after three months, hoping to get it at the end of four. If I have to go back to the old Battery, I will stand it as long as I can, but I expect that would curtail my programme somewhat. You are now au courant of my prospects and intentions. I hope they will leave me with 224. as long as possible. They are a most amicable set of fellows here: four of them are gentlemen, which is of course a very high percentage in six officer units nowadays. Be kind to Miss S[aunders]. Have you seen my Miss Godd yet?   Cheerio, my priceless old top!   W.L.

Archies and Lewis guns: Antiaircraft and machine guns.
Brummagem: A slang word for the city of Birmingham.
Miss Godd: Lewis's play *The Ideal Giant,* originally entitled, *Miss Godd and the Ideal Giant,* was published by *The Little Review* in a limited edition in 1917 and reprinted in *The Little Review* 6 (May 1918): 1–18.

Introduction to Letter 68.

Lewis's enlistment in the army had been delayed by a serious infection which developed from the gonorrhea he had contracted several years before. As the following letter shows, he feared a recurrence of his venereal complaint when he fell ill shortly after arriving at the front. But his illness was actually trench fever, and he was sent to the fever-hospital at Étaples, near Boulogne. After the critical period of his illness passed, he was sent to a convalescent hotel for officers which was supported by Lady Michelham. The facility was soon filled with gassed officers, and Lewis was sent rather prematurely back to his own battery, which was now in Nieuwpoort, near Ostend, in Belgium. He remained in this position until October 1917, when his battery was moved to the salient near the French town of Ypres, where Lewis fought in one of the worst English defeats of the war, the battle of Passchendaele. Lewis wrote in 1939 that he did not fully recognize the significance of the war until he "found himself in the mud of Passchendaele, and dimly discerned that he was present at a great military defeat. . . ."

"military defeat": Wyndham Lewis on Art, eds., Michel & Fox, p. 340.

68. TLS–1. [June 1917]. [5, Holland Park Chambers, Kensington. W.].

Mon Cher Bummbadier:

I should be much inclined to doubt whether your trouble were the clapp, glleet or ghonnerrrreaa, but rather a natural secretion caused by the continual lucubration or friction or pricktion of the route or rut march. You should state whether same is accompanied by redness, soreness, irritation or whether it be a gentle deposit in the said longish foreskin of white gelatinous substance sans peur et sans reproche. Nothing but the actual presence of the baccillus ghonnococcae in the said secretion would induce us to assume that the same was caused by the aforesaid c. g. or g. Even in the case of redness, soreness etc. the result may be merely a recrudescence of certain simple afflictions of puberty whence the more innocent young are in their teens so like to be afflicted with melancholia and cynicism and fears diverse and obscure. In any case the phystian [*sic*] who attended your earlier troubles would be the most likely person to prescribe at a distance. If he, however, be out of reach, I will approach a grave and reverend person of my acquaintance who will be deeply shocked and charge me accordingly. You should however state WHEN you were last a prey to the gleetish activities. also your habits !!!! . Unless you notice a definite soreness or pain I dont think you need be in any way worried, and even a soreness, so that it be not pustulent, is not of vital import. At any rate send ample detail before I go to said practitioner.

I have spent the day in your service, having had to go again to Sheldon. Also to Weaver with part II. of Tarr. I think this part is the easiest to cut very heavily. I have not got to the end of the mss. but the next sections seem to me more closely packed and more essential to the main movement of the tale.

Returning to the main movement of this epistle: if the discharge be perfectly clean and white and of jismatic appearance I think you can put it down to simple superabundance plus the friction of pedestrination. ⟨You apparently have no other symptoms of anything wrong?⟩

solemnly yours
E.P.

69. ALS–1. [France].

24/6/17.

Dear Pound.   I am still in the Casualty Clearing Station: but expect to be moved down to Base this afternoon. As soon as I arrive there will send you address. = My ailment is not serious: 2 or 3 weeks at Base I expect, though. My letters will be sent on from Battery there in a packet.

Yrs   W.L.

70. ALS–1.

29/6/17.
46th Stationary Hospital.
B.E.F.
France

My dear Pound.   The above title means that the Hospital will not move away: <u>not</u> as you doubtless imagine, that it is full of writing paper. There is practically no writing paper to be had here.

My disease is better: — practically well. I shall be back in Battery in 2 or 3 weeks. —I am bored. —I wish I had some nice wound instead of this stupid complaint. Still, even the Champ de Bataille has its dull moments. —I dont know to what part of the line I shall be going next. Further north still, I hope. I have not heard from my Battery for 7 days now: so a letter of yours dispatched 10 days ago will not reach me for another 3 or 4 days. I came down the line yesterday, & am only now despatching this address to my colleagues.   Yrs.   W.L.

71. ALS–1.

46th Stationary Hospital.

B.E.F.

France.   1/7/17 [1 July 1917].

My perfectly priceless old Bean!   I am in the best of <u>jolliest</u> and <u>jauntiest</u> health and <u>Humour</u>, you will be glad to hear! I shall soon now be <u>back in the Battery</u> (the new battery, I hope, 224). I am posting you the Soldier of Humour, & perhaps another Petrograd letter or two. = I am considering at present whether I shall try to write a little play. I expect I shall not. My head is swarming with dramatic fragments: if they could be integrated into an 8. inch Play, they would make a fine black fountain of dung and smoke in the midst of the Unseen Canaille, detailed charts of whose positions I have long been provided with!   How is the [Little] Review going? If you are not going to send me free copies, put me down for a subscription. I am anxious to see your launching number. Cheerio, my absolutely priceless old Turnip!   Yrs.   W.L.

old Bean: Lewis imitates the mannerisms of the music-hall comedian George Robey. See Letter 73.

82

Petrograd letter: The original title of the "Imaginary Letters" that Lewis published in *The Little Review* was "Letters from Petrograd." Lewis's persona, William Bland Burn, writes the letters from Petrograd, where he has gone to investigate the results of the Russian Revolution.

72. TL–2. [Fragment]. [July 1917]. On stationery embossed: 5, Holland Place Chambers, Kensington. W.

Cher Veend'aam:

Subscription be bugggar'd.   I have long since sent you a copy of the May L[ittle].R[eview]. It is very hard to get spare copies, as importation in bulk of periodicals is verboten.

If you want copies sent to anyone, send on their names and I will have the N.Y. office mail the paper direct.

Bundles of typescript from Q[uinn]. He says he has written you, if it [was] via me, the letter hasn't yet come.

I am a little vague as to the nature of your Promethean Vulture. But trust it will keep you out of shell's way for a seasonable period.

I have been in action, mental moral and physical uninterruptedly for some days. I am really beyond the point of communicativity. Heard from Bobby [Roberts] yesterday, no particular news.

I will put £10 into your bank in a day or two whether I hear from Q. or not. (£7 on drawing, and £3 from Review.) Less than half of the years review money has come, so you may have to wait for the other stray ha'pence therefrom. There will be £12 from the other drawing, later in the month. I see, by consulting Q.'s note that his cash for you wont be likely to arrive till Aug.

I believe the review is going O.K., I have dined several times on subs[criptions].

Two bundles of the best poems Yeats has done (June, 7, and seven more in Aug.) ought to announce to the desert places that the magazine is reel, refined litterchure. The respectability of Lady Gregory's name (cast it is true on a blasphemous and unchristian play) may we hope "put over" the indecorous and indelicate Cantleman, and foil the wiles of the decency prosecutors.

The corpse-like Waley has sent me some translations of fine Chinese poems, (rather damaged in transit), I dont know whether I can do a deal with him or not.

Eliot emits from time to time, and discretely. I hope you will live long enough to read my dialogue of Poggio, "Aux Etuves de Wiesbaden". and that a line or two of my "L'Homme Moyen Sensuel" which accompanies your "Preface" in Sept. number, will bring a smile to your war battered countenance.

DO YOU want me to buy up some "Timon" for you, @ 2/6, with slight reduction per dozen. I think it a good investment. Knopf is going to take the remainder from the Coptic. But if you want me to get a couple of £'s worth first I will do so. I've got four or five copies for myself.

⟨Re/ review – "The Pink" once did a good job. and may let⟩ [end of text].

Yeats: The following Yeats poems appeared in *The Little Review* 4 (June 1917): "The Wild Swans at Coole," "Presences," "Men Improve with the Years," "A Deep-Sworn Vow," "The Collar Bone of a Hare," "Broken Dreams," and "In Memory"; the seven poems which make up "Upon a Dying Lady" appeared in the August 1917 issue.

Lady Gregory's . . . play: Hanrahan's Oath appeared in *The Little Review* 4 (November 1917): 6–38.

"Aus Etuves de Wiesbaden": This imaginary dialogue appeared in *The Little Review* 4 (July 1917): 12–16.

"L'Homme Moyen Sensuel": Pound's satiric poem appeared in *The Little Review* 4 (September 1917): 8–16.

"Preface": Lewis's "Inferior Religions," which he planned to use as a preface to the comic short stories of *The Wild Body,* appeared in the *Little Review* 4 (September 1917): 3–8.

the Coptic: Pound refers to the printer of Lewis's *Timon* portfolio, Max Goschen, whose office was on Coptic Street.

73. ALS–2. [46th Stationary Hospital. France].

7/7/17.

My dear Pound. We may now, I think, dispense with George Robey's "perfectly priceless old Bean". This Hospital is stagnant with weekly and monthly literature. In the May number of the Red Storyteller, Robey claims to have initiated the above combination, especially Bean. = You know of course that it is now proved that Gilman and Robey are one?

Your letter received yesterday. = My balls are smaller and less troublesome: I have less (or usually no) pain in my eyes. I am almost well.

Thank you for copy of May Number of L[ittle]. R[eview]. Nothing has
yet come to me from the Line. I feel as though the whole Battery, all
record & trace & even memory of it, must have been blown into the sky.

What does Q[uinn]. say? = I dont know if I told you what I wrote him
before I came out, apropos of BOOK [*Tarr*]. I told him in half a dozen
words of my family mix-up, to make clear to him the necessity for my
getting best terms I can for book. The thing is clearly in Q.'s hands: that
is he could get as much out of Knopf as Knopf is willing to give, if he
liked. It is useless asking me how much I want. This I explained. I
spoilt Tarr as a book in this country, at least reduced its freshness 50%,
by giving it to Egoist. Any people who had read a chapter or two in the
Egoist, & got sick of the serial nuisance, will never read it as a book etc.
I dont want to further fritter the book away by an unremunerative sale out
there. —On the other hand, for the first year or so, there will nowhere be
much money to be made out of it. However, in short, to be worthwhile
publishing in New York, Knopf would have to pay something.

Have you seen "Miss Godd & the Ideal Giant"?—That, by the way,
is not for Review—not in any case a suitable size. But let's hear what
you think of it.

Hold the Soldier of Humour back till you get that revision.

I was sorry to hear that that you had been overdoing it for a few days.
What have you been doing?

Please buy me £2 worth of Timons at 2/6 each, as you suggested. Remember me to Mrs. Pound.   Yours ever   W.L.

74. ALS–2.

46th. Stationary Hospital. [France].

7/7/17.

Dear Pound.   Should you be leaving the Capital at any time, will you
give me ample warning? For why? Because my only chance of getting that
transfer to the Intelligence would be through you, – short of being in

London myself, which is impossible (except through wounds) under 6 months (Christmas). I dont know if you got my letters, all of them that is. Did you get one treating of that subject? I want to be in another Push or two. After that, there will be nothing to gain by remaining at the Front, practically nothing more to see or experience; & thenceforth I should be more useful to my country where my great gift for languages, & knowledge of France & its language, could be put to military use. (Or Spain is in a delicate state?) I am afraid that the War that has made Epstein, & set John on his feet again etc. etc. is going to continue for some time yet. Life as you know is only justifiable as a spectacle: the moment at which it becomes harrowing and stale, & no aesthetic purpose is any longer served, War would be better exchanged for Diplomacy, Intelligence!—or something else.—I told you in my letter that I thought in about 2 1/2 months that time would arrive. That, believe me, is giving myself a good number of opportunitys of ending existence. [The bottom of the first page of the letter, which ends here, has been cut away.] All that is required, with my linguistic accomplishments, is a little military good-will somewhere. If some bureaucrat whose Bureau was the Intelligence department, of or over the rank of Major, were favourably disposed towards you, Intelligence you would become. = If you have answered the other letter, dont trouble to answer this one. (This is only an Annexe to the other letter I am sending you today.) But bear the point in mind, & precipitate the movement if necessary. Normally, it should be left till after August. Enough, Hush. A la revista,

W.L.

75. ALS–2.

9./7/17 [9 July 1917].
46th stationary Hospital.
B.E.F.
France.

My dear Pound. Quinn's·letter arrived. He said that he had also sent one to you: I suppose you got yours by same mail. So you should be au courant. = What had I better do about English agent for Tarr, do you think? Could you fix anything up for me? Do you see exactly what has to

be done? As to Quinn's ideas on Executorship: will you be my literary
executor in the event of my death? If you accepted that post, I wonder
if I should send you a legal document resembling a will. I had thought
that you, Sturge Moore and the Captain [Baker] (who, although a more
recent friend, is a very kind and true one) might consent to execute for
my children, & keep an eye on my boy occasionally. But I feel these parts
of my arrangements, in the light of Quinn's letter, are not very complete
or precise.

==

I also got the Egoist yesterday [containing an episode of *Tarr*], & see that
in the duel scene Soltyk, one of the two principals, takes a pillule of oxide
of Bromium and Heroin. Now, here we have another of my bloody dum-
mies. That is to say I wanted to specify the sedative tablet taken, & for the
time being put down the above extraordinary concoction. It is just like
the German occurring all through the book.
Obviously before appearing in book form these things must be dealt with.
Alec Shepler [Alick Schepeler] would be useful for the revision of the
German, & has consented to do it.
    What have you done about missing page?
    What do you say to Quinn's three years more of war? Thats the stuff
to give 'em, eh? Those are blythe words for a war weary warrior, eh, my
nebulous old top?
    Getting up in a day or two now.   Cheerio Yours

                        Wyndham Lewis

76. ALS–1.

46ᵗʰ Stationary Hospital.   10/7/17 [10 July 1917].
    B E F.
            France.

My dear Pound.   I have just sent off to Miss S[aunders]. the revised beginning of Soldier of Humour. I have cut it down by about half, & much
improved it. There is nothing now to alter. If you cant get it in as it is,
do not print Soldier of Humour. I will send you something in its place.

==

Please give the enclosed note to Miss S when you see her, or send it if you are writing her.

Yrs   W.L.

77 ALS–2.

46   Stationary Hospital. [France].

17/7/17.

My dear Pound.   Thank you for Little Review, just received. Cant you freeze out the lucubrator at the end? Magazine has a sympathetic exterior & form. I read your ⟨version of⟩ Tagore again with great pleasure. I have just received a letter from Bobby [Roberts], who remarks that Jotsindranath [Jodindranath] must have been "a very sensible man." I dont know what Bobby means.

Bobby has been on the Somme and at Vimy: he seems somewhere else at present. ⟨(Since my Battery has moved, by the way, the veil of secrecy may be lifted, and I suppose I may now tell you that I was behind Wytchecte and on the morning of the big attack in an O[bservation]. P[ost]. facing Messines, which I believe I gave you a veiled description of.)⟩ = Bobby's letter recounted many trials, but chiefly the loss of his boots on the Somme, which seems to have left the most painful impression in his mind,⟨& filled several pages of his letter.⟩ He is at present in a situation of comparative safety and comfort: ⟨(—not very either.)⟩

I have just completed the Petrograd letters, & despatched them to Miss. S[aunders]. = They are better than the stories (Cantleman & the other) especially the last letters that you will shortly see. I wish I had written the first two more carefully. ⟨I am going to work on them forthwith.⟩ = Will you keep this letter, & I will proceed to tabulate one or two points I should like observed, & one or two observations about this very important piece of work.

I.   The title should be "Letters from Petrograd" (but of course not to be altered now in Review.)

II.   I find that the printer is a careless fellow. He changes "Not need changing back" of mine into "most need changing back", which is the exact opposite. Still, if he always sticks to the exact opposite in his changes it will not be so irritating as some of Leveridge's [the printer of BLAST] subtleties.

III. When you come to read my fourth or fifth Petrograd letter tell me what you think about "hillocks" with reference to the Public. I think it is allright.

IV. I suppose Colossi is the plural of Colossus?

V. What was the date of the deposition of the Czar? As you read my last two Petrograd letters keep your eye on the date at top of letter, & modify if essential. = But I think it is allright. = By April 28th the Revolution period was well past the first days.

VI. (I had to pretend that Bland didn't roger his friends for obvious reasons.)

VII. Miss S. will give you two copies, one of which will contain a certain passage, one of which will not contain the passage. It is the one that does not contain the passage that is to go to New York. Under no circumstances, as you love me, allow the copy with the passage to go. = But I should like you to see the whole thing. = Miss S. tells me that she has sent off to you Miss Godd & the Ideal Giant. Not for publication, of course. Have you time to read anything remote for the moment?

I am sending 10 drawings (small ones) to Pierce. You may possibly see them. I am going to a convalescent home for a week or two. I shall employ myself there in writing a play about 2 old ladies. = It is easier to write than draw under present conditions. I can attempt nothing new in either branch of my dual activity. I need an extra play or story more than I need an extra score of drawings for my work as it stands. So I shall do the play. Bien à vous.   W.L.

lucubrator: The concluding piece in *The Little Review* for May 1917 was a windy prose poem, "Prose Coronales," by Morris Ward.

version of Tagore: "Jodindranath Mawhwor's Occupation," *The Little Review* 4 (May 1917): 12–18. This story was inspired by the personality of the Bengali poet.

"hillocks": Lewis may have wanted to use this word to describe his character Burn's posterior, as in Letter 89; the word does not appear in the "Imaginary Letters."

2 old ladies: Lewis apparently did not write this play.

78. ALS–3. [No. 8 (Michelham) Home for Convalescent British Officers. France].

26/7/17.

My dear Pound.   A letter sent by you to 46th. Stationary just received. = Also June number of Review (Little). The printer, as you remark, is a bugger. When the MSS. is typed there is no excuse for changing <u>divine</u> to dévoué (page 25) which, on account of its accents, must be much <u>more</u> difficult to print.

Congratulations on your interview with Rabelais. You might have exaggerated still more his un-Rabelais-like delivery. That remark of his about not ringing <u>bells</u> gave you your opportunity! I shall look forward to further hours with the gently resurrected. = Where has his reading stopped, by the way? He knows Stendhal: does he get Reviews where he comes from? He is obviously ignorant of present day conditions, though not of books.

As to these Petrograd letters. As you well know, I had no intention of your printing those first two: they were rough. The new ones I am sending you are allright for printing. But I have rewritten the first two, and given Burn a better tongue. I have also sacrificed a little naturalness, & got more in.

Miss S[aunders]. will I hope give you the new stuff in time for the next issue of Review. But I will ask her also to send you my revised first two letters. <u>Villerant</u> remains the same, but Burn is better defended. I had to step in <u>and help</u> him a little more.

Please be my literary executor. I thought I had said that in one of my parting documents. Should it ever come to executing my remains (as Heaven forbid it should!) consult Sturge Moore a little. You are much more in touch with me than he is, and of course he couldn't, and wouldn't, undertake to deal with such revolting matter as mine. But I have a very great liking for him, and believe in his taste in many ways. And he helped me a great deal, a half dozen years back, and took considerable interest in Tarr. =

If literary contact with Moore worries you, cut it out, however.

If a Memoir has to be done at any time on me, I should of course rather that you did it than anybody else.

There would be no necessity for anyone to execute my offsprings if their present guardian lives (as she probably will do, judging by health and precedent). It was only in case of a second decease, supposing mine first should happen.

Did I tell you of my intention to write a play here? I have not so far done it. I am beginning to do some writing today.

I have just heard from my servant. My original Battery, to which presumably I shall return, has moved dead north. I think there can be no objection to my telling you that we are now attached to the Navy. How amphibious I am likely to be I cannot say. I prefer the salt brine in my nose to the dust of more central regions. It is also pleasant to turn one's back on the Ypres salient, my short stay having convinced me of its unsalubrious character. Although no longer much of a salient, the Germans appear desirous of keeping up the 'Salient' atmosphere as far as possible. = We were in front of Wytchecte, our observation post on the Wytchecte Ridge. The Salient really ceases about there, but you still were enfiladed from the north.

My servant, writing on the 9th, tells me that one Irishman in my enfiladed sub-section has been killed, and several gunners wounded. —May mine be a Blighty one if it comes, with just enough temperature to take me across the Channel. = I am living like a fighting-cock in this Home, and enjoy[?] very much the familiarity of the town. Other familiarity there has been none, so far! The young French ladies seem to have made up their minds on one point. All who have seen the Americans agree that they are ugly. (Nothing to look at is one expression: 'ugly' the most common.) —I wonder what those little pets expected?

Yrs   W.L.

interview with Rabelais: Pound published his dialogue of a student with François Rabelais, "An Anachronism at Chinon," in *The Little Review* 4 (June 1917): 14–21.

Villerant: A friend of William Bland Burn and his wife Lydia in the "Imaginary Letters."

my offsprings: Lewis's mother was caring for his two children.

79. ALS–1. [No. 8 (Michelham) Home for Convalescent British Officers. France].

31/7/17.

<u>My</u> dear <u>Pound</u>.   I am leaving here this week, I expect. So dont send any more letters or Review to this address.=I will send you Battery address. (Same as at first, I fear. But I hope near Dunkirk.)

I am sorry that the Petrograd Letters cannot go in without intervals. But I suppose this is unavoidable!

Remember me to Mrs Pound.   Yrs   <u>W.L.</u>

80. TL–1. [Fragment]. [August 1917]. On stationery embossed: 5, Holland Park Chambers, Kensington. W. ⟨8⟩

Dear Lewis:

I write in one [of] these fits of august lethargy when the lifting of a digit is a formidable and rather impracticable labour.

I have "as per instructions" gekauft £2/ worth of "Timon", slightly reduced rate under 2/6 the copy. = 19 clean copies and one dusty one.

Miss S[aunders]. has not yet turned in "Soldier of Humour". I will give her your note this p.m.

I have done nothing about Bertha's letter [in *Tarr*]. But will send on as much mss. as I now have to Knopf.

///

I would rather execute your books than your children. Perhaps it would be better for me to execute the books and duly deliver proceeds to your regular executors???? I dont know. I will of course do whichever you like.

I think it would be well for you to send me at least a formal letter saying you want me to execute, and also authorizing the "memoir" on you.

///

I sent you a second copy of May L[ittle].R[eview]., and a copy of June day before yesterday.

The **PREFACE** will, presumably, appear in Sept. Cantelman [*sic*] in Oct.

Lady Gregory's play fills Nov. I shall presumably put all the Soldier of Humour into December., and then go on with letters to Lydia, if Mr Burn has done any by then.

Mr Villerant has written some letters for Sept. Oct. and Nov. to keep the "reader" in mind of the existence of the Burn family. This literary rape and adultery is most underhanded and scandalous. But Mr V. has unexpectedly come to life, that is by the time he gets to his second epistle. He will perhaps annoy the "public" and provide B. with Aunt Sallys. He is not controversing with B. but discussing matters other, and of interest to his effete and over civilized organism.

///

Barclays have sent me a receipt for £10 to your account. £7 on ink drawing of fishermen, and £3 from Little Rev. £2 on Timons, will also count of Review stuff.

The National Service shook its head over me this a.m. they had never had anything like it before, finally decided that I was fit for something neither "manual" nor "clerical" [end of text].

PREFACE: Lewis thought of his essay "Inferior Religions," *The Little Review* 4 (September 1917): 3–8, as a preface to his stories in *The Wild Body* collection.

Mr Villerant: Pound himself wrote "Imaginary Letters," which were only loosely connected with Lewis's, in *The Little Review* for September 1917, October 1917, November 1917, May 1918, and November 1918.

Aunt Sallys: Puppet heads set up, as at a Fair, to be knocked down with sticks or balls.

81. ALS–1. [August 1917]. |Niewpoort, Belgium]

My dear Pound.   I am back now with my old Battery. I have come to a tedious spot. It is really extremely bad. The parapet of one of our guns was smashed last night. We were shelled and gassed all night: I had my respirator on for two solid hours. There is only one bright side to the picture: a good concrete dugout.

I hope Miss S[aunders]. has shown you my revised Petrograd Letters. Also the drawings I sent over you may care to have a look at. Le Feu contains good things: have you read it? I got a lot of books during my stay in the delightful back areas. I am now not so far from the port where I did my Timon drawings one summer.

What news? = I am writing Quinn. = Address me number of my
original Battery. 330 Siege Battery. R.G.A.   B.E.F.   France.   Yrs   W.L.

Le Feu: Henri Barbusse's *Le Feu: Journal d'une Escouade* (1916), the fictional
journal of an infantryman.

82. TLS–2. On stationery embossed: 5, Holland Place Chambers, Kensington. W. ⟨8.⟩

Dear Lewis:
                    Glad to hear from you after so many days. I am afraid news
is at a fairly low ebb. Save what's today from the front, which looks good.
Baker is, or was, depressed when last I saw him, says he will be where he
is until the end of the war. I have not read Le Feu, Dorothy has and I got
a breath off the top, when she quoted chunks of it. You will see that the
L[ittle].R[eview]. have looked at an Egoist review of it. Thus knowledge
spreads. I have been reading Elizabethan translations of the Classics, at
the [British] museum, with honour, pleasure and profit.
        The female who bought your £12 picture [Georgie Hyde-Lees], told
me last night she would send on the cheque, she is already two weeks late,
but her bank account is solid if not extensive, so it will in due time come.
I dont imagine you have much use [for] it where you are.
        Have had only an unintelligible cable about Joyce from Quinn. The
L.R. however write me that he ⟨J.Q.⟩ is a noble defender.
        Miss S[aunders]. has duly delivered the revised Russian letters. I dont
think it advisable to STOP the magazine quite yet. However she has taken
them away again to make certain OMISSIONS as per your order.
        I think the last four excellent BUT....... one or two passages might
...etc....

The Soldier of Humour much improved. Am using it for Xmas number,
all in one issue, if possible.
        I have got Tarr together, all together at last and Miss S. is going
over the foreign expressions, which when corrected, it will to America be
despatched.
        You will be pleased to know that Miss K. Lechmere has sent in 7/
for the review. Thus knowledge is disseminated.
        Ed. Wad[sworth] writes that he has nobly defended my reputation in

Mudros (I suppose against McKenzie, I dont know what other budding literatus he would have encountered in them pa'ars.

Arthur Symons very anxious to join the ranks of the L.R. contributariat. Is this a compliment? He apparently prefers our company to chance of payment from "Drama".

I have a vague feeling that if I post this before six it may reach you sooner than if I wait.

Good lungs to you, and dont get 'em obfuscated.

yours
E.

Ezra Pound
17–8–17

Baker: Pound writes of Baker in Canto 16, p. 72:

> And Ole Captain Baker went to it [the war],
>   with his legs full of rheumatics,
> So much he couldn't run,
>   so he was six months in hospital,
> Observing the mentality of the patients.

83. ALS–2. [Pmk: Army Post Office, 20 August 1917]. [Nieuwpoort, Belgium].

<u>Sunday.</u>

My dear Pound.   A horrible phonograph played by my horrible brothers-in-arms renders intelligible writing difficult. The unspeakable, vulgar brutes have introduced The End of a Perfect Day and a score more obnoxious pieces into a dugout 12 feet by 8. — There are only two, one in which we sleep, the other in which we eat and live. —Both are pitch-dark, dank and chuck-full. – This particular human combination is the 'comble,' however. They've just put on "Sympathy"; may their next fart split up their backs, and asphyxiate them with the odour of their souls! = I have been on duty from 4:30 this morning till 8 this morning. We have been under shell fire all day – as all days, and all nights. They got a direct hit on our dugout 4 days ago as we were having lunch. We were shelled this morning

with 11 inch, just before breakfast. Craters big enough to put a horse &
cart in. It is a bad spot. There is no possibility of doing any work ⟨writing⟩
here. I dont know how long we shall stop. [Censored] was a spectacle.
This is the cock-pit. = Our Battery position [Censored] constantly [Cen-
sored]. The other side of the road is the weird desert alright. Shells rain
on it all day. As you probably know, a shell is most dangerous when it
falls on top of your head. It is next most dangerous at from 200 to 400 or
500 yards — a big one, that is. We get nothing but big ones. Well, we are
at from [Censored] these agreeable obus habitually descend. At from 5 to
any number of feet they spray outwards, worst laterally, and with a tendency always to drive back rather than forward. We have earthworks
fortunately, but they are only partial, of course, & not always at the right
angle. It is not at all uncommon for a splinter to whizz between your face
& that of another man. Why it doesn't hit one of the faces more often is
one of the mysteries of this Great War. We have had several killed, however, but not in the gun positions. One of my men was wounded in the arm
yesterday. The splinter flew off a man's tin hat on to his forearm. We have
a very much worse time to look forward to. = Now so far I dont mind
this in the least. In fact I am both glad and ashamed to say that I rather
enjoy it. But there is one awful shadow over my existence here: and that
is the too frightful incompatibility of my companions. I should go stark
staring mad if I had to witness their awful archness, their abominable
skittishness, and bathe in their banality for very long. That hysterical little
thing I introduced to you is still in command. During my absence one of
the other subalterns has practically taken command of the Battery; as you
can suppose, this is not difficult for a pushing young man to accomplish.
Meantime from Captain they have reduced Clarkson to 1st. Lieutenant (his
captaincy was only acting rank, & they want his extra 6 months money).
He has sent in a recommendation for promotion of one of his subalterns. I
do not think that will be me. Thank god; but it is nevertheless annoying.
(His object is to be able to say "I am, you see, in command of a Battery;
but one of my subalterns is of the same rank as myself! Why dont you
either take the Battery away from me, or make me a Major?") = You
can imagine how a sort of competition, which I refuse, & which is nevertheless thrust on me, by the New-Cross Bank Clerk or the Canterbury
Board School Master, endears them respectively to me, & makes me more
readily suffer them. = I will continue this letter in a day or so.

Yours   Wyndham Lewis

P.S. In any case I will stick in this Battery till they are over their bad time. Else you can imagine what they could say! = But mon dieu que la vie militaire is difficult.

[*Censored*]: Letters from the front lines were censored either by inking over or slitting out sensitive information.

84. ALS–2. [August 1917]. [Nieuwpoort, Belgium]. On stationery imprinted: The Salvation Army. Recreation and Reading Room for His Majesty's Troops [crossed out by Lewis].

Monday

Dear Pound. I find myself today (monday) in [Censored]. I seize this opportunity of continuing my letter. I will tell you a little more of the life I lead at present, in case you should adopt the popular notion of the heavy gunner living in the lap of ease, miles from war, never smelling any powder but the whiffs of cordite that emanate from his own gun-barrel. = We are in front of all the heavy guns, as a matter of fact: on either side of us we have field Batteries, one of which was knocked badly yesterday. You can take it from me that our gun position is neither a sweet, safe, nor salubrious spot. As I left this morning from the distance I & the engineer officer who accompanied me had the satisfaction of seeing an 11 inch shell fall in the middle of our gun positions. Last night three shells fell slap in the middle of my gun-pit. The whole neighbourhood is not one to stroll in. = Now this is exactly as it should be: for what is the good of going to the War if you never see war? But you might imagine, did I not inform you of these simple & daily events, that my reticence was due to the notorious quietude of the Heavy gunner's existence. Disabuse yourself, mon pauvre vieux. I shall be under heavy & constant shell-fire every day that I spend in this position. No hour has passed so far that I have not heard the song of the little hot hunks that pass over or by you, or come down "plock" at your feet. = Enough of war: but my interest in other things being momentarily eclipsed, I can only turn to the more introspective side of the same dream. — The mounds, and charred stumps and bangs have a very great and definite charm. It is only by death-spreading explosions among gray and empty lunar landscapes that you can get our particular Hell. A few men move about the stumps of trees all draggingly and as though wounded, because they know it is no good moving quickly. = All the decors of the living quarters are excessively <u>romantic</u> in their untidiness, squatness and desuetude. It will require many a steel structure rising in bright security among harmless clouds after this bloody war to eradicate the loose intensity of the dugout, dump and camp.

 I have bought a guide-book on Touraine, full of old drawings [censored] photographs. = Did Miss S[aunders]. give you the Figaro cutting? = Remember me to [Mrs.] Pound. Yrs. W.L.

P.S. It should not be difficult in 3 months to get me a job as <u>R. T. O.</u> (Railway Transport Officer) at some small station, <u>D. A. P. M.</u> (Deputy Assistant Provost Marshall) or <u>District Purchasing Officer.</u> = Do not take this enumeration of the likeliest posts that my French would fit me for, coupled with my account of the horrors of war, to be a suggestion to activity on your part. I must see this Battery through its bad time first, try then to get transferred; after that, if it cant be managed otherwise, I will apply for one of the above posts, or a job in the Intelligence.

 = Give me news of all & everything. W.L.

85. TLS–3.

5 Holland Park Chambers,
Holland Park.

Dear Lewis:

   "Tarr" has been gathered into a lump and been sent to America. As that sentence can not possibly pass any censor, let me say clearly "The manuscript of your novel" more or less correct (Miss S[aunders]. having been through the furrin languidges) has at last been dispatched by registered post.

 I have also a receipt from Barclays for £12/12 (sent to [be] sure to Miss E Pound. but passons). That's for your Egyptian drawing. I forget the name, and cant be bothered looking it up. I have asked them to print the "Soldier of Humour" all in one number (Dec).

 As to Mayfair, I wrote you months ago that I hadn't seen anybody for ages. My letter was sent back with a statement that your whereabouts was uncertain. It was just after you had gone to hospital. My tidings were then stale, and no use.

Miss S. has sent you the letters, with request to expurgate. I'd rather you did it yourself. I am using the Preface "Inferior Religions" in Sept. and "Cantleman" in Oct. Lady Gregory's respectability in Nov. supposed to placate the reader.

I am doing a series of "Studies of Contemporary Mentality" in the New Age. Entertaining, laborious, unimportant. Am also plotting a book of essays for American publication [probably *Pavannes and Divisions,* 1918]. That's not of very breathless interest either. Really I feel as I had writ an article a day for a month. am trying to get "caught up".

The Figaro cutting was entertaining. Miss S. did not say it was from you. Probably never entered her head that anyone would suppose it to [be] her own, very own, unaided discovery. Baker is worried about you. I do not think I picture your life as one of satin coated ease. However it is just as well to emphasize things. I have not read Barbeuse [Barbusse], Dorothy did. Baker dont feel like reading it either.

I dont see what the hell any writer can add to one's imagination of things. However.. that's no reason for not trying. And again neither Baker nor I can be taken as types of average imagination. All these books should ultimately be very useful. [lacuna] has done one on the hospitals. "La vie des Mar [lacuna]s"

I on the contrary have b[een] writing of Larforgue [Laforgue], Elizabethan classicists. etc. etc. Vildrac said "Ce serait bien plaisant, passer sa vie e[n] [be]lles etudes.

I believe my two cousins who certainly dont care a hang for European civilisation have both been called up. Such is the irony of thin[gs.]

Theres an American employment something or other, which has told me to go away and [be] quiet, that in time our own troops will give us all t[he] employment etc ...

None of which things will in the least temper the sounds of "The End of a perfect day" or kindred gramaphone records; or stay off crumps from your parapet.

I wish you would get a decent and convenient wound in some comparatively tactful part of your anatomy. Say the left buttock. But that makes lying in bed uncomfortable. Really it is difficult to choose a part suitable for mangling. Hell. Such gossip as there is, [is] NOT amusing. The Strand Magazine for Sept. assures me the [lacuna]s are effective.

The morning Chronicle assures me my compatriots are called "Teddies", which is one in the eye for Mr Woodie Wilson. However transpontine politics may not amuse you. I have sent on the July Little Review. I suppose the Aug. will arrive sometime, but it has nothing of yours.

etc.

Yours ever.

E.

25.8.17.

"Tarr": Pound sent the corrected manuscript of Lewis's novel *Tarr* to the American publisher Alfred A. Knopf.
"Studies of Contemporary Mentality": Pound did a series of twenty articles under this title for the *New Age* between 16 August 1917 and 10 January 1918.

86. ALS–2. [Nieuwpoort, Belgium].

26./8/17.

Dear Pound.   Many thanks for letter. Will you please pay in the £12 to Barclay & Co. 1.Pall Mall East. = I am glad you liked the remaining letters (Petrograd.) That portion in which I quote the Masque of Anarchy must under no circumstances be printed. I should make an enemy at a time when I cannot afford to; for no doubt the eminent man referred to reads the Little Review. = I liked your contribution very much. Eliot very amusing.

I have sent Miss S[aunders]. a sketch "The King of the Trenches." Have a look at it. = Also before my batch of Dieppe drawings are dispatched to the place I destine them for, examine them, please. (See Miss S.)

Has she shown you the "Ideal Giant"? (Not for publication.)

Since my sergeant was killed, there is a little extra work. Otherwise humdrum. Our place has had five direct hits now, & today we are building it up anew. In the last twenty-four hours several shells have fallen 5 yards from our front door (& only ingress & exit.) My sleeping bag, airing in the doorway, has been brutally transpierced! If we get any very heavy stuff over here ever our shelter would be smashed up at once. It is a matter of pure chance, under these circumstances, when, how and how much you get pipped. Sooner or later it is difficult to see how it can be avoided. = We are pretty badly off here. But some Batteries are worse off than us. The only thing is that if our bad time comes, it will be as bad as any. = As soon as this time I refer to is over, I shall do everything in my power to extricate myself from this Battery, if I am still here. With this hysterical little matoid, Clarkson and the cockney officers' chorus, there is I fear <u>nothing</u> to be done.

I have <u>written</u> Quinn, giving your address.

Yours ever W.L.

Masque of Anarchy: In the deleted passage, which is now among Lewis's manuscripts at the Olin Library, Cornell University, Lewis quotes from Percy Bysshe Shelley's poem on the "Peterloo Massacre" of 1819, "The Mask of Anarchy." In Lewis's attack on revolutionaries who seek only personal power, he quotes Shelley's lines on Lord Castlereagh: "I met murder on the way—/ He had a mask like Castlereagh."

"King of the Trenches": This story was published posthumously in *Unlucky for Pringle: Unpublished and Other Stories by Wyndham Lewis,* eds. Fox and Chapman.

your contribution: "Jodindranath Mawhwor's Occupation," *The Little Review* 4 (May 1917): 12–18.

Eliot very amusing: A reference to Eliot's brief fiction "Eeldrop and Appleplex, I," in which the characters are in part modeled on Pound and the author, in *The Little Review* 4 (May 1917): 7–11.

87. ALS–1. [Nieuwpoort, Belgium].

28/8/17.

My dear Pound.   Miss S[aunders]. has sent me the typed copy of the [Imaginary] letters. But she has lost or forgotten to type the emendment I sent of the <u>second letter</u>. This however does not affect you. As to remaining letters; if there are any offensive passages, have them out, if it does not destroy sense. Otherwise let me know page & lines, & I will overhaul passage. (I have copy here, as I said.)

Despite my excellent protection, Heine has just dropped one (a big one) remarkably near. I therefore will repair to our solid refuge.

Yrs   W.L.

88. TLS–1. [5, Holland Place Chambers, Kensington. W.]

30/8/17.

Dear Lewis:

What the devil is the mask of Anarchy ??? Has Miss S[aunders]. sent you the letters for deletion of "impossibilities"? Or do you want me to remove the pink young man on my own.?

And why in heaven shouldn't we publish the "Ideal Giant"? I enjoyed it immensely.

Barclay have sent me receipt for £12/12. It is only chance that the Giant hasn't gone to U.S.A. already.

Have just sent you Aug. Little Review. Inferior Religions is in Sept. "Cantleman" in Oct.

Shall try to see Miss S. sketches etc. have been turning out an article a day for weeks, also book,.. Am doing "studies in Contemporary Mentality" in New Age. That also will make me a few MORE friends.

Baker was up and dressed in his wheel chair Tuesday and a bit more cheerful.

Your detested Watts [possibly A.P. Watt] from Italian front more or less exact replica of your emotions re/ la vie militaire. Why you two loathe each other with such acharnement...... when all traces of intelligence are so bloody rare and so much to be conserved ....'!!! However it is not my affair. etc. etc. etc.

⟨I can not say with the French wife "I write to you because I have nothing to do. I stop because I have nothing to say." However, I stop.⟩

Yours

E.   Pound
zra

deletion of "impossibilities": Pound was concerned that Lewis described the physique of his persona in the "Imaginary Letters" too graphically.

September 1917.

France

Dear Pound. We have been suddenly plucked up from our position in the North, and have since then journeyed many a mile. So the climax of that story has, I expect permanently, been skipped or missed. ⟨I will tell you some day, when we meet, what that was.⟩ Before going to our new position (a bad one, they say) we are billeted for 4 days in a pleasant country.

I think I told you we had a new C[ommanding]. O[fficer]. He comes from Hull, from its slums undoubtedly, and its Sunday Schools. The proud Naval men to whom we were attached would hardly speak to him, and wondered once more at the ways of the Army, in giving such unspeakable, foolish and dismal muck a Battery. ≡ Bad as are the things I have been witness of, I have never seen as bad a case. I am now absolutely sardine-packed with the quintessence of the prosperous slums of a Protestant country. = Two of these charming 'boys' today have been to a neighbouring bourg to buy a few pictures to decorate our dugout, — the one in which we shall have to live, probably, through this warlike winter. Yesterday, when for the third time this individual had attempted to prevent my having a square meal in a restaurant, there being nothing to do, I said to him; "I am in your Battery, not in your Sunday School." He considers, apparently, that a meal in a restaurant and the accompanying half bottle of wine is a treat for little children, indulgently provided by a kind O.C. every 3 weeks. = He drummed with his fingers for some minutes after my remark, and blushed as — one of Edward [Wadsworth]'s uncles blushes. = He stoops, is going bald, and has a hanging crimson underlip.

Excuse me for harrowing you with this picture of war. But I am very full of it at present.

Otherwise nothing further to report. Happily this awful situation has its interludes and entr'actes which if I weren't so damnably near to my chief colleague at the present moment, & if it were not for the acrobatics required to avoid giving information of use to the enemy, I might more profitably tell you about: = a weak-minded and hoary old Area Commandant, who, when he hears wheels, tumbles out of his Office and regulates traffic like a Policeman: the inhabitants of these farms etc. The beauty of these farms, by Christ! = But I shall forget the ugliness as soon as I turn my back on it, and it helps me to forget it communicating it to you (excuse me, once more) whereas the excellent thrills, and the scene and the humour, are a possession, undoubtedly. (Sentimentalized into an importance out of all proportion with what they are.)

Remember me to Mrs. Pound.   Yrs   W.L.

90. TLS–1. On stationery embossed: 5, Holland Place Chambers, Kensington. W.

Dear W.L.

Your last reaches a truly literary intensity. I hope the new position is more downy.

Re/ the Burn correspondence, I have deleted about four brief sentences. I shall risk it at that. I have not changed the sense or altered Mr B's Socratic temperament. or the shape of his posterior.

So that's that, and you needn't be bothered emending. Tokens of esteem begin to arrive. If we can hold out for a few years the review will I think manage to be permanent. How lucrative? heaven alone knows. August is a wasted number: I should have got the first six numbers into the first five. BUTTTT, one has to send off stuff so early, and I had to be sure of a feature in every number.

I shall probably get ALL the Soldier of Humour into Dec./ 3d. letter in Jan./ and the remaining three letters, 2 of which are so short, into Feb.

That leaves War Baby, and Ideal Giant.

My present existence is that of a highly mechanized typing volcano. Amusing note from Bobby [Roberts], a day or so ago. Must answer that also. Hope Hartley has found you.

yours ever

E
zra Pound

10–9–17 [10 September 1917]

shape of his posterior: In an "Imaginary Letter" published in *The Little Review* 4 (March 1918): 23–30, William Bland Burn refers to his "objectional buttocks that protrude."

91. ALS–2. [Pmk: 22 September 1917].

France
September 1917.

Dear Pound. Thank you for letter received today. = First of all, Hartley is unlikely to find me if you have given him 224 as the Battery number. = 330. is the Battery I am with. I believe you have also persuaded the unfortunate Mademoiselle S[aunders]. to address me 224. So shunt her onto the right number when you next see her.

I am very glad that you can print Bland without chopping his backside off. I hope that the five short sentences contain nothing of the spiritual importance of a rump. I hope for the best.

It is at present an hour when the vitality is not high, and I have had much work & little sleep lately. I have to sit up here because some officer must be awake, and consciously in the Battery. I am taking this opportunity of writing a few letters, but so far they have not said quite what I wanted to say. = My domestic troubles in the Battery have in one sense diminished. For some reason my C.O. is not unfavourably disposed towards me. On the other hand an open rupture has occurred with my most active colleague. We sit dead opposite each other in the Mess, and henceforth do not exchange conversation, or extend to each other the usual courtesies. – The Battery position is ten thousand times less shelled than the Nieuport position. To counterbalance this (very much) we have to do a lot of forward observation. Ainsi, I was F.O.O. (forward ob[servation]. officer) of the Group three days ago, and on that occasion had the extreme gratification of seeing, in the midst of our barrage, a large Bosche fly into the air as it seemed a few feet beneath me. From the ridge where I was observing things I looked down into the German front line as you might into Church Street. I was, as a matter of fact, 400 yards behind our own line, & 600, I suppose, from the Bosche. We were shelled steadily for three and two hours respectively, and I eventually left with my party of signallers through a 5.9 barrage. The journey to this particular O.P. is long (2 hours walk or more) and shelled for half that distance, especially at night. You meet plenty of dead men. I stumbled into one (of two) with his head blown off so that his neck[,] level with the collar of his tunic, reminded you of sheep in butchers' shops, or a French Salon painting of a Moroccan headsman. He was a Scot, & had been killed a few hours before. Every track & road is spasmodically infested with shells. Two officers on the following evening were wounded, one very badly, in performing my trick, = the famous dive through the barrage round this notorious O.P. So

105

you see —. The O.P. amuses me. I volunteered for the F.O.O. job as an opportunity of leaving the Battery for a bit. But lack of sleep, military competition, and such human society as I find here m'excéde, exceeds me; is more than even I bargained for "when I first put this uniform on." In a few months I shall see about Intelligence, Camouflage or something. = Another thing I notice is this: that when I was registering a Battery on a church the other day as F.O.O. I was glad that it was a presumably empty ruin that I was guiding the bursts upon. I am truly not sanguinary except when confronted by an imbecile: not, thank God, from lack of stomach. Too much sense. Alas, too much sense.

Farewell. Rappelez-moi a nos amis.   Yrs   W.L.

"this uniform on": from a song in Gilbert and Sullivan's *Patience*.

92. ALS–2. [Pmk: 8 October 1917].

Oct. 1917.
France.

My dear Pound.   I was glad to hear that Tarr had got sold. = Most of your letters have reached me. (Little Review, Sept. just arrived.)

I am glad drawings please you. = I am sending you three more: which examine, please, & hand over then to Miss S[aunders]. sometime for mounting. = As to what you find lacking in those designs, of course nothing new can be tackled out here. Indeed, that much was only done because I happened to fall sick. The Market Women, L'Horloge & a few others are however quite up to the mark.

I dont think where there is much of anything else that style is worth maintaining in pictures—or books. Examine the Market-Women & a few pen drawings of Rembrandt, and you will notice– I hope not with an air of amazement & discovery – that the Market Ladies possess a similar character & a very similar quantity of Style. Sometimes I am a bit careless and harsh. But in the majority of those mounted drawings you have there is nothing to worry about on that score.

As to writing: the King of the Trenches I can improve a bit. But I did not attempt to write it. It is only a scribble containing information towards a fiction that could be made given me by an amicable young fellow.

All as usual here. Three nights ago I had all my first gun-detachment except two men knocked out— the new sergeant among them. This is the second sergeant in 6 or 8 weeks. I have lost, I am sorry to say, many a pleasant companion by this – Old Bill, amongst them, much better than Bairnsfather's Bill. He dreampt [*sic*] the night before that the whole detachment had been wiped out. = The mud & cold is unutterably disagreeable. I liked your poem greatly. Have not yet read Appleplex.

Yrs   W.L.

Tarr: The contract to publish Lewis's novel with Alfred A. Knopf was dated 18 September 1917.

Market Women: This drawing, but not "L'Horloge," is listed in *Wyndham Lewis, Paintings and Drawings,* ed. Michel.

Bairnsfather's Bill: Bruce Bairnsfather's cartoons of the British "Tommy" Old Bill were famous. In Bairnsfather's best-known illustration, Old Bill tells a fellow soldier, "If you know of a better 'ole, go to it!"

your poem: Pound's "L'Homme Moyen Sensuel," *The Little Review* 4 (September 1917): 8–16.

Appleplex: Eliot's fiction, "Eeldrop and Appleplex, II," appeared in *The Little Review* 4 (September 1917): 16–19.

93. ALS–2. [Pmk: Army Post Office, 12 October 1917].

Oct. 1917.
France.

My dear Pound.   Thank you for letter & forwarded letter from Quinn received. I herewith enclose 1 of the Contract forms, which please send on to Quinn. The other form I will send you in a day or two. (You are supposed to witness my signature, I believe).

Miss Weaver has sent me copies of Egoist, & I will attempt to supply missing pages: although it is difficult without context.

Were those parallel lines = Quinn mentions kept going by The Egoist, or not? They occurred all through the book in the typewritten MSS. Could not they be disinterred, & used by Knopf?

If Miss S[aunders]. will send me the King of the Trenches, I will improve it a bit for you. = Talking of trenches, I am going up tonight to a spot 200 yards behind our most advanced shell-hole, from which the towers of Bruges may be observed. I volunteered for this muddy job as the officer to whose lot it had fallen, in rotation, had twice running been to the worst sort of O.P., whereas yesterday for the second time running a comparatively comfortable Operations Post, & not Observation Post, had fallen to my lot. The young man in question, —a sharp-featured, horse-toothed, narrow-browed, vain, crotchety young board-school master accepted my offer at once as though he were conferring a great favour upon me. Why treat these animals like human beings? I shall not in future offer my skin in place of the cheap pink trash that covers the absence of brain, heart and stomach of pedagogic or other colleague.

My gun-pit has been a melancholy place for the last few days. My first detachment of ten men only, reinforced by employed men, & some from the relief detachment, etc: has been crawling about like a mutilated insect. There are two or three letters to be written to mothers and wives. They are perfectly easy to write, for the more crudely conventional the better. But it is a nasty official task.

Mrs. Haselden wants to know if she may bring a Mr. Haynes to one of your dinner evenings. I thought she certainly might. She is a sensible woman.

Send me on the indecorous Cantelman [*sic*] as soon as you get him. I am posting you a few more drawings.

Yrs.   W.L.

P.S. My officer colleagues or most of them, are really as poisonous refuse as you could wish to find. One is standing outside the door of my gitoune [*guitoune,* a trench shelter] at present, with a thick Hebraic neck, scant hair, and a foolish curved sentimental mouth, a cross between a fish's and a baby's.   Cheerio.   W.L.

---

parallel lines: The double-dashes (=) Lewis uses to break up and emphasize his sentences were used, as Lewis wished, in the Knopf edition of *Tarr* but not in *The Egoist* edition.

94. ALS–3. [Pmk: Army Post Office, 18 October 1917].

Oct. 1917. France

My dear Pound. I have just received your note. I was glad to hear that the Little Review is going well. = I also received various copies of the Egoist. But God alone knows how I am to write the missing pages [of *Tarr*]. It is like trying to remember the shape of a cloud: the context under my hand is so incomplete. Nevertheless I will try.

Last night I went to a town some miles back, & had a good dinner. After a ten-mile walk through endless morasses & deserts, and having negotiated a number of barrages, I felt hungry. I went up on the day of the attack, the last attack, & the Bosche was laying down barrages everywhere. I got round some & through others, was sniped with pip squeaks & by planes, &, as I say, returned with a prodigious appetite. If you wish to visualize me these times, imagine a bulging figure covered with mud, with haversacks, field-glasses etc. hanging round it, plodding through a spacious and sinister desert, at the head of a small party of signallers, loaded in their turn with coils of wire, lucas lamps, telephone-cases etc. – all suffused with mud. — Well, I went to the town & had the dinner, & who should I see at the next table but an unusually ugly little monkey of the name of William Orpen. This monkey provided me with whiskey, which he said he knew was good, as he got it from Haig's Mess that morning. He has a crown [of a Major] on his shoulder, lives in an excellent Hôtel, & occasionally visits Hell, as he calls this neighbourhood. He is doing sketches, which one day will become panels, I expect, in the Houses of Parliament or elsewhere. = John is coming out, Orpen tells me, on the same job. Nevinson has likewise been here painting: Bone too; & God knows how many more! Barbusse says in his book [*Le Feu*], & this surprised me with the French, that "trés peu d'artistes ou de riches ont risqués leur figures dans les tranchées," or something like that; those were the words I think. Well, I dont, as you know, aspire to be a military hero. I shall shortly have 6 months service in France to my credit, during which time I have risked my "figure" many times; more than you think. Of the two detachments on my gun, only half the men who came out with me are left: several killed, the rest wounded. I have discovered no panic-streak in myself so far, & am fortunately not of a timid disposition. I could no doubt (the chances of war permitting) remain here another 6 months, and another after that. But there is one thing to be remembered. Nature & my training have made me curiously sensitive to ugly & stupid influences. The whole point of Me is that (& not that I don't happen to be over physically nervous.) This causes me to suffer a great deal more than most

people by my surroundings. Again, as I have cogitated a good deal
throughout my days, the futility, trickery, the element in fact of despicable
inhuman swindle in all this dreary & rotten business is borne in upon me
more sharply than upon most people. This has its effect. You remark
that I might apply for my Intelligence or Interpret job. It's no good my
doing that unless there is someone somewhere to receive my application
at the other end with benevolence. There are crowds of jobs that practically
eliminate risk & discomfort. Any soldier could enumerate them for you.
Only a fourth of the British Army is in the fighting line. The interstices &
accumulations of the Auxiliary Services extend all the way back through
France to Havre, & all over England, Scotland & Wales. Mrs. Strang
boasted to me that she had got all her four brawny sons out of the
trenches, or the Line; none of them spending more than 3 months here.
One she got into the Clyde R. G. A., one into the Camouflage section of
the R[oyal]. E[ngineer]'s, I think it is ETC. ETC. = Any benevolent &
weighty person could do the same for me with ease, I have done my bit
out here. My health is not good! There is the Ordnance: there are the jobs
of R. T. O. [Road Transport Officer?] out here (French useful) District
Purchasing Officer, Prison Camps, Deputy Assistant Provost Marshal; Intelligence jobs, & War Office jobs. Also there is the Clyde R. G. A. & other
Coast Defence services of the R. G. A. =
I think if you consulted with Baker, you might manage to work something. You see Languages are something definite, and of great use. I
could get German into line with French & Spanish without much trouble.
I could myself write to Lady C[unard]. but if you have not squabbled
with her, you could do it better there on the spot, perhaps. You remember
that Bingham got his leave instantly & with éclat. Why not benefit his
country by putting at its disposal a Linguist, and an Intelligence & being
instrumental in causing The Bombardier & My Battery (the former would
be the gayer book) to be outlined.

                    Yrs. W. L.

Orpen: This meeting is described in Part III, Chapter X of Lewis's *Blasting and
    Bombardiering.*

95. TNS–1. This note may be a fragment of a letter.

Re the "missing parts" of the novel [*Tarr*]. The whole text went to N.Y., it is merely the "=" marks that Q[uinn]. wanted put back.

I should think it would have to be done from the proofs. GOD knows what the printer has done with the original typescript.

(Damn Orpen anyhow)

Yeats was married on saturday. To the purchaser of your £12 drawing, at that. I dont know that that was your intention when you composed it.

God bless you, and Eaven 'elp you.

yours   Ez

Ezra Pound
22–10–'17

Yeats: W. B. Yeats married Georgie Hyde-Lees, a friend of Dorothy Pound, on 21 October 1917.
"=" marks: See note to Letter 93.

96. ALS–2.

Oct. 1917. France

Dear Pound.   I again dined the other night with Orpen. R. A. (Major) (Royal Academy, not Royal Artillery) also with a youth in the Intelligence De Trafford or de Travers; — only remaining son of Sir Humphrey de Trafford. This youth told me that Gen. Sir John Charteris is the head of the Intelligence department at the War Office. When I last heard of him (if it is the same man) he was a Major in charge of the department of Flight. Tonks is a friend of his, & gave Bob [Roberts] a letter to him at the time Bob wished to enter the Flying service. As he knows Tonks, he doubtless likes Art. (I am not suggesting you should send him Inferior Religions. Art was my word, & I was thinking of avenues of approach.)

There are many Intelligence jobs I am quite competent to do, dont forget that for goodness sake, if you move, should you be able to.

MacEvoy [McEvoy] threatened to come out here as a Major, & peep through a periscope at the Mist from Boulogne. But Diana Manners put her foot down.

111

No Little Review this month yet. — Did you have time to look at my revised [Imaginary] Letters. They are what the first should have been.

Yrs   W.L.

P.S. Have you seen Bob?

Introduction to Letter 97.

Lewis had told Pound that he wanted to stay at the front while there was still anything fresh to experience, but the preceding letters show that he was now eager to leave the trenches, particularly if he could utilize his experiences in his painting. When he was called back to England in November 1917 because of his mother's illness, his friend Captain Guy Baker recommended him for Lord Beaverbrook's Canadian War Records project. Pound immediately mobilized recommendations for Lewis, including one from John Quinn; and Lady Cunard arranged a series of leaves for Lewis until he was officially appointed. His first assignment was to paint a howitzer battery on the Vimy Ridge. One of his paintings, *A Canadian Gun Pit,* is now in the National Gallery of Canada, Ottawa; and another, *A Battery Shelled,* is in the Imperial War Museum, London. The hazards of war were not over, however, for Lewis became seriously ill during the postwar epidemic of influenza and pneumonia which took the lives of his mother and of Guy Baker.

97. ALS–1.

> War Records Office.
> Headquarters Canadian Corps.
> B.E.F.
> France.
> Jan. 1st 1918.

My dear Pound.   I was sorry to leave without seeing you: but I think I told you I was going off. I shall be here only 3 weeks I expect. I am installed in a good billet, met with great hospitality, & have facilities for getting my material together. I was taken out sight-seeing today, with a dismal & angry feeling I passed the place, through the fields, anyway, where Gaudier was killed. The ground was covered with snow, nobody about, and my god, it did look a cheerless place to die in.

I wonder if Baker came up to town after all? He was trying to get up yesterday for a day or two. I asked Miss S[aunders]. to bring those drawings back to Holland Place Chambers. = Well. À bientôt. Best wishes for this New Year, for you and Mrs. Pound.

Yrs W.L.

Gaudier: Henri Gaudier-Brzeska was killed on 5 June 1915 during an attack on a German position at Neuville St. Vaast.

98. ALS–2.

War Records Office.   9/1/18 [9 January 1918]
Headquarters. Canadian Corps.
          B.E.F.
                    France.

My dear Pound. Work is proceeding, or strictly speaking commencing, amidst the snow. I have located a dandy gun-pit: 2 weeks, perhaps 3, and I shall have got my material together. = The Major (John) has arrived. Tout comme de certains rois, he made his debut by falling down outside the front door. He lent me two copies of the New Age last night, with contempor[ar]ly psychology by you in them, which he praises: but says he feels all the time that you are rather a cox-comb. What is a cox-comb? Nothing to do with a varlet, I hope. In any case you bite your thumb at him, dont you?

Should you see or have occasion to communicate with Miss Weaver, tell her that that Epilogue [to *Tarr*] (which I will send on to the Egoist) is to be a preface: & secondly, that those passages from Montaigne I showed you are to be the device of the book, & come somewhere at the beginning. Paris looks real fine, dandy: it is bondé de Yankis. I could see no signs of Art anywhere. All traces of it appeared to have vanished. But I expect I didn't know where to look: et puis j'étais surtout occupé à dipper mon wick. La prochaine fois je serais plus tenace.

I liked your article very much: Forget-Me-Nots: noticed no trace of the mediaeval epithet, & would much like to read the rest. = When I come back I will get you to lend them to me. They are certainly the best things the New Age has contained for many a day.   Yrs   W L.

Major (John): Augustus John was an official war painter. In *Blasting and Bombardiering,* Lewis claimed that John's beard and manner led the troops to confuse him with King George V.

New Age: Pound wrote twenty "Studies in Contemporary Mentality," analyses of the British press, for the *New Age* between 16 August 1917 and 10 January 1918.

Montaigne: Lewis used two passages from Michel de Montaigne, which recommend a natural prose style, as epigraphs to *Tarr.*

Forget-Me-Nots: a reference to Pound's "Studies in Contemporary Mentality . . . XV.—A Nice Paper," *New Age* 22 (13 December 1917): 129–30, which analyzed *Forget-Me-Not,* a "penny weeklie" that serialized popular fiction.

99. TLS–2. On stationery embossed: 5, Holland Place Chambers, Kensington. W.

Dear W.L.
        Re/ Coxcombs, Cockscombs etc.

A coxcomb or cock's comb is the large red object which flops about on a rooster's head, this is carefully to be distinguished from the small red object placed at the other extremity of the rooster, i.e. and to wit, the cock's cock. I judge that Augustus [John] is trying to distinguish between my temperament and his own, i.e. pointing out that I fly my flag over my intelligence (such as it is) whereas he flys [*sic*] his over his penis, (such as it is), or over his flies, or buttons.

        In my so naive and undeveloped country men take the penis for granted, the percentage of actual eunuchs (natural eunuchs) is perhaps lower, or at any rate the American suddenly discovering his impotence is, in most cases, both annoyed and surprised, but rather more surprised than annoyed. The Englishman, on the contrary, gives in with the morne and desolate air, of one who says, "this is but what I had expected."

        In my case, there is but the one tribute, that of a well known continental sculptor. As to Augustus, I think you will agree with me, that cock's COMB would be a misnomer for him, whereas at his last exposure of painting there were many canvasses which might have been done by the lower organ, alone and unaided by brushes, pallate [*sic*] knife or the usual intermediaries of the craft. You will be grieved to know that the Little Review lost its case, despite J.Q[uinn]'s noble defence "The man who wrote THAT Story can NOT be a sensualist" etc. I have all the papers of the case and some of them are rich and refreshing reading.

I have been too busy with the XII th. century to take any further steps in the matter. The job is now about done, and part of it decently.

I enclose more on Augustus, springing from the Castalian fount of the Chenil.

VIRGIN'S PRAYER

> Ezra Pound
> And Augustus John
> Bless the bed
> That I lie on.
>
> > (authorship unrecognized,
> > I first heard it in 1909.)

It is emphatically NOT my own, I believe it to have come from an elder generation. However it is not pertinent to the subject. No one else has ever coupled our names. Orage hopes to get the Contemporary Mentality published as a book. It is not an important fandango. Enough of this.

yrs.
Ezra Pound

13–1–18

one tribute: Henri Gaudier-Brzeska's "phallic" treatment of Pound in his sculpture, *Hieratic Head of Ezra Pound;* see Pound's *Gaudier-Brzeska: A Memoir,* plate XIII.

J. Q.'s noble defence: When the October 1917 issue of *The Little Review* was suppressed by the United States Post Office on the grounds that "Cantlemen's Spring-Mate" was obscene, John Quinn unsuccessfully defended the review in court.

XII th. century: Pound's "Homage à la langue d'Oc," *The Little Review* 5 (May 1918): 19–31.

100. ALS–1.

My dear Pound. Enough, as you say, of coxcombs. But when you say that many of those paintings might have been done by the wise old Cock itself, I must demur. The Cock would paint pieces of interest to other Cocks. And in going round the exhibition I noticed no signs of interest down below, any more than up above!

Miss S[aunders]. writes me that your medievalalities ["Homage à la langue d'Oc"] are very fine. If they are all as good as the one I read, you are on the point of producing an important book, even if the Contemp. Mentality will not be one.

I am contending here with unfavourable conditions, chiefly bad weather & scarcity of cars. All the same, I shall soon have enough to go on with.

Bobby [Roberts] writes me that he has practically got the Canadian job: that is Watkins (Records Office) has written him, asking if he is willing to do the painting on spec: if not found suitable, no £250 but expenses paid. This since "their advisor cannot guarantee his not doing a Cubist picture" or something of that sort. He naturally accepts, with amertume, on any terms.

I enclose the passages ⟨2 passages⟩ from Montaigne I want stuck at the front of Tarr. = Should you ever be my executor, allow no one to publish any <u>poems</u> of mine. I looked through them the other day, and I should be <u>very</u> sorry to see any of them published.

I expect in a week I shall be coming back.

Yours ever
W.L.

poems: Lewis's unpublished poems of the prewar period are in the Olin Library, Cornell University.

101. ALS–1. On stationery imprinted: ENDSLEIGH PALACE HOS-PITAL for OFFICERS, <u>Endsleigh</u> <u>Gardens</u>, <u>London</u>, N.W.1

March 8th 1919

Dear Pound   Is this my first letter since I have been here? I got Flu, then pneumonia, as you know I expect. I am now still on my back, but am well and normal again—no fever, having, as my amicable young doctor said, staggered about a bit, but eventually rolled down the right side of the hill!

I expect I shall be <u>out</u> of this place in 2 weeks' time. Then a spell of convalescent home somewhere or other.

Can these things be avoided? No, Pound, nothing can be avoided.

I am sending you round a few cuttings. I want you to see how we stand as regards our Press. Please peruse and return.

I get good accounts of you & Mrs. Pound from people, or rather Miss S[aunders]. That is satisfactory.

How are you both?   W.L.

Who is O.R.D. Westminster Gazette?

O.R.D.: Probably the art critic O. Raymond Drey, who later became Lewis's friend. He wrote in "War Pictures by Mr. Wyndham Lewis," *Westminster Gazette* (24 February 1919), p. 2 about Lewis's one-man show, "Guns": "The whole exhibition is a work of remarkable intelligence and passionate contemplation. . . ."

Part III
Campaigning
1920-1940

We see two hostile ideologies contending for the mastery of the world—Communism and Fascism. Both advance their policies (they cannot do otherwise) in a paralysing atmosphere of martial law. And the constraints, the pseudo-religious intensity, of these systems, do not lend themselves to the relaxations of the senses, nor to the detached delights of the intellect, what ever else may be claimed for them.

—Wyndham Lewis, *Blasting and Bombardiering*

But to hitch sensibility to efficiency?
grass versus granite. . . .

Canto CXIII/ p. 788

Campaigning 1920–1940

When Lewis returned from the Great War, he was too weary of conflict to carry out the cultural battle plans he had announced in *BLAST*. He wrote in 1939 that trench warfare convinced him that "the community to which he belonged would never be the same again: and that all *surplus* vigor was being bled away and stamped out." He attacked what he called a shell-shocked society in his satiric fiction, but he was himself so deeply shocked by the war that he distrusted the avant-garde values of his Vorticist period. In *BLAST* he called for the "dehumanization" of the arts, but he tells us in *Rude Assignment* that when he saw the shell craters and ruined trees of the battlefield, he recoiled from a landscape "so consonant with the austerity of that 'abstract' vision. . . . And before I knew quite what I was doing I was drawing with loving care a signaller corporal to plant upon the lip of the shell-crater."

Lewis never entirely abandoned abstract for naturalistic styles of painting, although his new concern with realistic portrayal seemed like backsliding to Pound. Lewis briefly reassembled the Vorticist painters in 1920 in an exhibition held under the noncommittal title of "Group X," and in the preceding year Lewis's short book, *The Caliph's Design: Architects! Where Is Your Vortex?,* called for England's painters to lead the way to a visual revolution that would revitalize society as a whole. In 1921 he started an art journal, largely written by himself, called *The Tyro,* which Pound considered too limited by the London milieu to be fresh or effective.

During the years 1921–26, Lewis used a small inheritance to stay (as he put it) "underground." He published relatively little but read and wrote voluminously and perfected the draughting and painting skills he had neglected in his Vorticist phase. Out of this period comes the enormous "Man of the World" manuscript, which he describes to Pound in Letter 121, and a mastery of draughtsmanship that made him one of England's great portrait artists.

Pound also sensed that the "surplus energy" had left London and departed for Paris, where the war had strengthened and not destroyed the avant-garde. Pound urged Lewis to join him in Paris and to contribute to the journals and small presses that were Pound's natural element. But

Lewis was wary of Pound schemes; he wrote in *Blasting and Bombardiering* that "I entertained a most healthy suspicion of all Pound's enthusiasms—was I not one of them myself?" Lewis rejected the idea of moving to Paris because he thought his own individuality would be lost among the multiplying avant-garde "movements" of the world's art capital, and perhaps Pound left Paris for Rapallo, Italy in 1924 for a similar reason. He found in Rapallo not only a beautiful seacoast and low living expenses, but also a town where his presence would be unquestionably central (as in the music concerts he organized) and where he could imagine he was helping to build a new society. The remarkable volume of Pound's letters was necessary if he was to maintain his reputation as a cultural impresario. Typical letters to Lewis urged him to publish or exhibit his works in Italy. Lewis's view was that Pound was "buried alive in a Fascist State," and in any case Lewis was bent on isolating himself as a writer. In his virtually one-man periodical, *The Enemy,* he declared himself the "Enemy" of romanticism in the arts and revolution in politics. He claimed he was in "solitary schism" from the intellectual world and proceeded to prove it in works such as *The Art of Being Ruled* (1926) and *Time and Western Man* (1927) by attacking figures such as Bertrand Russell, Alfred North Whitehead, James Joyce, Gertrude Stein, and Ezra Pound himself. He accused avant-garde writers of uncritically fostering the revolutionary propaganda and social nihilism of the postwar period. The "Enemy's" reputation became even more notorious when he satirized former friends and patrons, such as the painter Edward Wadsworth and the Sitwells, in *The Apes of God* (1930). In *Men Without Art* (1934), Lewis even criticized T. S. Eliot for not being reactionary *enough.* Yet Pound and Eliot remained his loyal friends. Pound wrote in *Guide to Kulchur:* "Mr. W. Lewis, calling me in one place a revolutionary simpleton, makes honourable amends, calling himself a chronological idiot in another."

The conservatism of Lewis's intellectual position is even clearer in his political journalism, such as *Hitler* (1931), *Left Wings Over Europe* (1936), and *Count Your Dead: They Are Alive!* (1937). The subtitles of *Left Wings* ("How to Make a War about Nothing") and of *Count Your Dead* ("A New War in the Making") reveal that his political commentary was conditioned by the fear of another war which would again damage the arts. He wrote with great but belated insight into his political motivations in 1942, when he confessed to a liberal friend about his fears for the "tribe" of artists:

> Our tribe suffered terribly the last time it went to war: when I heard the war-drums rolling again I was almost madly concerned. I turned upon the left-

wing you remember, because it seemed to be from that quarter that the
war-psychosis came. —It is now very apparent to me that I thought too
much of our tribe: too little of the "genre humain." . . .

World War I had left Lewis genuinely frightened of any violent political
movements and committed to law and order at all costs. He believed that
right-wing authoritarianism was more likely to bring peace than left-wing
social revolution. Lewis was grotesquely wrong and yet sincere when he
wrote in 1931 that Adolf Hitler was a "Man of Peace" who would contain communist violence. In 1939 he publicly apologized for his Hitler
book and the political naiveté behind it when he wrote in *The Hitler Cult*
that he had indulged "in efforts at 'appeasement' beside which those of
Mr. Chamberlain pale in comparison."

Pound was more willing than Lewis to see violence used, as in Italy's
invasion of Abyssinia, to achieve political ends. Yet the political views of
both Pound and Lewis were motivated by a desire for a stable society, and
both writers thought that their gifts as artists guaranteed the soundness of
their political insights. Pound wrote to Lewis in 1951 (Letter 220),
"Dunno as political ideas are so dif/ from canons of writing. Ez saw the
Georgians were NOT the cream of the cream / same kind of perception
wd/ show Ooozenstink [F. D. Roosevelt] an ASS." Lewis could never
have applied aesthetic criteria to politics so reductively, but he also had
an unfounded faith in his own political perceptions. In a rejected chapter
of his second autobiography, entitled in manuscript "The Burden of Dullness," he wrote that "As a portraitist I feel I should have detected the
awful symptoms" of a power obsession in Hitler. He explains lamely that
he was fooled by the "platitudinous exterior" of the "little figure" with the
"disarming toothbrush moustache." This explanation is particularly significant and revealing because it comes from a satirist and portrait painter
who held that the artist's eye could always discern the truth about a person or situation from the surfaces of reality. Both Pound and Lewis
imported into politics something like Pound's "aesthetic of glimpses."

The years covered in this section of the Pound/Lewis correspondence
take us from their great creative years in the twenties, culminating in 1930
with Lewis's *The Apes of God* and Pound's *A Draft of XXX Cantos,* into
the troubled and finally disastrous thirties. Their artistic achievements
were still impressive in these years, but as they sometimes recognized
themselves, they gave too much energy to journalism—not only because
of the troubled times, but also for the small sums it could earn for them.
The thirties were additionally hard for Lewis because of a series of ill-

nesses and operations between 1932 and 1937 which left him deeply in
debt. His portraits of T. S. Eliot and Ezra Pound in 1938 and 1939 increased his reputation as a portrait painter, and he hoped to solve his
money problems by securing portrait commissions in America. When the
war broke out, Lewis was stranded in Canada with no means of returning
to England. Both Pound and Lewis lived through the war years as aliens,
and though Lewis was not in an enemy nation as was Pound, his living
conditions and isolation were even worse. Lewis, who called himself an
"outsider," and Pound, who referred to himself as an "exile," then had to
play these difficult roles in earnest.

"surplus energy": Wyndham Lewis on Art, eds. Michel and Fox, p. 340.
"lip of the shell-crater": Lewis, *Rude Assignment: A Narrative of My Career Up-
to-Date,* p. 128.
"Pound's enthusiasms": Lewis, *Blasting and Bombardiering: Autobiography
(1914–1926),* p. 284.
"buried alive": Blasting and Bombardiering, p. 13.
"chronological idiot": Pound, *Guide to Kulchur,* p. 234.
" 'genre humain' ": The Letters of Wyndham Lewis, ed. W. K. Rose, p. 328.
"efforts at 'appeasement' ": Lewis, *The Hitler Cult,* p. viii.
"toothbrush moustache": Lewis, "The Burden of Dullness," Olin Library, Cornell
University. Lewis decided not to use this chapter in *Rude Assignment.*
"aesthetic of glimpses": Hugh Kenner's phrase in *The Pound Era,* p. 69.

102. ACS.

　　　　　　3 rue de Beaume
　　　　　　Paris.

Can you send me a TIMON for adv[ertising] purp[oses].
=
also suggest you let me have six top notch drawings of different modes.
for purp. of prop[aganda]. = if you feel so dispogd. [disposed] enclose
'em in Timon—small sketches wd. do if show the gut. Linati & [indecipher-
able] want show in Milan.

　　　　　　a vous
　　　　　　E

21.6.1920

Linati: The Italian critic Carlo Linati; see Letter 109 and glossarial Index.

103. ALS–2.

14th July [1920]. 3 rue de Beaume. [Paris].

Dear W. L.

Thayer (The Dial) wants to know by cable whether they can use "Those Lewis articles" = I don't know which of the Athenaeum articles = some or all. But for Christs sake please cable assent. = They probably have files of Athenaeum, but in any case dont refrain from sending further copies as you intended. =

Also they want to use the drawing of me which appeared "in folio" (presumably portfolio) and in the Apple—unless some other American paper has permission to do so first, or is known to be about to do so. Please therefore wire to Thayer direct either "yes articles" or "yes portrait," or preferably "yes both" as that will save time, & I am not sure I can cable in english from here.
address.

Dial
152 W. 13th St.
New York

Will refund on cable in a fortnight.

yrs
E.P.

"Lewis articles": The articles on modern art mentioned in Letter 104.
drawing of me: Lewis published a drawing of Ezra Pound Esq. in his portfolio *Fifteen Drawings* (1920).
Apple: Pound published an article on the "pest and epidemic of museums" entitled "The Curse," in *Apple* (*of Beauty and Discord*) 1 (20 January 1920): 22, 24. See *Ezra Pound and the Visual Arts,* ed. Zinnes, pp. 158–60. He also published an article entitled "Obstructivity" in the *Apple* 1 (July? 1920): 168, 170, 172.

104. ALS–1. [July? 1920].

Dear W. L.

Dew fer christ's sake send on your story & also permission to use in U.S.A. anything that has come out in Athenaeum; also carbons of any new Athenaeum stuff.

125

They partic. want "Prevalent Design"; and from present indications they are already being so smacked for having reproduced a Cézanne that I think they will soon have to go the whole hog & really become an active periodical. =

The Dial. 152. W. 13 th St. New York.

Quinn has his eye on the paper, so you wont lose his attention by sending the stuff. Also advtg. for U.S. circulation & pub. of your books.

yrs
E

address.   Hotel de l'Elysée
             3 rue de Beaume
                  Paris.

"Prevalent Design": Lewis published a series of articles under this title about the relationship of art to "Nature" in *The Athenaeum* in November and December 1919 and January 1920. See *Wyndham Lewis on Art,* eds. Michel and Fox, pp. 117–28.

105. ALS–3. [July? 1920].

3 rue de Beaume [Paris].

Cher WynDAM

I agree with you that a rev. of Instigations [published by Pound in 1920] is mutual washing. = It is not, in the first place, a book that you are intended to read; it is a primer for barbarous americans, a substitute for bochized American university course.

Shd. of course like an article by you but shd. rather save it for a vol. of poems. or something with more centre. =

If you answer Thayer's letter; it wd. be, for general reasons, well to say that we agree that it wd. be mutual washing for you to review book mentioning you (damd inadequately.) but that on the other hand you dont disdeign [*sic*] my work—either Instig. or other. but wd. prefer to wait for vol. of poems (needn't commit yourself to do it.) =

Your opinion of poems wd. be of interest.

Our opinion of Instig. can only be that it is crowd-police work, intended to keep the mob in order; and that opinion shd. be kept to ourselves.

Or possibly that I have all the Xtn. virtues & none of the defects of that morass. That I have with the patience of an animal made a large clearing, wherein it is to be hoped etc.

=

Tributes to one's character being but one plank more in the gen. conviction that one is a blasted bore. I think it about time we chucked my character, & began prospecting for the coup de genie; the divine eclair etc. =

Probably a bit late to send yr. drawings if they haven't already started; as drawing-room to which I intend to take 'em is closing for summer.

=

I shall also close for the summer, in I hope a fortnights time. at any rate shall see you, I hope, before end of month.

Dial's europeeing staff promises to be excellent. & worthy of its organizer. Have even scratched up some good stuff here.

Benedictions

E

Dial's europeeing staff: Pound became correspondent for this American magazine in March 1920.

106. TLS–2.

52 rue des Saints Peres

Paris VI.

Dear W.L.

Cant see that TYRO [Lewis's art journal] is of interest outside Bloomsbury; and having long sought a place where

Sound of shit and shitwell is forgot

And Roger's visage overcast with snot

Absent from the purlieus, and in fact

A freedom from the whole arseblarsted lot

Am not inclined to reenter.

Am taking up the Little Review again, as a quarterly; each number to have about twenty reprods of ONE artist, replacing Soirees de Paris.

Start off with twenty Brancusi's to get a new note.

You have had since 1917 to turn in some illustrations for L[ittle].R[eview], but perhaps the prospect of a full Lewis number will lure you.

Also, as I have never been able to get a publisher for a book on you, I have the idea of trying one on "Four Modern Artists" IF you can collect sufficient illustrations. I know there is difficulty re S.kens[ington]. stuff and re/ Quinn's stuff.

I however give you this chance for a communique to Quinn. Tell him I am contemplating the book.

(He has just bought some Brancusi, by the way, and shown good sense in so doing.)

I should take you, Brancusi, Picasso and surprising as it will seem to you Picabia, not exactly as a painter, but as a writer. He commences in "Pensees sans paroles" ["Penseés sans langage"] and lands in his last book "J.C. Rastaquoure" [Jesus-Christ Rastaquouère].

& There is also more in his stuff ⟨designs⟩ than comes up in reprod.

Also the four chapters wd. give me a chance to make certain contrasts etc.

Format of L.R. will be larger, and reprods therein as good as possible. It will also be on sale at strategic points here.

Yr. correspondent Marcoissis [Marcoussis] is an industrious and serious person who has "done som beeutiful graiynin' in 'is time", not a titanic intellect, but has german market. Very very much concerned with execution. Gleizes isn't. Bracque [Braque] I have only seen for two minutes and am inclined to like. =

⟨You ought to get Eliot out of England somehow.⟩

yrs
Ezra

27 April
1921

---

shitwell: Both Pound and Lewis considered the Sitwells artistic dilettantes whose influence helped to trivialize England's intellectual life.

Roger's visage: Lewis founded his art journal *The Tyro* to help British artists counter Roger Fry's insistence on the supremacy of modern French painting.

S.kens[ington]. stuff: The collection of Lewis's drawings bequeathed to the Victoria and Albert Museum (South Kensington, London) by Guy Baker.

107. TLS–1. [Autumn 1921].

70 bis rue Notre Dame des Champs

Dear W.L.

Will you as soon as pleasable send off 20 to 25 photos of your stuff to the Little Review, 27 W. 8th St. New York. And let me know when you have done so.

Dont know whether you have seen the Brancusi number [Autumn 1921], very handsome and well printed. Please insist however that they print your reprods on one side of paper only. It will be more forcible from you than from me. Printing on two sides a silly economy, though the number cost 1000 bones to print.

Send also any other mss. that you have on hand and dont want for Tyro. You still have a Soupault thing, I believe. ⟨translated with English.⟩

yrs
E.P.

⟨unless of course you've changed yr. mind. In which case wd. you let me know. & I will let F[rancis].P[icabia]. go on preparing the Picasso number—which shd normally be the 4$\underline{\text{th}}$⟩

108. ALS–4.

Firano [i.e., Fermo] in Posta 5
Siena   April.[1922]

Caro Mio:

There is no use my giving you advice re/ yr. own affairs. – I have never known you to take any – anyhow.

Don't see that Bel Esprit cd. ever do much more than provide you a studio – –

Certainly can't start on you – as you have to the public eye had nothing but leisure for years – nothing to prevent or to have prevented your doing any damn thing you liked – save yr. habit of fuss & of having a private life & allowing it to intrude on yr. attention. =

Try New York — I mean emigrate. England is under a curse. also re. Bel Esprit. Joyce worked for years as language teacher. & I have done all sort of little jobs at £1–1 a shot.—

I had left Paris before you wrote re/ Schiff. —I left on March 27[th.] – Dont think wd. have done any good my meeting him. as it wd. be exagg. to say that I find him a kindred spirit.

Re. Bel. Esprit. vide New Age for Mar. 30th.

---

anyone who can afford to can buy annuities or place capital in Lloyds. = most of the subscribers cant.

T. [S. Eliot] bound to be sceptical until the actual sum is in hand. at present there is £120 a year = He wd. in Time earn something by his pen. annuities @ £180 on T's life are obviously the preferable form. =

Good will counts for something also the possible spread of the society & there being a larger fund than T's £300 to fall back on.

The £120 is already flanked by several people willing to give £20. but who ought not to be allowed to do so. = That margin acts as insurance. =

If there arent 30 or 50 people interested in literature, there is no civilization. & we may as well regard our work as a private luxury, having no aims but our own pleasure. = You cant expect people to pay you for enjoying yourself.

yrs
E.

Bel Esprit: The title of Pound's scheme to find enough donors to support T. S. Eliot financially and allow him to leave his job at Lloyds Bank and devote full time to poetry. If the plan worked, Pound hoped it could be used to support other needy and worthwhile writers; but the plan embarrassed Eliot, and Pound later admitted that Bel Esprit had been a failure.

New Age: Pound describes and defends the Bel Esprit scheme in his article, "Credit and the Fine Arts. . . . A Practical Application," New Age 30 (30 March 1922): 284–85. See Ezra Pound and the Visual Arts, ed. Zinnes, pp. 146–49.

109. TLS–1. [July? 1922].

70 bis N[otre].D[ame].de C[hamps].

Dear W. L.

While in Milan I visited the Bodega di Poesia, which has three excellent rooms for exhibiting pictures.

It looked good to me, and as I liked the people, I suggested to Linati that it was time they had a show of W. L.

He said he wd. discuss the matter. Have just had a card from him saying that Ferrieri (who now has the Libreria del Convegno, is going into quarters more sumptuous than the Bodega, and that HE, Ferrieri, wants to have the show; or several modern shows.

The Convegno is a very serious monthly review. I like Ferrieri, and Linati is absolutely solid and reliable.

We spoke of expense of shipping, They wd. be willing to frame the stuff.

I shd. think if you sent two large oils, and twenty drawings it wd. be worth while.

Milan is a fairly active non-italian city. and thinks itself the capital of Italy.

I absolutely wash my hands of the matter if
you try to take a troop of british artists.

But I think I can assure your having their best
gallery to yourself, whatever else may being [*sic*]   yrs
going on in the other exhibition rooms.
⟨Bel Esprit is progressing.⟩   E

110. TLS–3.

70 bis, N[otre] D[ame] de C[hamps].

14 Julliet [1922].

Cher VVwvyndammmn

The Libreria del Convegno in Milan offers you an exposition on the follerin terms. As I know nothing of these matters I cant tell whether they are good or bad.

If you pay the carriage of the stuff they will "organnizare la mostra", pay for the printing etc. and "occupy themselves largely with the matter in their review," which is a sober and serious production, and take 10% on sales.

The situation is this. I saw the "bodega" people and liked them and their gallery. I suggested to Linati that they shd. improve the quality of their expositions.

(I was in Milan only 24 hours).
I also saw the Convegno people (or rather Ferrieri who is the Convegno), he has a small place BUT he is taking on the Palazzo Scotti;

and
Linati assures me it is a swanker gallery. And that Ferrieri is less out for himself, meno commerciante etc.

You can write to Carlo Linati, 24 via San Spirito
in English
Or to Dott Enzo Ferrieri, Il Convegno, ⟨in French⟩ Via Canova 25
Milan.

If you want to wangle about the matter.

I think Milan is alive, and worth using as a base of operation.

I might even manage to be there during part of the show.

But I CANT argue about the matter either with you or Ferrieri. I will forward a letter if you prefer to write to me. rather than to them.

I also think they can be made to frame the stuff.

I suggest that you send 24 drawings, unframed and make them frame them. (That point isn't covered in their letter)

You might write to me asking IF they will do it; or send me a statement of terms on which you will expose [*sic*]. (ONLY for Christs sake get your letter typed.)

The Little Review [Spring 1922] has reappeared with   yrs
the Picabia stuff. A dull number.   E.P.
The next number is yours. IF you
want to make it count, you might write
to them direct, and jazz 'em up a bit.

Simply ask 'em if they want to jazz up. I have abandoned them, they will be delighted to push any manifesto you care to make

(at least I believe so.)

It shd. save you the printing exp. of a Tyro.

They've reproduced the Pic[abia]s. better than the Branc[usi]s. and are probably open to suggestion to improvement.

They have bungled my death mask, sheer stupidity. I told 'em something was coming, and they hadn't sense enough to reprod. the documents. You have to guide 'em hand an foot.

I am not having any further immediate communication with them.
But you can enquire when and IF they are bringing out another number.

They may be a little agitated at a note I wrote last week to the Two Worlds [ed. Samuel Roth]; telling the two Worlds to take over all unpub. L.R. stuff and prepare a W.L. number.

An idea which ought to galvanize the L.R.

You might even suggest in your letter that I have definitely abandoned them (the L.R.) "as might be expected seeing's as how they have never even had the energy to review any of my books or in general show any interest whatever in my activities".

You might also tell em that Guillaume Apollinaire died some years ago, and that his book on Cubism is a little out of date.

Ask whether they really are going to bring out YOUR number SOON, whether they want a Blast from you to liven it up;

or whether you shd. turn over duplicates of the reprods to the Two Worlds?

yrs
E.

⟨you might send me a red & a black blast [*BLAST*, nos. 1 & 2] & a Timon to show to Decharbres [Descharmes].⟩

death mask: Life mask of Pound by Nancy Cox McCormack.
book on Cubism: A translated excerpt from Apollinaire's *Les Peintres Cubistes* (1913) appeared in the Spring 1922 *Little Review*.

111. ALS–1. [July 1922]. [London].

Dear Pound. I am sending you Blast 1. & 2. & all of Timon that is creditable to me. (Who is Descheuel [Descharmes]?)

If you are indulging a disappointment with me, leave me alone for a bit.

At Leicester Gall[ery]. & Goupil (one man show) I sold only to people I personally knew. Outside of that Quinn is the only person to whom I have sold. All other forms of exhibition are useless. L'honneur sans argent n'est q'une maladie. We all have glory enough & to spare.

If you wish to remain a friend of mine observe the 4th. & 5th. line down (above.) ["If you are indulging . . . leave me alone for a bit."] Until I can produce something unassailable, & better than I have up to the present, it is perhaps best to leave me alone. It is too early yet, you can believe me when I say it, to write retrospectively of me.

(Hueffer I hear is active in this latter sense in my behalf in America).

Let me alone for a little, that will be best. You will have plenty to talk about before very long: and all your talkative, generous, burbling instincts be satisfied. Forget me for a year, say.

———

Meantime the Milan thing is no good. I will write to them if you like, saying that I have 2 exhibitions (1 here & 1 Paris) coming off in the Autumn, & have no work to spare. I am writing Little Review. Sorry to hear that you are de puntos with them.

W.L.

112. TLS–1. [July 1922].

70 bis, N[otre] D[ame] de C[hamps].
VI

Dear W.

I am not suffering a <u>deception</u> or disappointment. I had already written my second letter about Milan, when your note came saying you cdnt be bothered. I thought you might as well know what the terms were.

It wont do the Milanese any harm to wait a year. You needn't answer. I will write, saying you cant bother with it now. Other vaster affairs prohibiting; and leave the thing open for some later year, if ever you do want to go.

benedictions

E

113. TLS–1.

70 bis, N[otre] D[ame] de C[hamps].

Cher W.

  Was asked yesterday for name of best portrait painter and his prices. Said I thought it was about £40 for drawing and £200 for oil, but that I wd. enquire definitely. Also wd. enquire probable date of his exhibition or next sojourn here.

  Drawing of me, as in ROd. portfolio, approved. Wanted rather more face than in the girl at table [*Girl Reading*] in the Tyro.

Funds solid.

//

Little Review pulluling to me about stuff for the W.L. number. Didn't you say you had sent them the photos? They seem ready for outburst. You might send em any instructions you think of. Also that story of Soupaults if you still have the mss.

///

I think the portrait thing is solid. American business methods. Wants good article and is ready to pay market price.

⟨Didn't you get £250 for Prax[itella].⟩

E

7 Nov. [1922]

drawing of me: Ezra Pound Esq. in Lewis's portfolio *Fifteen Drawings* (published by John Rodker).

Prax[itella]: a highly stylized portrait of Iris Barry which Lewis painted in 1920–21. See *Wyndham Lewis, Paintings and Drawings,* ed. Michel, p. 30, plate 67.

114. TLS–2.

11 Nov. [1922]

70 bis, N[otre] D[ame] de C[hamps].

Paris VI

Cher W:

I will continue the matter of portrait with Monsieur N. this evening. Re/ Little Rev. the [special Lewis] number ought to be properly organized, 25 photos, and a series of article[s] on and by you.

I have asked A[gnes].B[edford]. to go through files of N[ew].Age, Egoist etc. and collect anything of interest, and to submit result to you for expurgation. (Dias [Pound's pseudonym as an art critic] remarks, if there are any good ones, can be transferred to me.)

I have suggested to Ed. Wad[sworth], that he and Etchells write something; also that Mathers and Kreymborg be enlisted. Kreymborg is at 51 Hunter St. Brunswick Sq., W.C. 1.

The thing ought to be an improvement on the Brancusi number. The Picabia number dont rank.

There ought to be NO reprods. save of your stuff. but as much other copy as you like.

What about ten pages of aphorisms, taken from your various BLASTS, notes on mod. art etc.

I dont know who else can be enlisted. The thing CANT be properly organized from here.

Kreymborg has done a good deal of commendable editorial work. He should be a very serviceable luogotenente.

I am writing to him again. You might try to smoothe over any asperities existing between him and the N.Y. office. (I dont know that they do exist) Also exploit any rancour that may exist between him and his late associate Broom.

He might make the selections from the Blast stuff, if you haven't time. etc. will discuss and try to nail portrait affair, this evening.

E

Broom: Alfred Kreymborg was co-editor of *Broom* from November 1921 to February 1922, when he resigned over a disagreement about whether American or European experimental writers should be featured.

115. TLS–1.

70 bis, rue N.D. des Champs   6. Sep[tember 1923].
Paris VI.

Dear Wyndham:

I wrote Eliot a letter last week pointing out, in no mea-
sured terms, the bhloody dullness of the Criterion. He has replied in a
rather satisfactory manner, admitting that 3/4 ths of the stuff isn't worth
printing.

BUT he says he has done his utmost to get you to collaborate, and
that I can't name one author of first rank whom he hasn't tried to get.

This last, is to the shame of conthemporary litterchure, true.

Of course you are on the ground and can judge better than I can
from a distance. Possibly the success of the bhloody Adelphi may indicate
a position further to the left for our financial editor (??) Possibly he is
fed up with the mauvais frequentations which you mentioned when last
here.

At any rate, I am putting together a more lefterly outburst for some
future number of his organ.

He says it (the organ) is the best there is.

I don't know that the time has come for a new onset (???) protest
against the earthquake in Japong, or whatnot. I dont know that there are
any forces to be reorganized, or recruited, or anything.

yrs
E.P.

Adelphi: John Middleton Murry founded the *Adelphi* in 1923, and over 15,000
copies of the first number were sold.
earthquake: Pound refers to the Tokyo earthquake of 1 September 1923.

116. TLS–1.

70 bis, rue Notre Dame des Champs
Paris VI

Dear W.L.

There is a new review [*Transatlantic Review*] starting here;
which pays contributors (mildly, all reviews pay mildly when at all)

Policy of the review certainly favorable to yr activities; though I have heard you express unfavorable opinion of the editor [Ford Madox Ford]. ANNY how I can assure you that yr woik will be opera grata to management. Anything you're not using in Criterion. Stories of course the hardest thing to get; as Ford does NOT intend to dally with the Lawrence, Murry, Mansfield contingent.

Leading off with Robert [McAlmon], Cummings, myself, Steffens, Deschrames [Descharmes] etc. To be handled by Duckworth in England and some other firm in america, and printed here.

I understand T. S. E[liot]. is sending his benedictions. The thing seems to be properly financed. And there seems to be no intention of muzzling anyone. Only limit is the Brit, Customs House, against which there appears to be no appeal.

Fer wot its woif; this infermat'n.

yrs

E.P.

7 Oct. [1923]

117. TLS–3.

Hotel Mignon, Rapalla [*sic*],

3 Dec, 1924

Wall, ole Koksum Buggle:

I have just, ten years an a bit after its appearance, and in this far distant locus, taken out a copy of the great MAGENTA cover'd opusculus [*BLAST*, no. 1]. We were hefty guys in them days; an of what has come after us, we seem to have survived without a great mass of successors, save possibly the young Robert [McAlmon] (NOT with the terminal -s) and in another line the young Gawge [George Antheil]. (I think I asked A[gnes].B[edford]. to deliver you a copy of my leetle Blarst on that subjek.)

I have never been converted to your permanenza or delayed dalliance in the hyperborean fogs, ma!! Having rejuvinated by I5 years in going to Paris, and added another ten of life, by quitting same, somewhat arid, but necessary milieu; etc . . . . .

Am also letting out another reef in my long job [the *Cantos*]. Installment of which should soon be inspectable. (XVI) have gone on, I think with more kick, since arrival here.

Question being (now that we have emerged, or if you like, now that I have emerged from VARIA, that you found alien. Can we kick up any more or any new devilment??

I am going down to Etna, d[eo], v[olente], in a fortnight. Have you any suggestions?? I dont know wot the bullsht you are doing. It strikes me that ten or a dozen BLACK designs about the size of this type sheet, wd. be serviceable.

(Cant remember whether I have ever discussed Straters initials with you. Need something for press, etc. etc. etc. proportion of design lines to type. lot of boring detail had to be cooked between printer and ornater.

neither here nor there. but perhaps ten or a dozen designs for the two cantos dealing with Hell [Cantos 14–15], might be circulatable. As that section of the poem can NOT be circulated freely.

You did years ago in Kens[ington]. G[ar]d[en]s. discuss a book of verse and designs. In this case it wd. be designs only but with cantos as reference.

You will readily see that the "hell" is a portrait of contemporary England, or at least Eng, as she wuz when I left her.

I dont know that the designs need have much to do with the text, or anything. Merely that I have failed on various occasions in attempts to RAM unrelated designs of yours into the continental maw;

and shd. like a try at ramming designs related, or supposed to be, related to something that had already gone in.

The de luxe had more than paid for itself some time ago. 2 of 100 buck copies had gone, when I last heard, and requisite number of the 25, also some of the 50.

Anyhow, wait till you see the text, and if you approve, or if it starts you. I shd, be glad to try either to make Bird print 'em, or to get some other sort of bally hoo in action on the matter.

Have also iron in fire for some more general sort of publishing that the 3 Mts [Three Mountains Press] offers, and more satisfact. than afforded in Eng, or Am. pub. circles.

(In parenthesis, I aimed a kick at that bastard D.B. this morning. this purely en passant. of no importance.) Really a country that will tolerate that pyper for any purpose, even that of wiping pig's arses, is beneath the jo level.)

It rained yesterday, the feast of St Bibiana. That is said to mean rain for forty days. So that I shd. have leisure to attend to your correspondence if there were any.

Benedictions.

E.P.

You understand this suggestion of designs for the hell is merely an idea that came to me as I was writing this note. If you can think of something better, blaze away. Only I think the idea of ten or twelve BLACKS of size that cd. go by post, and that cd. be done in line block; might be useful. No use trying to drag J.J.A. [possibly Lewis's friend A.J.A. Symons] or W. Rob[er]ts or anything or anyone else into it. The rest of our companions presumably HAVE belonged to the decade just past. Apart from Robert [McAlmon] and young George [Antheil] I think the rest of the buds, have disappeared in unblossomed fragrance.

Whether we can produce further and larger detonation by a new combination, I leave to yr. wisdom to konsider.

I cant, and dont believe in Mr. Ingres. In-gress. NOR Seurat, nor Greco, nor . . . . oh damn it all . . .

I am not very sure about Cezanne. But I like Rouseau's Baboons; and the warts on Feddy. Urbino's nose.

And I think . . . . some of the chunks of Manet's execution picture. . .??? The Timon, on Plate V of Blast still looks O.K. etc.

May your cock's shadow never grow less.

E.

leetle Blarst: Pound's *Antheil and the Treatise on Harmony* (Paris: Three Mountains Press, 1925).

Straters initials: Henry Strater designed the initials for Pound's *A Draft of XVI Cantos* (Paris: Three Mountains Press, 1925).

bastard D. B.: D. B. Wyndham Lewis wrote a column for the *Daily Express* between 1919 and 1925. He was often confused with Wyndham Lewis.

Rouseau's Baboons: There are a number of jungle pictures by Henri Rousseau which Pound might have in mind. For Pound's comments on Rousseau's importance, see *Ezra Pound and the Visual Arts,* ed. Zinnes, p. 304.

Feddy. Urbino: Pound probably refers to Piero della Francesca's *Portrait of Federico da Montefeltro, Count of Urbino,* although the warts are on his cheek and not his nose.

chunks of Manet's execution picture: One version of Edouard Manet's *The Execution of Maximillian,* a large oil painting, was cut into pieces; two of the fragments are in the National Gallery, London.

118. AN–1. [December 1924].

> address
> probably.   Hotel Roma
>   Siracusa
>   Sicilia

Cher W:

  Here in Taormina. ex convento S. Domeningo 16ᵗʰ century vorticism—quite pure except for intrusion of Picasso's fat foot (one foot.)

119. ALS–1. [1925].

> 61.Palace Gardens Terrace.
> Kensington. W. 8.

Dear Pound.   Many apologies for my long delay in answering you, but I was uncertain as to where to aim my letter, indeed I am now. I could not have done what you wanted [the initials for the "Hell" Cantos], as such an important task would have taken some time, and I have had none to spare from my present work. But I should very much enjoy reading the Cantos you mention. I hope I shall be able to get them somewhere here. Miss Bedford tells me that you are still in Sicily: but I gathered you did not intend stopping, as it was too expensive: but I hope this will be forwarded. Are you returning to Paris? I shall be there I hope in a few weeks time & perhaps we shall meet. How are you getting on with the Dial—do you still write for them? We have had a lot of bad weather here, but I expect it has been much the same over in Italy. Most english people who can afford it seem to be settling in France and Italy, but there does

not seem to be much difference in the winter months anywhere north of
Africa. The W. Indies seem to be becoming very fashionable. Nassau
must have a delightful climate. Why dont you go there? —Let me know
(in a simplified form) what your movements are likely to be & when your
book is being published.

> Yours
> W.L.

120. TLS–1.

> Via Marsala 12, int 5.
> Rapallo.
> 14 April, 1925

Dear Wyndham
        I want one or two drawings of the Red Duet, or later Timon
variety, if they exist. I still think Ingres is competent stupidity. Dont
know what your present prices are. I send enclosed anticipatory, no use
canning it. D[orothy]. will select the drawing when she next gets to London. I send her cheque, as my account is in Paris, and it will probably be
easier for her to deal with London cheque.

> yours
> E.P.

Introduction to Letter 121.

    In a bad-tempered letter to Pound in June 1925, Lewis says that he has
had a "long and unpleasant struggle to get my present work completed."
The struggle to earn a living and publish his works in the early twenties
was the inevitable consequence of his satiric temperament and his dedica-
tion to art. The following letter shows that he was not content to market
his works in the way of ordinary men of letters. Between 1921 and 1926
Lewis lived in semiretirement and near poverty to write a gigantic anatomy

of post-World War I England called *The Man of the World*. T. S. Eliot warned him in January 1925 that "it would be in your own interest to concentrate on one book at a time and not plan eight or ten books at once. . . ." Lewis received related advice from Pound, who said of Lewis's volume of social criticism, *The Art of Being Ruled:* "It wd. be hypocrisy fer me to say that books all erbout everything in general are of any gt. interest to me in partikiler." (Letter 140.) Lewis ignored Pound's warning but was forced to see the merit of Eliot's. The fragments of *The Man of the World* named in this letter all went into separate volumes when Lewis could not find a publisher for the complete manuscript. *The Lion and the Fox* was published under that title in 1927. "The Politics of Philistia" became *The Art of Being Ruled* (1926), with the inclusion of "Sub Persona Infantis" as Part IV and "The Shaman" as Part IX of the book. "The Politics of the Personality" became Lewis's major work of political and philosophical analysis, *Time and Western Man* (1927). "The Strategy of Defeat" might have gone into either *The Art of Being Ruled* or *Time and Western Man.* "The Great Fish Jesus Christ" was never published and possibly never written. Fragments of the satiric fictions "Joint" and "Archie" are in manuscript at the Olin Library, Cornell University. "Joint" mingles narrative, discussion, and fantasy in the manner of Lewis's fiction *The Childermass* (1928), and "Archie" prefigures Lewis's great social satire *The Apes of God* (1930).

The difficulties of publishing these manuscripts at the length and for the price Lewis required embroiled him in arguments with publishers and editors, including Robert McAlmon of Contact Publishing Co., Ernest J. Walsh and Ethel Moorhead, who published the journal *This Quarter* in Paris, and even the patient Eliot, who told Lewis about the sections from *The Apes of God* which he was publishing in *The Criterion:* "it is worthwhile running the Criterion just to publish these." Lewis distrusted the editors of *This Quarter* so much that he refused to let them do a "Lewis" issue, and he quarreled with McAlmon when the Contact press failed to publish a volume of his social criticism and even with Eliot over the terms for *The Apes of God.* Lewis also quarreled with his patrons, the "wealthy friends" of the following letter. This group, which included the former Vorticist painter Edward Wadsworth and the writer and painter Richard Wyndham, set up a fund to give Lewis a monthly allowance. This fund led to the same problems that plagued Pound's Bel Esprit because it seemed more like charity than patronage. Lewis would have preferred that his admirers commission and buy paintings from him, and when he quarreled with them over the terms of the agreement the funds were

shut off. The tensions accumulated in years of furious work and frustra-
tion were poured into the satire of *The Apes of God,* in which Lewis's
former friends and patrons were masterfully caricatured. We may assume
that the satire was a catharsis for Lewis, but the letters of the thirties will
show that his character lost none of its impatient and acerbic qualities.

"eight or ten books at once": The Letters of Wyndham Lewis, ed. Rose, p. 151.
"Joint": Excerpts from "Joint" were published in *Agenda* 7–8 (Autumn–Winter
    1969–70): 197–215.
"just to publish these": The Letters of Wyndham Lewis, p. 140.

121. ALS–2.

61. Palace Gardens Terrace.
Kensington. W.8.

29 April./25.

Dear Pound.   Thank you for cheque (£20. twenty pounds) and you or
Mrs. Pound shall have the drawings when you wish.

You must not be offended if I am wrong: but your letter left a doubt
in my mind as to whether one or other of my wealthy friends, who some
time ago left me in the lurch, were not using you to affect still to be
"helping" me. I should not like for a handful of silver to put myself—or
them—in that position. = This in case the matter should have been misrepresented to you, and you have lent yourself to that manoeuvre. If there
is nothing of that sort behind your cheque for drawings, I hope you will
not be offended. You will understand my desire to be fixed on the point
of that not being a treacherous bounty; and that in any event I am not
implicating you.

It may interest you to know that I now have many books completed
or almost completed. After one attempt only I saw how difficult it would
be to find a publisher who would give me what I wanted for my five
hundred thousand word book, The Man of the World—(longer than War
& Peace, Ulysses & so on). Luckily its form enabled me, without very
much additional work, to cut it up into a series of volumes. In each part
of the original book I had repeated the initial argument, associating it with
the new evidence provided by the particular material of each part. I daresay even, as it turns out, it will be better as a series of volumes, which I

can assemble under the title The Man of the World. —One of them, as you may have heard, is to be printed by Macalmon [McAlmon]. That is all about the question of CLASS, but I have not got a title for it yet. There is a hundred thousand word volume, called The Lion & the Fox about Shakespeare, principally. There is one called Sub Persona Infantis which deals with a particular phase—you know the one—of the contemporary sensibility. The Shaman about exoliti & sex-transformation. The Politics of the Personality (100. thousand) principally evidence of philosophy, one (100. thousand) called The Politics of Philistia & one called The Strategy of Defeat (40 thousand). Then there are 2 vols. ⟨(not of course part of the Man of the World)⟩ of The Apes of God (fiction) the first of which is nearly done. Joint (sketched & partly done) Archie (complete, thirty or forty thousand). —The Great Fish Jesus Christ (45 thousand). The rehandling for definite publication of these things is taking some time. Macalmons I hope will be ready next week. Two of them are out. I will give you a few more details when I hear from you.   W.L.

122. TLS–2.

Via Marsala. 12 int 5.

2 May. [1925]   RAPALLO

Dear Wyndham:

I hasten to assure you that work or works of art ordered on 20 quid cheque are for personal consumption on the domestic hearth of la famille Pound; and that purchase of said works was instigated by NO outside pressure, suggestion or other occult or other influence.

Have wanted another drawing of "that sort" ever since I was honest enough to let Q[uinn]. have the red duet after I had bought it for him.

I heard from my belle mere [Olivia Shakespear] a day or so after my writing to you that she had recently acquired a vorticist drawing, but this was sheer coincidence, AFTER and not before the fact of my request to you.

I did not see the Shitwells [Sitwells] after my return from Sicily i,e, the last time I saw them was in Dec. before my trip south. (if they are the ricos to whom you allude.)

At any rate the cash does not come from external peripheries.

Now that I have a little strength and time I am ready for any dark intrigues that might conduce to our ultimate glories. I have, as matter of fact written both to Tauchnitz and Liveright [publishers]; though dont know how useful they can be. For moral effect and to BUST the goddam strangle hold of Smiff and Son [W. H. Smith and Son, Booksellers]. I think Tauchnitz is to [be] encouraged, though there is hardly any direct payment to be got out of him.

Dr. Curt Otto the head of the firm writes me he is going to London in June. Do you want to see him?

Of course Tauch. has up to the present done only reprints; but Otto says this is not imperative. And that now that they have recovered a bit from the lyte hostilities they wd. like to do a bit-er-igh-Brow stuff. (He used much more dignified langwidge).

Dont fer Xt's sake mention that I am in touch with T. to any one. A flank move again the buggers, bastards, Squires, Geeses [Gosses] etc. of no val. unless it succks seed.

ALSO IF you have terms for an Xpensive edtn. with McA[lmon]. you cd. deal with T. schnitz for reprint later. AND if MCA. gets a few vols. into type before June tant mieuX.

Pussnly. IF MCA. is doing the whole thing, seems to me better to label it ONE book. However, I dont want to go off half cocked re/zummat I haven't seen.

Yrs   E.P.

red duet: "Red Duet" (1914), an abstract drawing. Pound purchased this picture from the John Quinn Estate; one sees it in the background of the photograph of Pound in his *Gaudier-Brzeska* (plate XXIXA).

123. ALS–1.

61.Palace Gardens Terrace.
Kensington W.8.
May 7 / 25

Dear E.P.   Thank you for letter & I am glad to find that my suspicion was unfounded. I will certainly for the daily consumption of such an organism as yours provide something if not worthy of it at least the best I can do. (With the constipated Shitwells [Sitwells] I have had no economic contretemps).

As to the book, the milieu was too much for it, and it has been compelled to sink to a lower type, has reproduced itself, and is now, multiplied by six, a series of independent units. In the process I believe I have considerably improved the material. The Shakespeare volume (the Lion & the Fox) is now sold, & should be out in October. The publishers reader reported that it was the greatest book on Shakespeare in the english language. This excited the publisher very much, but convinced him at the same time that he would not sell very many copies. Also he says that owing to a few passages <u>no american</u> publisher would set it up. He is however communicating with Liveright. ⟨With Methuen I have only contracted for one vol. of almost 100 thousand words, which I call <u>Critique of Class</u>.⟩

I have heard from Liveright, and shall send him something. Eliot told me last year that Liver. was peculiarly unreliable. What do you think? What would he give me for the Enemy of the Stars, with a forty thousand word essay supplementing it attached?

In a few months if you still feel up to mischief something might be done. I shall be in Paris fairly often (I am going again next week). Perhaps we shall meet there. This Quarter received.

Yrs   W.L.

P.S. Offer just came in for <u>whole book</u> from publisher (a new one). Present arrangement is best, however.

Critique of Class: Probably an early title for Lewis's *The Art of Being Ruled.*
Enemy of the Stars: Lewis revised his Vorticist drama, which first appeared in *BLAST,* no. 1, adding a commentary entitled "Physics of the Not-Self." It was finally published by Desmond Harmsworth, London, in 1932.
This Quarter: A literary journal edited by Ernest Walsh and Ethel Moorhead.

124. TLS–2. On stationery imprinted: Via Marsala, 12 Int. 5. Rapallo.

12 May. [1925]

Cher Wyndham:

If you have written an interesting boK, on Shikespeer it will be the first one, on a damnd uninteresting subject. I dont suppose the pubs reader has read ALL the others, there are nine million. Neither have I. I suppose the book is about something else and uses Shukes. as a start off.

///

I dont think murika and Liveright are ripe for Enemy of Stars. Neither do I think there is much use trying to circulate books of controversy or criticism, unless one is advertising ones friends, or their supposedly vendible products like moozik or baindings [paintings].

////

How much of this new opus is story?

///

Bob [McAlmon] seems a bit worried that you haven't correlated Fraser [Frazer] and Havelock Ellis and some of the later profs. with Morgan and Begorrah, sorr. or at least thinks you'll get jumped on for not doing so.

I shd. think Tauchnitz, Liveright, and This Qtr. wd. all want novel or stories, rather than criticism.

This Q[uarter]. OUGHT at last to do the forty reprods of your designs. Historique, as they have done the Brancush [Brancusi], getting a better lot than those I grabbed for the L[ittle]. R[eview].

Liveright wont care a damn about the "few pages" he'll put in a note saying it is 'fer parsons, scientists, lawyers et cie, and charge two bucks more: as he did with my Remy. I think Horace [Liveright] is quite as likely to send you money as anyone. At least he has sent ME more than anyone else ever has. (not that that is such a hellovalot.)

Yrs
E.P.

Morgan and Begorrah, sorr.: Lewis expected McAlmon to publish a volume which eventually became *The Art of Being Ruled.* Since the book contained arguments drawn from anthropological and sexual studies, McAlmon may have expected Lewis to cite Sir James Frazer, Ellis, and C. Lloyd Morgan (a popularlzei of scientific and philosophical ideas who was associated with the phrase "emergent evolution"). Begorrah is apparently a comic name, and "sorr" may be Pound's abbreviation of "sirs" or "señors."

Remy: Pound's translation of Remy de Gourmont's *The Natural Philosophy of Love* (1922). The first edition had a slip which asked bookdealers to use discretion in selling it.

125. TLS–2. On stationery imprinted: Via Marsala, 12 Int. 5. Rapallo.

6 June [1925]

Dear Wyndham

I met Walsh [editor of *This Quarter*] in Bologna four days ago. I couldn't answer questions about your new stuff that I haven't seen. They had a copy of AHT woik with an article of yours in it etc.

BUT Moorhead had also on her own had the idea of doing a set of reprods of you. before I mentioned it. She studied with Whistler in the year 1830 or zummat.

They seem to me pure in heart, or at least ready to attack the bastile. and to pay for cost of having photos made, etc.

Also you cd. probably get a payment, not gigantic, for the right to print the reprods, and they wd. buy tyro cliches, or other from you IF they were right size.

I know DAMN WELL that the L[ittle].R[eview]. Brancusi number brought cash to Brancush. I saw a persecuting attourney ⟨not Q[uinn].⟩ walk in an buy something, meself.

And your stuff damn well IS NOT KNOWn to a lot of people, some not born, and others still in the bush when Blast appeared.

This does not mean that they wont use and pay for your text, but it does mean that they are definitely ready to lay out on doing a decent W.L. art supplement; you may remember, or you mayn't, that I tried to get Lane et al. to take a book on you, by me, WITH illustrations back in 16 or 17.

I have wanted the thing done for a long time, and hope, this time, something will come of it.

I have also told em that rather than use bad art they ought to do a number simply 50 photos of machines and parts.

If ther'Z anyfink I can dew to elp; such as trying to get photos out of J[ohn].Q[uinn]. executors etc. lemme know.

Important thing is to have ENOUGH reprods altogether, as they have done in case of Branc[usi].

They have sense enough to see that Picasso is no longer useful as a special feature. In fac. I think they ought to be encouraged.

E.P.

AHT woik: Lewis's "The Politics of Artistic Expression," *Artwork* 1 (May–August 1925): 223–26.

126. TLS–2.

61. Palace Gardens Terrace.

June 11 / /25.   W.8.

Dear E.P.   I do not want a "Lewis number" or anything of that sort in This Quarter or anywhere else, at this moment. My reasons are my own affair, although I indicated them as much as was necessary. Have I said this to you or not? You insist on disregarding what I write to you, is not that so?

Please note the following: because in the glorious days of Marinetti, Nevinson, machinery, Wadsworth[,] Wormwood Scrubs [the London Prison] and Wyoming, we were associated to some extent in publicity campaigns, that does not give you a mandate to interfere when you think fit, with or without my consent, with my career. If you launch at me and try and force on me a scheme which I regard as malapropos and which is liable to embarrass me, you will not find me so docile at Eliot.

If you are offended with me because my note written to you in Sicily had not what Macalmon [McAlmon] calls "abondon", and are disposed to be troublesome, in consequence, then I am sorry that my letter had not more zip, and will endeavor not to repeat that performance. Does this undertaking help to clear your mind, or your bile?

Recently a painter [Michael Sevier]—who I daresay is a friend of yours, as I understand you see a number of people from England in your italian home—came to ask me to contribute something to a show he,

Wadsworth, Nash and other people were getting up. I did not wish to exhibit with him or with his friends at all, although the advertisement they would derive from exhibiting with me would be very attractive to them, no doubt: for some of them had proved that in the past. I said I did not want to exhibit at the moment which was also true. He said he was sorry, and went away. When the show opened, in the middle of the wall hung a large coloured drawing of mine which Wadsworth had sold to the Gallery, or put into Sothebys, where it could conveniently be bought. For that I had no redress, except such as would have been only a further advertisement for Sevier and Co. I am sorry to have seemed to have afforded the world precedent for such treatment of an artist. I will endeavour to make up for it presently.

You knew that I wished, for the sake of the money; to have a section of my book [*The Man of the World*] in any paper that would print a substantial section of it, and pay me properly; you knew that the book was not fiction; yet when it comes to the point, you say that your paper, or your friends paper, "does not want anything but fiction" and gave me the advantage of your opinion that the only sort of writing that should be done is that that is likely to get ones friends out of prison, sell their work, etc.

I have had a long and unpleasant struggle to get my present work completed. You seem inclined to step in at the last minute and harass the final stages of my work with, I hope sincere, but certainly misplaced, offers of help. Please answer this letter at once.   Yrs.

W.L.

Note to Letter 126.

Pound returned this letter to Lewis with marginal notes. In the first paragraph, beside "Have I said this to you or not?" Pound wrote, "No. you have not said this until now." Beside "painter" in the fourth paragraph, he wrote: "Unknown to me. I have very little interest in painters in general." In the fifth paragraph, beside "your paper," he wrote "no not my paper"; and beside "sort of writing that should be done," "buncumb." At the end of the letter, he typed a note:

Cher W:

I trust these three negatives are perfectly clear.

And hasten to assure you that I shall take no further steps

whatever regarding any activity of yours until requested by you to do so.
Goody bye, and good luck.

To elucidate my note on page 1 "unknown to me". By this I mean
I have no knowledge of any show by any painter arranged in London;
neither have I seen any painter English or french since leaving Paris,
last october, nor been in communication with any painter likely to
have had a show in London. (At least I suppose you do not refer to
Mr Beerbohm, the caricaturist.)

There are some matters in which you really do behave like, and <u>some</u>
⟨some not all⟩ lines in this letter of yours in which you really do write <u>like</u>,
a God damn fool.

                              candidly and
cordially yours
                    E.P.

127. TLS–1. On stationery imprinted: Via Marsala, 12 Int. 5. Rapallo.

                    6 Sept. 1925

Dear Wyndham:
          It stands like this. I've got some money promised me from
America. Kristnoze IF it will come; if it does I can send you twenty quid;
if it dont, I cant.
          And if it dont I have no means of making the americano send it;

                    yours ever
                    E.P.

128. ALS–1.

                                        61. Palace Gardens Terrace.
                    Sept 12/   Kensington. <u>W.8.</u>
                         /25.

Dear E.P.   Very many thanks for your promised help. The sum you mention would keep the bailiffs out until I could begin touching the first in-

stalmont of my book money. I would eventually pay you back: but could not guarantee repayment till say January, by which time I should bo fairly straight. Lets hope your Americano does as you say he should.

Enraged at my writings (such as Apes in Criterion) and fearing worse, the big Rolls Royces have tried to starve me out! —Its a pity I am not somewhere where it would be possible to consult you on a few points as regards what I have done: but I only have one fair copy of most of my things. Eliot here I have not seen for a long time: he seems very peculiar and ill.

Should you be in touch at any time with american or other publishers desirous of dealing in my sort of writing, you can let them know that I should like to arrange for the publication of The Enemy of the Stars with a 40,000. word essay attached, and large cover design (on Timon model).

I want to get out of England for good: but have to lay my eggs first, or rather get them marketed.

Yrs   W.L.

129. ALS–2.

61. Palace Gardens Terrace.
Kensington. W.8.
Sept 22/
/25.

Dear Pound. I have been away on a money-hunt out of London. The cheque for £20 which I have just touched was providential, and I am your eternal debtor for this timely help. —I owe you a couple of drawings already for the other cheque, and these I propose to despatch, as you suggest (Mrs. Shakespear). If I get some money quickly I will pay you back this last cheque, or half of it to start with. But I will avail myself otherwise of the generous spirit in which you have offered it to me to the extent of leaving things as they are until I am a little straight as regards money.

The two drawings I shall send you are the best I've got at the moment. One of them (an alpine scene) I should like to have for a month if I arrange a show. As I go along I have to sell drawings of course; so when I have a show, if it is to be representative, I must borrow a certain number from different people. (I hope to have half to sell, & the other half lent.)

Again, my profoundest thanks for the cheque.

Yrs   W.L.

130. ALS–1.

61. Palace Gardens Terrace.
W.8.
22 Sept/
/25

Dear Pound.   I carried a letter to you about for a time, and then was not able to express it, as I had intended. So I am sending this to make sure.

Thank you very much indeed for the cheque for £21. It came in the nick of time and drove away three wolves. I am very grateful. — As to repayment, unless you are meantime pressed yourself, I will keep it till I am a little straight. Two drawings are yours on the strength of the first cheque, & I am sending them out by Mrs. Shakespear. I hope you will like them = if not, I will send you some photographs of others.

Well god bless you — my other letter will probably have reached you.

Yrs   W.L.

131. TLS–1. On stationery imprinted: Via Marsala, 12 Int. 5. Rapallo.

1 Oct. 1925

Dear Wyndham:

Orl rite; send 'em when you get ready; That is to say keep 'em for your show; and send 'em afterward, and dont fer gawd's sake bother about the 20 quid.

For the drawings, registered post seems to be safe now, if package is WELL wrapped.

Saw Walsh the other day, he is now ill again, hemorrage. He says

Robt. [McAlmon] had nothin to do with your disagreement, chief point being that he ⟨WALSH⟩ had only 10 quid to spend per contributor, and was not prepared to go higher or to take on such a large wad of matter. Too late to do anything for this number; think you can place 10 quid worth (NOT MORE) with him in later numbers, if you think it worth while. Let it set for the present.

(i,e, 10 quid per number, two or three times a year, while it lasts. Think it will go on as long as Walsh himself does, but he is not a very good life; allus spittin blood.)

Etc. so it goze.

E

ill again: Walsh was dying of tuberculosis.

132. ALS–1.

61. Palace Gardens Terrace.
Kensington. W.8.
Oct. 7/
‾‾/25

Dear E.P.   With regard Walsh: for a long time past I have been very hard up indeed: during that time I could have got money by doing things I didn't at all want to, and refrained: contributing in any way to Walsh's paper is now one of the characteristic things that I decidedly have no intention of doing. When he says he could not print, and did not want, a large section of my work, he is lying: because he first asked me for [it] & repeated it throughout our correspondence that he wanted, a big wad, or big bunch, anything up to 40 or 50 thous. words. He also agreed to give me £30 (which he had heard from Macalmon [McAlmon] was my figure) so again he lies twice—once in saying he was only able to pay £10, & once in saying that he got nothing from MC.C [McAlmon] on my circumstances.

That Walsh has consumption interests Miss Woodpigeon but does not interest me. MacC. told me in Paris that the Ford motor-car millions were somewhere behind This Quarter. I see no reason why I should advertise a fifth rate poet & his friends, none of whose compositions appear to me in any way necessary, without being paid for it. I dont see why I

should slave in a London room and be flung a fiver by MacA. & a tenner
by Walsh occasionally. If Walsh & MacA. now say that there is no backing for that huge costly venture, again they are lying, as they will always do.

You are the patron saint of This Q. & it is useful to you—that is the
only way in which I can imagine it being useful. Your connection with it
was indeed the only reason that made me contemplate contributing to it.
This note is hurled past your head, & I am sorry it has to come so near it.
All the best blessings of the season on that shaggy head. Another note
following tomorrow on drawings about to leave.

Yrs   W.L.

patron saint: The first issue of *This Quarter* was dedicated to Pound.
Miss Woodpigeon: Probably Lewis's satiric name for Ethel Moorhead, Walsh's
    patroness.
motor-car millions: Walsh was born in Detroit, but neither Walsh nor Moorhead
    were associated with the automobile industry; and Walsh himself had little
    money.

133. TLS–3. On stationery imprinted: Via Marsala, 12 Int. 5. Rapallo.

23 Nov. [1925]

Dear Wyndhamn:
            I dont know whether you wd. consider it beneath yr. dig-
nity to apply for Guggie's 2500 dollars per annum.

I dont know even whether you have heard of the endowment. It is a
very decent scheme, as intelligently planned as any such endowment can
be, with no strings that I can see attached.

I wrote to them in Feb. that the only way they cd. do any good to
the arts was to subsidize the men who cd. produce the stuff.

They replied that I wuz puffikly right

"absolutely coorrect in yr. estimate of the purposes" etc. and
that they knew yr. pubd. work. would I send further details.

I sent 'em ten pages on you; saying that I did not think they
ought to write to you until they were pretty well convinced that they
wanted to send you the 500 quid.

If it is any compliment, you may know that I put you first on

my list (and young George [Antheil] third). I have already admitted that
you do not come specifically under outline.

Paris is worth a mass.

They still have the "research" idea; but it is the first big subsidy to include a lot a art. (licherture moozik etc.

I think my ten pages to them wd. satisfy you. I at any rate said you were
the best value they cd. get for their money. That they ought to run you
for five years at least. I put in a good deal of general instruction for their
souls' good. I also said they ought to arrange a show for you in N.Y. at
the end of a year or so.

OF COURSE I CANT GUARANTEE ANYTHING. I merely made
my statement as strong as possible. That if they wanted to boost the production of the best possible stuff they ought to pay for YOUR time, FIRST,
and then subsidize anyone else they chose. AND that I didn't want you
bothered until they were ready to act.

In my second letter, in reply to their asking for fuller detail I sent ten
pages on you, seven on Eliot and three on Antheil.

                                ////

Will you return me Moe's [Henry Allen Moe, secretary of the Guggenheim Foundation] letter enclosed, s,v,p, ..

                                ///

I shd. think the best thing for you to say, IF you consent to say anything,
is that the suggestion to apply at all has been sprung on you. That your
only qualification is your past work, and capacity for MORE.

That you understand from me that they are more interested in ACTUAL
PRODUCT, than in your coming strictly into the quota of "25 to 35" etc.

TYPE THE DAMN THING. Make as LONG a list as possible of paintings, important drawings, mentioning Quinn, the S.Kensington, Canadian
War (comment of no more than three lines on any one item) List of
stories that have appeared. call 'em uncollected, in various magazines,
naming the more respectable.)

And say that twenty years <u>hard work</u> have brought you scant
monitary reward.

High price of studio rent, or any other facts that you think per-
suasive. (NOT domestic details, or what wd. be considered immoral
revolutionary ideas)

Hell, IF Guggie is pourin out his 20 thousand quid a year he ought
to spill a little of it in the right spots.

And there is the one solid fact, i,e, that you cd. do more if you weren't bothered about living expenses.

So far as I see there can be no publicity about the matter unless they do subsidize you, and if they do, they have a stake in the matter, and ought to help advertise your work.

Etc. ennyhow, thaar it is; dew as ziou like.

E

Guggie's 2500 dollars: Simon Guggenheim established the John Simon Guggenheim Memorial Fellowships in 1925 in memory of a son who died in 1922.

ten pages on you: This letter to Henry Allen Moe, secretary to the Guggenheim Foundation, is reprinted in part in *Ezra Pound and the Visual Arts,* ed. Zinnes, pp. 294–99.

Paris is worth a mass: Statement attributed to Henry IV of France upon declaring himself a Catholic for the sake of unifying his nation.

S.Kensington, Canadian War: Pound refers to the collection of drawings that Guy Baker bequeathed to the Victoria and Albert Museum (South Kensington, London) and to Lewis's service as a Canadian War Records Artist in World War II.

134. ALS–2.

> 61. Palace Gardens Terrace.
> Kensington W.8.
> Dec.8./
> ⁄25

Dear E.P.   I must apologize for the long delay in answering your letter. For a week or so now I have been very much occupied, and could find no time to write a letter.

With regard to the Guggenheim grant: I am not clear as to whether you want me to apply or wait till I am written to. But it appears to me very unlikely indeed that I should be successful. The first objection that of age (what age did you say I was?) could, from the wording of the form, be got over. But the other difficulty, namely that I am not a United States citizen nor have ever been one and have always been domiciled in England, would eliminate me at once.

If you think it would be worth while I could write them a letter, stating the two disqualifications, and asking if under the circumstances it was any use applying. But much as I should like £500. I dont see how I am eligible for it under the terms of the circular you have sent me.

Before in future taking any action on my behalf, you consult me, do you hear? You might do me a lot of harm, with little chance of any compensation. This time it's all right, I think: but we must make a rule of that, because your judgement is at fault so often. —In general, references to the distressed condition of artists is not appreciated or of any use to them. The fact that you might associate conventionally the genius with the distress would never, with such folks as you are apt to talk with about these things, make your references any the less damaging. In my own case, I should today be on perfectly friendly terms with everybody (of the McAlmon & every other sort) and no one would ever have dreamed of departing from a courteous and friendly attitude to me, if it had been known that I possessed say £300. a year. —Your assumption that the majority of people are compassionate, full of a delicate consideration for other peoples difficulties, distressed on hearing about them, incapable of feeling satisfaction on hearing that another person is ill-provided with money, —incapable of being insolent in consequence—feeling they could be so with impunity, —disposed to give more money, not less, because they know it is badly needed—where do you get that from? —Not content with helping people yourself, you want the most unlikely people to share in the task of supporting what they hate most—namely talent in another person: you make me by god since you are no fool almost feel that you are doing it on purpose.

Excuse me once more for putting obstacles in the way of your impulses to befriend: all I mean to say is for the love of Mike be discreet, never never say your friend is hard-up (you will make people sick, so they'll at once go and attack him for getting into such a disgusting state): only to a select minority ⟨and I must be on the selection committee⟩ confess that pictures sometimes sell for relatively modest sums, especially if they are good (if you advertise this fact don't you see that you will ruin everybody in time?): say so and so wants another twenty pounds to make up a million that he will then have earned in the course of the year, so breaking a record in his own line.

Yrs
   W.L.

P.S.   Could you get me the Nobel Prize next year? or do you want it yourself?

135. TLS–4. On stationery imprinted: Via Marsala, 12 Int. 5. Rapallo.

11 Dec. 1925

My Dear Wyndham:

These people are not shits. They are definitely trying to do what, for ten years I have been saying people with money ought to do, namely to keep up the arts.

My correspondence with them occurred last Feb. when they made their opening announcement. I wrote to them, and they replied that I was dead right in my estimate, and that what they wanted to do was to increase the artistic power of the country, and that they weren't going to be tied by regulations. Though naturally they have to make a general outline.

As the time is short, what you'd better do is to fill out the blank, AT ONCE, and send it with a letter putting all the blame on me. Saying that you would never have thought of applying, that you aren't strictly inside the quota; but that having had an American father (at least you once said you had) you have always wanted to establish relations with N. America, and that possibility of coming over with a show, etc.... wd. mean more to you than the subsidy.

Say that you can live by sales, short time work, etc. but that of course leisure for longer work uninterrupted is always of use.

by the way

N.B. all my letters to them (two in fact) were written long before my note to you saying I wd. keep my hands OFF your affairs.

////

There will be, so far as I can see, NO publicity save possibly a printed list of the people who receive the fellowships.

You can say after (all)

"if my work is sufficiently known to the committee, or if they consider it of sufficient interest ...." to waive the general specifications etc.

/////

What I have hammered into their heads. (using chiefly my own biography and Yeats's to show) is that people are always or often ready to pay one for something OTHER THAN one's real work. Namely that in my own case for years every time I had a chance to make ten quid or over it was with the condition that I QUIT work and offer a substitute.

////

I dont know how much I have to do with the whole foundation of the endowment. Pam whom I read the riot act to in Rome two years ago was a friend of Gugg. He got to point where "SOMETHING ought to be done fei aht", it was "subsidy fer life" that he struck at. Couldn't see what wd. prevent a man's lying down and doing nothin the minute his bread was safe.

////

I think that a few decent people ought to take the subsidy, in order to make it effective. I think Gugg. ought to be encouraged. (However ..... I think you have suffered enough. I don't want you martyred to a sense of duty.)

AND OF COURSE I cant guarantee action on the part of the committee. If you want time to finish your present set of books, you have an excellent ground on which to ask for leisure. A mass of work nearly finished and the call to interrupt it for immediate gain.

Nothing to prevent your letter to Moe being confidential.

HOWEFFE R !!!!!

If you want to do anything, write to them AT ONCE. otherwise it will be too late for this year.

Their age limit is only approximate. Read their damn slip. They say "usually between 25 and 35"

En parenthese (how much do you want for taking out nacherlization papers??)

Would you go to Murka for three or four years if they wd. make you a nest there??

NO, the Nobel prize is for idealists. That is for people who dont mind international combines of munitions makers, and makers of canon. who see only the beautiful symbolism , ,,, etc....

E

AT ANY RATE, as per my letter to you of a couple of months ago (written AFTER my negotiations with Gugg's company),

I will henceforth
forth refrain from allusions,,,etc,,, allan sundry ... to circumstances .....
etc....

tranquilizezzzz vous....

I have, you know, told people that your paintings, were a good investment. You mayn't believe it ,,, they usually didn't either .... but still ....   E

Pam: Pound had asked Max Pam, who had supported *The Little Review,* to contribute to the Bel Esprit scheme for T. S. Eliot.

136. ALS–2.

61. Palace Gardens Terrace. Kensington W.8.

Jan 15/
/26.

My dear E.P.   Excuse me for my long delay in writing you. I have been extremely occupied and thought I would wait till I had a breathing space. —I dont think the Guggenheim scheme was contrived for me. I met your friend[s] Bap n Bom in Paris, I have also seen them over here. It is wildly improbable that such people would encourage me to produce masterpieces.

I enclose a page or two (title page & Foreword) of a book, which should appear next month (when I will send you an early copy). 6 months after publication in England it has to be setup in or arranged for in America, else I lose the american copyright. As you will see it is a book of about 440 pages. I know nothing whatever about american publishers— except Liveright, who Eliot tells me is very dishonest. Have you any information? Are you on good terms with any american publisher—one not too closely in touch with the bohemian millionaire world (I have several reasons for that clause) wealthy and whose idea of loot at the expense of "authors" is not too highly percented?
If you do, shoot me a high-velocity note with his name (and qualifications, address, any facts I should know, whether he hates you or merely despises you, his record of hold-ups and larceny "under the armpit," denomination, speculative range etc.) I am sending you a packet, & shall write you again at once.

I have 2 copies of the uncorrected proofs of this book ⟨not in galleys but pages, as you see,⟩ complete, now, I could send off at once. Liveright offered me 3 years ago £100. for a book (I dont know what he meant, but that was the figure). I should want a £100 advance. W.L.

Bap n Bom: These comic names may be references to two associates of John Quinn, Max Pam and the painter and art critic Walter Pach.
(title page & Foreword) of a book: The Art of Being Ruled, which was published in England on 11 March 1926. It was published in America September 1926 by Harper & Brothers, who also published Lewis's *The Lion and the Fox* in 1927.

137. TLS–3.

Cher W: I think Eliot's U.S. publisher is Knopf and not Liveright; NO, hold on. Knopf started and Liv. continued. But the dishonesty consisted I believe in doing the Dial. I. E. leaving 'em stalled with 400 copies of editio princeps [of *The Waste Land*], while he rushed out 2nd. edtn.

This in favour of the author and to the detriment of the bloated.

HOWEVER. Liveright is my publisher, and the only one I have any dealings with.

Huebsch I believe to be dishonest, perhaps only when really bankrupt, which he mostly is.

Knopf broke his word to me, so I nacherly am shy of him. The American McMillan is known to be a bandit.

LIVERIGHT HAS BEEN KNOWN to send cheques abroad. I shd. think your list of contents wd. scare him into next week.

Can CHATTO [& Windus] DO ANYTHING. Probably if they cd. they wd. want to sell sheets; which wd bring YOU practically nothing.

AT ANY rate Liveright is the only man I know in America with enough pride to WANT to bring out a book.

The rest are worms, humble worms, with no self-respect to appeal to.

Liveright has mistrusted my judgement ever since I told him Coué was bunk. thus costing him millions, as he took my word for it, and failed to think of the bunk-profits.

He mistrusts my opinion thoroughly; though admits that he lost some years of sales by not grabbing Morand sooner. Still having got him in the end, he probably knows that it is almost as profitable to WAIT till popularity is assured.

The only way ... oh hell ..... Have you his letter offering you 100 quid???

The only audience in america for "serious sociological" is prob. the readers of the "Nation" / american not english, and the New Republic.

Never heard of anyone getting 500 dollars advance royalties for a serious book in America. But go ahead.

There is Dr. Collins, but I imagine he wants ALL the market for himself. Have Chatto send review copies to Nation and New Repub.

dont know how Ernest Boyd will react. He also probably wants all the space for himself.

If some american reviewer thinks it a GRREAT WORRK he might do

something about am. edtn. .... but usually they want to repel the foreigner unless they can live on him.

Liveright much to my surprise is bringing out a collected edition [*Personae,* 1926] of me, whether he will think that ENOUGH sacrifice to the
high-brow for one year ....

Instigations has sold out, but I dont think he has any intention of reissue.

Besides he may not agree with what you say in the book.

I dare say the best thing to do is to keep up your price.

Try: Dear Liv: the book we spoke of five years ago is now ready.

only

dont blame me for results.

Or have a shy straight at Harper or some of the crusted old shits. Harper
has reputation for being good to his authors (Louise Morgan Sill, and
other refined old ladies.) Chatto's name is aged and conservative.

A kike named Frank (brother of Waldo ditto, edits their magazine ....
complete curds; pseudo intelexual slush .. "Making of America" "how I
refound america" etc. a little flattery to Waldo: perhaps he's your meat—
dont fer Xt's sake mention me.

Noncommital note 'Waldo Frank, co Harpers Bros.
        49 E. 33rd. St.
I am told (not saying by whom) that you are the one man in america who
can tell me where to pub. a serious work. 'How to beG,' pub. by Chatto.
        Conceited little shit of chew.
                    40 to 1 Chance.
I am sending you a copy of Harpers. recd. yesterday in hope of reclaiming
me. I have not read it, and the markings are not mine. excep on one ad.

It will tell you more about America than I know or want to know.

The other perioducles are as said Nation and new Rep[ublic].

Putnam's are an old house, but I think not yet touched with the new
pseudo-intellectualism. Probably wd.nt print Strindberg.
                    2.W. 45th, St.

There was once an agent: Jean Wick, Aeolian Hall. N.Y. but I dont know
if still in bisniz, or if handles anything but rattle snake fiction.

Of old houses Harper only one, sfar as I know where you stand chance of snowball in hell. either via Waldo, or by straight attack.

Write simultaneous to Harp. and Liv. and see which answers soonest.

ZETC.   E.P.

edits their magazine: Harper's Magazine was actually edited by Thomas B. Wells during this period. Waldo Frank's series of articles, "Re-Discovery of America," appeared in *The New Republic* in 1927–1928.

138. TLS–1. On stationery imprinted: Via Marsala, 12 Int. 5. Rapallo.

9 Feb. [1926]

Dear Wyndham:

Here apparently is your chosen angel and messenger. A chap with editorial job on Morning Telegraph in N.Y.; BURRRning with desire to prove to me that America is the promised land.

By all means write to him. He may be able to sell the stuff twice, once serially and once in book.

As his ZEAL is abs. fresh, and no mss. or anything yet intrusted to him, you the CRRREam of his young youth and zealotry.
Judging from clips. of ONE of hopeful starters. New Asses [*New Masses*], BLAST has just got to the Bowery; you[r] day shd. be about to dawn, unless they wanter [*sic*] each BLAST fer hisself. Do mind returning the cuttings. This Price, ought to be our Price.

Thass all. His letter just in, and time to get noon post.

yours
E.

Name an address on his own note.
JOHN M. PRICE

47 W. 48 th. St. New York

Price: An American literary agent who assisted Pound with his journal *The Exile.* See Barry S. Alpert, "Ezra Pound, John Price, and the Exile," *Paideuma* 2 (Winter 1973): 427–48.

139. ACS. [Pmk: Paddington, 27 March 1926].

33. Ossington. Street.

Bayswater. W.2.

note new

address

I'm glad to hear Tome arrived although no room for it in flat. T. S. E[liot]. is so angry with me that he refuses to hold any further communication with me except through his lawyer or secretary. (Something to do with book.) Every publisher in America is clamouring for books. Knopf has intervened and put in a fifty-year old option claim in Tarr contract, about which I know nothing. If Miss Weaver is not too indignant to write hope to get details from her.   Yrs   W.L.

Tome arrived: The Art of Being Ruled was published 11 March 1926.
T. S. E[liot].: Lewis and Eliot had quarrelled about the terms for Lewis's contributions to *The Criterion.* See *The Letters of Wyndham Lewis,* ed. Rose, pp. 152–54.
Knopf: Harper & Brothers's publication of *The Art of Being Ruled* was delayed because Knopf claimed that it had the option to publish in America any of Lewis's books which followed *Tarr,* which Knopf had published in 1918.

140. TLS–2. On stationery imprinted: Via Marsala, 12 Int. 5. Rapallo.

30 Marzp [March 1926]

Dear Wyndham:

Riight yew are, go to it. If "all" the bloody publikers are clamouring mebbe you can make a few of 'em pay.

Knopf hasn't any opt. to git a book fer nothing. His money is as good as anothers. Ennyhow you're supposd to have about six books ready.

Re the rages of Eliot, Weaver, et al. ich weiss gar nicht. I spose they all hav their sorrows.

          ///

I didn say there wuz no room fer the book; I sed there wuz at moment of its arrival, no room fer me own behind.

It wd. be hypocrisy fer me to say that books all erbout everything in general are of any gt. interest to me in partikiler. Have turned out too much generality myself to care a damn whether there is any more done or not.

It is however a satisfaction, usually, to the author to git his heterogenious notes about "life" etcetterer more or less straightened out, or at least printed and out of his own desk-drawers.

That Kruschen feeling. NOT Rhooshun, but KKKKruscian or however they speel it.

I dont see why it shdnt. go like hot cakes in the better murkn magerzines. all except some parts. Hell they read Bertie Rustle [Russell], and Wm, Jim. [James] an a lot of high brows.

Moi, j'aurai "preferé le moindre saltimbanque."

I,e, Cantleman or any of the huskies, from Sigismundo to Miss Codd. (which had, to my mind, a certain vigour and distinction.)

Re Kruschen. I spose the Rhoosian feeling (Dustyoffsky etc,) is due to bad action of the bowels, opposite of Kruschen.

As fer edderkating the pooplik:

> Oh the Henglish wuz so stoopid
> They'd fergotten how to fook
>   Till Mrs Doktor Mary Stoops
>   Com to skow them wid her book.

> She sez: O Jhon do mind the moment
>   When her oviduct is full
> And then go in
> An' play to win
> And show- ye- are . . . . . . JOHNBULL!

I dare say yr. book is a good move politically, to git you your place in the sun etc. Wish it luck to that end. Publik oviduct in proper condition, le's hope.

And ov course, a series, a lot of books in line, even about everything in general, is useful to publikators.

Hoch!
Yrs   E.P.

Kruschen feeling: Pound refers to an advertisement for Kruschen salts.
"le moindre saltimbanque," Cantleman, Sigismundo, Miss Codd: Pound thought
   that Lewis's strength as a writer was his delineation of character. He refers to
   Lewis's stories "Les Saltimbanques" and "Sigismund," which were published in
   The Wild Body (1927), and his play *"Miss Godd" and the Ideal Giant,* which
   was published in 1917 as was "Cantleman's Spring-Mate."
Doktor Mary Stoops: Marie Charlotte Carmichael Stopes, controversial advocate
   of sex education and contraception.

141. TLS–1. On stationery imprinted: res publica, the public convenience Via Marsala, 12 Int. 5. Rapallo.

18 Aug. [1929]

Dear W.L.

Wd. it in least interest or profit you to make an alphabet; caps. for printer, not tied to any particular text. General style that of yr. late Timon (after portfolio) or your most latest as you see fit. The late Timon wd. go very well with Caslon. In fact Ed Wad[sworth]. set for Ovid press were quite good but you cd. nacherly do the job better.

I dont want to start agitating unless you wd take the job. Cd. you say what you wd. want for it and what size (minimum) you wd. want the caps to be in order to show yr. designs with due honour and geelory.

No restrictions save that obscene caps wd. be less useful than non= obscene. In fact the people prob. cdnt. afford to pay for an obscene set, at least not enough to make it worth while. A good alphabet wd. need four or five T s. Some of the letters like X. wdnt. really be necessary but it wd. be more bother figuring out the omissions than it wd. be worth. Better figure on 30 letters, alphabet with 4 Ts and 2 Ss.

E.P.

Caslon: A style of typeface.
Ed Wad[sworth] set: Edward Wadsworth designed the letters for the Ovid Press portfolio of Lewis's *Fifteen Drawings* (1920).

142. TLS–1. On stationery imprinted: res publica, the public convenience Via Marsala, 12 Int. 5. Rapallo.

5 Sept. [1929]

Dear W.L.

My suggestion was "general" and i dare say ANY time wd. do if you ever felt like it. I dont think the Cavalcanti wd. stand anything modern, and I dont think the prose wd. be printed so as to take caps big enough to use your work on it, but in a general way I think printing ought to get prodded up, and the cap. seems to me to give good chance for purely abstract composition.

As one can't get architecture or even mural stuff DONE one retreats to printed page . . . . (or not as case may be.) At any rate a chance to see something done right in a chaotic environment.

Nor worth interrupting anything else for.

etc.

Possibly useful in breaking up a state of mind; something O.K. but unfamiliar strikin the eye. etc.

EP

Cavalcanti: Pound's *Guido Cavalcanti Rime* (Genoa: Edizioni Marsano, 1932). For the publishing history of this book, see Donald Gallup, *Ezra Pound: A Bibliography,* pp. 152–54.

143. TLS–2. On stationery imprinted: Via Marsala, 12 Int. 5. Rapallo.

13 Feb. [1930]

Dear Wyndham

Some virchoos murkns seem disposed to give me the faculty for printing a series of critical monographs, cheaply.

plus my asking to extend it to woiks of licherchoor. (short, odd sizes, scheme as I see it, meaning to print here where it is cheap and distribute there.

I don't know whether this can be of ANY use to you. I cant see a poss. profit to author over five or ten quid per item. (at least not unless a wave of intellexshul hunger engulphs them states in a moss onlikely manner.

Still you have the honourable misfortune to be the first person to whom I am writing re/ the proposal.

Whether there was anything of yours in the Little Review that they cd. now use??

With all this war stuff abaht it might do no harm to indicate that you did in 1916 or 17 (Cantleman) what the lot of em are now cashing in on. Can't remember whether Cantleman was suppressed or not ?????? However things have moved since.

I don't see the scheme as useful for new stuff as printing new matter (not already copyright in U.S. one wd. lose copyright.) It might be used for some things that no one else has the sense to print, but I rather imagine you wd. make more by printing 'em in Enemy [Lewis's journal, 1927–1929].

Largely question of what of yours is out of print and not for the moment "yielding" usufruct to its author.

I don't want to bother with the scheme unless it can be some use.

Is the Caliph [*The Caliph's Design: Architects! Where is Your Vortex?*, 1919] in print?
Has Inferior Religions been reprinted?

Do you see anything by anyone save ourselves that is worth ramming down the amurikan gullet?

etc. "please write stating terms" if any. ⟨plus conditions on which you think such scheme might be useful. = even title of books that ought to be available at 50 cents. or prise of bloody frawg books.⟩

ever

E.P.

virchoos murkns: Pound had proposed to Lincoln Kirstein and R. P. Blackmur that they publish books by Cocteau, de Chirico, Frobenius, and his own *How to Read.*

144. TCS.

8 april [1930]

DearW.

Am sending you copy of Indice with good intention. It is most active fortnightly or other rev. in Italy.

IF you have any photos. you wd. like reproduced, send em along. I think they will print about anything, esp. if I give em a little letter press.

Do you see Variétés?

yrs.   E.P.

via Marsala   I2/5 Rapallo

Indice: Pound wrote for the Italian journal *L'Indice* in 1930–31.

Variétés: Pound was planning to edit an American number of this illustrated periodical.

145. ALS–1. [before June 1930]. On stationary imprinted: ARTHUR PRESS. 113a Westbourne Grove. London, W. 2 [crossed out], with Lewis's drawing of Pegasus.

53. Ossington Street.
Bayswater. W.

My dear Ez-roar! Please overlook my prolonged silence—when your letter came I was too busy to attend to anything at all except what I was doing. —As to the things you want—there is I am afraid nothing available. The few rough war-stories & sketches (Crowd-Master included) have been all used for a large war-book which I started 2 years ago, have not so far gone on with, but hope to soon. [*Blasting & Bombardiering,* 1937]. The other stuff I shall revise & bring out with Arthur Press. I am sorry, & I hope you will have success with your plan. Who are your friends?   Nancy C[unard]. or WINN perhaps?

Very soon now my Apes of God will be published. Your copy shall go to you at once. The reason for the delay has been that I have added a great deal to original version. It is now about 1/4 million words.

With best wishes to you & Mrs. P.

Yrs
W. Lewis.

P.S. This has been delayed a long time until I could find your address.

WINN perhaps: Possibly Winifred Henderson of the Aquila Press.

146. TCS.

via Marsala I2/5

I4 Sept. [1930]

All right. Keep it up. Glad to see antient sperit of BLAST and 1912--17 still survivin'

yrs.
E.

147. TLS–2. On stationery imprinted: Via Marsala, 12 Int. 5. Rapallo.

25 Jan [1931]

Dear Wyndam

This lunatiQUE Bard means well. He can afford to pay moderate fees. If he gets round to inviting yr/ collab/ I recommend him to yr/ mercy. He swears he is going to wipe off his past errors and run his magazine properly. I have taken him at his word to the extent of reviewing the past ten years of Britain's shame. Damn it all, somebody ought to reprod/ yr/ designs; even if you don't care to write fer the blighter.

He was decently educated in Budapesth and Vienna/ he had sense enough to direct my attention to Frobenius. . . . wot th' hell.

he can be made to fight the Criterions' deadness. I <u>think</u> he has sense enough to recognize some sort of proportion. He do NOT know a damn thing about art, and will have to be told.

I am a tellin' him some. But damn it all, I am not an authority, I can't live out here doin' me yeown job and know who is doing decent ⟨plastic⟩ work.

I suppose in a general way that you, Brancus', Dali, Pic[asso]/ and Pic[abia]/ etc//etc//

The man is soft/ but NOT tied up to the bloomsbuggahs [Bloomsbury Group]/ and would I shd. be inclined to think, swaller 'em.

What about APES // any chance of a pop/ edtn ???? There is a stir in america: but no one with both the sense and the capital to bring out so large a vollum.

Mindful of yr/ past cussin' I have refrained to butt againt solid walls in the matter/ but have not putt it out of mind.

I suppose Linati sent you his article in Pegaso; some time ago ??

oh well, cheerioOOOOO !!! I did say a word about Apes// can't remember where/ long ago. . . .

Another pt//what about wop/ translations. I am trying to set up a proper series here. Yr/ short stories shd. take. Have you a pubd/ vol. of 'em?

Perfectly willing to buy it. Am trying to get a printer started who will pay (not that wop pay is much, but it can be used as pointer to frogs an huns.) and the hunyin do pay fer his books.

etc// appy noo yr/
E

lunatiQUE Bard: The young American writer Samuel Putnam founded the *New Review* in 1931. Pound wrote for the first issue what he calls here a review of "the past ten years of Britain's shame" in an article called "After Election" (January/February 1931, pp. 53–55), in which he comments on his post as associate editor.

Pegaso: Carlo Linati, "Wyndham Lewis," *Pegaso: Rassegna di Lettere e Arti* Part 2 (1929): 437–48.

148. ALS–2.

53. Ossington St.
London. W.2.
Feb. 17 1931.

Dear E.P.   Thank you for nice bit in New Review (just seen). What is N. R.? Who is Putnam? Is Putnam a publisher? Is he the great american pub? A 'Putnam' does things here. Is it possible to place literary objects with Put here? —or there? I would like to find a Pub for odds and ends— here—and there—I do so much. I have a fine book—"The Roaring Queen". It is a novel. Can you put me through to Put? (You seem a great guy with the big noises on the "New"!)—"Apes" found no Pub. U. S. A. (Rhinehart [Rinehart] full of fulsomeness but no big rhino. Must have rhino "Apes". Good book).

Congrats smack Jimmie Joys in "New View" —Jim J. insinuating ivernian barstard—all my congrats hence. Wot else? —Nuffin cept woots the odds when yew stops fartin' re 'Bob' [McAlmon]. —But all my congrats. —Please occupy best wits cogitating up transatlantic Pub. "Apes." America cant afford not to pub. "Apes." Disgrace Stars and Stripes. Hoover under cloud. Orefill! See toot—look to utt! ——————————— Goot-pay! Gooot-pie!

W.L.

New Review: Pound wrote in "After Election" (p. 54; see note to Letter 147): "Nevertheless I prefer THE APES OF GOD to anything Mr. Joyce has written since Molly finished her Mollylogue with her ultimate affirmation." Pound also praised McAlmon in this article.

"The Roaring Queen": Lewis's satiric fiction about the book publishing world was turned down by Chatto & Windus in 1930 because they feared the retaliations it might provoke. The novel was accepted for publication by Jonathan Cape, Ltd. in 1935; but after the book was in proof, the publisher decided that it was libelous and suppressed it. It was finally published by Secker & Warburg (London) and Liveright (New York) in 1973.

149. TLS–1. On stationery imprinted: res publica, the public convenience Via Marsala, 12 Int. 5. Rapallo.

20 Feb. [1931]

M deah WnhDAMN

Putnam no relation of the plooto/pubr. Has more intentions and excitability than resources physical (down with dysentery) or fiscal (some sort of guarantee for printing bill of N;rev[iew] and the HOPE of going to Chicago may be for more.

Best way to whet appetite wd. be to start with sending him a brief ms/ ⟨for N. Rev.⟩ saying I suggested it. He can only pay slightly and to those absolootly needing it, so it wd. be inadvisable to give the effect that you have a great lot goin' cheap.

///

Whenever I have suggested any Particular am/ pubr/ you have (historically speakin) usually (if I remember correctly) demurred.

I slld say that anything one Putnam wd. do the other wd. NOT (emphatically NOT)

///

I dont think England amounts to more than half a horse terd or that any
of these new american or continental editors will care a damn about local
measures to clean up any particular gob of Bri'sh garbage.

///

One of the milder Yanks has got to essayin "The premature apotheosis
of Mr T. S. Eliot".

What wd. "put you over" wd. be brief CONSTRUCTIVE statements on
matters of more than local interest
paradox and funny bizniz at no premium.
Or t'putt it nother way. Anything you might write to ME in a letter might
be printed, but attempts to educate Pelman students and the Brish publik
of no use.

Photos of yr/ noo paintin's might be advisable.

More money prob. from Time an Tide [*Time and Tide,* a journal] ???

Murkn money is in weakly revs. like N.Y. herald "Books" the Shitardy
Rev. of Licherchoor [*Saturday Review of Literature*] etc. . . . .

"in applying at this office" ⟨via Marsala⟩ please state clearly whether glory
or cash is main obj. of partic. etc. . .as it wd. save time on computation.

any DETAILS re/ any ONE obj. save waste on impractical conjecture.
    Wot ells.

E.

"T. S. Eliot": Sherry Mangan's "A Note: On the Somewhat Premature Apothe-
    osis of T. S. Eliot," *Pagany* 1 (Spring 1930): 23–36, discusses the effect of
    Eliot's pessimism on young writers.
Pelman: "Pelmanism" was a popular psychology that claimed that everyone had
    the ability to become socially and financially successful.

150. TLS–2. On stationery imprinted: res publica, the public convenience Via Marsala, 12 Int. 5. Rapallo.

15 March [1931]

Dear Wyndamn

Wot I have to say re/ last artcl/ of yrs/ in Time and Td/ poss. better in letter than in print.

re/ credit cranks and yr/ not understanding 'em. No doubt this the only way to introduce the topic in that milieu.

English universities I believe to be useless. I have spent some time kussing the defects of American Univs.

In fact you being the only, so far as I know, contemporary with ANY intelligence who has not undergone univ.

you constitute a special case of a general category the rest of which is empty.

Am. univ. and all univs. bad in many ways // nevertheless may have one or two of the qualities of their defects.

When you say you can't understand credit cranks (economics etc.) I don't believe it is from inherent nature of the subject, but simply that you haven't made any systematic attack on it.

Have you read Marx, analyzed him and then proceeded to read the later authors who are NOT liked by Pigou[,] Keynes and co/?

Are you sufficiently interested either to read them OR to indulge in criticism of them

If you are sufficiently interested I will write out a list of books; some of which I have read and some of which I intend to read// on advice of people whom I more or less trust.

Univtarirism // dead and deadening in that all the "products" have read the same books in same order with same criticism applied.

autodidacts good to stir up

BUT they carry some extra load and have their own difficulties to git over. cant have it both ways//

anybody who rousts about in the unorthodox or uncodified, constantly gets disparate stuff and lumps it together. (Fault in both our writings)

Am perfectly willing to "attack" you publicly in print now and again, if you prefer that to private correspondence.

Ez

Time and Td/: Lewis's "Hitlerism—Man and Doctrine: Creditcrankery Rampant," *Time and Tide* 12 (14 February 1931): 182, 184–85. This was part of a series of six articles which became Lewis's *Hitler* (1931). Pound misunderstands Lewis's tone in this article. Lewis's ironic claims that he cannot understand social credit theories are meant to dissociate him from those who think that economic reforms alone can solve political problems.

151. TLS–1. On stationery imprinted: res publica, the public convenience Via Marsala, 12 Int. 5. Rapallo.

28 Nov. [1931]

Dear Wyndham

I nclose part of a note from Fr. Monotti a good egg; post war, writes art crit' to live not because he fancies hisself as a arsethete a la Valery and Clive Bell.

Old question of whether you <u>want</u> a show. You ought someday to have a room at the Venice Biennale.

There ought to be and to HAVE BEEN a book on yr/ stuff years ago; etc. god damn publishers anyhow.

E

Venice Biennale: A biannual international exhibition of modern art. See Pound's comments on the Biennale of 1935 in *Ezra Pound and the Visual Arts,* ed., Zinnes, p. 215.

152. TLS–2. On stationery imprinted: Via Marsala, 12 Int. 5. Rapallo.

31 Jan ⟨1932⟩

Deer WynDAM

My belle mere [Olivia Shakespear] seems to think you are in MOrocco/ quindi, I prob/ shall not hear from you fer a long time. Hence this somewhat previous note.

Having brought out my Cavalcanti despite all the de la Merrdres and marmelade tins in Shitain I am lookin fer a new scrap.

I have, az you know, considered it for 18 years a bloody outrage that there is no book on you at a decent price//

mentioned it to young Harmsworth but he (on or without consulting you?) seems to think it wd. be no money maker.

BALLZ, I am vurry near the point of bringing it out myself. 16 good reprods/ and three brief essays by me, in Eng/ french and wop/ (not translated one from other, but a dif statement in each of the lingos.)
to the effect/

A. you are the only Brit' (or half=brit) artist I shd. think mentioning seriously to any serious yourapean//

B. That the Apes deserves more attention.

///

I dunno how much objection you are going to raise. The reprods/ wd. have to be a sequence/ sort of biog// from 1912 to present/

They wd. have to be what I thought wd. convince a certain number of people. (not merely the part of your work that you happened to be interested in at the moment.

Though I shd. naturally prefer something that we cd/ both agree on.

I think a page the size of my Guido [*Cavalcanti Rime*], or not much smaller, is wot I have in mind.

My letter press wd. cover abaht 8 pages. attempt to keep price down to 5/ bob.

ennyhaow// awaitin yr/ objections
I remayne.

E P

MOrocco: In the spring and summer of 1931 Lewis and his wife were traveling in North Africa.

de la Merrdes: Richard De La Mare, production director of Faber and Faber. The firm had considered bringing out Pound's Cavalcanti book.

153. ALS–1.

Feb. 16. 1932

Dear Ezra. Your letter to hand. Very well. But give me some details. What books will you discuss? Which pictures will you choose? ETC.

I have only just got your letter—beneath is my present address:

⌈ PALL MALL SAFE DEPOSIT.
| Carlton Street
⌊ Regent Street. W.

(the Ossington St. address no longer the best).

I returned the other day from Washington, D.C. —The Apes is to be published in New York on the 24th of Feb.(next week).

In very great haste. I will write you next monday more fully.

Yrs

W. Lewis

Washington D.C.: In November and December 1931, Lewis visited New York, Boston, and Washington. The American edition of *The Apes of God* (New York: Robert M. McBride & Company) was published in February 1932.

154. TLS–2. On stationery imprinted: Via Marsala, 12 Int. 5. Rapallo.

I9 Feb. [1932]

Dear W.L.

Question IZ more WHAT pixchoors can one git at? I've two decent ones here. Whazzis name hasn't even a negative of my illustrious replica; only a bloody "block". The goddam WarMoozeeum sez it has only ONE artillery drawing [*Battery Position in a Wood*] and the ???? Canadian war picture [*A Battery Shelled*] or wottell?

There are some things (Baker's lot) in the S.Kens.

I WANT, I shd. say four of the artillery things, there were several that were fuller and richer than the good one my mother=in=row possesses.

There are at least 4 good ones in the S.Kens. but I shd. like to get in as much variety as poss/

I don't think the viscera wd. be very serviceable. I shd. be glad to have on loan any photos. you can excavate. and wd. follow yr/ suggestions re/

179

aht wherever they didn't too violently conflict with what I thought wd.
GET ACROSS.

I am damn glad the Apes is to be done in the land of . . . .

I shant do much diskussin'. Constaterai./ I shd. emphasis [*sic*] the
existence of the stories, Tarr and the Apes.

I note you say "letter". I have sent you two if not three. However.
you seem to hev got the drift.

dev. vs

E

illustrious replica: Pound may refer to the charcoal drawing, *Ezra Pound Esq.,*
   which John Rodker published in *Fifteen Drawings.*
Baker's lot: Guy Baker's collection of Lewis's drawings, Victoria and Albert Museum, South Kensington, London.
mother=in=row possesses: Olivia Shakespear had purchased Lewis's drawing *'D'*
   Sub-Section Relief.

155. TL–2. [Summer 1933]. On stationery imprinted: Via Marsala. 12–5.
Rapallo, with a reproduction of Henri Gaudier-Brzeska's profile sketch of
Pound.

Dear Wyndham

Re/ poem. which D[orothy]. mentions to me [Lewis's
One-Way Song, 1933]. What I shall expect is something badly written
and a damn sight more alive than anything else now being produced in
England/

or rather as Bridson is also alive, etc. . . at any rate something NOT of the neo/georgian etc/etc/

Sorry I didn't know about it before sending my noo yanthology [*Active
Anthology,* 1933] to press, though I spose you wd/ have had some complicated etc/etc/ for not wishing to yappear in company of Z/Y/ and X

(includin the Rev. Possum [T.S. Eliot].)
All of which dont alter my opinyum that it wd/ have been detrimental
(slightly) etc. or bad strategeee to have printed the pos=baudelairian
verse you showed me in 1916 or 1919 or when ever it wuz, /I/E/ to
have printed it AT THAT TIME/

Now the newe Abercrombies are in flower, I cant say whether even that old material mightnt be exhumed with a date on it. Gord/ how Bloomsbury bloometh ever with the same cheese mould, ever with the same ole etc/ mumble and fumble.

As to technique; there aint nobody wot couldnt learn somfink both from Profile [Pound's anthology of 1932] and from my new anth (due out in autumn proofs been sent to press).

Have you any spare photos of yr/ noo paintinkz?? The "Mare" [*Il Mare,* an Italian newspaper] will print aht IF chichés are supplied.

if you've a few ole blocks, say three or four, you might send em along IF the whim takes you. Or I can try the photos of new stuff on "Quadrante"

⟨Have just seen announcement of Blast 1933?? yours or some thiefs? & if so has the thief had the decency to send it to you?
=
yet again P.S. puld. [publishers of *Blast* 1933] 55 W. Hope Place N.Y.= fake!!⟩

Blast 1933: A New York bi-monthly (September 1933–November 1934) with which William Carlos Williams was associated.

Introduction to Letter 156.

Lewis used the image of the "doppelgänger" to express his sense of the way Pound's character was utterly changed by his involvement in economics and politics. The reason that Lewis thought of this change as a "sudden eruption" may be seen in the following letters, which begin in 1936 after more than three years in which there seems to have been little or no correspondence between them. There is a disturbing change in the tone of these letters. Although Pound is certainly imperious and even arrogant throughout the early thirties, in the early years his many enthusiasms are subordinated to his passion for the arts. He never neglects the social conditions of the arts in the post-World War I years, but in 1936—to judge from these letters to Lewis—social and political conditions take over the foreground of his thought. Typical letters to Lewis are no longer pestering him to write a book or enter an art exhibition but rather to sign a manifesto or write a political tract.

The political climate of Italy seems to have conditioned Pound's responses by 1936. Noel Stock observes that "Pound and some of his friends shared in the national hysteria that accompanied the Italian campaign in Abyssinia and they began to dream of Rapallo as a centre of the new culture." In 1936 Pound published a series of articles in the Rapallo newspaper *Il Mare,* which urged that Rapallo should become a center of Fascist thought. After Italy conquered Abyssinia in May 1936, Mussolini proclaimed a new Italian Empire as the rebirth of the Roman Empire. Pound thought that this new order would permeate every facet of Italian life. He wrote in July 1936: "Now that the Empire exists, it needs a Center in which the intelligence and the strength of the race are concentrated, but from which in turn the light of its civilization spreads across and penetrates the lesser nuclei. . . . The New Order will speak from Rome in ways neither understood nor dreamed of, in ways forseen only by a few people who have an 'ardent imagination'. . . ."

The political jargon and pseudo-science of this passage are not redeemed by the irony that Pound's vision was tragically blind. If he could not foresee that the conquering of Abyssinia could never renew the "Empire" in Italy, then we cannot be surprised at the startling unreality of the political commentary in the following letters. In Letters 159–62, for example, he imagines a conspiracy behind Edward VIII's abdication of the English throne in order to marry Mrs. Simpson. He told Eustace Mullins in 1950 that "the cards had been dealt out in 1936, and the Second World War was all set to go. There was one last-minute obstacle— 'Eddie' refused to sign the mobilization papers. He had been through the veterans' hospitals just after the First World War, and apparently he could not bring himself to send men into that kind of hell again. 'That woman' rushed onto the scene, and 'Eddie' was hustled out the back door." Pound may be right to see the political dimensions of the abdication crisis as a struggle among the forces represented by the Baldwin government, the laboring class, and the Church of England. But his interpretation of the abdication, like most of the political analysis in the following letters, is simplified and heightened into a parody rather than a record of events.

Despite his own reactionary positions, Lewis was immune to Pound's efforts to involve him in his economics and politics and attempted to keep the renewed correspondence on a personal level. Letter 158 is as close to being a tactful letter as any Lewis ever wrote to Pound, and Pound was still too loyal a friend to allow political differences to divide them.

The new political intensity of Pound's correspondence is signaled in the following letter by the first use of Fascist dating, which takes Mussolini's March on Rome (30 October 1922) as the start of "Anno I."

"*new culture*": Stock, *The Life of Ezra Pound,* pp. 338.
"*'ardent imagination'*": Pound, "Marconi's Violins," *Il Mare,* 18 July 1936; ed. R. Murray Schafer, *Ezra Pound and Music: The Complete Criticism,* p. 393.
"*the back door*": Eustace Mullins, *This Difficult Individual, Ezra Pound,* p. 195. See also Andrew J. Kappel, "What Ezra Pound Says We Owe to Edward VIII, Duke of Windsor," *The Journal of Modern Literature* 9 (May 1982): 313–15.

156. TLS–2. On stationery imprinted: Anno XIV. 1936. Via Marsala. 12–5. Rapallo, with the Gaudier-Brzeska profile of Pound.

26/ Oct

My Dear Wyndham

                            Appropos of LEFT WINGS o. E. what about a little CONCENTRATED fire/

                            Hasn't the time come when there being a REAL agreement; it might be well to sort it out.

I dont know what you read (if anything) of mine. I printed the enc/ ⟨Vdit. 8.⟩ in 1933; after talking with B[enito]. M[ussolini].

Whether you noted my articl/ in Fascist Quarterly; current issue. whether you have looked at Impact [Pound's *Social Credit: An Impact*]; or told Nott to send you a review copy (with no ob/ to rev.) I dunno.

At any rate MONEY. its nature; its mode of issue is the one thing the XIXth century wouldn't and prob. couldn't THINK.
Marx and la Tour du Pin equally paralyzed.
Germany save Schacht is fairly ignorant. just IGNORANT.

I dont send you news of England because you may have means of getting some/ but garrnoze it AINT the press.

    and the Paris papers have been silent as the tomb ever since kikey Leon [Blum] got into office.

                            a fabian Manchesterguardian shit I believe (subject to yr/ correction).

Mor[ning]. Post printed about 18 of my letters. Then I got the boot for calling Hartley Withers a LIAR. which he is.

nacherly; being English he is a liar.

it is yr/ alien blood that disinterests you in mendacity.

If you care to outline yr/ ignorance of what I have pubd. I might get S[tanley].N[ott]. or someone to supply you with texts (free) unless you can plead prosperity on me.

I dont recall having used exact words bro. Marinetti quoted in recent Listener.

At any rate I am open to suggestion re/ manifestos/ or fire control. IF you think it wd. serve any useful purpose.

ALSO there is a news and travel mag/ starting in the FAR West that might print you. pays a LITTLE.

mebbe you get higher rates in London. I have just done 3 cantos on founding of Monte dei Paschi [Cantos 42–44]. and dug up some econ/ history that wuz smothered by Napoleonic wars.

thazz for the spring edtns.

I recommend Buchart's [Butchart's] anthology on MONEY/ also note an american weekly of that name which QUOTES/ as does faather Coughlin; useful historic etc//

communism on the way out/ Stalin having killed off five million mujiks because too stupid to set up ticket system.
I did tell you about a bloke named Douglas ⟨C. H.⟩ YEARS ago.

Kill J[ohn]. Bull with ART.
waaaal. ISNT it about time to FINISH off the Wellsians diarrhoea and the Shavian dry shitpowder and THAT epoch of Englands shayme?
I see you mentions hell's arse's last louse Inge, also.
Seeriously, cant you do a little piece on MONEY, its nature and mode of issue; and pub/ it somewhere that I can't.

you are welcome to any spade work I have done.
Faber wont print economics. Cape wont print ME.

anyhow: greetinz affer many days.
Zappa said he ran into [you] in the wilderness. ⟨Thazz some time ago also.⟩

yrz.
E.P.

⟨Cordially & greetinz to the ladies.⟩

Left Wings: Lewis's *Left Wings Over Europe; or, How to Make a War About Nothing* (1936); it argues that "bourgeois-bolshevism" was provoking another world war.

printed the enc/: Missing from letter–possibly a reference to Pound's *A B C of Economics* (1933).

Fascist Quarterly: "A Social Creditor Serves Notice," *Fascist Quarterly* 4 (October 1936): 492–99.

Mor[ning]. Post: Pound published twenty-four letters on economics in this London newspaper between 20 March 1934 and 13 September 1935; Hartley Withers was editor of *The Economist.*

recent Listener: F. T. Marinetti, "Art and the State—VI. Italy," *The Listener,* 16, no. 2 (14 October 1936): 730–32. Marinetti, the founder of Italian Futurism, wrote that "The well-known American author Ezra Pound declared: 'Marinetti and Futurism have given a great fillip to all European literature. The movement which I, Elliott [*sic*], Joyce and others have started in London would not have existed but for Futurism.'" Pound's letter to *The Listener* on Marinetti's article is reprinted in *Ezra Pound and the Visual Arts,* ed. Zinnes, p. 310.

157. TLS–3. On stationery imprinted: Anno XIV. 1936. Via Marsala. 12–5. Rapallo, with the Gaudier-Brzeska profile of Pound.

29 Oct [1936]

Dear Wyndham   (continuing from mine of about the 27th)

Whatever you think of it, and however it looks in London it appears to me; here, that time for concerted action IS. Manifesto against TREASON of the CLERKS. Damn and blast generation that left our generation the bloody mess it did leave us. The slobby and sniggery Wells=Shaw miasmus.

I.   Couldn't or didn't distinguish a TAX from a SHARE.

2.   The shitten lot did NOTHING to investigate MONEY; its nature and mode of issue.

3/ Historians and educational apes did NOTHING to dig out real history. as visible in quotations now being printed by Butchart, Buck and Coughlin. ⟨& Ez. P.⟩

4.   Educational system a treason. so called authors and specifically Authors Society did NOTHING to come to reality.

5. Kill John Bull, specifically Baldwin, Chamberlain, Norman.

   Baldwin symbol of negation of intelligence. POSITIVE hate of intelligence AS SUCH.

6. England unaware of fight between American Newspaper Guild and Roy Howard of Scriiis [Scripps] Howard chain. Howard for right of employer to pervert and suppress all vital news.

   The Guild 60 years behind the times; but England hasn't even a guild.

7. God damn all socialists for being too stupid to think about socialization of means of Exchange. And damn all communists for being too bloody sodden to consider communization of product.

//

subject to whatever additions and emendments you consider TIMELY. Question of who ought to sign. I think it ought to be OUR generation; such as it is. and possibly the next. I suppose Eliot; Joyce if not too soused; Bill Williams, then cummings, Osbert [Sitwell] and possibly not Huxley, the latter more use for ad[ver]t[ising]. purposes; but never had any spirit. I don't know whom you think worth putting on. I shd. say Hem[ingway]. Miller; Callaghan,

write yr/ own ticket if you have heard of any writers.

25 better than six. ⟨?europeans who wd. d/n few.⟩

That dozen signed letter on Soc. Credit was useful.

Form of the blast is indifferent to me.

Say that the generation of writers as we found em did nothing to break the idea that ALL books were made for money profit only. They accepted tamely the dictation of merchants. They welcomed it. The ideals of Kipling were horse piss and he typified his time. None of these he bitches really disliked the system they found. Man was a stomach and nothing more, and all collections of writers accepted that ideal.

   Marx had no curiosity about the NATURE of money, etc.

   You will probably think up ten (invalid) reasons against a third issue of Blast.

     From my pt/ of view it wd. be useful.

             Yr

             E.

Buck: possibly John Buchan, whose *Oliver Cromwell* Pound reviewed in 1935. See *Ezra Pound: Selected Prose,* ed. Cookson, 265–66.

158. ALS–1.

Dec. 1. 1936.

My dear Ezroar   Thank you for the 2 notes. I am very glad to hear your
roar again & should have written before but have been prevented by
accidents of all sorts.

—You cannot "kill John Bull" with economics any more than you
can with art. Besides why kill John Bull? A debauched & rather decrepid
police-dog! You might with advantage kill the masters of J. B. but I
doubt if you can do that with economic theory. (J. B. is quite impervious
to any theory— you might as well talk sanscrit at him). However, I will
write you again in a day or two. This just to wish you un petit bonjour &
start in a mild way a correspondence!

Yrs.
W. Lewis.

121. Gloucester Terrace. Lancaster Gate. W.2.

"kill John Bull": Lewis wrote an article entitled, "Kill John Bull with Art" for
The Outlook 34 (18 July 1934): 74.

159. TLS–2.

4 Dec. [1936]   via Marsala
Dear W.L.   12/5

⟨1.⟩

WOTTER condition/ that pigfancyiny shit [Prime Minister]
baldwin!! and nobody with brains enough to see
A/ that the show follows the Kink's display of human sympathy
to the miners/

System of moneylenders control/ stupify the bloomink monarch/ ole
Geo[rge V]. tied up to that stuffed sofa/ [Queen] Mary/ and druv. to
boose/
Waaaal//
hizzery repeats/ or not.
Of course the buggarin Bish/ is fed on human flesh/ and it will ALL
help to confuse the public suckers.

and Mrs. S[impson]// of NO mortal interest. and not a trace of intellect
in the whose [sic] sickly ambience.

   pity he prob/ wont accept Baldwin's resignation. A hundred pities.
That wd/ be too much like the real thing.

⟨2.⟩

WD/ B/B/C/ broadcast Enemy of the Stars if you did a radio version/
      ONLY way the stage direction cd/ be effective. Wd/ you bother
with doing an AIR version of it.?

1.

Og well/ wotter subjekk fer a satirist who cd/ get to a printink press/
         The utter sadistic shit of the brit/ govt. and the way things
play into the hands of the extortioners.
              If only the bloke wd/ let Baldwin resign tho I
dont imagine Bald/ WOULD even if Ed[ward VIII]/ told him to go to
hell. But something ought to be done to use the generated heat to damage
pigfanciers and the starvers.
              that is the one outstanding point.
and will ANYbloodybody in Eng/ see it EXCEPT otto Neimeier
[Niemeyer].

         and his gangsters?

E

Kink's display: King Edward VIII had visited the "Depressed Areas" of industrial
   South Wales in November 1936 and urged improvements in living conditions
   for the miners.

buggarin Bish/ : The news of Edward VIII's intention to marry Mrs. Simpson became public when Dr. Blunt, bishop of Bradford, called on the king to be a
   better Christian. However, Pound may be referring to the archbishop of Canterbury, Cosmo Lang, who with Prime Minister Baldwin encouraged the king's
   abdication.

160. TLS–3.

Waaal ole SawBUKK
                    When a furriner looks at Baldwin's MOOG in dh'
wypers he SEES why you orter KILL J. Bull (and or Buhl)
This note is written in pure idleness/ between TEE/ruffic heaves/
        largely to enclose the enclosure/ recd/ coTemporeous with yr/
hnrd/ epistle.
            so as to estab// DATE. It refers to a Blast by the undersigned/
intended as opining GUN IF the very reverend episcopal ELYot will
print it.
            I trust it will (IF it passes the edtr/ the 'ed=eater, the deaditor)
do more good than harm or at any rate cheer the worthy and infastidiate
the opposers of light.

So 'appened I had Blarst; the two bound up tother day as a young wanted
to look at 'em I wanted to preserve 'em.

By no means a wasted effork/ I mean that heave/ IF you gaze on
miserable epigons and too=laters.

Also feel all this flow of conSquishousness Gertie/Jimmie [Gertrude Stein,
James Joyce] stuff has about FLOWED long enuff.

Time also the APES [Lewis's satire, *The Apes of God*] was seen out of
human contingencies
            time and place wherein written and konsidered OBjekTively.

Talkin' with local printer other day/ GOOD working linotype machine
secondhand/ no more trouble to work than this typewriter worth about
400 quid/ i;e; interest charges wd. be 20 quid a year/
        DAMN deluxe edtns/
[Go]d damn it one lives so long to learn so little.

Epigons OUGHT to have been setting up texts for years// increment of
association//
How far did babysinia [invasion of Abyssinia] wake J/B ?? if at all

"The Emperor of Abys/" and "the EX–king of Spain" [Alfonso XIII]
            notes of Britsch press locutions.
    The Emp/ referring to Halitosis Sale-arseis [Haile Selassie].
of Gore and Kensington Gore [possibly W. Ormsby-Gore, Conservative
statesman].

ex of Gore/ caressed of old lydies.
waaal/ tis to excaecate and cacchinate.

/// Curious to say/ Scrutiny for June seemed at this distance
BETTER than years ago/ know this bloke Denys Thompson?
And as you might say/ without expecting to annihilate ALL J/B's ///
a little more sirloin might be purloined from his bastardly
butcher shop.
by concerted action? or not?
"giver of reasonable satisfaction
to those who have moderate expectations".
There are times for lone hunt// times when two or more brains more
effective than one.
Re Econ/ one part of my job is DONE
on that front
and I suspect publik not ready for the other harf of it.
At any rate contemplating a bit of shindy in the Kulchurl depts
If a half squad of LIVING animals etc/etc.

Lets cop the poLICEman's elmet. or as you like it.
you see Young cumming's [e.e. cummings'] EIMI??
among the few real book[s] of the epotch. . .
sorry Crevel croaked
hisself . . . nice lad/ bettern most.
nuff o this.

y E
—
P

enclosure: This was probably the "Manifesto" Pound prepared in 1936 to urge
the continuance of the "renovation of writing" that began in the days of *BLAST*
and *The English Review* and its extension into social and political life. See
Stock, *Life of Ezra Pound*, pp. 340–41. (T. S. Eliot refused to print the "Manifesto" in *The Criterion*.)
Denys Thompson: One of the editors of *Scrutiny;* see his "The Robber Barons,"
Scrutiny 5 (June 1936): 2–12.

161. ALS–1.

Dear Ez. As you say, <u>far too real</u> for King to say Hop it! to his outrageous P. M. So His Majesty has been bundled out of England at 24 hours notice & in the winking of an eye his successor stuck up in his place, but the people should give expression to their bewildered displeasure! Such is "democracy", for which they are about to be asked to fight the wicked "dictators"!

Why dont you keep your eye on Mario Praz? Why do you allow that semitic coxcomb to infect a Fascist State & misinform the Wops re. British Litterchur! Fie!

Yours

<u>W.L.</u>

What was the name — & address— of that bloke I met in Barbary?

121. Gloucester Terrace. Lancaster Gate. W.2.

met in Barbary: During his visit to Morocco in 1931, Lewis met Paolo Zappa, an Italian journalist and Pound's friend.

162. TLS–1. [Via Marsala. 12–5. Rapallo].

15 Dec. [1936]

Waaal me deah wynDHAMN

What am I xxpeckted to do about one frousty li'l purrferrer in Liverpool/ [Mario Praz] asphixiated by Herb Read and Baby/crumby [Lascelles Abercrombie] and the rest of yr/ Island singbirds? Blighter dont do it HERE.

and as fer Monarchy/ wot the Dily Mile [*Daily Mail*] sez muss be protected.

sure you frame him/ and then you pack him in cotton woolll and send him off to Sasoon's [Sassoon's] friends the RotSchild's [Rothschild's]

so az anyt thing wot Sasoon has tippedd 'em off to BUY can now be blamed on EdVardus wot iz known to look on the cup and the coctail some frequent.

and Montague/ ague/ sheeny/ skinner Norman [governor of the Bank of England] settin on a camp stewel outside the door in the EX/R's [Ex-King's] sleepink car/ hopin Edwardus snores in morse code/ so as to tiddle the tiddleede.

oh/ my gorr wotter/a gummyment.

Wop press down on Wilkinson's story about spionage around Mrs Simpson/

    D[orothy]/ sends regards. ⟨&⟩ Hopes you will make a DRAWIN of the kike on the camp stool in the slopping car.

Paolo Zappa wuz the guy wot you met in the jungle.

The dictator bizniz wuz either in N.Y. herald or somewhere/ about Stan [Baldwin] bein quicker an slicker///
wotcher yer know abaht the gnu sovrink [George VI]??? 100% cotton rabbit or god's greatest joke on England since X.Kolumbus??

    WOT about a gnu bk/ by W. L. "Lies and Lives of English
                      statesmun now linin' [lying]"

E

the RotSchild's: After the abdication, Edward traveled by train to Schloss Enzes-
feld, near Vienna, where he was the guest of Baron Eugène de Rothschild.
Montagu Norman did not accompany Edward on the train's special sleeping
car. But Pound's addresses on Italian radio during the war show that he believed that both Norman and Victor Sassoon were members of a financial cabal
that forced Edward from the throne.

Wilkinson's story: Ellen Wilkinson, a Labour member of Parliament, accused
the pro-German group that gathered at Lady Astor's Cliveden estate of using
Mrs. Simpson to encourage Edward's favorable opinion of German foreign
policy.

163. TLS.–2. On stationery imprinted: A tax is not a share. A nation need not and should not pay rent for its own credit. 1937 anno XV. Via Marsala. 12–5. Rapallo.

II Maggio [May]

M' deah WynDHAMM
                    Nidwit seems to be a ACTIVE and useful job of work.
        my CompleMongs !!
Now, about this ruction in Sanctuary Buildings/ do you know anything I ought to?
            They got me on the cover of B[ritish]. U[nion]. Q[uarterly]., ["Demarcations," January/April 1937] but they aint answered my last. AND I dunno whether they have sent copies to them AZ needs 'em.
            And I wd/ like yr/ opHinYum. . as to whether which . . .
                ///
Is Lovat Fraser any use apart from printin yr scintillations ?? I am doing a fire box fer Faber/ on KULCHUR [*Guide to Kulchur*].
            BUT they dont seem to incline toward seereeyus ECO-Nomiks. I spose the termination is too keltiK? they think its O'Moike or zummat.

I want that last B.U.Q. article chucked about a bit. Nott is tied, no cash. AND so forth.
        You might notice the Monte dei Paschi [a bank, Siena, Italy; see Cantos 42–51] stuff. Nidwit seems to me more to the point than his precursors. Whether my heavy cart horse ploddin' can pull any more than it does, or get into larger circ/ I dunno.
        You better send Nidwit to GLOBE/ ⟨157–1/2 W. 5th St.⟩ of course St Paul, Minn is a long way from Lunnon/ and whether what they pay wd/ be any use to you/ and whether yr/ chat wd. do anything but rattle the simple furriners GorNoze.
            An ov course gorNOZe whether Faber will wanna spell Kulchur wiff a C/
            or refine my next opus. They done purrty well by me so far, and I have ter allow fer ubicity.
    //

Whether you can boost my drive fer DEFINING the bloody terms/
    waaaaal; havva think. Launcelot might get into quite a good stew
trying that instead of cross woidz.

Orthology a new detifrice [*sic*] or wottell.
waaal, hereZow and keep at it.

yrz   EZ

Nidwit: Launcelot Nidwit is a character in Lewis's *Count Your Dead: They Are
    Alive! or, A New War in the Making* (1937). Although it is a political tract on
    the Spanish civil war, *Count Your Dead* contains fictional dialogues between
    the politically naive Nidwit and Lewis's mouthpiece, Ned.
Sanctuary Buildings: Pound refers to the incident in March 1937 when Oswald
    Mosely fired over one hundred organizers of the British Union of Fascists, in-
    cluding John Angus MacNab, who edited the *Fascist Quarterly*. Together with
    John Beckett and William Joyce, MacNab formed the National Socialist
    League. Mosley's headquarters were at Sanctuary Buildings.
Lovat Fraser: Lovat Dickson, not the artist C. Lovat Fraser, published Lewis's
    Count Your Dead.

164. ALS–1.

May 22. 1937.

121. Gloucester Terrace. Lancaster Gate, W.2.

Dear Ezrorrrrr.   My Launcelot [Nidwit of *Count Your Dead*] will do no
good— dont you believe it! Dont you remember that in 1914 we tried to
do a spot of good in the picture & poetry line! Nothing alters here. —I
dont really know why I take the trouble to write these disinfectant
treatises.

    As to Sanctuary Buildings. Several of the prominent Mosleyites were
recently dismissed, & have started a little show of their own, called <u>Nat.
Socialist League</u>. Mosley goes on just the same but it may be that some of
the present personnel at Sanctuary are not so amenab[le] to Credit
Theory as MacNab, who was not such a bad boy. (I dont know them;
only O[swald].M[osley]. He is not personally responsible for occurrences
at Sanctuary).

    Enclosed letter in "Statesman" (May 21). <u>Did</u> you give apples an
ethical status? Were you thinking of the apple in the Garden of Eden?

Did you mistake barking for singing, or vice versa? If so, I think you should apologize.

Dont think I'll trouble about Minnesota. Too far off.

Macnab tells me I ought to get your book Jefferson & [/or] Mussolini. Shall do so.

Yrs

W.L.

letter in "Statesman": A letter by Arnold C. Taylor to the editor of *The New Statesman and Nation* 13 (22 May 1937): 845, criticizing Pound's translation of *Homage to Sextus Propertius:* "Mr. Pound translates 'māla' (apples) by 'sins' (măla), which makes nonsense and won't scan."

165. TLS–1.

RAPALLO (via Marsala 12/5)   23 Oct [1937]

Dear WynDAMN

His somnolences [T. S. Eliot] asks why HE dont hear from YOU. I have givv him opinyum with some more on his parasites.

AND I admit that the mere simultaneity of you N me in the same issue of B[ritish] U[nion] Q[uarterly] seems to have been enuff to disrupt Os[wald] Mos[ley's]' lil' party.

Causal sequence obscure, or possibly not// animal life, at least Brit. an/ life unable to sustain the tension in them altichoods.

Nevertheless better a guinea a page than sheer humanism and the Criterion pays that. HELL 25 years after the fact it ought to be by now time for the Criterion to enter into more etc/etc/ action. ⟨I mean without losing its club scriptions.⟩

IF it wd. be any use to you. at least say 40 quid a year use.

If Butchart:Macnab: young D[u]nc[a]n EVER get off the mark with their l(il [*sic*] pubctn. [*Townsman*] that might also if not serve at least bark.

ALSO if you send review copies and/or photos to

    Kitasono Katue

        1649 nishi 1 chome

                magome machi

    Omori   TOKIO

They will probably get reviewed or reproduced; more likely the former in VOU [ed. Kitasono Katue]. a vurry lively and simpatique rev/ in the sun rise.

Only group now blastin and bustin.

Entirely unconnected with any Japs whom I used to know in London or Paris/

wrote me on their own and have since been doing nicely.

Zappa by the way has at last got onto BANKS, as per my suggestion when he did his guns. La Stampa, 3 of the series have appeared. I spose no use sending you my Italian articles on econ/ vurry seereeyus.

anyhow here ZOW.

and IF the egregious Possum his firm or his underlings dont deliver to you my FIFTH DECAD within one week of yr/ receipt of this phone 'em s;v;p; and say why the hell haven't they.

yrz   EZ

⟨I have cited Count Dead in Revista Monetaria for June.⟩

same issue of BUQ: Pound's "Demarcations," *British Union Quarterly* 1 (January/April 1937): 35–40 and Lewis's " 'Left Wings' and C3 Mind," pp. 22–34.
Revista Monetaria: not listed in Gallup, *Ezra Pound: A Bibliography.* However, Pound had offprints prepared of his three articles in *Rassegna Monetaria* in 1937. See Gallup, pp. 314–15.

166. TLS–1. On stationery imprinted: Anno XVI. Via Marsala. 12–5. Rapallo, with the Gaudier-Brzeska profile of Pound.

4 Nov [1937]

Dear Wyndham

AZ I hav just got roun' to readin' yr "Heetlair" [Lewis' *Hitler,* 1931] strikes me mebbe you have not seen my "Jefferson and/or Muss[olini]"

IF not; I will have Butch[art] send you a copy, or you can drop him poscar/ to say I said so.

No use sending it to uncertain address & if you have already seen it.

NOW that mr Ward Price has got round to telling the stinking woild a
little of what we said in the decade before him.

I like the furst chap/ in yr/ nuvvle/ [*The Revenge for Love,* 1937]
damned form the nuvvle/ I have only got thru 3 chaps/ so will refrain
from goin orf half cocked re/ the rest. ⟨until I git on wiff it.⟩

Zappa turned loose in La Stampa/ on bankers of revolution. waaal; I
spose we both said something to him; yew in Afrikaaa an me here.

good lad

Zap/
Did I send you my "Holy City".?

yrz   EZ

"Holy City": Pound referred to *The Fifth Decad of Cantos XLII–LI* as his "Holy
City" because it told of beneficial financial and governmental reforms in seven-
teenth-century Siena. Pound subtitled this group of Cantos "Siena-Leopoldine
Reforms."

167. TLS–1. On stationery imprinted: Anno XVI. Via Marsala. 12–5.
Rapallo, with the Gaudier-Brzeska profile of Pound.

9 Dec/[1937]

Waaal; Soilent O'Moyle

EF I make mistakes fer want of guidance be it on
yr/ own head.
Editor of Purpose [A. Desmond Hawkins] wants me to review yr/ Memoirs [*Blasting and Bombardiering,* 1937]; but sez yr/ pubr/ is too stinking
mean to supply a rev/ copy.

ALSO I doubt my capacity to do it in less than a vol/ of equal length
and equal cheerfulness

I.E. ⟨cheerfulness⟩ fer the land part/

The mud (or fifth element) is beyond me. I.E. this refers to the red but
not bolshie/ or shd/ we say
the war front. I suppose really browner than red. Damn good.

Here is also a EYETALIAN magazene [*Broletto*] that wants to print news
of the few eng/ books that are worth mentioned [*sic*]. ⟨I am puttin a naval
man [Ubaldo degli Uberti] on to yr. Hitler.⟩

I find it costly to lend my copies to reviewers/ sometimes they come back/
BUT it is really the pubrs/ job to supply review copies/ can't be left to
the chance admirations of blokes like me who don't mind being the MAR-
KET sometimes, but care less to be the goat.

Why the hell was Doom of Yth/ wrindrawn, if it was withdrawn?

    ennyhaow, here'z fer CHRONOLOGY. and lemme know about En-
gland from time to time.

        I shall go on sending mss to Os/ Mos[ley] as he
seems to let R/Thom[son]/ [editor of the *British Union Quarterly*] print
'em and to take it straighter than the pink tea and Clapham contingent.

        I can NOT be expected to know what is suitable to yr/
locality/ not from here.

Cant you do a pixchoor of Cecil getting the piss prize [Nobel Prize, 1927,
for contributions to the League of Nations] at Nic[holas Murray] Butler's
banquet in Noo yukk//

    as figgers of fun; they need a little Rowlandson de nos jours.

              yrz   EZ

Soilent O'Moyle: Pound refers to Thomas Moore's song, "Silent, O Moyle! Be
    the Roar of Thy Water (Song of Fionnuala)."
(fifth element): See Canto 51, p. 250: "Fifth element; mud; said Napoleon."
EYETALIAN magazene: Pound enclosed a form letter from *Broletto, Periodico
    Mensile di Cultura e Turismo,* which requested review copies of Lewis's books.
    Pound added a note to the *Broletto* letter: "dare say 'Blasting and Bombadeer-
    ing' [sic] wd/ be a good start. or rather good for the next notice of W. L.'s work.
    yaas, ole top, action is gittin activ. EP."
Doom of Yth/: Lewis's analysis of the modern obsession with youthfulness, *The
    Doom of Youth,* was published by Chatto & Windus in 1932. It was withdrawn
    by the publisher when Alec Waugh threatened a libel suit over Lewis's remarks
    about Waugh's interest in schoolboys.
Clapham contingent: The Clapham Sect was a group of wealthy Evangelical re-
    formers who were concerned with many liberal and charitable reforms between
    1790 and 1835.

168. ALS–2.

Dec. 26 1937.

Dear Essror.   The compleemengs off the season!

Excuses for long delay in answering yours, but have been picture-making under great pressure, for a big picture-show (which has now come off, with much to-do and brou-haha)

and no time to eat or sleep, much less to write letters.

Many thanks for the Cantos [*The Fifth Decad*, 1937] which I have only just started reading. —You have been busy too, my Ezror! —As to what you say re. fascist-international, can do nothing about that, though think Brit. Government a lot of warts, and Mussolini he makes rings round them as a politician. But I am wearied of all politicians.

Publishers, they also give me a pain in the neck; and Mr. Jerrold, as a publisher, seems to me as bad as they make 'em, especially as he is a blasted "author" too. No use at all asking him for a copy of the book he published. I am not on such terms with the gentleman that I can ask him for anything, except for permission to kick him in the pants. I'm sorry, but he is a really excruciating bastardly coxcomb.

This hasty note is a reply of sorts, to yours now a month old. But I will write again in a week or two.

Yrs
W.L.

NOTE ADDRESS

| 29. A. Kensington Gardens Studios. |
| Notting Hill Gate. W. II. |

big picture-show: "Paintings and Drawings by Wyndham Lewis," Leicester Galleries (December 1937).

Mr. Jerrold: Douglas Jerrold was the editor for Lewis's *Blasting and Bombardiering* and insisted on being mentioned as an author in Lewis's autobiography. See Meyers, *The Enemy, A Biography of Wyndham Lewis*, p. 232.

169. TLS–1. On stationery imprinted: Anno XVII. Via Marsala. 12–5. Rapallo, with the Gaudier-Brzeska profile of Pound.

8 Dec [1938]

Dear W/L

      I havent forgotten the remaining fiver/ will send it when I have an INTAKE/ but lemme know whether it makes any dif/ whether you get it just before or just AFTER Jan Ist.

//

      More I think over that lot of yr/ early drawings the less I like the idea of them being wasted on the peerage etc/
D[orothy] will pick another of 'em' the EARLY ones, when she comes over somewhaere after April 5th.

      The Blue odalisque [Lewis's *Odalisque,* owned by Pound] is very satisfactory/
There are several more that I shd/ like to absorb IN TIME. ⟨with Mrs S[hakespear]. lot. the later "phase" is represented. & anyhow the early ones have associative val. for me that they wont have for the outer apes.⟩

/My daughter [Mary] wants a photo of me portrait/ will you send a dozen prints of it ⟨when convenient⟩, for which I will remit on receipt.

Also you might send me a list of CHEAP but clean hotels in Washington, N.Y. and even Boston/ and of people whom I might meet. I know NO-BODY in that b[loo]dy/ country.
But presence on spot MIGHT stop theft (disguised with flattery)

When are YOU going over? team work any use ? or better separate?

when

did you say you were going?

Does yr/spouse want EMBOSSED stamps ⟨vide. enc.⟩ (a spécialité, or only adhesives?)

      very few letters coming in, as have written none during stay in London.

Ez P

stay in London: After the death of Olivia Shakespear, Pound was in London in November and December 1938, when Lewis painted his portrait.

170. ALS—4.

Studio. A.
Kensington Gardens Studios.
29. Notting Hill Gate.
W. II. 						Dec. 17. 1938.

Dear Ezroar! I would have answered yours of Dec. 8 earlier but have
been submerged in flu germs—my wifes and then my own. Today I got
your registered letter with the welcome fiver. For the twenty you have
now so generously disbursed you can have either early or recent drawings.
When Dorothy arrives that can be settled. ⟨Or you can specify by letter
requirements.⟩

That is to say, if I am here: and that means if I am back. For long
before April 5ᵗʰ· I shall I hope be dropping over to the New World. —My
plans are these. The New York Exhibition opens in 5 months time. By
March 1. I should be ready to quit work. I shall then have a lot of paintings ready ⟨⟨& numberless drawings⟩⟩. My idea is to have the show in
New York, & to visit Boston, Chicago & so on, attempting to knock down
sitters here & there & to make "contacts." I should not mind being in
America for some months. So I may not be here in April, when Dorothy
is arriving. (How is she by the way? Much better I hope & not suffering
too much from Mediterranean cold.)

You say you are going to America too. That is I think an extremely
good idea. And let us have a little team-work by all means. As to hotels.
There is only one hotel to stop in in New York (if it is still there) and
that is the BREVOORT HOTEL (Fifth Avenue, corner of 2ⁿᵈ Street).
It is down-town, a stone's throw from Washington Square. At the back
of it is the Lafayette Hotel. ⟨good, too⟩ Both are French—the rooms large
and not expensive (probably 2 or 3 dollars a day). —You ask about
Washington D.C. There I stopped in the Mayflower Hotel. It is the most
expensive hotel in Washington but a small room is quite reasonably priced
& if you are seeing senators & people it is better to be stopping at a superb
hotel. I would give you a letter to Mrs Alice Roosevelt Longworth
("Teddie" Roosevelt's daughter). She is a great girl. Senator Borah is her
most intimate political friend —I interviewed him in the Foreign Relations
Committee bureau—and I think you would like him. —Boston hotel I
cant remember. I stopped for 2 or 3 weeks in a hotel in Cambridge (a
suburb of Boston, where the famous university of Harvard is situated).
From my windows (I was told later) I gazed into Eliot's sister's [Therese
Garrett Eliot] parlour. You would not desire to do this. But the hotel (the
name of which I could obtain—I have forgotten it) is good.

We should certainly synchronize our visits. You must arrange to stop there long enough to visit the various centres. I should contemplate if I were you a good long stay. However give me some idea when you are proposing to go.

As regards photos of portrait. I will send a dozen prints as soon as it is photographed: but that will not be until it [is] quite finished. There is still a little bit of thinking to be done about that. It has been greatly admired. ⟨It has aroused a quite unusual amount of approval.⟩ The peerage liked it better than any portrait of mine. The portcullises were also duly impressed. The Tomlins tittered approval. It is very good. But the problem remains. Here it is—

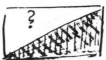

Perhaps the best solution is this

Anne my spouse thanks you very much for the beautiful stamps. The envelope in which they arrived was a philatelic masterpiece. Embossed as well as adhesives are greately welcomed. —The "Mr Bull' boycott is lifted; ⟨mysteriously lifted—by the mysterious Mr. Bulls newspapers.⟩ I was told today in the shops that it has been selling very well indeed. The Undertaker (as Lady Ott[oline Morrel]. called "poor Tom" [Eliot]) has been here to sit and I have done a lot of useful work on his face. His is going to be a very good portrait indeed. You will see it in New York, I hope. Spouse sends greetings,

Yours

W.L.

P.S. The Petition to the King (Coventry) people have got a shop immediately opposite to me in Notting Hill gate. [Th]ey are hooking in Christmas shoppers & getting them to sign.

P.P.S. Carlow says colour-blocks of O[livia]. S[hake-spear]. drawing of knitter is done. He is bringing it in, possibly tomorrow. Will send a pull. Better than photograph.

New York Exhibition: Lewis's painting *The Surrender of Barcelona* was being shown at the World's Fair in New York.

Alice Roosevelt Longworth: Lewis met her during his trip to America in November 1931.

portrait: Lewis painted Pound's portrait when Pound visited England after Olivia Shakespear died in 1938. It was finished in 1939 and is now in the Tate Gallery, London.

The peerage . . . The portcullises: "peerage" seems to be an allusion to Lord Carlow, and "portcullises" refers to Lewis's friends Hugh Gordon Porteus and Michael Cullis.

"Mr Bull": Lewis's *The Mysterious Mr. Bull* (1938) was an essay on the British character, especially as it affects English foreign policy. The "boycott" Lewis refers to is probably the lack of sufficient reviews of the book.

"poor Tom": Lewis was completing his portrait of T. S. Eliot.

Petition to the King: The National Unemployed Workers' Movement petitioned George VI for benefits for the unemployed during the Christmas season of 1938.

drawing of knitter: Lewis apparently confuses his drawing *Woman Knitting* with his *Girl Sewing;* the latter was owned by Olivia Shakespear.

171. TLS–1. On stationery imprinted: Anno XVII. Via Marsala. 12–5. Rapallo, with the Gaudier-Brzeska profile of Pound.

20 Dec [1938]

Waal

My instink IZ/ you let thet portraT ALONE. Az Jim Whistler said abaht shootink the artisk.

Ef you must diddle an MONKEY with problumbs you take a GNU canvasss or paper and you do a ABstrakk dEEsign about

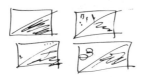

⟨until you git it fit to be lookd @⟩

but dont do piddlin round like Velasques/
three hosses hooves whaaar one orter be/ and Messin up the paint in that thaaar north west corner.

yrz. EZ

shootink the artisk: Whistler expressed his thoughts about the finishing of a painting in "Propositions—No. 2" in *The Gentle Art of Making Enemies,* p. 115. But I can find no instance of his expressing himself as violently as Pound's words would suggest.

hosses hooves: Velazquez reworked the paint of many of his canvases. Pound is referring to the *Equestrian Portrait of Philip IV* in the Museo del Prado, Madrid, Spain, which is mentioned among other Velazquez works in Canto 80 (p. 493).

172. TLS–1. On stationery imprinted: Anno XVII. Via Marsala. 12–5. Rapallo, with the Gaudier-Brzeska profile of Pound.

9 Jan [1939]

Dear Wyndham

What had YOU to do wiff the end of Criterion? Can any use be made of said END of an effort or uneffort?

Knocks me about 20 quid per annum/ but if it released any energy fer constructive labours etc// ⟨?⟩

At any rate I shd/ welcome any news IF you have it. whether YOU, me AND young Duncan altogether putt the kibosh on it. I dunno. He ⟨Possum⟩ said newt when I was IN London.

In fact was projecting continuance.
of course purse strings and Faber or ????? may have contracted.
got any dope ?

E

Criterion: The final issue of T. S. Eliot's journal *The Criterion* appeared in January 1939.

173. ANS–1. [Studio A. Kensington Garden Studios. 29 Notting Hill Gate. London, W. II.].

Jan 21 1939

Dear Essror!   Answer to your query to be found in enclosed cutting.

> **W. L.**

Thanking you for spouse for beautiful french & italian stamps. Your portrait greatly admired. Am attending to background: photos following shortly.

enclosed cutting: Missing from letter.

174. ALS–1. [Studio A. Kensington Garden Studios. 29 Notting Hill Gate. London, W. II.].

Feb. 20. 1939.

Dear ESSSROR.   Enclosed first notice I have seen of Laidlaws Gaudier [Laidlaw & Laidlaw Ltd. reissued Pound's *Gaudier-Brzeska*]. —Re. Laidlaw. I will not recount the vicissitudes of Roaring Q., but what in the end was agreed between Laidlaw & self was that he should publish all my utterances upon the Fine Arts, from Blast, Tyro etc. [*Wyndham Lewis the Artist, From 'Blast' to Burlington House,* 1939.] I have picked the best: also have written new pamphlet for him (entitled "Super-natural versus Super-real"). Caliphs Design had to be rewritten all through: Blast material taken off its stilts & resettled ETC. Laidlaw paid me £100 advance. I did not like to ask him more. (You warned me to temper my Wyndham to the shorn lamb). Laidlaw could put himself on the map here if he got known as an art-book publisher.

Re. Portrait Ez. P. The portrait is nearly finished. Within 8 or 10 days it will be photographed for Laidlaw's book. Also probably it will be colour photographed for a paper. (I will tell you more about this a little later.) There is a certain likelihood it will be bought for the Tate Gallery. It has been indicated by director as one of the pictures they wish bought. More next week, or when photographs of picture are ready.

> **W.L.**

shorn lamb: Lewis alludes to the proverbial saying, "God tempers the wind to the shorn lamb."

175. TLS–1. On stationery imprinted: Anno XVII. Via Marsala. 12–5. Rapallo, with the Gaudier-Brzeska profile of Pound.

2 Marzo [March 1939]

Deah wynDAM

   I hav bin TOLD that it is "necessary" to go FIRST CLAWSS to Amurika, if anything is to be accomplished. Waaal; wot have I got to SELL, that wd/ justify this eggspence?

Do you advise it. I shall go on Rex or something large / prefer 2nd. on colossus to capn's kaBIN on a small tub.

Purrvided they dont stik one 80 quid fer a foist.

    Tate Gallery Millbank/ UGH/uh
vurry nize IF.

    devMo
     yrz

⟨sig. chur fer use in Murka? or not.⟩

176. ALS–2. [Studio A. Kensington Garden Studios. 29 Notting Hill Gate. London, W. II.].

      March 10. 1939.

Dear Essror! Tonight by rotary photogravure your <u>image</u> will be stamped out one million eight hundred thousand times. I am to be sent (monday

I suppose) a dozen pulls for my private use. I will send you a few of these. —Your lawyers letter must have jolted Carlow but I am happy to say his esteem for me does not seem to have suffered in consequence: he has been away in Switzerland for a little, but a few days ago when I saw him I reminded him that the drawing of the woman knitting [*Girl Sewing*] should be sent back as arranged to you at Rapallo. He then told me about Shakespeare. —These rich, aristocratic, people, you know, are usually spoilt: but Carlow, although he has his weaknesses and blind spots (among which you figure so prominently, for he was very stupid not to acquire an important mss. of yours when he had the chance) is much better than most. Ever since last summer he has been extremely occupied with military affairs—he spends his time between his town-headquarters & airfield, air conferences & official dinners follow each other in quick succession): his civilian & cultural interests, his private-press, have gone by the board. Normally I do not think you would find him casual. Put it down to ARMS—and yet more arms!

The photograph (monochrome) of your drawing gives a poor idea of it. The collotype in colour Carlow has got is very good indeed. So far I only have one copy of that, and his only one. But as soon as I get an extra pull or two I will dispatch them, per registered post, between boards.

The World Fair (N. Y.) opens on April 30. I doubt if I shall be able to get there now before May 15, but I may make it sooner. As to whether it is worth your while to expend a first class fare to U. S. A. how can I say? It depends what you want to get there. If you go there with a fascist cockade you will git nothing, that is quite certain. On the other hand you would have a good deal of fun. If you would refrain from ramming Mussolini down his throat, you ought to establish useful connections with some publisher, and an editor or two. Why not pick up some money by lecturing to the Women's Clubs?

Yrs

W.L.

your image: The portrait was reproduced in *Picture Post* on 25 March 1939.
woman knitting: See note, *"drawing of knitter,"* to Letter 170.
The World Fair: Lewis's painting *The Surrender of Barcelona* was exhibited at the fair.

177. TLS–1. On stationery imprinted: Anno XVII. Via Marsala. 12–5. Rapallo, with the Gaudier-Brzeska profile of Pound.

12 Marzo [March 1939].

Dear W.L.

Buggar Carlow/ NO englishman is ever sufficiently evolved to stand civility. KICK the bastards in the jaw
FIRST.

Nothing but solicitor is any USE. The little squirt had MONTHS to get that drawing shifted.

They lie; they procrastinate/ =one must NEVER give way to ones natural instinct toward treating 'em as one wd/ human beings.
AFTER a good root in the jaw they sometimes behave.
//Waaal: I shall be glad to see the photos/ And az fer Murka/ I have something much more unpleasant / something that will rile 'em a lot more than Littoria or hackenKreuz/ I.E. and namely the CONSTITU-TION of the U. S. which they have never read.

I enc/ rev/ copy of my latest and briefest volume.

Ez. P

Of course if they thought I was coming to America to STAY
that wd/ rile 'em still WUSS

Buggar Carlow/: In a comment on this letter in his "Ezra Pound" (*Ezra Pound: A Collection of Essays,* ed. Peter Russell, p. 259), Lewis writes that it concerns "a young English bibliophile I had sent him in '38 to Rapallo. What happened I never knew: his letter contained the savage axiom: 'There's only one thing to do with an Englishman—kick him in the teeth.' His patience must have been sorely tried. . . ."
briefest volume: Introductory Text Book (3 pages), 1939.

178. TLS–1. On stationery imprinted: Anno XVII. Via Marsala. 12–5. Rapallo, with the Gaudier-Brzeska profile of Pound.

27 Marzo [March 1939]

Dear W/L   re/ enclosure

     Spit not upon the only young un that is capable of SEEING the difference between yr/ work and that of Brodsky.

Waaal/ yr/ copies of Pixchr/ Post aint come/

But I have sent one to Uncle George/ ⟨I'll tell him of course when I see him⟩ FER a reason/ in fact for TWO reasons. I must have you do some of that rough leonine stuff on him.

EZ

re/ enclosure: Missing from letter.
Uncle George: Pound was hoping that Congressman George Tinkham would commission a portrait ("rough leonine stuff") from Lewis.

179. TLS–2.

29a Kensington Gardens Studios,
Notting Hill Gate. W. II.

April 16. 1939.

Dear Ezz.   Help! Things have become like a madhouse here. I had been told that on the 20 April (next week) the Tate Committee would buy your portrait. I had fixed with the Director of Tate price and everything. Now the Committee, "owing to the crisis", is not to meet. Also, "because we may be at war next month", the Bond Street Gallery, where I was to have my show, will advance no money against sales. Everywhere it is the same thing; a complete paralysis. The shops even are not renewing their stocks (of needles and thread, blind-cords and whistling kettles) because they have to pay cash. If I could transport myself out of this madhouse I naturally would: but meanwhile merely to exist in it, I have to have a little money, and all the time I have put into pictures has been wasted. I am under these circ[umstance]s. ready to sell your portrait for a knock-down price: and if Dorothy (who I am told is here) would like to have a look at it, please let her know how things stand. – My poor old Ezz, we have fallen upon an evil time: whether war is imminent or not (and who can say how near it is, without being in the counsels of those who make the wars?) everything has at last come to a complete standstill in this country. —Carlow says he saw you in Rapallo: his best friend has just died.

Yours,

W.L.

180. TLS–2. On stationery imprinted: Anno XVII. Via Marsala. 12–5. Rapallo, with the Gaudier-Brzeska profile of Pound.

3 Aug[ust 1939]

Dear Wyndham

       I have burried pore ole Fordie in (of all places) the "XIXth Century and After" /

           only hole left. And an inadequate oration as they had room for "under 1500"

‧ and by the day after the day etc/

        an I think you cd make a beau geste and putt a penny on the ole man's other eye. No one else will.

       Kussed as he wuz in some ways/ when you think of Galsworthy's England etc/etc/

        and fer ten years before we arruv I spose he had NO one else to take the punishment from the frumpers//

          wuz again[st] the "mortisme" of our venbl. friend the Possum, and in short virtuous as these things in a world of Gosses, Royal Acc/ [Academy] etc.

He did NOT regard prose as mere syntax.
///
Have you seen Yeats Brown "European Jungle"/ good on jews and most of the Ital/ chapter/ also debunks, if needed, Spain.

----

and the Danzig pamphlet (Fuchs) is very good, calm; lucid and I shd/ think TOTALLY irrefutable.

Have you seen my "What is money for?"
>>2 pence/

Also any line on Wm Wiseman/ ex Brit. Information soivic [service] now Kuhn Loeb N.Y. / I spose you have had dozens of the enc.

Waaal; I am sorry you wuznt in Washntn/ and I hope you meet Uncl George [Tinkham] before he gits too tired of it awl. Nothing much else vurry PAINTABLE there/ though I can interjuice to the Polish damnbasdor/ Patocki. nice chap/ but got polish awt on th walls.

Why DONT you dig up Angold/ nearly as bad a corrispondent as you or Mons Eliot.

Daily paper in Grenwich [*Greenwich Time,* Greenwich, Connecticut], millionaire subub outside N.Yok open to Ez/ you might find it useful means of communicatin with some of the pubk/ if you go over/ or IF you want to print anything there. They favour a lit/ page by Ez/ but the financial pubbubblum!!!
>>also I onnerstan Barr (mod art mus/) iz lookin fer EARLY W.L. .. [Lewis's pre-World War I drawings].
>>damn I told you not to waste them drorinz. I might poifikly well have pinched the lot/ and sold 'em fer yr/ bean/y/fit. Blue gal/ [Lewis's *Odalisque*] reposin at my left. FULL of characteristics that wd/ prob/ distress you....

If you SEE Eliot, take a monkey wrench and find out WHAT the hell Morley [of Faber and Faber] means to do in N.Y. (IF anything save sink into the damnbience.)

There IZ also a lot of my econ/ writing available when young whatshisname gits bak/ I fergit wot you told me about Allen Unwin / or why the blighters never print me.

couple of young lads think them essays OUGHT to be available/ dunno if you can turn them ⟨the y[oung]. l[ads]⟩ onto any deaf ear ???

>>yrz
>>Ez

pore ole Fordie: See Pound's "Ford Madox (Hueffer) Ford; Obit," *Nineteenth Century and After* 126 (August 1939): 178–81.

Wm Wiseman: a British diplomat whom Pound believed to be the head of British Intelligence before he joined the New York banking firm of Kuhn, Loeb & Company.

enc.: Missing from letter, a prospectus for *What Is Money For?*

181. ALS–2. [Studio A. Kensington Gardens Studios. 29 Notting Hill Gate. London, W. II.].

Aug 10. 1939.

Dear Ez. I would willingly help you bury pore ole Fordie ("Fatty" as you used to call him) but 1 I know of no paper that would want an article about him, & 2 not having been a Fordie-fan or having been able to read more than 3 lines of any of his fiction, I should be extremely ignorant of my subject. Research would be necessary. I could (& would if I knew how) write a gossipy obit. He belonged to a happier & more cultivated age than this & should certainly be praised for having had the good sense to be born when he was.

The "Undertaker" as Lady Ottoline used to call him (you call him "Possum") I have not seen but will make it my business to do so and ascertain what the hell Faber's live wire [Frank Morely] means by running to New York. A healthy respect for bombs and ballyhoo is I suspect the answer. —How is it going to affect your relations with Faber & Faber?

I shall spend 2^d on your money pamphlet [*What Is Money For?*]. ⟨(Thanks for prospectus)⟩ Did you find Gods Own Country alive to the pernicious effects of Usury? Tinkham (Ev. Standard my informant) assaulted Roosevelt the other day. Would he like his portrait painted, did you ask him?

A friend of yours (Mr. Reid) has turned up. He's written rather a good book I think, about a small Canadian town. No publisher will do it here I should imagine because he speaks of little girls undoing little boys fly buttons. ⟨(Have offered to put him in touch [with] Hale.)=Trust he has [a hole punched in the letter obscures one or two words] with Pollinger).⟩ —He goes off next week.

I hope to get out of here very soon: will let you know when. What are you up to?

Yrs
W. L.

Missus thanks you heartily for stamps.

Tinkham . . . assaulted Roosevelt: Tinkham was a Republican congressman who criticized Roosevelt for being pro-British.

182. Telegram. [Pmk: Rapallo, 11 September 1939].

ADDRESS KING EDWARD HOTEL TORONTO CANADA MAIL ME ADVICES TINK-HAM ETCETERA ALSO NEWS POUND FAMILIES === LEWIS ====

183. TLS–6. [Via Marsala. 12–5].   Rapallo. 11 Sept. [1939]

Waaal me deah Wynddham

                    You do leave things till the ultimate moments.
As to how to deal with Uncle Jarge/ [Tinkham] he WUZ in Bastun on Aug.
24th. in which locality he is INvisible. If there is a special session of
CONgress he will be in Washntn/ and the way to him is to call at the
HOUSE office Building, first floor down the corridor/ to the leftish. one
of the FEW offices with two doors room 256 I think, but you better ask
the doorman.

You will there find Miss G. C. Hamelin anyhow, whom you shd/ treat
with deep courtesy/ the dark skin supposed to be due to Breton forebears/
as iz I believe the case. bright gal.

            Tell HER I said you were to paint Mr Tinkham's portrait and
that my ideas carry weight with you.

            As to how the pair of you are to PURRsuade the Tinkham.
I suggest indirect attack/ FIRST that EZ sez the job is to be done/
                                                                    2nd.
YOU got to live, but IF Unc. G. is elected president you suppose you can
sell the portrait even if he dont want it fer the family album.

Then there is his Buddha, and his tibetan fabrics/ that collection cd/ in-
spire yr/ interest/ a fourth century Bhuddist head etc//
[The following paragraph is typed in red.]
OR you cd/ say/ see here Mr. T/ you have been in CONgress 26 years/
the TENTH district will certainly hang a portrait of you/ do you want the
fate of Prexy Stryker (late president of Hamilton college) whose portrait
was executed; or guillotined post mortem from a fotograf by a austrian
lady portrait picturialist.

And "in any case, damn it sir, I think you shd/ be painted/ having seen
you, I agree wiff me ole friend Ez/ who has frequently been RIGHT
during the last 30 years of our acquaintaince.["]

You neednt be backward in saying that I want him to run fer president/
that his job gettin rid of prohibition and keeping the U.S. out of the stinking league of stinkin nations deserves some notice.

I admit it may have been impractical for him to have run for vice presi-
dency with Borah LAST time/ but it WOULD have got him into the
public eye/

            waaal, mebbe he has done better.

Of the men he interjuiced me to my pick is [Senator] Bridges/
if he (Tinkham) damn well WONT stir his stumps/

But I shd/ like to know what the hell IF ANYTHING
Bridges knows about money and the monetary history of
the U. S. A. ⟨ask Unc. G. that. it will keep the conversation going while
he sizes you up. you cd. tell him THAT also. It might draw a smile.⟩
Also America is damn well to keep out of the war/

[The following paragraph is typed in red.] BAD enough to have european
aryans murdering each other fer the sake of Willie Wieseman [Wiseman]
and a few buggarin' kikes.

Keep in mind that Unc. G. is male 100% / dont try to conceal anything
from his valid eye. He will know you want to paint him fer money, but if
you take a risk; and "hope" he will want it when finished etc/
    Besides the 10th district ⟨Be precise in these matters.⟩ should buy it
if he dont. something above level of usual senators portraits, as deserved
by a man above the level of 'em. And DONT try calling him senator. he
is a M/C/ [member of Congress].
                                    who cd/ have run for the senate and
didn't.
        I mean dont try little arts.

He is one [of] a dozen men who KNOW something. It don't happen to
cover Matisse and co/ or Rilke and P. Valery
    but what he sees he sees straight.

Use FACTS when you have 'em, and dont budge on THEM: but where he
has the goods, no use argifyin'.

He knows it is gold against Hitler.

    Now fer marginalia/ you better see Jas. Laughlin/ ⟨J. Laughlin.
New Directions. Norfolk. Conn. visible in Boston or N. Y.⟩ Pittsburg steel
is in the back ground/ his ma and especially aunt need portraits/
                                                        he and
Johnnie Slocum need portraits/
                        in fact where the lesser lights of letters
have not trod YET; there might be sales. Let young Ja[me]s [Laughlin]

guide you. (he is a penny-pincher; but no objection to getting you money.
I mean he is by NATURE barnZo [born so], an observer of ha'pence/
but wd/ motor you all across new england.
//
Another POSSIBLE avenue, but uncertain is Roderic Don O Connor who
has written a few stories fer I think the Sat Ev Post and is in touch with
money. Wife a sort of adopted daughter of the late Col. House ⟨he is "in
Wall St."⟩
                 he is with G. H. Walker and Co. 1 Wall St you cd/ phone him.
                       Say, I think, frankly, that you want to
paint GOOD portraits/
                              He is lonesome; no one to play with in between
stocks and bonds and the goodlife//
Likes to talk theology with the head of Jesuits/ etc. WANTS intellectual
conversation, and got me about the best I found in the U. S.
                       I mean he SAID he would and meant to and did.
Say I am sorry not to have seen Batchelor again/ and that I enjoyed
father Murphy, and Millar. the latter as good a mind as you need/
I spose Millar will be painted by some cawflik/ but a good
subject. head of Fordham Univ.
In fact you ought to paint him. There['s] some composition
in that head.
                 several old papal bokos that cd/ be suggested. Tell Don you
wd. like to meet Millar as I said he was a subject suited to yr/ vigorous
style.
Yr/ portrait of me being in Tate [Gallery] might weigh/ with his circle.
        Tinkham wd/ think it proper/
                                   young Jas. wd. know that it
dont d/n well matter & that the Brit. Acad/ and Galleries are full of
crap.
                       all this is rudimentary Baedeker, but may save you
time.
e/e/cummings' address is 4 Patchin Place/ N.Y. he is the one writer in
America whose mind is active. ⟨apart from Overholser "Hist. of money"⟩
You better accept him as the autochthonous comrad. One MUST distinguish the grades in the gerarchia.

He is a painter/ also. Damn it I dont know enough about his painting.
        It probably OUGHT to be in the Museum of Modern Art. IF he
wangles you in, you shd/ reply in kind. ⟨& get him in .⟩ You cd/ also sell

'em some of MY Gaudier drawings. The MORE they get the more they are likely to get.

You and Gaudier are the two hartisks whom they cd/ get FIRST, I mean before the european grafters and collikters have taken the pick of the swag.

cummings will do a lick of work for me/ and he is O.K. he wont undercut you/ in short as Zeus remarked of Odysseus... dont high hat him.

Then there is Baldy Bacon; 80 Maiden Lane.

dont go foolin round with Mrs B/ in fact you keep yr/ eye on paint. If the republicans win and the crisis passes, the old New England habit of family portraits might REVIVE and baldy bee in on it. ⟨That ass Quade might also fall.⟩

In washington the Capital [Capitol] Daily may awake/ look for H. H. Stansbury. a live journalist/ also Bargeron, at the press club.

I don't know what you wd. make of the Miss[es] Mapel 3301 P. St. they might putt you next to some sitters. and remember that gawd and the angels wd/ NOT impress Miss Ida and Adah Lee is perfectly c[ap]able of continun' to sip her tea quietly in the midst of a earth quake. The folk in the Congressional Library are not negligible/ Old Putnam has gone: and Arch MacLeish now head. you never went in for orient; but there is a japanese female Dr Sakanishi, head of jap dept, and VERY much on the spot. You wd. have to draw in yr/ hauteur re/ the orient. and take an interest in my views or her views. But a portrait of the Jap ambassador wd. be publicity   also a different line composition from some of yr/ setters an pigeons. and of course there is Borah whom you have met. But NOT until after you have done Uncl. George. If you dont do him ⟨Jarge⟩ first you will never get the chance. and there is only one Uncle George (Holden Tinkham) memorize the full name. and treat Miss H[olden, Tink-ham's niece]. with due deference which she will presumably return./

She is constructive/ you tell her a portrait of Unc G/ will be good publicity for HIM and not commit him to any set of opinions/ she will understand any-thing you say to her/ you won't have to grope around in a fog. ⟨⟨I have but she can't remember everything and there are 1/2 million elections⟩⟩

then there are licherary circles/ Marianne Moore 260 Cumberland St. Brooklyn, N. Y. via the underground.

[The following paragraph is typed in red.] You better do a build up of EZ/

on ground that I am their most distinguished writer and they OUGHT bloodydamnwell to DO something about it.

such as print me promptly/ NOT let London do it first. etc.

Whether Watson wants his picxcschoor too I dunno. ask Marianne

she is apt to think Watson has sacrificed all fer licherchoor. etc. you cd. find out if he is, or is not, still opulent.

any idea that he shd/ come to life again, she regards as a reach fer his pocket book. sfar as I know he died when the Dial did.

　　　no reason ⟨for him⟩ to stay dead unless he is stony dead broke. ⟨Marianne's ma reads the bible & they arent YET anti semite.⟩

yrz

EZ

That ass Quade: A friend of Francis S. (Baldy) Bacon who also struggled for suc- cess in the business world; see Canto 12, p. 54: ". . . Mons Quade who wore a monocle on a wide sable ribbon."

184. TLS–4. On stationery imprinted: Anno XVIII. Via Marsala. 12–5. Rapallo, with the Gaudier-Brzeska profile of Pound.

7/8 Feb [1940]

Dear Wyndham

　　　Am wonderin' whether yr/ Hitlerism [*The Hitler Cult,* 1939] was done 89% to get yr/ boat fare OUT of judaea? Am about half way thru 4;; of course you couldn't have printed or been paid for the truth about the war. War for usury, for gold monopoly/ for unutter- able stink/ with the poor bdy/ brit/ told he is fightin fer the rose covered cottage and tennis on Sat. p;M.

Rothschild/ vengeance running for 150 years/ Sas/ bloody/ shitten soon [Sassoon]; silver, and mass murder in China/ the cunt of all arseholes Mond being nickel; the Times; Hamboro/ Manshitster Stinkereen/ [newspapers]/ 60% interest; god save and so forth.

I can't honestly think that objection to this is necessarily ridiculous; unless any resistence to heavy odds is ridiculous. Also the German pavillion at the bloody biennale [the Venice Biennale Exhibition] was better than the shit in other pavilions, merely made for sale. You will be gatherin' the Hitlerism aint my favoureet among yr products. Also shows signs of yr/ reading the Britsch press which CAN NOT be good for even as strong a stummik as yourn NOT if ingurgitated over a 40 year period. The mond sasoon rothschild set up is cert/ worse than anything you have adduced vs/ Adolph. and, on the interlexchul plane, I begin to doubt that the yidd/ fluence has ever been anything but a stinking curse to Europe. ⟨from A.D. 1 to 1940. entirely apart from grease & bokos.⟩

One gets that way watching the various inflows from Athens, from roman law etc. as mixed up with the dirty old stinking testament in mediaeval writers before a wop named Galieleo [Galileo], and the XV century, largely wop, got us out the damnblasted bog.
In fact I object as much to semitism IN matters of mind as in matters of commerce? and god knows the earth stank with mercantilism in our young days. needed a nice big platitude to being [sic] a li'l daylight into the then matter of course acceptance of Pierous Morgan's dominion.

Proust and Freud are unmitigated shit/ they pass for intelligentzia because their shit is laid out in most elaborate arabesques; the ideas which they have swiped; from Galdos or H. James or wherever.

A good socking platitude in the jaw may be a perfectly good way of clearing off a lot of this sewage. Admitting that Goring [Goering] has possibly thrown out ten good paintings for every 99999999 Brodskys etc.

The art dealers stock in chew galleries of the past 40 years (or 30, so as to keep it in one's own immediate experience) has been 85% pewk; and never there for its merits when good.

Havin', as you know, plugged for latin clarity and the mediterannean ambience I am not going to tell the world about what happens north of the alps; apart from some lucid and coherent argument, and the Geheimrat Frobenius who was a man and a brother. I can't agree that all huns are comics, as seen by the british bombadeer.

And of course the idea of stranglin' 80 million, and yr/ tenderness for the unspeakable god damn rhoosians (there YOU are the sentimentalist) don't ring yr/ old kumrad's bell; not fer nutz.

Certainly HERE ⟨Italy⟩ is more freedom to print than under the shitten arse of the Times in London/ and more goddam chance for any man who wants to paint or carve anything of ANY merit (and a lot merely medi-ocre) than under the dirty behind of Selfridge. wherewith my benedictions.

yrz

[letter begins again]

Say the best fancy writer here is Malaparte/ YES, they took away his badge, and sent him off to think in the Confino/ but LET HIM go on writing newspaper articles from villiagature, and have now set him up with a big fancy magazine to talk about Breton and Elouard [Eluard].

much less fancy damn wiliness needed than when you are up against a mere vacuum cleaner for extracting 7/6 a shot from the Brits.

and I suppose the pooplishink woild in america is NOT above that of henkland.

Damn'd if I know anything seriously writ in search of truth that can't be published here. e. e. cummings's dirge went onto first page.

don't you go and fall for nickle plus and filagree in yr/ ripe and bloom-soming years.

and respex to the missus

Page II8, you've got nothing on Adolph. England has come about because the "elite" has so often been licked, no sphincter muscle/ the Cobbetts dont win/ BUT it ⟨explanation⟩ is O.K. as definition of the American revolution/ an elite/ betrayed/ comes to/ in fact three successive revolu-tions of the good guys, and then final betrayal, from which it hasn't yet recovered. debt created by civil war/ used to control nat/ currency.

evn ole Crumpwell [Oliver Cromwell] rebelling aginst sheer theft by the kinks [Charles I's] amorality can be just as brainless as ethics.

HAW HAW HAW/ as to the applesauce on p. I57/ this British charm etc/ nuts/ the average Englander of the kind I have met is a fat headed boor in comparison with the sort of Italian I have been meeting for the past I6 years.

tennis court for tennis court and all that. Part III chap 4 shows the orful result of yr/ readink britisch papers and not living on the continent, and nearer the balkans. / folk lore/ YOUR folk lore, out of the Irish plays. . . .

As to America's not making or knowing what to m/ of Eng/ again HAW! ⟨(I see by the U.S. paper that sour puss Hutton has a chob.)⟩ again HAW!! I found most of the blokes in Washington perfectly onto the Brit. govt. and

its comic propaganda// The minority of Americans who read ANY history can't do it without finding 170 years of god damned lies, bank buggars etc/ they either play with 'em or agin 'em, but they are
o   n   ON.

coOperative Me ARSE!! you hide from monetary question for the whole book/ O.K. only way to be printed in a usuriocracy with Astor at the top/ BUT this federation poop is just the same old Bank of Basil/ [Zaharoff] secret committee of shit, bleeding the world thru a money system///   it is NO go.
god damn it have you got down to Wells' level??

an uncontrolled secret committee of bank poops, calling itself the lag of nations or federal onion or NUTZ!!!

as to yr/ utopia/ nationalize profits on gold exchange/ nickel exc/ and silver exc//// The bare thought of it wd. take England out of the war. It is war for money lending and a few metal monopolies. Can you print that? Why all this slap stick about Adolf. . . ? wot you need is a bit of economic background.
Blessings on yr muzzy ole top

yrz   EZ

cummings's dirge: In *E. E. Cummings: A Bibliography*, George Firmage lists the publication of "Dirge" in the American magazine *Furioso* (Summer 1939) but not in any Italian publication. Pound quoted the poem in his *Carta da Visita*, which was published in Rome in 1942.

Page 118: of Lewis's *The Hitler Cult* (1939). Lewis cites a passage from *Mein Kampf* "in which 'the nation' is simplified for us, by Herr Hitler, into classes of good, bad, and indifferent citizens."

applesauce on p. 157/: of *The Hitler Cult,* in which Lewis claims for the French and English "advantages derived from our superior social charm and gentlemanliness."

185. TLS–1. On stationery imprinted: Anno XVIII. Via Marsala. 12–5. Rapallo, with the Gaudier-Brzeska profile of Pound.

8 Feb [1940]

Dear W/

Later post sets me off again/ Considering how bloodily bothered you are for money/ why the hell dont it occur to you that the lousy jews who run yr/ fahrt of an empire steal 7 bob to the quid from a mans royalties/ naturally loathing the idea that one shd/ produce literature in a language not yittisch/

Waaal it was a scotch louse [William Paterson] that started the bank/ and didnt profit/ and the brits are as bad as the yitts when it comes to theft and oppression/

so keep it economic.

But if any british buggar asks you WHY his farht of a govt. ought to be replaced by something clean/ tell him the tax system and the 60% steal of the public purchasing power for the benefit of lice.

I see by a press par/ that "sour puss Hutton" is said to be running the Intelligence (!!!) service for Eng/ in the U.S.

my KyRist/ do they think that face will elicit confidence.

This is no news, I have just read it in a month old U.S. paper.
I forget whether you have had the enclosed.?

I shd/ like to get it clearly into yr/ mind that British taxes go, (must be 80%) into the pockets of shits/ largely Mond, Astor Sasoon [Sassoon] and Rothschild and the buggars on the gold exchange.

in yr/ book on Germany you say nothing about the lousy britich DEELIGHT in paying taxes/ sheer masochism.

yrz   E Z

the enclosed.?: Missing from letter.

Part IV
Remembering
1946-1957

The scientists are in terror
 and the European mind stops
Wyndham Lewis chose blindness
 rather than have his mind stop.

Canto CXV/p. 794

Remembering 1946–1957

When Lewis returned to England after the war, he returned not only to his old debts and problems but also to a country where it was more difficult than ever to survive as an independent writer and painter. Yet he regained his reputation as a painter with a successful exhibition in 1949 and established himself as a lively and wide-ranging art critic for *The Listener* between 1946 and 1951. He wrote eight major books between 1948 and the year of his death in 1957, including his great autobiographical novel *Self Condemned* (1954) and his visionary fiction *The Human Age* (1955). These achievements were made in spite of the medical problems which continued from the thirties and the new affliction of a tumor that progressively damaged his sight until by 1951 he was blind. He did not "choose" blindness, as Pound writes in "From Canto CXV," but a removal of the tumor would have risked brain damage.

Pound's life in these years was just as creative as Lewis's and still more difficult because he was arrested in Italy after the war and accused of treason on the basis of the broadcasts he made on Italian radio. When he was judged mentally unfit to stand trial, he was imprisoned in St. Elizabeths Hospital for the criminally insane. He was to remain there until 1958, still producing polemics, translations, and Cantos, but acutely conscious of his status as (in his own words) a "jailed lunatic." Lewis and Pound resumed correspondence through T. S. Eliot. Pound sent the following message to Eliot, which Eliot then passed on to Lewis:

> Now as to ole Wyndham, whose address I have not, to thee & him these presents. While I yet cohere, he once sd/ a facefull, & apart from 3 dead & one aged arcivescovo who gave me 3 useful hints, ole W. is my only critic—you have euologized and some minor have analysis'd or dissected— all of which please tell the old ruffian if you can unearth him.

The four critics of Pound who are ranked with Lewis are probably Ford Madox Ford, Thomas Hardy, W. B. Yeats, and an Italian archbishop who once told Pound that he should not pursue too many ideas in the same article. Lewis could not have guessed the identity of his critical peers, but Pound's continued respect and affection for him was clear. Eliot sent Pound's comments to Lewis, who replied:

I will of course write to him at once. I am not very good at deciphering his
impulsive and temperamental script, but I believe I detected a note of humility
in one place. A bad sign I am afraid: although otherwise he seems much as
usual. There is one thing—probably he feeds better than we do, and it will be
part of the duties of the attendant psychiatrists to read all his Cantos and to
encourage him to discuss them.

Pound, of course, had no respect for those he called the "pussy-
KiKeatrists." It would be pleasant to think of Pound at St. Elizabeths
always out on the lawn and under the chestnut trees of the hospital
grounds entertaining his friends. But such occasions were rare compared
to the usual routine of hours in confined and noisy conditions with constant intrusions from the medical staff and the truly insane patients of his
ward. It was once again necessary, as it was when he moved to Rapallo,
to write voluminous letters to break through his isolation. In an echo of
Remy de Gourmont's phrase about the only pleasure of a writer, he said
that his letters were the "seul plaisir etc. of the jugged." (Letter 197) He
wrote to D. D. Paige, the editor of his *Selected Letters:* "Gtst difficulty is
to get people to write me enough letters to keep me aware of life outside
the walls." Even this pleasure, however, was spoiled by his consciousness
that the prison authorities were reading his correspondence. His wife
Dorothy, who was living under difficult conditions in a foreign country to
care for her husband, once wrote Lewis in 1947 that Pound did "not care
for too-lucid letters to go out through psychiatrists." The problem was
solved when Dorothy Pound took the letters out of the hospital and
mailed them herself. Many of the letters sent out under this system were
merely strips of typing paper without date or signature. Pound did not
want it known, however impossible this was for so voluminous a correspondent, that he was sending letters from the hospital. He thought of
himself as a "strictly anonymous" person (like the "no man" of the
Cantos) who was deprived of his rights as a citizen, and it is for this
reason that during this period he rarely signed his letters.

   Pound wrote to a friend early in 1946 that "I can't hold two sides of an
idea together but can live on memory if someone BRINGS it." Lewis was
scarcely an ideal, nor even a very sympathetic, correspondent for someone
in Pound's circumstances. He had once described Pound as "Man in Love
with the Past," thinking of his love for the classics and the Troubadours.
Now Pound was trying to revive in Lewis a more recent past, or what he
called in Letter 146 the "antient sperit of BLAST." In Letter 236 he asks
Lewis what he meant by a phrase Lewis had written forty years before in
BLAST, no. 2, and jokes that the question was meant "just to annoy yu

by retrospect." Yet they were both inevitably drawn to the past. One of
the first subjects of the following correspondence is a reminiscence of
Pound's early years in England that Lewis was writing for his autobiography of 1950, *Rude Assignment*. Soon after there are letters concerning
articles Lewis was writing for tributes to Eliot and Pound. Lewis considered it "Very difficult and unsatisfactory writing like this about contemp[orarie]s." (Letter 201)

Lewis felt that the best way to help Pound was to praise him as a poet
and man of letters. When he spoke to a group of Pound's British support-
ers in 1948, he argued that they should not attempt to justify his Italian
radio broadcasts: "For those . . . who are *not* passionate ideologists,
Ezra Pound's verse will *by itself* be sufficient to win their support for his
release." Pursuing this hope, he published three essays on Pound that the
poet himself liked so well that he wanted to publish them as a volume. He
also helped to convince Eliot to publish Paige's edition of Pound's letters
and hoped that their *"exuberance* would both amuse and endear." Yet the
public abuse of Pound that occurred when he won the Bollingen Prize of
the Library of Congress for the *Pisan Cantos* seemed to show that his
growing reputation as a poet might just as likely hurt his chances for a
pardon or a release. Lewis grew still more discouraged when he saw that
Pound in his letters continued to be obsessed with political and economic
themes. He concluded a letter about this problem to an American friend:
"I hope that Thomas Eliot will pray for him, for I dont know what to do
and thats a fact."

It was not only Pound's political hectoring that disturbed Lewis. He
was at times a reluctant correspondent simply because he could not respond to Pound's demands nor even at times understand his letters. Some
of Pound's letters are detailed notes on Lewis's works, such as Letter 225
on Lewis's volume of literary criticism, *The Writer and the Absolute.*
Pound's comments are so detailed that one needs to have the passage he is
criticizing open before one. Lewis admired Pound as a "pedagogic volcano," but he was now in his seventies and in no mood to take lessons.
In addition to such letters (or lectures) as no. 225, Pound sent Lewis what
he called "detailed notes" on *Rude Assignment* and Lewis's work of 1939,
The Hitler Cult, which Lewis simply ignored. Lewis could not, in any case,
have read these lengthy notes because he was blind. They were sent to
Agnes Bedford, a former close friend of both Pound and Lewis who had
now devoted her life to helping Lewis in his blindness. In a letter to Bedford in May 1951, Pound told her that he regretted being out of touch
with Lewis for so long and that he still hoped to claim him as an ally in his

economic and cultural crusades: "Had to leave Sodom in the 1920's/ but possibly cd/ hv/ maintained closer connections. However, no retrospects/ its whaaar do we go frum here?" But in this hope Pound was disappointed; he wrote to Bedford in July 1951: "Naturally difficult to direct W. L.'s thought to useful channels, or even find if yu hv/ read him the notes on Ru[de]/ Ass[ignmen]t/ and got any scintillas."

Lewis was not the only correspondent to complain of Pound's obscurity. Eliot, for example, told Pound that he was baffled by his references to strangers and unknown authors. Yet even when Pound's letters are annoying or offensive they can be witty and memorable. Pound resembles James Joyce in the way he verbally transforms everything he writes about into something that will fit into his own private universe. (A symptom of this tendency is the way he assumes that everyone will know whom he is talking about when he refers to personal friends by their first names or historical figures as if they were contemporaries.) Anyone who deeply interests Pound will be rechristened and so bear the mark of Pound's judgment upon him. Eliot of course is "Possum," Lewis is "Wyn-DAMN" or the "Vort," William Carlos Williams is "Dear Bull," or "W. the Walruss," and E. E. Cummings is "Kumrad Kumminz." These are some of Pound's heroes, but of course the villains are renamed as well: "Ooozenstink" is F. D. Roosevelt, "Weenie" is Winston Churchill, the "Rot-Schilds" are the Rothschild family, and "Nick Smutty Butter" is the former president of Columbia University, Nicholas Murray Butler. Renamed, Pound's friends and foes play out their parts in the "Pound Era."

Pound's leaps among levels of diction also reveal the vitality and the contradictions in his character. In Letter 220, for example, he scolds Lewis on the faults of *The Writer and the Absolute:*

> No use dragging in ethics as a world that tolerates Edens and Churchills s'en fiche pas mal de that sort of impedimenta. Without which it rots stinks putrifies etc. BUT on the plane of intellect, however much a swine, a plootbaloon puffed up by Weenie, and dont blame Weenie, think how tempting it wd/ hv/ been to Iago such a bag of foul air (privileged etc. re/ Owen Wistar's "Philosophy Four". he wuz WEAK in the head.

In this passage formal words such as "ethics," "tolerates," and "impedimenta" govern the colloquial expressions "dragging in" and "s'en fiche pas mal." The latter phrase in French, however, makes the colloquialness a curiously learned one. The same mixture of formality and casualness, and of high and low culture, is seen in the allusion to both Shakespeare's *Othello* and Owen Wister's racist short story "Philosophy Four." It is the cultured, expansive style of a man who is at least trying to make his learning vital and available. The vitality is unquestionable, but the availability is damaged by the multi-directional flow of Pound's thought. In this case it seems that the sentence which begins "BUT" is finally completed by the one beginning "he wuz." The "he" is uncapitalized to show it completes the main statement, yet it stands as a separate sentence as well to emphasize his judgment on Anthony Eden, whom Pound argues did not have the natural sense of ethics or philosophy that the Yankee students had in Wister's "Philosophy Four." When this statement finally completes the "BUT" clause, the meaning is that Eden is not so much immoral as stupid and empty ("a ploot-baloon"). One does not often wish to pause long enough to analyze a passage in detail, but the play of ideas and images is constantly arresting.

Lewis described Pound in 1915 as a "demon pantechnicon driver, busy with removal of old world into new quarters." He is still that in these last letters, but the moving van is now careening out of control. We do not read these letters to see what "new quarters" Pound will discover, for he has nowhere to go, but for the interest and excitement of the journey.

"*jailed lunatic*": Pound uses this phrase in a letter to Stella Bowen, 6 September [1947]; Beinecke Library, Yale University.

four critics: See Stock, *The Life of Ezra Pound*, p. 367.

"*old ruffian*": Ezra Pound to T. S. Eliot, April 1946; Olin Library, Cornell University.

"*attendant psychiatrists*": *The Letters of Wyndham Lewis*, ed. W. K. Rose, p. 394.

"*outside the walls*": quoted in C. David Heymann, *Ezra Pound: The Last Rower* p. 206.

"*too-lucid letters*": Dorothy Pound to Lewis, 1 May 1947; Olin Library, Cornell University.

"*thats a fact*": *The Letters of Wyndham Lewis*, ed. Rose, p. 476.

"*Love with the Past*": the title of Chapter XV, Book I, of Lewis's *Time and Western Man*.

"*amuse and endear*": *The Letters of Wyndham Lewis*, ed. Rose, p. 473.

"*someone BRINGS it*": quoted in Heymann, p. 206.

"*support for his release*": Lewis, "Introduction to Peter Russell's Reading of the *Cantos* (Poetry Society, 1948)" [Draft and Notes]; Olin Library, Cornell University.

as a volume: Only Lewis's "Ezra Pound" was published, however, in an Italian translation by Mary de Rachewiltz: *Ezra Pound: Un Saggio E Tre Disegni* (Milan, 1958).

to take lessons: the phrase "pedagogic volcano" is used by Lewis in "The Rock Drill," in *Ezra Pound: Perspectives,* ed. Stock, p. 198.

"*any scintillas*": These two passages from Pound's letters to Agnes Bedford are quoted in Appendix III of Toby Forshay's edition of Lewis's *Rude Assignment* (Santa Barbara: Black Sparrow Press, 1984), pp. 263–64. Appendix III (ed. Bryant Knox) contains nineteen pages of Pound's detailed notes on *Rude Assignment.* Six pages of Pound's notes on Lewis's *The Hitler Cult* are published in Black Sparrow's BLAST 3, ed. Seamus Cooney, pp. 183–96. There are seventeen more pages of Pound's notes on *The Hitler Cult,* as well as two pages on *The Writer and the Absolute,* in the Lewis collection at the Olin Library, Cornell University.

unknown authors: T. S. Eliot to Ezra Pound, 11 August 1956; Beinecke Library, Yale University.

"Pound Era": Pound's own phrase in 1922; see Stock, *The Life of Ezra Pound,* pp. 246–47.

"stinks putrifies etc.": This phrase is an allusion to Lewis's "The Code of a Herdsman," which he published in *The Little Review* IV (July 1917): 5: "matter that has not sufficient mind to permeate it grows, as you know, gangreous and rotten."

"new quarters": BLAST, no. 2 (July 1915): 82.

186. TLS–2.

Studio A.
Kensington Gardens Studios,
29 Notting Hill Gate,
London. W.11.

July. 1946.

My dear old Ezra.　How are you, and what are you doing with yourself? T.S. Eliot sent along your letter and I was rejoiced to see your handwriting again, and receive your messages. I am told that you believe yourself to be Napoleon – or is it Mussolini? What a pity you did not choose Buddha while you were about it, instead of a politician! – To turn to more serious matters, I was in several bookshops in the Charing Cross Road not long ago, and saw, in each, piles of your books. I was informed they were selling well. Eliot told me you were projecting a volume on Confucius, which seems an excellent idea. It is a good time to sell books over here, for everything is in very short supply, ⟨a big surplus goes into books.⟩ If your publishers can, or will, find the necessary paper (which alas is in short supply too) you can be sure of every copy selling. Fifteen thousand copies should assure to you a royalty of 2000 pounds sterling ⟨(9,000 dollars?)⟩ minus of course taxes.–I heard with the greatest concern about your money difficulties: this might be a way to solve them. The buying of books has simply become a disease of the English; I went into a large bookshop the other day, but it was so full of people I could not get near the shelves I wanted. It doesn't seem to matter what the book is. – When I got back here I found myself with a considerable debt and have not been able to catch up with things yet, or I would have offered Eliot my widow's mite towards the fund which I understand has been raised to help you, and I suppose poor Dorothy. I have nothing much to report regarding myself. For six years I moved around America, painting portraits wherever I went. You will remember that in World War I my career as a soldier ended in the painting of war-pictures. But the organising of such things this time was in different hands and I honestly do not know how I should have kept alive had I remained in England. I met an old schoolmate of yours, Carlos Williams, up in the Genessee, and saw Laughlin once or twice. He puts his riches to good uses, but I got none of them, because he thought my price for portraits too exorbitant. – The North American continent is an amazingly beautiful place. I still prefer the American people ⟨(the "people" as understood by Carl Sandburg)⟩ in some ways to any other: but I think it is going to be tough organising life there in such a way that the artistic man will have a chance. There is an immensity of talent, which is frittered away in the most trivial tasks. But the future lies there, if anywhere. What a pity it is that the lure of history kept you locked up in the dusty old Mediterranean. The Hudson River Valley would have been a better place. – Are you writing anything? Please drop me a line; and if I can get you any books or anything of that sort be sure I will do so. With all my best wishes.

Wyndham Lewis.

P.S. My wife sends you her best wishes, and hopes we shall all see you again before too long.

W.L.

Confucius: Confucius: The Unwobbling Pivot & The Great Digest (1947).

187. ALS–1. On stationery imprinted: J'AYME DONC JE SUIS

St. Elizabiths Horspital
Washington D.C.

24 Lug [August 1946]

W. L.

INcurable Borrovian. Le Chateaubriand de nos jours—still enamoured of the primevul forrest—

Waaal you aint vury au courant (factual) re EZ—but I whope you will douze with the Possum wen he gets bak to Eng. & keep 'um from dozing.
=

Yrs
E P

Borrovian: Lewis's early work was influenced by George Borrow's stories of his travels, especially among gypsies.

188. TLS–2.

Studio A,
Kensington Gardens Studios,
29 Notting Hill Gate,
London, W.2.

Sept. 24. 1946.

Dear Pound.   Unless I answer letters quickly, I am apt to lose them, and I have lost Dorothy's. What is her address? —As to your note, I have not seen Eliot for many months, though I believe he is back from America. If I come across him I will suggest he publish something of yours, though I have no influence with him–and I doubt if he is able to influence Faber and Faber to do anything they dont want to do. It is to my mind a tiresome conservative firm, and Faber himself a terrible old snob. – The book-boom maintains itself, though people are now able to go tripping about and that will take some money away from books. – Why does not Laughlin publish something in New York? He now has an office I see in Fifth Avenue. But I am not, as you say, au courant, and perhaps he has already done so. – I am sorry my views about America provoke your mirth. I enjoy a great many things, you must remember, that have not the same appeal to you: the wonderful landscapes met with everywhere in

America: and simple pleasant people (butchers, bakers and candlestick makers) whom you would despise. But believe me I am not blind to the horrors of Hollywood or the universal ballyhoo. Then what appeals to you very much – the <u>historical</u> – leaves me cold. It even makes me uncomfortable to be in a place where something happened four hundred years ago, but that has fallen into decay. I prefer Willow Run to that. You should chuck all politics, get out of that place, and become an American. Boogie Woogie is better than Sole Mio.–But perhaps again I am not au courant!

Yrs ever,

Wyndham Lewis

189. ALS–1. On stationery imprinted: J'AYME DONC JE SUIS

Day of Thankgivink
28 Nov [1946]
St Elizabeths Hospital
Washington D.C.

Buttt my deerly beeloved Wyndham:

Aapart from the botany & geology?

The most uninteresting country on earth beecaws it takes the least interest in truth.

Tho' dare say France is rapidly approachin that nadir.
Non! l'homme n'est pas descendu du singe, mais nous y arriverrrrrrons.

---

regards à Madame.

Yrs

E P

190. TLS–2.

Studio A.
Kensington Gardens Studios,
29 Notting Hill Gate,
London. W.2.

April 9th. 1947.

Dear Ezra. I often think about you: and I have been writing about you too. At least a year must elapse however before the book in which that bit occurs sees the light. Shortage of paper etc. etc. makes it very long. I never know what to say to you when I sit down to write. Do you find time to write anything (verse or prose) or rather – for you have time enough no doubt – are you able to? – In what way you had served our not very deserving kind was the subject I referred to in passing. How would you answer that – I mean <u>poetry apart,</u> for there it is obvious. It seemed to me that you were responsible not for Joyce of course but for Joyce getting heard about in the way that he did – seeing that you sold the idea of Joyce to Miss Weaver, which was the nearest approach to supernatural experience Jimmie J. ever knew – and the intervention of the supernatural world in his personal affairs was the theme of quite a lot of his conversation. – Then there was 'Cathay'. That Hueffer described as 'the most beautiful book in the world' I remember. But other people (who were Chinese experts) thought that too apparently: and you started a translation racket, with which the name of Waley (or Whaley?) is conspicuously associated. Correct?

Any information of that sort I should welcome. – Have you been visited in your retreat by any literary lights? Cummings for instance? I saw him when I was in N.Y. But he was such a jumpy and peppery little creature it was impossible to talk to him much. He has succeeded in writing some very excellent verses. As Washington is so near to N.Y. I suppose you may have seen him. – My wife sends her kindest regards. If there is anything I can do – !

Yrs,
Wyndham Lewis

writing about you: in Lewis's second autobiography, *Rude Assignment* (1950).
'beautiful book': Ford Madox Hueffer (Ford) wrote in his review of *Cathay* in 1915: "The poems in *Cathay* are things of supreme beauty." See *Ezra Pound, The Critical Heritage,* ed. Eric Homberger, pp. 108–9.

191. ALS–1. [1947].

S. Elizabeths Horsp[l]

D C

Dear Wyndham

     me dorter & g[d] son @f at l[ast] hv. arruv. in yr. island – gal translated some Cantos into wop. rather better (I thought) than the local wop Bloomsburrys.) – infant sd/ to be calm & house-broke but conditions transport. Shd/ like her to dine wh you (poss. suitable friend fer M[me] W.L.). if she gets to london.

     anyhow you might drop her a line.

Mary Baratti	consort
Shutters. Dale Rd	wop—russ
Spondon nr Derby.	not yet
	in Eng.

yrs

EZ

me dorter: Pound's daughter, Mary, had married the Russian-Italian Prince Boris de Rachewiltz in 1946. Mary de Rachewiltz visited England with her recently-born child, Walter, for two months early in 1947. See Mary de Rachewiltz, *Discretions,* p. 283. She has published numerous translations of her father's poetry in Italian.

192. ALS–3.

S Lizabeths Orspl

Wash DC.

17 Ap[ril] 47

(1)

Dr Wm

     Yais—that iz, I tried to sell idea of keepin' up lit. but to q[uo]t[e]. you, he (J[oyce].) threw himself on it like starved dog. & swallowed enough to have publish'd the necessary of the 4 footmen. (the drive for bro. Possum [T. S. Eliot] backfired an' Valleryed. 'Arriet [Shaw Weaver] swallowed the 'ook line an sinker & that ended the fishin.

②

Yes. I cert did show the   that chink cd/ be made into english
but Not dilutation aint the ultima parola – cert. the —— —— —— was paralized
before the gate wuz op'd. =

3.

I sd/ there wuz blanks fer adjectives in Shell[ey]. — I mentioned
Crabbe (not Dryden. Dry. iz Possum's.) I was cert. not exclusiv' provençal
rrrrromance in fact there wuz Gautier as deestinkt from Laforgue on ole
EZ's bk-shelf. & Olivia [Shakespear] gimme my Gautier. So if Adam (not
Smiff) etc. nothing without efficient ecc- [etc.]
Ps on – Elizabethans – in general,
               ⟨—— Next. or Today⟩
a pseudo Sweed [Charles Olson] wuz mentionin' Lion & Fox as about the
only ecc. & [?] at least the Sweede's "awake".

          wha' hae not   only on
             with Shx @ mermade   Chewsday
I cd. indeed a boom unfold if you & I ecc. anyhow I do occ.ly mention
mental activity as distinct from embalming ("I presume",) & that what
little crit. has been done ecc. as distink from.
yais. bro. I am still on the town.

                                        yrs
                                        EP

nothing without efficient ecc-: Pound has attributed the principle that "nothing
    happens without an efficient cause" to both Aristotle and St. Thomas Aquinas.
    The "ecc-" is the Italian abbreviation for "etc."
Lion & Fox: Lewis's *The Lion and the Fox: The Rôle of the Hero in the Plays of
    Shakespeare* (1927).
Shx @ mermade: Pound refers to the gathering of such poets as Shakespeare,
    Donne, Beaumont and Fletcher, and Ben Jonson at the Mermaid Tavern in
    London; "only on Chewsday" may refer to visitor's rules at St. Elizabeths.
"I presume": Lewis's *America, I Presume* (1940), which is based on his experi-
    ences in the United States and Canada.

193. ANS–1. On stationery imprinted: J'AYME DONC JE SUIS

19
Dec
1947

Appy Xmas
    to you n your'n

        note usual
        time
        lag

yrs
EZ

time lag: A newspaper clipping was enclosed with this note:
      "John Bull, Dies at 85
      St. Helier, Jersey, Channel Islands,
      Dec. 18 (AP)–John Bull, 85, retired
      circusman who once trained animals for
      P. T. Barnum, died at his Jersey home
      yesterday."

194. TLS–2.

Studio A.
Kensington Gardens Studios,
29 Notting Hill Gate,
London. W.II.
Jan 27. I949.

Dear Ezra. Good luck in the new year, is my tardy salute. Christmas holiday etc. is with me a lump of knots in the otherwise reasonably level stretch of day to day. Good luck I hope may take the form of a relenting on the part of Uncle Sam.

    The deadline given me by Paige was February I think – but <u>when</u> – for the article. I search, frantically, for his address. You sent me a cutting announcing the decease of John Bull (are we still interested in such events, such entities?) and it will not surprise you to learn therefore that one of John Bulls houses – the one in which I dwell – is dropping to pieces, afflicted with a disease known as "dry rot". We found one of our windows wobbling about in its socket: we informed the landlord. It was a case of dry rot! Workmen were already engaged upon dry rot cases in other parts of the building. As a consequence for many weeks we have lived upstairs (where you sat for your portrait). Yesterday we came downstairs. The workmen now go upstairs, where dry rot abounds. The beam on which the glass roof rests is full of it: they will, I think, remove the roof. – From these few remarks you can see that there is considerable disorder, and things might easily get lost. If by any evil chance I have missed the Weiss number, I know where I can plant an article by itself.

There is completely nothing to talk about regarding books and things here. Most people live in the country–they have not come into London again to live, only to work, and go back to country. This greatly diminishes sociability. But the cost of a bottle of whisky does not help matters either. The great expense in a good restaurant, and very poor return for your money, is another discouraging factor. – I spend most of my time, when not working, with my lawyer, trying to keep my publishers in order. England, like yours, is a lock-up, its size unimportant really. However, I have certain privileges you do not have. – When are you having published that Confucius book? Keep well!

Yr.

W. L.

deadline: Lewis wrote an article, "Ezra: The Portrait of a Personality," for a special Pound issue of the *Quarterly Review of Literature* (5 [December, 1949]: 136–44) edited by Theodore Weiss.

dry rot: Lewis wrote a brilliant comic story about this situation, "The Rot," in his book of short stories, *Rotting Hill* (1951).

195. TL–1. [St. Elizabeths Hospital. Washington, D.C.].

day after ground hawg day [February 3] 1948 in the era of pestilence.

⟨re. enc⟩

Dear W. . .DAMN

Yew 'n' ole Bill [William Carlos Williams] wuz made to onnerstan' each other. g[rea]t PITY you never did, as he has on several occasions (dont know if actually in print) expressed perception that some minds are NOT dead.

    esp/ on one occ/ to me re/ my havin' perceived W.L. when he, W.C.W., hadn't.

Now I WISH you wd/ lend a hand / IF either of the Doktors /doc⁷/ O.M. [T. S. Eliot] and Doc. W. [William Carlos Williams] medico plus / cd/ be persuaded to LOOK at the Areopumpk / or pump ship /ika [Milton's *Areopagitica*] they wd/ or possible SHD/ see that to give this hodgepodge of deceased vocables to ANY

    young Bobby Roberts ("I said it's buddin', Yakob") [Jacob Epstein?] of licherchure WITHOUT

        the Poison label on the bottle is a CRIME of first magnitude vs/ the future.

Of course if you wd/ send five lines to the Texas steer⁺ to this effect it wd/   #ded-eye Dallam [Simpson])
  AID

   and how, in that thaaar "organization" of etc/

         that you were talkin about 2 years AGO/
even if you (amid the dry knot of rotting hill) can't see why and how.
   This is a request, and dont argue.

I think Tate did his damndest for you. He has left Jolt and Co/ in disgust.
   and ought to be backed in whatever attempt he next makes to putt you over (i.e. into print in this marasma.)

       Give me respexx to yr/ Missus /
I spose she still cooks.

    [Note added by Dorothy Pound:]

    DP adds: four lines or six, would help
    out the Texan—if you can bring yourself
    to focus on it—<u>and</u> please ole Ez enormously./

          DP.

re. enc: An article by William Carlos Williams, in *Four Pages,* a Poundian "little mag" edited by Dallam Simpson ("ded-eye Dallam") in Galveston, Texas. Williams's article, "With Forced Fingers Rude" (February 1948, pp. 1–4), deplores the revaluation of the importance of John Milton's poetry which T. S.

Eliot made in a pamphlet published by the British Academy in 1947. Eliot's
piece (in a revised form) is included under the title "Milton II" in his *On
Poetry and Poets* (1957).

O.M.: T. S. Eliot received the Order of Merit from King George VI in 1948.

"organization" . . . *that you were talkin about:* Probably the organization of
a democratic society Lewis urged in "The Cosmic Uniform of Peace," *The
Sewanee Review* 54 (Autumn 1945): 507–31.

Jolt and Co/: Allen Tate was an editor for Henry Holt and Company from 1946
to 1948. Lewis sent Tate his *America and Cosmic Man,* which Holt did not
publish.

196. TLS–2.

Studio A.
Kensington Gardens Studios,
  29 Notting Hill Gate,
    London. W.II.

Feb. 28. 1948.

Dear Ezra. Your letter and enclosure gave me great pleasure. At the
moment I was unable to answer properly as lawyers and publishers were
on my chest, in my ears and navel and surtout in my hair. Having
profitably disposed of them I blow my nose and turn to you. ——I will
write for that production you sent me: I like Williams's little article about
Milton. I think that our old friend T.S.E.'s business about Milton was
merely a feature in his long build-up of self. Groomed and disinfected
as he is for the long dreampt-of dubbing ("rise Sir Thomas"!) in a
protestant country it is not a bad thing for a poet to advertise his partiality
for "Paradise Lost". Like all these manoeuvres of our honoured colleague,
this one was quite misunderstood – and he, forseeing ⟨(as usual)⟩ that it
would be taken as a serious literary contribution, playfully miltonised all
over the globe. It would be better of course if people took no notice of
him. Carlos Williams got quite worked up about Milton however! – I will
see if I can get worked up about something which I should like to make
an exhibition of myself getting worked up about in public. I'm sure I can.

Why do all Americans without exception pretend that everything
they do and have ever done and will ever do is for the young? I am not
worked up about this believe me, but somebody ought to be. Both Eliot

and Carlos Williams writing about Milton speak as if art were a department of education. Also, il y a de l'idée du progrès ladedans.

Looking out from that funny old place you've got yourself into you
may notice that the world is in an extremely unsettled state. Will write
you soon again.

Your

W-dam

lawyers and publishers: Lewis was having difficulties over the publication of
America and Cosmic Man.
that production: Four Pages; see notes to Letter 195. Nothing by Lewis appeared
in *Four Pages.*

197. ALS–2. On air letter form.

4 March [1948]

S Liz

Dear Wyndham

They wd/ de facto have to "fr. the young" as the adult
population is practically non-existent. =As a Yourupeean you hv/ got
the @. fᵒ 'abit of pre-supposing an adult pubk or @ least an adult element
in the goulasch. =

yes, rumours of a unsettled state reach the cloisters via a d[ail]y/
press that avoids ref/ to the vital.

I hv/ ever held that a academic cock-shy has its uses. – but it shd/
of course cast back the coconuts.

⟨re arising⟩ [of T. S. Eliot] in a long-since & monumented past you
sd/ they w[oul]d/n't—& S that they w[oul]d/. & to carry on. I now suggest that it will go beyond one dub. Them animals are arborial & reach the
high branches.

Met a friend of yrs tother day who 'nquires. Onnerstan also that
Mons. Beckwith's shelf is stocked largely with you, me 'n' ole Bill &
Stendhal (who I regret to state is in cardiac difficulties.   i. e. Bill not
Beyle [Stendhal].
Mr Kuminkz also shares—on the finding of Par/ᵈˢ Lost. = e.e.c. razor
blade without a handle—but a[?] relief.

     & so on
Saluti Madame & beeleev me

I like to get letters:
seul plaisir etc   EP
of the jugged.

198. TLS–2.

Studio A.

March 30. 1948.

Dear Ezz.   Since all my time has been fully occupied writing 3.000 words for your memorial number none remained for correspondence. Probably the stuff arrived too late. I hope if you ever see it you wont disapprove of it too much. – No news this end – unless a sort of centenary volume that I have promised to write something for, celebrating Eliot's sixtieth birthday, is news. A book has appeared called "The last of the Pre-Raphaelites," by a certain Douglas Goldring. He was Hueffer's secretary in the English Review days. Of course Goldring has arranged Ford upon a suitable biographical pedestal: or so it appears, for I have not read the book. This has turned the critical columns of the press, I am afraid, into a coconut shy with Ford as the Aunt Sally. Goldring was obliged to confess for instance that his hero was an inveterate liar. It was impossible to disguise the fact that he was a social snob (more than half his departures from the truth involved with this fact). But seeing what England is in the matter of social snobbery, it is difficult to see how one snob more would make any difference. And I thought some reviewers need not have devoted all their space to his untruthfulness – his fabulous baronial estates in Prussia and his imaginary schooling at Eton – but have spoken of his doings as a critic. That they dismissed, however, with the statement that he attached too much importance to the young. Hueffer was never a favourite of mine: but several times ⟨in the past few weeks I have⟩ felt like providing an answer to their attacks. – In my article re. yourself I mentioned Hueffer.

The war I imagine will be a year or two in arriving. Meanwhile in a food parcel from one friend I have Cuban Honey, and in a parcel from another friend a dozen packets which enables us to make loaves of dazzling bread.

A little hasty good wishes,

Yours

<u>W. L.</u>

P.S.   In 4 or 5 weeks my book about the U.S.A. will be published. As it is something you know all about I shall not of course send you a copy. It is a fact, merely, of camaradish interest. I forgot to say that I will certainly do something for the outfit, copy of which was sent me [*Four Pages*]. I will just draw breath, do the bit about Eliot, for his centenary volume, then take up the 3 pages of "little mag" prose.

centenary volume: Lewis wrote an article, "Early London Environment," for *T. S. Eliot: A Symposium*, eds. Richard March and Tambimuttu (1948), which is as much about Pound as it is about Eliot.
Aunt Sally: A puppet used as a target in games.
Goldring: Douglas Goldring, *The Last Pre-Raphaelite: A Record of the Life and Writings of Ford Madox Ford* (1948).
book about the U.S.A.: America and Cosmic Man (1948).

199. ALS–2. On stationery imprinted: J'AYME DONC JE SUIS

S. Liz   6 Ap[ril 1948]

Waal my dh W—ⁿ
as you hv. seen <u>much</u> more of it in the past 40, than I hv. & az I njoyd "I presume" so <u>much</u> – you send it on. <u>even</u> if I hv. to acquir' by purchase— all you can tell is welcom. my iggurunce iz VAST. ⟨& the no/ of writ^rs whom I can rd/ without nausea SO FEW!!⟩

Yaas. D. Gold[rin]g did a xcellent "S. Lodge"   is this a reissue. or a new vol? – send yr/ copy when done with. — The old walrus hd/ his pts. & ∴ they kuss him.   ————————————
? I giv you the kid's [his daughter's] address?
Mary Baratti
    @ Shutters, Dale Rd. Spondon, nr' Derby.
        greet's to Mme.   yrs

EZ

"S. Lodge": Lewis referred in Letter 198 to Goldring's *The Last Pre-Raphaelite* (1948), not to his *South Lodge: Reminiscences of Violet Hunt, Ford Madox Ford, and the English Review Circle* (1943).

200. TL–1. [April 1948]. [St. Elizabeths Hospital. Washington, D.C.]. On a half-page of typing paper.

Strictly anonymous info/ fer poisnl benefit of W.L.

The egregious, the O.M. the Pos/O.M. [T. S. Eliot] hove into v/ between
BLAST No. I   (view)
and BLAST No. 2 [1914–1915].
The Wyndam then bombadeering ergo
saw less of the REMARKable animal than London habitues.
ONLY forgotten fact is the ardour, not to say recklessness of said
marsupial in its early phases
with venbl/ Ez restraining
it in time to prevent such calamities as hav since befell W.L.

i.e. calamities to it, the sd/ marsupial.
wich is prob/ why the said Ez
has more patience with the later marsupial habits
than them wot do NOT
remember the headlong impulses
(now ALmost incredible) of MiLord the rizen TOM.

HELL. fill in with wot you do remember of Gaudier, and the ineffable Yakob [Jacob Epstein], and Rebel Awt / [Rebel Art Centre]
    set the bloody scene/ with a dab of S.Lodge, Frieda [Strindberg], etc. the courting of Possum by x.y.z. wich you prob/ dont recall and the resistance.

201. TLS–2.

Studio A.

May Ist. 1948.

Dear Ezra   (I) Thank you for your letter re. Eliot. I of course, being a red-blooded chap, respond suitably to what you report re the violence of his passions at the time in question. To what particular 'calamity that befell W.L.' you refer I do not know. But aware as I am that wise old Ezra prefers at all time[s] the allusive and mysterious I am silent. It would be like expecting answers from a boozy Magus.

(2) Why Ronald Duncan?

(3) Do your papers inform, Eliot made Grand Knight Commander Legion of Honour?

As you must have heard, Eliot and Valéry racing neck and neck for Nobel Prize. Should imagine Legion of Honour bestowed by enemies (in Académie Française) of Valéry.

———

You might almost have contrived this climax to your respective careers: yours so villonesque (though there has been nothing else of the Villon in your sedate existence) and Eliot's super-Tennysonian (though he will never make the House of Lords nor even get a 'dubbing').

Have written the article upon T. S. E. as first met. Very difficult and unsatisfactory writing like this about contemp[orarie]s.

Yr.

W. L.

Legion of Honour: In 1948 Eliot received the Order of Merit, was made a Chevalier de la Legion d'Honneur, and received the Nobel Prize.

202. TL–2. [1948]. [St. Elizabeths Hospital. Washington, D.C.]. On both sides of a half-page of paper.

May the coolth, in fact coldish

Cheer UP

He can't git the Collana of the Annunciata. cause it was writ by the gt poet anonimo

Vino

Non fino
Nessuno vuol
Umbertino.

and evn I dont expect him to be made Garter King at Arms. This a.m's
noozprint, by the waye bears the effigy of the Yapock [an aquatic mar-
supial], "or water opossum" of french guiana.
HAVE you seen THAT?
Well who's this D(?rity) Sturge Moore wot writes in the Specked-ater
[*The Spectator*]? I been meanin to ask wot ever bekum of ole T.Sturge?
is this some degenerate rampoll?

waaal of course you british SUBjects see things with a other eye.
Too bad you didn't do a bit of observin on the spot like you did in that
admirable work [Lewis's *Hitler,* 1931] wot got suppressed in Choimunny.
I mean down south.

And as fer the rest ole Erik Satie said a mouth full wot I wont repeat. And
I know one guy who declined.

of course you may know more about young Dun/Can [Ronald Duncan]
than I do / I occasionally like direct observation of active particles of the
cosmos, by reporters capable of sd/ DIrect observation. Certainly active.
and partisan / sometimes puzzling. You yrslf/ once had a [Rebel Art]
CENTRE in Ormond St/ feeling the use of such combined etc/ mebbe
you wasted time on Bobbie [Roberts], but I dont believe you ever regretted
it. By the way. ever read Dizzy [Benjamin Disraeli] on Bentinck? the
slouch gives away on the unconscious. Also ef you want to soothe grampop, lemme know if you find anything fit to read. Rostovtzeff very limited.
have you read Brooks Adams and Kitson YET? (Law of Civilization and
Decay by B/A.)

The real stalwart is the Rev. Swabey. That you can depend on.

No. not calamity to You / calamity to the abovementioned Marsupial due
to its own IMpetuosity/ I know it sounds like a mythological age. but so
it was. I mean it was so.

No, the wypers here, sfar as I saw / didnt headline the fr/ avatar/
frogvatar of the celebrity in question. I spose you mean Gide? Valéry
croaked, didn't he [in 1945]. demised OBIT. / how's Suzanne Lenglen
comin on?

Collana of the Annunciata: The Collare dell'Ordine dell'Annunziata, an Italian
order of knights whose origins go back to 1350 A.D.

Umbertino: The verse Pound quotes seems to refer to the lack of public enthusiasm for Umberto II, who became Lieutenant General of the Realm in 1944
after the liberation of Rome when his father, King Vittorio Emanuele III,
stepped aside.

Erik Satie: Pound may refer to the avant-garde composer's comic attempts to
be elected to the French Academy in 1892, 1894, and 1896.

one guy who declined: Pound could be referring to the French playwright
Georges De Porto-Riche, who was never officially admitted by the academy
because he refused to address it after his election in 1923.

203. AL–1. [Draft]. [Probably not sent]. [May 1948]. [Studio A, Kensington Gardens Studios, 29 Notting Hill Gate, London, W. II.].

Dear Ezra. Your letter, tortuous comme d'habitude, but a few clear
spots. —Eliot could be of great use to you and my remarks were not an
invitation to join me in a less than respectful attitude towards our mutual
friend. I was giving you the news, that is all. Just for the record let me
say that you have not especially afforded me your support in the past,
except during the recent war when you wrote about me, with a view some
might think to drag me into the silly mess where you had landed yourself.
To try to help drag you out of that mess I have given you such support
as I am able. And in writing me do understand that I am politically a
complete agnostic. No theory of the State interests me in the slightest. It
is a waste of time talking to me about social credit, because I take no
interest in it. If you would take my advice you would throw any books
you possess dealing with economics out of the window. As to politics,
you only have to open the newspaper in the morning to see that politics
are all nonsense. You are in a chaos. Why not face the fact and sing the
chaos, songbird that you are?

Yr.

you wrote about me: Pound referred to Lewis in *What Is Money For?* (1939)
and in *Carta da Visita* (1942). Pound also mentioned Lewis in his wartime
radio broadcasts from Italy.

204. TL–1. [1948]. [St. Elizabeths Hospital. Washington, D.C.]. Verso headed "strictly anonymous notes fer W . . d . . . L . . . . s"

W. L. CONfound him, comPOUND him. Has three devotees, AT least not countin the zombie J[ohn]. R[eid]. and the antient wreck in the big ⟨the prefix is BUG⟩ house whence cannot LEAD. These blokes will never do, until TOLD.

    They shd/ damn well manifest against difficulty of getting the only books worth reading.

    DAMN it all manifestos work; count; there are traces of intelligence and disgust. all of which need focus.

ONE known spot where intelligent orders can be printed.

Possibly other devotees known to WL and not to the anonymous.

potential shovers can be listed EVEN in England under the curse.

NOT necessary to stick out the neck. There are points which do NOT subject pointER to blackmail. MAINLY positive statements which Bevin cdnt/ identify with human decency, or Joad and McCulloch spot as inimical to their infamy.

30 years ago even ole Santayna [Santayana] was weepin over coral insects/ one does NOT have to submit.

If WL dont KNOW what is wrong, one cd/ tell him, but he must have noticed a few defects in the present shystem.

Does he ever READ anything now?

                 and

                  so

wd WL read a few intelligent   on
authors (damnfew)
if told who they are
benedictions etc/

Sieze, sieze the lyre,
seize seize the liar
RESOOM the lofty strain.

TELL 'EM
wot to DO
and if you dont
know, you can be
TOLD
wot they
OUGHT

205. TLS–2.

Studio A.

July 20th 1948.

My dear Ezz. The writing (and reading) you would have me do is impossible. It takes me all my time to keep alive, I have none on my hands at all. Eliot however – who is over in the States, someone told me, but no matter – has more time than I have by far. Thank you for the cutting. It was not the accepting of honours I had in mind, it was rather the disposing of one's life in such a way as to attract them. As to your implying that my remarks were motivated by envy of the dangling crosses and those letters you stick after your name, oh sir, has my life been that of one prizing the values of the career-man or directing his gaze ahead to covet the dignity of knighthood? You know it has not. Every day I have lived is my witness to the contrary. At least I am privileged to speak of those things without the risk of what I say being imputed to envy. – Perhaps I was suddenly over-vocal, on account of my awakening to a certain disagreeable fact.

Meanwhile my American book [*America and Cosmic Man,* 1948] is announced for publication July 26. Other books will drift out I expect this year – if there is not another war. In the latter case you are in much better position than I am. Indeed a so much better position that there is no comparison. I should be locked up in the island, with hardly any means of earning a living, with practically no food I could eat, with a variety of disgusting missiles raining down (if the place was not actually invaded) and this would last indefinitely. – However, if war holds off another 12 months, a few books will be published.

In speaking of your situation in this unceremonious way, understand that mine is quite respectably unpleasant, because of the awful state this country is in. But I never take your incarceration for granted. A petition ought to be started up at the proper moment: say next April.

Yours,
W. L.

206. TL–1. [July? 1948]. [St. Elizabeths Hospital. Washington, D.C.].

W. L. must have misunderstood something / cited Satie's "surtout de ne l'avoir merité" in what I believed (correctly) to be W,L,'s attitude. no suggestion that he minded TSE's rise, but that such elevations CAN be utilized,

> tho seldom are.

Ef one had been TOLD name of yr/ blinkin bk/ or pub/r it wd/ be easier to get in these emporia?

why dont Giovanelli or some of yr/ ADmirers come across with some printable

> BOOSTS ??

a guy like S[locum]/ wants to do something to boost W.L. to proper position,

> re/ Joyce inflation etc/

> > > AND WL and HISNs spend 9 months being found.

> PROportion

like wot Ez has several times indicated, and that nobody properly takes up, insomma, Uly/bloosy/liaases / Eimi/ Apes
cd/ be COMpared if the only critic of the age warnt in bug house/ in fact he DID first.
only it takes 'em three or six years to find it out/
also shd/ revive the ONE WAY [Song].
also git books into circ/

---

only critic of the age: Pound discussed Lewis's *The Apes of God,* E. E. Cummings's *EIMI,* and James Joyce's *Ulysses* in "Augment of the Novel," in *New Directions in Prose and Poetry, 1941,* pp. 705–13.

ONE WAY: Lewis's satiric poem *One-Way Song* was republished by Methuen in 1960 with a foreword by T. S. Eliot.

---

207. ALS–2. On air letter form.

> > > > S. Liz 25 Jan[uary 1949]

Dear Wynd. Landseer
I mean the equiv—a slight slip in Rough [*Rude*] Assignment—not distinguishing Ez Walter Scott 1909 & Ez 1949 (or '38) serious curiosity startin' @ death of Gaudier re: why.

> in short study of grampaw wd hv. done u as much as some of those continental fadists wot you hv. read.

you cd/ defend by three words, making the "Troveurs" (Troubadours) line apply to pre-1914 ⟨re which [word] true⟩

other slip one x in Madox you made one good hit re Fordie not blind to other writers————'ow diff fr 98% of his contemporaries

@ Rugby

yrs

EZ

1 shall mention the bright spots= the 'Landseer' dont ref W. L. 1949— but to the dawg.

Rough Assignment: In *Rude Assignment* (p. 41), Lewis wrote that "Pound has lived too long with the trouveres to regard war as anything but a romantic institution." Lewis misspelled Ford Madox Ford's name as "Ford Ma*ddo*x Ford."

continental fadists: Lewis was interested in such writers as Léon Bloy, Julien Benda, Albert Camus, Charles Maurras, Georges Sorel, and Jean-Paul Sartre.

Landseer: Sir Edwin Landseer (1802–73) painted a famous portrait of Sir Walter Scott with his dogs.

208. TL–2. [1949]. [St. Elizabeths Hospital. Washington, D.C.].

IF W.L. can git hold of a copy of Frobenius :Kulturgeschichte Afrikas. He will find poor [proof?] that the German whose name Gaudier cdn't remember, but from whom he learned, wuz the Geheimrat (per es/ that triangle on the Dancer's face). Waaal naow as WL wondered about organizin, and as the Wilde Steer of TexAS, the Dallam [Simpson] is the only visible trying to make up time-lag and boost the abovesaid W.L., and certainly NEEDS a line from W. L. over W.L's signature, to estab/ his prestige and squish the bedbugs, cockroaches etc. and as the EZ. is from force of circs / incapacitated from making sd/ communique re/ the abovesd/ Henri Gaudier Brzzxxqzzk. [Brzeska] and as in order to abbrevate time lag, all ready night millenar,,etc. AND as the boost of Frobenius is part of the TexAS program (no metaphasis expressed), said Dallam havin appealed to various and NOT been able to get much re/ Frobenius, The said WL, cd/ with very small loss of time and labour, putt the above facts into ten lines of effulgent prose, and help the Dallam

advertise "I Presume" wich McLuhan sez irrrrrritttated the godam Kenuks. juh git me?
answer to Texas, or to the bug house with leave to forward.

You prob/ fergit the gt/ Hamitic WORTEX, at back of blast, and prob/ never conversed enough with yr/ distinguished colleague (cert more distinguished than the Wad/ [Edward Wadsworth] or the Bob/ [William Roberts] enough to remember that H[enri]. G[audier-Brzeska]. HAD been browsin in Bib[liotheque]. Nat[ionale]/ de Paris when Appolinaire was robbin the Toccerdero, etc. and had heard about cave-men.

Breton by the way has pubd/ a photo of the Prince des Penseurs, visitin' the Penseur de Rodin. so I now know wot happened the day after I left. (Anthol. Humeur Noir, with nize pome by Cros' papa, the orig. Charles) AND so on.

respex to the lady, and I think you will like Vals' [A.V. Moore's] head. Why shdnt you paint a few bassadors (in anticipation).

and so on, respex to the lady AND so on.

Nothing in the note you do (or dont) to indicate PRESENT utterance by EZ, but if you need, you cd/ remember IF necessary, the query as to wot Teuton Gaudier had read.
The aim bein to GET Frob/ printed, so that PART of the pubk/ can understand CONTEMPORARY expression by us or whomever, without our having to spell out and EZplane c a t KAT a domestic etc.

Titl, /re the KOnexshn of Frob/ with contemporary thought, or Einfluss etc.

etc.

[To this letter, Dorothy Pound added the address of A.V. Moore, whom she recommends as a subject for a portrait]:
"not Holbein, Velasquez," says EP.

Frobenius: Leo Frobenius, *Kulturgeschichte Afrikas* (1933). There is no evidence that Henri Gaudier-Brzeska read Frobenius; however, the triangle used in figure 56 of this work does recall the use of the triangle in Gaudier's *Red Stone Dancer*.
"I Presume": Lewis's travel book, *America, I Presume* (1940), was a characteristically satiric look at the United States and Canada.
Hamitic WORTEX: Gaudier wrote a prose "Vortex" in *BLAST,* no. 1 (pp. 155–58), which gave a brilliantly condensed history of sculpture from primitive to modern times.

Toccerdero: The Palais du Trocadero, a museum and exhibition hall. Pound seems to be referring to the incident in 1911 when Apollinaire was implicated in the theft of the *Mona Lisa* from the Louvre.

Prince des Penseurs: The French semanticist Jean-Pierre Brisset is shown in front of Rodin's *Le Penseur* in André Breton's *Anthologie de L'Humour Noir* (1950). Works by the surrealist Charles Cros also appear in the anthology. See Canto 80, p. 506: "when they elected old Brisset Prince des Penseurs . . . before the world was given over to wars. . . ."

209. TL–1. [May? 1949]. [St. Elizabeths Hospital. Washington, D.C.].

W.L.

might indulge his notable capacity fer analysis and narrative in communicatin some data re/ the personnel of a gang of newts called "Poetry London", and a few sidelights on the injunction alleged to have been worked thru that sewer and/or or plus "Longman's Orient" fer preventing the sale of the "Unwobbling Pivot" Calcutta edition. Dunno if W.L. has seen the murkn edition. Singular opacities occur in London news. Not to say the singular stupidity of our noted friend the O.M. [T. S. Eliot] the minute you git to Frobenius or Confucius or anything outside the fugg of the Xtn. whatever, sometimes called a religion.

The Calcutta implement of Longmans bears the suspicious name of Dutch, né possibly Dutt, whether mesopotamian or untouchable not yet ascertained. Obviously the wholedamgang will be reborn as rats and/or camels, but in the mean time a few schede penali or whatever wd/ be suitable subject fer dith[y]ramb.

Some of the dirtiest ornaments of the american obscene are gittin their names in the news BElatedLy. Dunno as it leads to freedom but still diversifies the snoozeprint.

Ef WynDAMMMM aint seen [*The Unwobbling*] Pivot, a cawpy cd/ be provided, not az itz up his particular alley, but to indicate the natr of mayhem etc. and the perspicacity of wm.SHX [Shakespeare] when dealin with similar subjects.

London news vurry slack the past months, as most of the compos inhabitants of yr/ Isle liv in the country. cmon, unleash a postage stamp and letter flik.

"Poetry London": New Directions published *Confucius: The Unwobbling Pivot & The Great Digest* in 1947. Editions Poetry London planned to publish this work in England, but before they could an Indian edition was brought out by Orient Longmans Ltd. in 1949. Editions Poetry London then decided not to bring out another edition. "Dutch, né possibly Dutt" may have been an Orient Longmans agent.

210. TL–1. [St. Elizabeths Hospital. Washington, D.C.].

W.L.

any light on N[ew]. E[nglish]. W[eekly]. demise /i.e. for many sins, or the very rare uses?? Who the hell cd/ you collaborate with or BOSS, do you still see Porteus?

  Young Pete [Russell] silent. (? private life) learning the hard way, I purr-zoom. Vacuum ought to be USED, cant think that any of NE.W gang are useful save Port [eus]/ and what's this about Sisson? sign of brightness.

  Shd/ appreciate survey of state of chaos on Timz [Thames]. W. L. feeling active ?? (as usual).

Only possible program wd/ be W. L.'s regular i.e. better be alive than dead (in the top end).

  "England I presume", wd/ make nice backbone, regular weekly item, on state of island. Purchaser ready for ten copies at least of the former noble work (I presume).

  OR are you bein spatial. paintal, etc.

      nobody ever sees anyone else. And W. L. the true surveyor of why, usually. What become of Port's friend the son of the char lady? git refinement, or wottell.

best to Madame,

[Dorothy Pound added at the bottom of the letter]: "D. C. Sept. 24 [1949] Saluti cordiali D. P."

N.E.W. demise: After A. R. Orage's death in 1934, the *New English Weekly* was supported by his widow and friends under the editorship of Philip Mairet until 1949.

211. TL–1. [December 1949]. [St. Elizabeths Hospital. Washington, D.C.].
On a strip of typing paper.

WnDM

BLAST in 1/4 lt Rev. [*Quarterly Review of Literature*] duly recognized.
Effort being made to git Laughlin to do a proper vol/ of SEEElect W. L.,
the non-abstract hunks of WL. // a series of political pictures by DIF-
FERENT writers (if there is a 3rd. worth including) wd/ also be desirable... Someone, possibly WL might show curiosity re/ the Mensdorf
letter, M/ was Ausssstrian rep/ of the dirty Carnegies, and sent 'em a
letter on the causes of war. Wich nacherly Nick Smutty Butter did NOT
thrust into the lime light back there in or abaht 1927.   Ol Santaclausiana doin nobl/ in Pete's [Russell] lil garland of posies.   These
here ROT-icles ⟨i.e. WL on Rot hither and ROTyon⟩ O.K. we commend
to WL 'Zatenshn the Hudson Rev.   Manly tone in autumn issu. Giov-
[ane]/lli gone soft on hoss-racin'. Escape mechanism or wottell.   E[liot].
told them bize to do a vol/ on WL. but you cant steer a jelly.   AZ
uzual the labourers in the Lard'z gdn be few. Noted pious words re/
EdWad. [Edward Wadsworth died in 1949]. I dont spose THAT has released any resources. Relict [Mrs. Fanny Wadsworth] not taking up publishing or building memorial gallery? (9/8ths Ed. and a back room for
contemporary effort)

BLAST: Lewis's "Ezra: The Portrait of a Personality," *Quarterly Review of
Literature* 5 (December 1949): 136–44.
Mensdorff letter: Pound and Count Mensdorff sent a letter to Nicholas Murray
Butler, chairman of the executive committee, Carnegie Endowment for Peace,
concerning the causes of war, which was ignored by Butler ("Nick Smutty
Butter"). The letter and the reply of the endowment are included in Pound's
Impact: Essays on Ignorance and the Decline of American Civilization, ed.
Noel Stock, pp. 281–83.
Ol Santaclausiana: Apparently one of the contributors to *Ezra Pound: A Collec-
tion of Essays,* ed. Peter Russell.
pious words: Lewis wrote an article on the occasion of Edward Wadsworth's
death for *The Listener* (30 June 1949); reprinted in *Wyndham Lewis on Art,*
eds. Michel and Fox, pp. 421–22.

212. TL–1. [December 1949]. [St. Elizabeths Hospital. Washington, D.C.]. On a strip of typing paper.

wynDAM
"bugbear" eh? BUGbear, sez W. on p. 142. and we dont mean the State Boudoir either.
the omniverous (often to his delay) W. L. go down to the Brit. Messium and look at Alexander Del Mar's 30 vols of FACT wot Ez/ hadn't read in 1930, and then talk about BUGbears, Bugcubs, etc..
        An just as I git ready to start Johnnie S[locum]/ on a useful career, he ups and sets me, that he TRIED to have a youseful Kayreer and yu spit in his eye.. Naow ef yu kin tell me when (i say WHEN, and whenever) grampop giv yu bad advice, yu tell me. I dunno Az itz enny yuse, I tole Johnnie not to mind a little saliva, as it wuz just one ov yr/ picturesque habits. But these denizens is sensitive. like squirls and other sylvan fauna.

"bugbear": In the special Pound issue of the *Quarterly Review of Literature,* Lewis wrote: "Economist Pound certainly is immeasurably more sophisticated than William Jennings Bryan, we know that. . . . But with him Gold is a great bugbear too." See Lewis's essay reprinted in *Ezra Pound: A Collection of Essays,* ed. Peter Russell, p. 263.

213. ALS–1. [Draft]. [January? 1950]. [Studio A, Kensington Gardens Studios, 29 Notting Hill Gate, London, W. II.].

Dear E.P. I perceive I have offended—though what in my article provoked retaliatory biographical .... I cannot guess. (1). Were I to become an active addict or partisan in the economic crusade which still engrosses you, I might soon find myself like yourself in a place of detention; but I have not a wealthy wife to do me the services yours does for you. Nor, I will be bound, would people be writing nice long flattering articles about me, trying to assist my case. No: you should not be cross on that account.
  2 . But something or everything in the social-biographical part caused an unpleasant reaction? The article was wholly benevolent. I wish I had not written it. At least I shall not make the mistake of consenting to write other things of this nature.

                        W.L.

wealthy wife: Although Dorothy Pound had a small independent income, she was not wealthy.

214. ALS–1. [January? 1950]. [St. Elizabeths Hospital. Washington, D.C.]. On stationery imprinted: J'AYME DONC JE SUIS

WL
You can take it from me that you are almost only [one] who has writ any real criticism of [*crossout:* me] ——— work (fools called it attack.)

---

                                                      got

the point esp. re no originality —
precisely the not-to-be desired
i. e.
unless it
happens

                                              benedictions

                                                   E_z

5 useful phrases
        from 5 others.
     not uttered
        as analysis.

5 useful phrases: See p. 255.

215. TL–4. [February? 1950]. [St. Elizabeths Hospital. Washington, D.C.]. On both sides of two strips of typing paper.

W.L.
    "VOIX de Napoleon", à paraitre prochainement Editions du Milieu du Monde, Geneve et Paris.

MONEY in translation rights fer someone. Actual sayings of Nap. reported direct by Roederer, Molé, Talleyrand, Metternich, Narbonne, Caulaincourt and Benjy Constant (l'in-)

Not the least doubt that the bloke who gets the translation rights (prob. be some goddam pubr/ who will sweat a hack) BUT still somebody decent ought to have a try fer the $.

        vide review in MURK-ure de Frog [*Mercure de France*], fer Feb. 1.

pass on if no can use; allus someone needZit.
WL got any henchmen in occid[ental]/1/2 except the racing-expert Giovanelli?
one copy each of 2 vols WL in circ/ BELATEDLY.

WL go'r a nopinion of March, Botterl [Ronald Bottrall] and co? now the Tumbi [Tambimuttu] is tumb out?
March writ nize le'r sez HE didn't do the sabotage.
WAAAL, who did? who t'll is Longmans in person?

In short, only nooz fr/ Lunnon is in wop-wyper re PosO.M. [T.S. Eliot] and the pup. they talked of REEsponserbility.
        Did he take Rita Heyworth to S.Afrikaaaa?

W.L. 2. [Second strip of typing paper.]
idea shd/ be, ED-ited before putt into circulation.
Wot bout Wine-dealer's address, which I hv/ not. Anyhow sympathies to Fanny [Wadsworth]. Endowment of a vorticist room at the/Tight [Tate Gallery]? something to distinguish the era from post-messism, and pathologic tremors. I aint got the gal Zadress. Ed did some clean work, not full of slop. Not his fault he wasn't born Goya. She cant expect a Wad/room ⟨egg-sklusive, but a VORT-room, whytellNot.⟩ I wd/ cheerfully contribute a strip, say 12 ft/ by two of big Gaudier charcoals. Stipulate not more than one of the marginal purr-formers. after all they cant run forever on sWatts [George Frederick Watts, popular British painter], hope, soap etcetera.
        greetinks ovthe seezun, and to th Missus. you may or maynt hv/ noted that the Vivaldi ms/ in Dresden were soaked to hell. Music saved by Ez/ having got it in microfilm.
        viddy VERSO [of strip of paper]
        Proper FOR½MU½lah: a gift of Wad's paint[ing]s, and certain Sum fer

the purr-chase of works showing understanding of basic forms, both in natr/ and ON the kanVASS, or "cohesion and proportion of forms" or that wd/ GIT to be called Vort-room in time. wottell.

"VOIX de Napoléon": ed. P. -L. Couchoud (1949).
March, Botterl and co?: Editions Poetry London; this concerns the "sabotage" of Pound's *Confucius* (see letter 209), which Editions Poetry London failed to publish.
S. Afrikaaaa: Eliot visited South Africa for six weeks in the winter of 1949–50 accompanied, not by Rita Hayworth, but by the Geoffrey Fabers. Eliot was at the time sharing a flat with John Hayward.

216. TL–1. [early 1950]. [St. Elizabeths Hospital. Washington, D.C.].

W.L. with due etc/
Olga [Rudge] has managed to publish foto reprods of FOUR Vivaldi con-
certi/   originals
lost in carpet bombing of Dresden, and text saved ONLY cause Ez/ has had 'em microfilmed.*

She rushed up to Lunnon to see his eminence [T. S. Eliot] before I knew of her time table, otherwise wd/ have asked her to see you.

There are about 36 MORE concerti in micro/ which I shd/ like pub-lished/ BUT the MO-RAL effek could or SHOULD be.

It shd/ not be smothered under bushel. O[lga]. R[udge]. not having talent for publicity etc/

Naow ef W.L. has any bright ones. SPILL 'em.
Or hold it in back of mind till when a favorable opporchinity arises
Not up W. L. partic/ alley, but anyhow Vivaldi so good Bach made use of his stuff.

MORAL heave re/ Ez's Utility /
                                    publicity usefully steered onto   Count
Guido Chigi Saracini / [founder of the Accademia Musicale Chigiana]
                                    cause with enuff spotlight he might print some
MORE/
                But that really is of less moment than moral benefit to Ez/
**might note that the Chigiana has ALSO completed the Cavalcanti pa-

leographic text wot the fat lady [Winifred Henderson] with her AQUILA
press left hung in mid air, with typical brit/marmalade retroscena.**
more details if W.L. can use 'em. VERY hard to git any NOOZ from
Sodom on Thames/ wot bout World Review?? the pollok [the co-editor,
Stefan Schimanski] fired fer his virchoos or the reverse?
In short wd/ like greater influx of data/
earlier EPizl wuz re/ party b'name ov Slocum. (since evaporated) but
then they do / drift in twilight /

$\qquad$ member that touching passage in H.
J[ames]'s bout the dissolving view ??

Dunno ef W. L. ever got the bearing of advance in philology registered in
that Genova edtn/ of Cavalcanti..

$\qquad$ but also wd/ take CONsiderable weight,
in cf/ what the bubfessers [professors] do with their eddikashunt.
The attrition of years etc/ waaal there iz a limit to awl things/

$\qquad$ patience,
O.K. to a point. and our centennaries will be rollin in in another four or
less decades. BUT still .... being TOO still (and/or anchored) etc.

list of able bodies denizens of ThemezGulch [London] might enlighten.
* the careful hun putt mss/ in bombproof cellar but the damn thing
leaked, and water got 'em.
** by't'way WOT evr bekum ov that ole tubo'guts ANYhow an severl
others? Brigit [Patmore], fer ezampl?

Vivaldi concerti: Antonio Vivaldi: Quattro Concerti Autografi (Siena, Italy: Accademia Musicale Chigiana, 1949). R. Murray Schafer writes of the story that
Pound's photocopies saved some of Vivaldi's manuscripts: "The rumor seems
to have spread that the originals were destroyed during the war and that
Pound's microfilm was the only form in which these Vivaldi works survived.
This is both true and untrue. A few of the Dresden manuscripts, including
those obtained by Pound, were 'badly damaged,' but the collection as a whole
remains intact." (*Ezra Pound and Music,* p. 329.)
AQUILA press: When the Aquila Press in London failed, Edizioni Marsano in
Genoa, Italy took over the printing of Pound's *Guido Cavalcanti Rime* (1932).
Winifred Henderson was managing director of the Aquila Press.
dissolving view: Pound also attributes this phrase to James in Canto 87, p. 575.

217. TL–1. [Pmk: Washington, D.C., 22 November 1950]. [St. Elizabeths Hospital]. On air letter form.

wynDAMMMMn
When asked our EMinent colleague [T. S. Eliot] re/ "intellectual life" in them Isles, he sd/ I hd/ "taken him unprepared." Invite exchange of views. Personal being that W. L. got a bit of Yangite nonsense stuck in his giZZard 45 years or 50 ago/ and that it bein contrary to his inborn/ it has stuttered him sincely. However, wot the O. M. [Eliot] gits twisted is more on the surface/ might observe that the Kenner shows signs of de-vilUPing into a KUNDiger, and will cert/ do as well,
waaaal, I shd/ say prob/ do better fer yu than anything else on the hori-Zont. Whether Rangery [Lewis's American publisher, Henry Regnery] can be of use. seein his contagious ambience, I dunno. The O. M. hadn't heerd Tambi's wuz knowd as "Tomb of T/" [*T. S. Eliot, A Symposium* (1948), eds. Richard March and Tambimuttu], how li'l intercommunica-tion occurs even at higher levels. An awareness of outer world cd/ or at any r/ SHD/ be developed. Even yr/ prize gorilla W[inston]. C[hurchill]. wanted to attack thru the balKANZ.

AND yu gittin no knews, afar az known, FROM this gorFerZaken,,, shdn't fergit that 1951 aint 1940 or even '46 or '7.

ANY goddam information WL. can collect and SHIP wd/ be valued. re/ anydam/ there being almost none save in crank pubctns/ Is there anything in partic/ the Blastodizer WANTS/ gentle dame wrut las' week: when I think ov wot yu and WL wuz doink in 1914.

waaal thazz bri'sh elegy at the turn of the 1/2 hunderJahrzeit.
Anyhow, yr/ stealin the Tomb from Tambi[muttu] has had a chicago re-print [Chicago: Henry Regnery, 1949], under the damAdlerz' [Mortimer Adler's] schnozzle. Didja pick up and dope on THAT outfit while "I–presuming"?   Of course they mayn't kno yu are IN the wollumk [volume], and think it pewer as the cowslips in the dell, a wreathe of posies possumd.

Cant get any DIRECT answers, even re/ who hell is nu edtr/ World Rev/ ?? ole Fitz[Gerald]'s son? or wottell?

an wot wiff Lunnon Weaklines [*London* weeklies] mimeographed looks like the doghair waz growin'. The blithering bumability of angSax's re/ affairs of ALL other parts of the terrestrial ,,, is sumfink fer adjectivs.

Wy dont yu encourage the Belgion? seems to be a late-blossoming better than when Quarterlied in the Morterarium [Eliot's *Criterion*].

Infact godDDDAAAQQMMMMbit unleash a postal stamp/ no ned of air mail.

ole Fitz's son: Max Wykes-Joyce wrote to Pound on 8 September 1951 (Lilly Library) that the Fitzgerald of the *World Review* was no relation of the Irish revolutionary Desmond Fitz Gerald.

218. TL–1. [Pmk: Washington, D.C., 6 December 1950]. [St. Elizabeths Hospital]. On air letter form.

W.L.   sometime in Dec/ '50
Have corrected la Raine, pintin' aht that yu were THERE before I was, and noticing things I didn't, ergo if debt it is tother way on. Some of the things were a d.n nuissance, and even when note worthy, in the sense that clogged sewers need unclogging, weren't what I wanted to notice/

i.e. sometimes the L[ewis]/ suspected my nose deficient in perception. and SO on.

re/ yr/ remark p. 260 in Peter's Posies / "as POSSIBLE" line 2, after the quote. UGH, 'ow possible is it?

wot do YU reely fink of the brz in Sodom on Thames? waaal, no, that wdn't git thru the mails.

briky-brak? yes, and if it warn't there? wd they swaller the pills wiff aht the pink sugar coating?

Paris cooking? CHRONOLOGY, mebbe one cd/ git the INgredients. Ham not all fat or zummat.

Ole Fordie [Ford Madox Ford] gettin' sprayed with laudatory goulasch by all the slugs and bat-worms, but his real job hardly recognized. Th iggurunt crediting me with some of it.

sales resistance still strong to anything like debunking. Did I tell yu to read Del Mar?

and so on
SEEZUN'Z greetinks, and regards to yr/ consort.
⟨PS⟩ few days ago I at last got in a radio, thinking to save eyesight or praps different rest from playing solitarie. Might be useful fer someone OUTside, to note the filth, the god damned ignominy of all that I can

manage to hear/ in contrast to Europe / the DIStance from organ in Berlin Dom/ [Cathedral] or me tellin the wops I was damned if I wd/ transmit along with merda musicale / made 'em finally give all Vivaldi with my talks, for as long as their records held out/ Bach-Vivaldi axis.

vs/ no

sense of poison or fluorine in water etc/ Never yet got any attention to "Studies in Contemporary Mentality" (yu prob/ bombadeering at time) anyhow tellin the goddam Brits wot was pizin'em via print on noosestands. Even the O. M. [T. S. Eliot] cdn't see the utility, when I tried for a reprint in volumette. and now lookat their goddam hempire.

anyhow peril to all life above that of newts and dungworms via the "air", the auditory or whatever.. slusch, goddam trype, tunes used to sing in 1895 and ROTTENLY done at that. gheeze the B.Bloody C. [British Broadcasting Company] is an empyrean by contrast.

mebbe it don't git

transmitted to abroad, but 150 millyum peasants being turned into robots. and not even metal robots, but slushpots.

Anyone send yu a Hudson Rev/ with Jaime [deAngulo]'s Injuns in it? blast all, ole J/ dun died, a few days after he got his copy. thus reducing the adult population of the 1/2 sphere by about 50%

la Raine: Kathleen Raine, "Il Miglior Fabbro," *The New Statesman and Nation* 40 (25 November 1950): 510–12.

Peter's Posies: Lewis's article on Pound for the *Quarterly Review of Literature* was reprinted in *Ezra Pound: A Collection of Essays,* ed. Peter Russell. Lewis wrote: "Although my feelings with regard to the Englishman are as different as possible from those of Pound, nevertheless I would endorse everything he says above as to their cultural delinquencies." (p. 260.) Commenting on Pound's dislike of England and the English, Lewis writes that Pound "was more in his element in Paris. I actually believe he cooked better in Paris than he did in London. . . ." (p. 261.)

Jaime's Injuns: Jaime deAngulo, "Indians in Overalls," *Hudson Review* 3 (Autumn 1950): 327–77.

219. TL–1. [Pmk: Washington, D.C., 15 April 1951]. [St. Elizabeths Hospital]. On air letter form.

W.L.   13 Ap/ ad interim.

Detailed note on Hit/ Cult going ⟨to W.L.⟩ in installments slow post. Verlag der Arche [Pound's German publisher], ZURICH 44, Susenbergstrasse 63 who are doing two vols bosche of Ez/ and obediently gittin the best german translator, write AZ follerz "We are really interested in Wyndham Lewis' "Rude Assignment" Could yu send us a reading copy?" Will W.L. git hiz Huctchers [Lewis's publisher, Hutchinson] or pubrs to send same.

In case he dunt know it, best german translator is Eva Hesse, Bauernstr/ 19, iii
     Munich-Schwabing.
also suggest review copies of WL's woiks be sent to Dr J.M. Alvarado, Casilla 1701
     La Paz   Bolivia
Yung Fjelde done a goodish note on WL in Western Review just recd/ along with Sister BERnettaaaaa [Quinn] on Ez an Ovid / nice subject fer cloistered soul.??
waaal more so purrhapz than WL.

Hope Cairns is behaving nicely.

P.S.

     Santayan [Santayana] has just sent his
     Dominions and Powers / [Santayana's *Dominations and Powers,* 1951]
     chapter on p. 249 ["The Middleman in Trade"] might be worth yr/ attention. I dont spose he will
     git vurry far down to partic/ remedies
     bk/ just come, no time to do more than open it

Hit/   Cult: See introduction to Part IV, pp. 227, 229–30n.
Yung Fjelde: Rolf Fjelde, "Time, Space, and Wyndham Lewis," *The Western Review* 15 (Spring 1951): 201–02.
Sister BERnettaaaaa: Sister M. Bernetta Quinn, O.S.F., "Ezra Pound and the Metamorphic Tradition," *The Western Review* 15 (Spring 1951): 169–81.

220. TL–1. [April? 1951]. [St. Elizabeths Hospital. Washington, D.C.]. On verso: W.L. surface.

O.K. ole ROCK-drillaHHHH

Vurry nobl blast, but I dunno az on the interlexshool plane I can accept all yr/ dicta. The BASIC fact is that Ez wuz sending his OWN stuff, NOT axis. Naturally it riles the cockroaches to hear that a wop country had sufficient respect fer awtANle'rs [art and letters] to give a mere goddam Schriftsteller Freedom of the MIKE.

Dunno as political ideas are so dif/ from canons of writing. Ez saw the Georgians were NOT the cream of the cream / same kind of perception wd/ show Ooozenstink [Franklin Delano Roosevelt] an ASS. as now several admit.

No use dragging in ethics as a world that tolerates Edens and Churchills s'en fiche pas mal de that sort of impedimenta. Without which it rots stinks putrifies etc. BUT on the plane of intellect, however much a swine, a plootbaloon puffed up by Weenie [Churchill], and dont blame Weenie, think how tempting it wd/ hv/ been to Iago such a bag of foul air (privileged etc. re/ Owen Wistar's [Wister's] "Philosophy Four". he wuz WEAK in the head.

AND note the SAME zone of ignorance in Hull (Hill billy) Stilwell, good guy, Leahy rubber stamp fer the conviction, and Mme de Chambrun.

1878/ "trying to keep some of the NON-INTEREST-Bearing national debt in circulation as currency."

70 years aint got THAT into the muttheads.

Thing to hammer on is difference between quoting Brooks Adams AS WRIT in 1903, and sending stuff dictated by EVEN the more civilized end of the Axis.

and keep hammering on fact that NOBODY gave the faintest drift of a hint to Ez re/ contents. And that dear ole jew Serao quite amused when I said "I had had freedom PROBABLY because none of 'em had the faintest idea what I was talking about.. I mean wdn't hv/ understood a damword of it.

Vurry nobl blast: Pound refers to Lewis's review of *The Letters of Ezra Pound,* ed. D. D. Paige: "The Rock Drill," *The New Statesman and Nation* 41 (7 April 1951): 398. Lewis concludes his review: "This greatest living American exile apparently did not realize that politics was a different dimension from literature, and now they have him boxed up in the nation's capital . . . ; he will hardly regain his freedom, once more to sing and scold by the Latin Sea, alas!"

OWN stuff, NOT axis: After 29 January 1942, Pound's broadcasts on Italian radio were introduced by a statement that he had written himself: "Rome Radio, acting in accordance with the fascist policy of intellectual freedom and free expression of opinion by those who are qualified to hold it, has offered Dr. Ezra Pound the use of the microphone twice a week. It is understood that he will not be asked to say anything whatsoever that goes against his conscience, or anything incompatible with his duties as a citizen of the United States of America."

dear ole jew Serao: Possibly Serafino Mazzolini, foreign minister of Italy's Salo Republic. In 1944 Pound discussed the American charges against him for making his Rome broadcasts. See Stock, *The Life of Ezra Pound,* p. 406.

221. TL–1. [Summer? 1951].

3215 Tenth Place, Washington S.E.
D.C.

wynDAMMM

use this address [Dorothy Pound's] and not worry about pussyKiKeatrists. hellup power of resistance by a little THOUGHT re/ points raised in notes on Rude Ass[ignmen]t, i.e., a little nutriment for jailed.

in general a battle of EDUCATION, solid, not mere hat tricks needed.
fight vs/ falsification of history in universities.
" " vs/   idem of news in papers.
a little comprehension of the facts / correlation of Ez' publications, uncollected, to select vital points such as last or almost last art.l in "Action" re cultural level.
WL might even review Del Mar /
as Swabe[y] and O[mar].P[ound]. abandoning the sinking island, recommend
Max Wykes-Joyce, 58 Birkhall Rd. S.E. 6

there are two other live kids, Gilling[-]Smith, and Neame, but dont see that they cd/ be of much use to W.L. but suggest Mx W-J (NO, goddamit no, relation of James Jheezus) as vice-Omar in absence of the latter IF he abs/

No suggestion of selections from One Way [*Song*] but of reprint
/ at any rate let WL say what would be USEFUL to him
The Sq/$ pair are ready to be of USE. it dont mean much spondooliks,
but it does mean 10% royalty AND personal distribution to the best grade
of peruzer. and of course grade A. company / no cigarette butts of the
late J[ames].J[oyce]. or other spent rockets. AND as a lot of the early
stuff is NOT covered by cawpyrite in this kuntry, it wd/ be clear gain,
and thin edge of wedge. Sloke [Slocum] is in Choimunny on Hicob/ wafts
thru here once in every five years, the magnif/ lepidopterus.

Curiosity, damBit, KU-RI-osity / as to source of lies / of slanders/ W.L.
has occasionally stimulated thought / let him steer the good guys onto
CURiosity. Hownd-dawgz on trail.
ALSO useful to get two or three or FOUR people to agree on BASIC
dissociations/

this guy Barker seems willin. If WL cd/ spot anyone in London with free
time to look up data in Brit/ Mouseum that wd/ be useful. I.E. WL asks
about being useful / waal when it is said that some (possibly incomprehensible DETAIL of work would be USEFUL dont eggspekk grampaw to
write a whole encyclopedia to explain WHY it wd/ be useful.

A very stupid y[oung]. m[an]. named Rowan has got to london (pizond
wiff Marx) I dont know that ANY use can be made of his plodding energy.

Another USEFUL line might be that grampaw believed in horse-sense
while the Bugsons [Bergsons], Possums etc/ were chasing fads, and pipple
trying to find something they COULD believe instead of gitting down to
what one CAN believe. WORRTEX, as Gaudier used to say. And all the
slimers going in for space plus relativity, or the smearing of Euclid.
Rockets to the dogblasted MOON.

and so on/ ossy keep hr/ taiLUP.

wot I mean is that if SEVERAL writers focus attention on a FEW dis-
sociations, it wd/ emBareArse the henemy.

and fer CONservatives, there is a SANE tradition, to be found in Mencius,
Ocellus (possibly in Pythagoras, but I dunno bout that) Dante AND
Agassiz.

and of course there have been historians / and Alex the Gt/ paid his
sojers' debts, as distinct to guaranteeing loans from the scrougers.

"Action": ". . . Mr. Chris Hollis in Need of a Guide!" *Action* 182 (19 August
1939): 11; or "Gold Brokers," *Action* 163 (8 April 1939): 12.

Sq/ $ pair: T. D. Horton's and John Kasper's Square Dollar Series published short
works, such as Fenollosa's *The Chinese Written Character* and Pound's translation of the *Confucian Analects,* which sold for one dollar.

222. TL–1. [Winter 1952]. [St. Elizabeths Hospital. Washington, D.C.].
On a strip of typing paper.

wynDAMM

it got here goddamit with MONTHS of delay
NNjoying Rot Hill / but p/ 290/
depends whether yu include Confucianism in term "religion" ideogramic
mind: what IS, has been and will be, unless exception or sequence noted
and/or emphasized.
naturally jew/ xtn etc/ largely trype/ and lust for ecclesiatical benefice /
bishoprichs rising from pagan temple property /

BUT Mencius the most modern book in the world/ straight tradition,
AXIS / Mang Tze [Mencius], Dante (scale of values, in the vital part /
Agassiz / that is Dant[e] minus the trimmings a Solid core lasts thru the
lot/ respect for the KIND of intelligence that enables cherry stone to grow
cherries. /

command me.

Rot Hill: In his book of short stories *Rotting Hill* (1951), Lewis wrote (p. 290):
   "Religion is an immovable block of dogmas, anchored in the past; it belongs to
   the past, in order to survive, it must prevent people, at all costs, from getting
   too far away from the past."

223. TC. [Pmk: Silverlake, New Hampshire, 11 August (1952)].

[Pound lent Lewis's *Rotting Hill* to E. E. Cummings and received the following comment on a post card: "Rotting Hill on its way back to you,
with many thanks—by all means send us the other WL. Et bonne

chance!!!" Pound then wrote the following on Cummings's card and sent it on to Lewis.]

W.L. as indicta[i]v[e] of spread of Kulch/ inter barbaros / signature that of Kumrad Kumminkz / author of EIMI and other notable woikz/ They will stand live stuff if brot to 'em.

224. TL–2. [January 1952]. [St. Elizabeths Hospital. Washington, D.C.].

Yes my deah ole wynDAMMMMM

           Will this happy new year's greet (with enclosures) conduce yu to consider that one is not dealing with Coke, Lyttleton, Blackstone and men of LAW.??? Three stinks to start with/ the administration/ the beaneries/ and society piffle / plus the slicks / and SO forth.

AND another point, my Wyndam/

           Instead of asking me to ask myrrh from skunks/ NOW that a few people have noticed the stink of the big foundations/ someone might notice the TYPE of goddam parasite, non-producer that these mutts hire at astronomic salaries/

           and if someone wd/ state in LOUD clear voice that Ez hz done MORE for civilization and international communications than the whole piddling lot of 'em. Saving Vivaldi texts, translation, etc.

the pewkers wd/ have a damn hard time to show the contrary / wd/ prob/ funk it altogether.

           I cant say it because the idea that megalomania affects anything larger than a louse prevails among nitwitz.

and as for the Viennese sewage [Freudianism]/ 40 years and not produced ONE interesting work/

           in fact hoax for paralyzing the will of the victim, like the wopse or whatsodam that lays egg in caterpillar, thru providing MEAT fer its progeny. W.L. has allus IGNored the univ/ stinckg/ not having been putt thru that wringer/

           and of course having his more proximate cloacae, Apes etc/ to occupy or disthract [*sic*] him.

as fer hiking the price of gold/ yr/ proximates have diamonds cheap as coal, or almost, and vaults full of emeralds

and I doubt if an up of gold wd/ increase brit/ bread allowance /

save possibly for a few months as camouflage.

enclosures: missing from letter.
Saving Vivaldi texts: See note to Letter 216.

225. TL–3. [Summer 1952]. [St. Elizabeths Hospital. Washington, D.C.].

W.L. Riter an Abscheroot/
Imposbl/ to git a pipSQueak out of yu / BUT still to indicate that I am in course of perusin' yr/ ult/ [*The Writer and the Absolute,* 1952]

As to Mistaking Mus/ for Jeff/ that is a pinwheel / at times stuck in yr/ formidable hat to catch conies /

I did however live to see Jeff/ quoted on a fascist poster/ statement of which simple item which were it not supported by other witness NOT confined to buGhouse/ might lead to conviction on part of Winchell's pubk/ that one   SHOULD be confined in obvious manicomio [mad-house]/

as to Clowns / if a distinction were drawn between a Barclay Gammon named Churchill and some of the limey variety / and the kind (if yu in-sist on the term) that get swamps drained/ grain grown so that a country need not sink into debt to the great stincgkers who are so effectively de-britaininzing the antient isle/
give me the variety that DOES get the grain grown / the swamps drained. O.KAY.

** also a distinction between ideas WORTH putting into action and the mere drivvle of frawgs, Mal/whichwhat / and Mau/tother.

/ alZO ain yu a bit late in observing the lignification / fixation, in short death of mind in frogland/
or let us say / precisely because it WAS NOT a milieu fitted for uncondi-tioned writing/ I got out of it in 1924 and went where Uniformity was NOT required/

of course even yu dont get rid of the idea that dagos cant think/ however,
yu may take time out to reflect that Italian writing during the ventennio
was NOT prevailingly pro fascist /
                                        the best of it was constructive / but
along with the live thought there was
the non conforming thought / naturally my Doug[las]/ and Gesellism
had NO italian origins/ and was NOT part of govt/ program BUT it was
not suppressed for NOT being such/

and a lot of second rate liberaloid palukas / such as Croce and Einaudi
burbled along /
                        beside Gentile (probably a better egg/ tho I wasn't reading
abstract discussion at the time/

I merely saw him in Pisa when the filthy BBC or some other brit/ source
was burbling about shame of his being exiled to the penal isles.

So far ⟨up to p/ 90⟩ that is all the dissenting notes on Wr/ and Abs/

after woptalia the worst strain on bak of one's nekk in this continent is
the goddam iggurunce and frivolity of the alledgedly edderkateds.

And again / yu can find serious sentences / serious definitions in M[usso-
lini]'s writing/
                        not such a whale of a lot of 'em / but enough to qualify as
"serious character" in Rebel Art Centre usage of that term.
                                                            Whether ANY
of the dambastids responsible for destruction of european balance of
power can have as much sd/ for 'em / I leave to yu.
                                                        Cert/ not the
Churchills, Ooozenstinks [Roosevelts] and Edens ?
                                            (or have
yu evidence that this aint so.
        dunno if yu ever revise/ but cd/ tighten use of "oriental" when yu
mean that source of all filth / the mogoloido mespot/ mess that interrupted communication between the two centres of decency / China Mid
Kingdom/ and the Mediterranean basin /   clear from context that yu
mean the goddam muscovitobabylo etc/
and of course all forms of idiocy hv/ also appeared ⟨in China⟩ and largely
got registered in ideogram /
                        serendipity/ chinoiserie etc/
vs/ the sanity.

waaal yu sure do like cleanin sewers / and more powWoWer to yr/
HELLbo.   Ole BURGlar alaRRum in a land where there aint no
mental cops /

        my more finniky natr purrfurring hunt water supply/ BUT
the shovel is useful. As per 30 years / LACK of communications no ad-
vantage/

If yu havent noted. Beck / Dernier Rapport / Adolf [Hitler] decided Eng/
not serious re/ Pole guarantee when Soapy Si [Sir John Simon, chancellor
of the exchequer] "lesinait" on a (7 million I think it was, anyhow
SMALL) loan to la poLOGne [Poland].

Spampanato [an Italian journalist]/ "Contromemmoriale/" Money-issue as
sovereignty/ only 3 lines/ too bad I didn't meet him 20 years ago/ also
Muss called him down fer overlooking the U,S.Consterooshun.

    which yu can putt with Jeff/ quote / and conclude / Nacherly I cant
PROVE I edderkated manyDAM wopz. But dont YOU goddamit go to
thinking I was swoonink in idolatry rather than trying to plant a few
seed[s]. Incidentally while the island apes are being bled (with vaults,
safe deposit, still (one supposes) stuffed with emeralds/ and the S.Af/
diamonds pullulating like lice) Italy now chief creditor country in la vielle
YouROPE.   which must indicate that some dagos had more alertness
than the squalid disciples of the Sodom on Thames Univ/ or school of
kneeconomikz [London School of Economics].

Mus/ for Jeff: In *The Writer and the Absolute* (1952), Lewis wrote (p. 41):
   "As to Ezra Pound, previous to his incomprehensible intervention in World
   War II (when in some moment of poetic frenzy he mistook the clownish Duce
   for Thomas Jefferson), he never revealed any interest at all in politics, only in
   Douglasite economics."
Mal/ whichwhat: In *The Writer and the Absolute,* Lewis discussed André Mal-
   raux, Claude Mauriac, François Mauriac, and Charles Maurras.
ventennio: il ventènnio fascista, the roughly twenty-year fascist period in Italy.

226. TLS–1. On stationery imprinted: Studio A, Kensington Gardens Studios, 29 Notting Hill Gate, London, W. 11. Lewis's postal code is W. 11 from this date on.

Sept. 10. 1952.

My dear Ezz.   Thank you for your communication re <u>Writer</u> and <u>Absolute</u>. It is no use protesting about your <u>absolute</u> nationalism, of course. But I know you are not such a fool as to think that it makes any difference whether you live beside the Thames or beside the Potomac. What <u>does</u> matter is <u>how</u> you live and the sooner you get out of that Asylum the better. Do <u>you</u> think Oozenstink as you call him might be inclined to forget your insults to Mr. Roosevelt?

It wearies me your remaining where you are. To take up a strategic position in a lunatic asylum is idiotic. If I dont see you make an effort to get out <u>soon</u>, I shall conclude, either that your present residence has a snobbish appeal for you, or that you are timid with regard to Fate. – Ask your wife to give the signal to your horde of friends to go into battle for you. Anyhow, my love to you and Dorothy.

Your,
Wyndham L.

Oozenstink: Lewis may have thought that Pound referred to President Harry S Truman as "Oozenstink" when in fact Pound was referring to Franklin Delano Roosevelt.

227. TL–1. [Fall? 1952]. [St. Elizabeths Hospital. Washington, D.C.].

wynDAMMN

on reflection will probably concede that it wd/ have been useless for me to reply to his ult/ at an earlier date.

Noting the element of TIME in the goddam morasses of western 1/2 sphere/ etc. timeLAG in Regnery, fer ezampl and "Revenge"

and recording ole Fordie's favorite: hypocrisy to seek for the pussn of the Sac/EmPEror in a low teaHouse.

I think the next advisable move wd/ be strictly in the suburbia of licherary crizsm/ to DISTINGUISH between those authors whose minds possessed some quality which prevented them fer falling fer the tide of red poison/ pinko snobismo etc.

notable among which are W.L. / Mr cummings (as of EIMI) and one or two more whose names will occur to yu.

There have been diversives/ there still ARE. Archaic fads / leading of discussion from focal points / failure to consider that the kulch/ level niv/ etc. of a conducting nation cannot SAFELY be allowed to descend to the level of Adamic and Mickey Rooney.

and so on /

with, as usual, my considering and respectful saluti.

any line on this bloke Oakeshott ?

"Revenge": Lewis's novel *The Revenge for Love* was published in England in 1937 and was not published in America until Henry Regnery (Chicago) brought it out in 1952.

228. TLS–1. On stationery imprinted: Studio A. Kensington Gardens Studios. 29 Notting Hill Gate. London, W. 11.

5 Dec. 1952.

My dear Ezz. Thanks for yours, and was glad to hear my letter had reached you: you say that Regnery has printed something without my knowledge, but <u>what</u> you do not say. Reg did not send me a copy of the book. Will try and get copy.

Yulish greetings.

W. L.

229. TL–1. [December 1952]. [St. Elizabeths Hospital, Washington, D.C.].
W.L.

not abserOOTly certain
but as far as can recall
Regnery's little SURprise fer whnDAMM

wuz "revenge fer luVV" / [Lewis's novel, *The Revenge for Love,* 1952]
                    lent perused vols/ to Mr French father of two
females /
      his wife took 'em fer bedside reading
                    and the THIRD French de-
scendent hastend out one month in advance,
                    and
                      naturally
                        MALE.
                      appy gnu yeah

[Dorothy Pound added the following note:]

The prof. had "Rotting Hill"   Regnery   & the jacket
said, shortly to be brought out.
                    R. for Love
                    Tarr
                    Wild Body

Mr. French: William and Gloria French were friends of Pound and often visited him at St. Elizabeths. Their third child, born on 11 December 1952, was named Luke Ezra French.

230. TC. [Pmk: Washington, D.C., 27 January 1953].

the herMITT rektor of Warleggan
(ef we spel it rite, as fr/ radio noise
one more iteM fer WynD/L's anglican
KO lexshn

anglican KO lexshn: Pound was apparently suggesting a subject for a short story by Lewis. Lewis had written about two Anglican clergymen in *Rotting Hill:* the Rev. William Feast (as the Rev. Samuel Hartley Rymer of "The Bishop's Fool") and Pound's friend Rev. Henry Swabey (as the Rev. Matthew Laming of "Parents and Horses").

231. TN–1. [St. Elizabeths Hospital. Washington, D.C.]. This note was included in a letter to Agnes Bedford.

26 Ag   "53

WynDAMMMM
waHHHH waaaal, I be-blowed.
D[orothy]. h[a]v[in]g/ at outrageous cost got hold of a cawpy of SNOOTY [Lewis's novel, *Snooty Baronet*] I cannot, i.e. it taint worf me while to take the trouble to refrain
from / GOSH.
I naturally have NOT opened a page of D. H. L[awrence]. since 1912 or '13 or whenever he did a couple of short stories/ but I'm damned if I knew it was cow-slop
to the degree of passage
quoted by yr/ rivrince [reverence].
How well and how wisely I did to
EMERGE quitely from yr/ greasy isle
decades ago, to the less
cumbered frawgland, and thence to the Ventennio [Fascist era in Italy].
    NoozZITEM; Carter's W. L. issue eggzists/ Ash Brown had one, and I am still waitin fer a bound copy.

passage quoted: In Chapter IV of his novel *Snooty Baronet* (1932), Lewis parodies D. H. Lawrence's style.
Carter's W. L. issue: The "Wyndham Lewis Number" of *Shenandoah* IV (Summer/Autumn 1953), edited by Ashley Brown, Thomas Carter, and Hugh Kenner.

232. TL–1. [St. Elizabeths Hospital. Washington, D.C.].

W. L.

    dunno whether Kit Kat [Kitasono Katue, editor of *Vou*] sends yu his products / his last vol   250 pages,/deewotes some to yu p. 127 az I dunt read jap / I dont propose to plow thru dic/ for chinese ideograms and guess at the rest. I dont know what partic/ USE this jap stuff is / Kit Kat at least not owned by Bloomsbury, tho too much small frog infiltration / may be jap trans/ ultimately acts as indirect leverage VIA froggery / If yr/ pubrs have spare review cawpies might need some to
    Kitasono Katue

1649 1 tiome nisi

MAGOME   ota M.Omoriku, Tokio, JApan.

*** Marg Anderson wantin to git yr soul filled wiff sweetness and light via some Gurdjieffite femme now in Paris

I have told her I am unable to promote this action.

But, of course, if yu are feelin the NEED of such operations I will be glad to transmit yr/ reactions to M.A.

Did yu henquire re/ the Widdy CARUSO / if so, he was a wopera singer who woptained q. a lot of pub/cty in his time. rhyming, as Time sez, with Rrnsn [Robinson] Crusoe.

23

Ot [October]

53

Gurdjieffite femme: In a letter to Pound of 9 October [1953] at the Beinecke Library, Margaret Anderson suggested that the shock of Lewis's blindness might make him more receptive to religious experience and that a Parisian follower of Gurdjieff, Mme. Vera Daumal, would be able to present the Russian mystic's ideas to Lewis persuasively.

Widdy CARUSO: The widow of Enrico Caruso, Dorothy, who was a friend of Margaret Anderson.

233. TLS–1. On stationery imprinted: Studio A, Kensington Gardens Studios, 29 Notting Hill Gate. London, W. 11.

Nov. 19th 1953.

Dear Ezz.   You have been doing your best to transform a late celebration into a 1914 (strictly pre-war) Blast. But how are you? Is your health passable?

Your Japanese suggestions appear to me too implicated with Korea, North and South. That is perhaps a mistake. Regard the United States as more immediately important to myself, and somehow or other to get better understood there – not blurred and misrepresented.

W. L.

234. TL–1. [St. Elizabeths Hospital. Washington, D.C.]. On air letter form.

W.L.

13 Dec 53

Waaaal, me old VORT

        CAN a kat laugh louder / the CBS raDIO nitwork
just doink "inVItashun to learnink"
Bryson. L.evans (ex-lie-bury-em of Konkruss) [Luther Evans, ex-Librarian of Congress] and some hindoo /

    Evans now head of Unesco (known as Nabisco) tellin the listenink
woild how Unesco shd/ purrmote interchange, and translation of great
buks from oRIent.

Now were I at large and some other Giauscutus in jug/
the proportion between wot Ez has done fer kulchurl eggschange/ and
what all these fahrts hv/ accomplished/

        with millions of oil, steel, buncomb
aluminum/ etc..

    wd/ raise at least one eyebrow in iRONY

    thazz enuf fer one letter/
dont let me disthrakt yu with minor itemZZ
but wyper here sez the Beaver [Lord Beaverbrook] is weepink cause Dexter
White DECEIVED that buncosteer Keynes.

    (were AV I heerd thet nayme?)

Yr yung frien Pete HRRRusl [Russell] hasn't YET managed to get copies
of ABC to this address.

Forssell's sweedish select Ez poEMZ sold at once, and F/ amused that his
pubrs/ had (nacherly) destroyed the plates and had to set up 2nd/ edtn/
ex novo.

Giauscutus: In American folklore the Guyascutus or Guyasticutus is a ferocious
creature of indeterminate form. Traveling showmen would offer to show it to
a crowd of paying spectators. The showmen would panic the crowd by claiming the creature had broken loose and then disappear with the money.

Beaver is weepink: Harry Dexter White, American director of the International
Monetary Fund in 1946, and Lord Keynes were co-authors of the Bretton
Woods monetary pact and co-authors of the International Monetary Fund. This
relationship was in the news in 1953 because White had been accused of being
a spy for the Communists.

ABC: Pound's *ABC of Economics,* second edition (May 1953).

Forssell's sweedish select: Pound's *Dikter,* trans. Lars Forssell (1953).

235. TL–1. [St. Elizabeths Hospital. Washington, D.C.].

13 Mz [March] 54

W.L.

minor matter / but as several ikles make a mickle. Question of COMpensation. You may or may not remember Tami Kume's paintings in my studio in Paris/ but you could remember 'em. I mean it is not inherently improbable, or strictly impos/

You SAID that the portrait of the prince (never remember his name and yu prob/ never knew it. two spheres, and a serene expression. To be exact you said nowt re/ the big ten by 12 ft/ swish and swirl /

BUT fer the purposes of valuation, you might risk yr/ rep/ that the pair were worth at least $2000.

NOT ov course that the market . etc. we know about markets. The point is they were in house rented to a wop/ and I spose he bein a painter (did my portrait, and I did not buy it, nacherly,) but he HAD a market, tho supposed to live on "cambiali."

Anyhow, he presumably cut up the big painting cause canvas was scarce during the late unpleasantness. ⟨& the other disappeared.⟩

My name shd/ NOT enter the question, as my status is as yu know.

But if yu cd/ limber yr/ conscience to state that you think the valuation of $2000 for the two painting[s] is very moderate and probly much too low/

it might assist.

Gornoze the dagos took more than the woikz of awt.
⟨Just 2 lines typescript & siggychoor.⟩

With espressioni di alta stima / etc.

B.B.C. says it is projectin some Sophokles Ezd/ on the 25 Ap. prox.
I suppose the chit shd/ read.

In my opinion two painting[s] by Tami Kume, a large canvass about 3 metre by 2–1/2 and a smaller portrait, both in low tone buff, yellow and blackish are undervalued or at least very moderately valued at $2000.

Kume's paintings: Pound held a show of Tami Koume's paintings in Paris in the 1920s. The "big ten by 12 ft/ swish and swirl" is *Tami's Dream* (mentioned in Canto 76, p. 462), which was hung in Olga Rudge's house in Venice. Her books and paintings were damaged during the war, and Pound was apparently

279

trying to obtain compensation from the Italian government. The painter who cut up the painting for canvas was Guido Tallone.

Sophokles Ezd/: Sophokles: Women of Trachis, trans. Ezra Pound (1956). It was first performed on the BBC's Third Programme on 25 April 1954.

236. TL–2. [St. Elizabeths Hospital. Washington, D.C.]. On air letter form.

19 Nov. 54

Yuss. my beamish buckO ! this IZ some book.
above ref/ to "Self Condemned" [Lewis's novel, 1954] wich 'as at larst reached me. Now at page 245.

An' do oi recall the wife of a DIStinguish -ed ex-official and author of AWT woik, assenting re/ fee given him

that
"Of course, bribes".
Even the distinguished and successful KANDIDAT is bowdlerized when reported in the N.Y. Slimes [*Times*], according to pipe line (said to be from one present at interview via partner of the DIStinguished visitor transmitting.)

Campa cavallo, che l'erba cresce. I don't see how my telling the intelligent Sweede (who says some sweedes reads) is goin' to take effect in time to be of much use.

There OUGHT to be more and quicker communication between the 34 men of good will/

YU allus were a lousy correspondent, but as Fred Manning once remarked there are or, perhaps in the singular, is a what the hell was it: "extenuating circumstance".

I have time to read, and something the nrg/ to do so. If yu have heard of any other buks projuiced in Britain since the late (and continuing) unpleasantness I wd/ take under CONsideration yr/ indication re/ their eggzistence.

"Constantinople our Star" (just to annoy yu by retrospect). You can't have KNOWN much or in fact anybollodywhatsodam particular re/ same. But Baynes and Moss "Byzantium" contains a chapter by Andreades ["The Economic Life of the Byzantine Empire"].
It was writ long after yr/ hunch.

Fordie wd/ have had to admit S[*elf*]. Cond[*emned*]/ is a novel, At least I think so.

He (F.M.F.) once did a SHORT book, I spose pot-b[oiler]/ and to order for a lousy series / it wuz called "The English Novel" / never 'eerd tell on it, till this month, or last.

The Coll / NO the SElected Essays of Wm. the Walruss Williams (hay-stack) contains several needles. Or tacks fer TSE to rise from when in cathedra. or in the act of inSEDation.

Buzzard [Williams] wrut a lousy Autobiog/ but 50 years writing NOT for money, in fact almost NEVER for $ / has paid off. God knows who did the selecting. Even he may have done it. And the bugocracy doin' him dirt. Front page headline scandle, re/ his being non-investigated, but kept out of job. Local Ch/ of Commerce, givin' him dinner. These minor items will NUT reach the Brit/ Press/ BUT as yu still follow current events (the HELL yu do "follow") as yu still adjourn in the wop sense / i.e. take note of current collapses/ I go on hittin the keys. Of course WCW dont KNOW enough. He often muddles but does not fake.

There are three or four young livin in '54 mental chronology. Campa cavallo.

My friends (or gang) write good books, the others do NOT. The IDIOCY of the whole damn system, basic, is making LEGAL crimes of non-criminal acts like selling beer or lugging diamonds from one place to another / this DONE under idiotic superstition that the buggars need to TAX something to get revenue.

Racket shown up or understood 300 years before Kublai [Khan] / J. Adams pre-Gesell / recently (or since my cantos) pubd/ letter of J.A. to Rush / "devaluation for benefit of the WHOLE people" (1811 .. 5 years before Jeff/ to Crawford. Have you read (or even recd/ the Benton [Square Dollar] reprint, and the Del Mar?)

Carson Chang / "Third Force in China" / haven't yet got hold of it.

alzo Waddell (dup up fer yanks by "Alfalfa Bill" Murray / who alzo did chapter on Swabey's fight fer local school/ ex-gov. of Oklahoma / now 83.

Wonder cd/ yu educate Pegler. Methuen SHOULD damn well send him review copy of Self. Con.
address Westbrook P. King Features, 235 E. 45th . N.Y. 17

He is now aware that he did NOT accept invitation to write fer Exile/ / He COULD be useful to YOU.

No reason MORE am/ profs/ shdn't follow up Kenner and Shenendoah. One of the best Clark Emery bx/ 1265 S. Miami, Florida.

in strictest ANonyMity. y[ours]. v[ery]. t[ruly].

Campa cavallo: This may be a proverbial saying: "Horse get going, the grass is
   growing."

some sweedes reads: a reference to Lars Forssell's translation of Pound's *Dikter.*

"extenuating circumstance": In a letter to Olivia Shakespear in 1909, the poet
   and novelist Frederic Manning wrote that " 'He (Ezra) is not as other men
   are – He has seen the Beatific Vision[.] Which is an extenuating circumstance.' " See Pound and Litz, *Ezra Pound and Dorothy Shakespear: Their
   Letters 1909–1914,* p. 9.

"Constantinople our Star": In one of Lewis's "War Notes" in *BLAST,* no. 2 (July
   1915): 11, Lewis hoped that Russia would conquer Turkey and turn Constantinople into a cultural capital: "The traditional amenity of the Turk helping to
   make the Southern Russian Capital the most brilliant city poor suffering humanity has ever beheld, not excepting Paris and Vienna."

headline scandle: In 1952 William Carlos Williams was offered the position of
   consultant in poetry to the Library of Congress. His liberal politics of the thirties, however, came to the notice of the *Washington Times Herald,* and as a result of the controversy he was never officially approved for the position. Luther
   Evans was chief librarian at this time and did not support Williams.

J.A. to Rush/ . . . *Jeff to Crawford:* These letters are cited, respectively, in
   Pound's *What is Money For?* and *Introductory Text Book.* See *Ezra Pound,
   Selected Prose,* ed. Cookson, pp. 313, 296.

local school: Lewis wrote of the Reverend Henry Swabey's attempt to stop a local
   school from being closed in his story "Parents and Horses" in *Rotting Hill.*

Shenendoah: A special "Wyndham Lewis Number" of *Shenandoah* was issued
   for Summer–Autumn 1953. Hugh Kenner's *Wyndham Lewis* appeared in
   1954.

237. TLS–1. On stationery imprinted: Studio A. Kensington Garden Studios. 29 Notting Hill Gate, London, W. 11.

Dec 2nd 1954.

Dear Ezz.   Your letter with approval of Self-Condemned gives me great
pleasure. A constant stream of rumors reached me about you. – The latest,
that the U. S. Government were releasing you, and sending you to China.
I hope that this is true. It is also said that you have officially finished your
Cantos. Is that true? Give me, from the horses mouth, the latest. How

is the little old health. It is a very good sign that you are working. Me pongo a los pies de su señora.

<u>W. L.</u>

238. TL–2. [St. Elizabeths Hospital. Washington, D.C.]. On air letter form.

6 Dec/ [1954]

W.L.

to confirm HIGH opinion of "Self -Cndd"/ [Lewis's *Self Condemned*] it and Rot-Hill all post 2nd/ hell lit/ yet discovered among ruins of Albion. Shd/ git yu the Nobble [Nobel Prize].

Cantos damn well not officially, or any howsodam FINISHED // Hudson [Review] was going to print 85 / but the print shoppe has anti-McCarthies and Dex Whites placed to throw monkey wrenches / I spose munition woikz in same shape/
F[rank].M[orley]. in S[outh].A[frica]. till tenth / proofs for NEXT issue [of Cantos, *Section: Rock-Drill*] promised ten days ago have NOT arruv / and wont till he goes down and sets the type himself. IF then ...

Buzzards (and cockroaches) trying every wheeze to get me into congeries of mouse-traps and to put up a false defence to OBSCURE all the real issues.

DUTY of citizen (when senator can't) to Warn his buggard compathriots that they are being sold down the river. Charter Oak in Connecticut, not getting any publicity, let alone enough.

Free speech nuts now without radio free/ I think it was Manchester Guardian quoted that line/ but had to be TOLD to do so.

Naturally the decent chinks wd/ LIKE to have me teaching the iggurunt about Confucio/ BUT Knowland cant

git more than 25% of the senate/
                              and they dont agree with each other about
nuffink wotsodam.

S. Amurika or Mexico via isolated individs thinks they wd/ more appreciate my curious talents than the inhabs/ of Baruchistan [America] / etc,
campa cavallo.

Do you want nice kid [probably Stephane de Yankowska] to help Agnes
[Bedford] read to you?
Or does she regard it as a privilege not to be shared?
Modest candidate did NOT suggest herself, but has just come up with the
ONLY summary of St Augustine that seems useful: sic:

Love God and do as
you please.

Someone ought to correct errors in "Panorama de la lit/ contemporaine
auZZ etatZZ uniZZ" by John Brown.
pubd/ by GallimeRDE.
I dont think in malice, just propagatin iggurunce of
fact I had FREEDOM of microphone.

th owld Admiral [Sir Barry Domvile] wonders WHY all this build up of
W[inston].C[hurchill]. (yr/ national figure)?
Tenzone / p/s/ various that I cd/ write re/ Self/Cndd
/tenzone with Cantares / W.L. objecting to grampaw's vision of the world
as ice-cream soda ⟨Incidentally Possum is all WET when he tries to set my
2 canto vignette of the mind of London 1919 against ALL Dante' hell.⟩

Both works highly necessary. Defence vs/ W.L.'s earlier objection / there
ARE several unpleasant items mentioned in Los Cantares. and so/ on.
any CONversation occur in the Olde Capital in
these later times?

I dont spose yu saw Geo[rge]. Biddle / curious way of expressin his horror
of war / had job of sketching the generals (Nurnberg trials) but fer his
own. went down to the BOTTOM to inspect the torturers etc/ / very
mellowed and humane, after interval of 22 years. I didn't think to ask him
if he has stopped off in London.
    PS. continued
Gt/ comfort to see another adult. One bulgar has immigrated, but I only
see him once in three years. Aldous [Huxley] alzo ripened a bit.
    Talleyra[n]d was a bit older when he said: all contemporaries are
now friends.
    Ever hear of John Burnet : "Early greek philosophy" 1892 / some
items on numbers by diagram, as dice and dominos/ frog named Milhaud

evident source re/ gk/ mathematics. Also a few quotes from Empedokles. Get Blackstone back into print / esp/ if yu seeing Possum, who COULD

if yu light a fire under him. Want some Benton? or other improvin readin matter?

Hudson [*Review*]*:* "Canto 85" was published in the *Hudson Review* 7 (Winter 1955): 13–27.

Charter Oak: Pound refers (as in Canto 74, p. 447 and elsewhere in the *Cantos*) to the story of the citizens of Hartford hiding the charter of Connecticut in an oak tree when it was demanded by the British governor general in 1687.

Free speech nuts now without radio free/: One of Pound's favorite tags; see Canto 74, p. 426; "that free speech without free radio speech is as zero."

John Brown: He wrote in his *Panorama de la littérature contemporaine aux États-Unis* (1952) that Pound spoke on fascist radio as a propagandist for Mussolini.

Possum is all WET: In *After Strange Gods* (1933), p. 47, T. S. Eliot described Pound's "Hell" Cantos (XIV–XV) as "a Hell for the *other people*."

John Burnet: Pound refers to Chapter II, paragraphs 46–50, of Burnet's *Early Greek Philosophy*, in which Burnet cites Gaston Milhaud's *Les Philosophes-Géométres de la Grec.*

239. TLS–1. On stationery imprinted: Studio A, Kensington Gardens Studios, 29 Notting Hill Gate, London, W. 11.

Dec 31. 1954.

Dear Ezz. I greatly value your good opinion, so what you say about Self-Condemned gives great pleasure. About June a very big book [Lewis's fiction, *The Human Age: Books 2 and 3,* 1955] is appearing: I will send a copy to Dorothy: if I sent it to Saint Eliz the Management might not consider it suitable reading for you. I hear rumours which are promising regarding your probable freedom. Hemingway was helpful I believe.

Omar [Pound] seems to have settled in what is a very pretty city [Montreal] for N. America and it is his ambition to teach oriental tongues. There is no reason that I can see why Canuck's should not learn to converse in the language of Omar Kayam.

I have just been reading a Babylonish cosmogony by an admirer of yours. Many echoes of your private lingo.

Best wishes for freedom in New Year.

Yrs.

W. L.

P.S. You speak of doing some "promotion". I, of course, welcome any action of yours.

Babylonish cosmogony: D. G. Bridson's *The Quest of Gilgamesh* (1956).

240. TL–1. [St. Elizabeths Hospital. Washington, D.C.].

9 Jan or thaaar9bouts [1955]

Know then, **O Man**

if up to hither thou hast or art in a state of non-knowing, that in Baruchistan [America]

IS: "The murkn SOCiety for Aesthetics."

with a "Journal of Aesthetics and" awt crizism.
And our cigarette butts are to be preserved in aspic.

in yr/ case by Geof Wagner, un tel, impossible to make out if among those present were Ed. Wad[sworth] AND his uncle, or if Ed Wad WAS the unkl of Geof. Wag.

If yu collect, or incline toward aspic containing yr/ cigarette butts, the issue for Sept. 1954
contains the artl/ "W.L. and the Vort. AESTHETIC."

at 6$ buks a year. –NO price quoted on single issues.

I spose the aesthete who brot/ the Sept. issue MIGHT lend it to you/ I dont see how either of us can extract 6 bucks worth of juice from another cawpy.

I spose Rostand said all in "co/ko-Ri-ko".

"Journal of Aesthetics": Geoffrey Wagner, who was the nephew of the Vorticist artist Edward Wadsworth, wrote "Wyndham Lewis and the Vorticist Aesthetic," *The Journal of Aesthetics and Art Criticism* 13 (September 1954): 1–17.

"co/ko-Ri-ko": The cry of the rooster in Edmund Rostand's verse play *Chantecler* (1910).

241. TL–2. [St. Elizabeths Hospital. Washington, D.C.].

20 Jan 55   W.

                                                                               L.

AND seriously, is there NO way to get anything printed in england until it pleases the totally DEAD mentality of The Nursing Mirror?

Conditioned by a cut or cut back to at least one and possibly more parasites?

Whether there OUGHT to be time for me to cash in on having mobilized the various Harriets (M & W) [Harriet Monroe and Harriet Shaw Weaver] etc.

Check / you did mobilize Pete Russell. And Pete got something started/
        I don't make out just what sands he has run into / probably vendetta from the s.o.b. cutting his overdrafts etc/
                        That high degree of liquidity, first checked, I believe, in the case of Cecil Palmer, about 1920 or before.

You kno poifikly well that a commercial house is no damn use for life of the mind /
        What has functioned since old Harriet [Monroe], I dunno.
You noted my absence from the country/
                        and ....
Seems the frogs got a paper called "RIVAROL" /
        hv/ yu seen any other attempts at a ⟨frog⟩ comeback.??
        Got to be means of printing for sake of SUBJECT matter not merely one firm tolerating an estabd/ author / one author per firm.
        Possum [Eliot] willing to print the more approx
Xtn/ parts of Ez/ Forget who pubs/ you, Methuen or someone BUT does NOT, so far as known, print any other author showing traces of mind.
        WORTEXXX, gorrdammit, some convergence/
The fact that I leak thru, in furrin translations, dont hellup yr/ gordorful isle.

Neither do one or two clandestine reviews printed in the J[ewnited]. S[tates]. and no use seeing snakes/ but alzo no use cultivating oblivions re/ industrial espionage and sabotage, in print shoppes as well as in munitions plants/
high % of military air-crashes, in proportion to Civil aviation's. Has Kenner, by the way, a good list of translations of W.L. into heathen tongues?

Have yu heard from a s.o.b. who sez he has writ a bk/ [Leopold Infield, *The Evolution of Physics,* 1938] in colab[oration]/ with Einstein (god damn him)*. and now proposes a work on woild lit/ from Adam to us ? or at least Adam to Ez.? he hrites a vunny englisch vrom sVVizzerlandt.
   * Einstein, not the s.o.b.
The s/o/b. seems to be documented up to about 1930.

Did I mention Waddell? whom you did NOT tell me about 20 years ago ???
and why NOT ??
     now dead, of course.
discovered fer murka by Alfalfa Bill [Murray], who has unfortunately read the Bible/
   BUT is otherwise sound of wind and limb at age of 83.
Of course you ought not to be bothered re/ anything but makin pixchoors of INDIVIDUAL kurrAkters, portraits.

at the same time we NEED and like HELL we need a little controversial writing.

Can't yu find any bright young things to SET TO WORK on same? I am gittin bloody near fed up with bein' in jug.

there is no doubt that this is the MOST god damned UNinteresting country in the world / and that IT WAS NOT always uninteresting. In fact from 1750 to 1870 it was worth inhabiting. ⟨mebbe to 1880⟩

There were individuals/ and it is now inflicted with blotting paper and wooden clocks. The total piffle is beyond belief.
   with which mansuete and urbane reflections I
     fer the moment, close.

The Nursing Mirror: The Nursing Mirror: Pocket Encyclopedia and Diary, one of Faber and Faber's most successful books.

242. TLS–1. [Carbon]. [January 1956]. [Studio A, Kensington Gardens Studios, 29 Notting Hill Gate. London, W. 11.] The unsigned carbon of this letter is at the Olin Library, Cornell University; but the second paragraph is from a signed, typescript fragment at the Beinecke Library, Yale University.

Dear Ezz.   Your last letter undeciperable, just cannot imagine what lies beneath the words. Have you anything really to say? I have something to ask you. Do you remember some drawings (water colour and ink, vertical and bright) that Mrs Shakespeare [*sic*] bought, and which I believed went to Rapallo? If you know present owner, will they allow them to be collected by the Tate Gallery, which is proposing a retrospective exhibition? No time fixed as yet, but it will be soon, and I will send you details soon.

How did you and Dorothy get through the Christmas and New Year? Did the Warders and Doctors sing you Carols, as the Nurses and Doctors did in hospitals here? Best wishes, anyway, best wishes to both of you. I expect you heard that He, you call Possum [T.S. Eliot] lies in the London Clinic. It is not, I understand, in anyway alarming.

Yrs,

W.L.

some drawings: See notes to Letters 244 and 245.

243. TL–1. [St. Elizabeths Hospital. Washington, D.C.]. On air letter form.

27 Feb/ [1956]

Got stuck trying to read yr/ nut [note?] on Richard [Aldington] on Tommy L[awrence]/ naturally wdn't have tried to read it if it had been by any one else.

Trouble is the buggar was NOT a first rate mind. Kid brother, Will, must have been flower of the flock. killed in 1915.

Tom L/ night he came to H[olland].P[ark].C[hambers]. wanted to talk about modern art / wdn't talk about you, blithered about god KNOWS which of 'em,

Nevinson or Duncan Grant	I dont
or zummat. # # #	think it
Do yu need to eat ALL of a egg ...	was as good
	as D[uncan].G[rant].

Albion seems has got a NEW low, name long familiar but odour wuss than thought, as of course the name sepulchres might lead to expect.

as he had been with Lard Geo[rge]/ and the frogblastador [French ambassador]
, yes. yes, might well want to keep off matters of
interest, especially with a furriner, but
to gravitate to second or third rate art....
                    that is the punt I am smackin'.

Tommy L/: Lewis reviewed Richard Aldington's *Lawrence of Arabia: A Biographical Enquiry* in the *Hudson Review* 8 (Winter 1956): 596–608. Pound also compares T. E. Lawrence to his younger brother William in Canto 74, p. 444.

244. TLS–1. On stationery imprinted: Studio A, Kensington Gardens Studios, 29 Notting Hill Gate, London, W. 11.

April 26 1956.

Dear Ezz.   Thank you for letter, some days or weeks ago. I prepare or help to prepare with Rottenswine [John Rothenstein] of the Tate a retrospective Show. I should have liked the group of bright coloured watercolour and ink panels bought by Olivia Shakespeare [*sic*]. But it is too late, and the Rotten Shit unwilling to spend money. Also, do you know, individually, where your things are in Italy?

When is the American Law going to release you? Loving and respectful greetings to Dorothy.

Yours
W.L.

P.S.   Eliot has sailed from here. Is visiting you I believe.

water-colour and ink panels: Three panels with the single title *Abstract Drawing,* which Lewis did in 1926.

28 Ap/[1956]

    revered colleague and ancient bombshell / It aint the LAW that keeps me in. Aint yu never heered of the Persecut Atty/ of Phila "All I'm in'erested in is BUNK, seein wot yu can putt over."

    When, if EVER, freedom of the press extends in the Jewnited States beyond struggling fortnightlys and fly sheets the steps ad BugHouzum may get printed somewhere the popLik can see 'em.

Several wild men now mention the Constitution/ and there is a new ten cent edtn/ NOTING, as it always has/ the WHEN habeas corpus may be LEGALLY suspended.

        i.e. in times of invasion or rebellion when the pubk/ safety demands it.

        as there warn't no invasion/ yu may jedge the terror of rebellion that prevailed.

I thought I DID/ send yu detail re/ the large bright once belonging to O[livia]. S[hakespear]. now in keeping of Bacciagalupo [Bacigalupo], at Rapallo/

    gornoze
where the rest are/

        BUTTT are prob/y more use ⟨potentially⟩ to you in woptalia than under the rottin stone/

        I mean, lookin forward, grampaw's in'erest in W.L. might even in another couple of decades git his ⟨⟨(WL's)⟩⟩ name past the wopDogana.

You will soon git a sample of Scheiwiller's capacity to reproduce in colour / HOW long it will take Wildt's grandson, and his father's nobel scion to get VORTik, i dunno.

        he, despite family loyalty finds his gramp's work troppo leccato. BUT dont say that, he is forcing Ez/ into decently printed etns / where De la Mare's [a director of Faber & Faber] pals cant Bowdlerize the text unbeknownst. (of course from most politic and explainable reasons etc.)

        ever examine Faber from the ethnologic angle ??

        never occurred to me that there cd/ be one/ but the mind roming in tranquility sometimes flops onto unsuspected.

At any rate/ there is NOW a mendment to our Consterooshun [the twenty-second amendment] to prevent any ambulating dunghill to reside for more than 8 years in the seat of Frontage/ before it had been unwrit law respected as custom.

And I see the wops got a Jeffersonian party, at least by program, but aint sure it is kosher. Got to look into it. Several good items in ole Santayana's Letters / might be used in blasting the kulchurd but timORus brits.

I hear that Borin had never heard of Ashberg [Aschberg] till 3 weeks ago in Orstralia [Australia], so the MusKyvites are az iggurunt as frogs/ or Hull, Leahay [Leahy], Stillwell, and Mme de Chambrun.

I dunno if I can move Vanni to do 8 colour prints of wot ⟨W.L.⟩ I LIKE/ Wich wd/ be Red Duet / at least 2 Timon / one female [*Odalisque*] that belonged to O[livia]. S[hakespear]. Grampaw as in the Tat [Lewis's portrait of Pound in the Tate Gallery]/ because Vanni's fledglings will print ANYthing connected with yr/ aged friend and DO not care much about art (except as practiced in the peninsula) which is NOT why I stayed IN the Peninsula. wot three W.L. wd/ be most likely to knock the top off the Mediterranean occiput?

The kid (aetat 21, and ergo the world's greatest marvel in the publishing woild. was chasin Brancusi
the KEWratter of the Gug[genheim Museum, New York]/ sent me fotos of B[rancusi]/ show in J[ew]. Y[ork]. to disprove allegation of a smaller kikessa that he had eggsposed 'em with their backs to the wall so nobuddy cd/ see more'n one side of a stachoo.

33 years time lag after Litl/ Rev[iew] 33 years post obit W. Shakespeare Cromwell decapitated Charley [Charles II]/ 50 years lag after Shx [Shakespeare]/ hizzery plays. W.L's cycle evidently a 50 not a 33.

Dick UB/ [Riccardo M. degli Uberti] has at last got some facts into print in Corriere della Liguria/ freedom of press creeping back.

Dunno if W.L. wants to do a biography of [Natalie] Barney?
or cd/ get Aldington to do one / that'd be a yoke/
a vostre serVIce, Monsieur
accuse reception our most etc.

large bright: Lewis's *Abstract Drawing*, which is mentioned in Letter 244.
Scheiwiller's capacity: Vanni Scheiwiller published *Iconografia italiana di Ezra Pound* (1955) and a small book of the paintings of Sherri Martinelli (including a portrait of Pound), *La Martinelli* (1956), with an introduction by Pound. Vanni was the son of Giovanni Scheiwiller, who published Pound's *Profile* in 1932, and the grandson of the sculptor Adolfo Wildt.

Mme de Chambrun: Pound told D. G. Bridson in "An Interview with Ezra Pound" (*New Directions in Prose and Poetry,* 17 [1961]: 176–77):
> While I was in the bughouse, I ploughed through four sets of memoirs— Hull, Leahy, Stillwell and Madame de Chambrun. . . . You get Hull, the plodder, who is . . . well, you just go round him. And then you get Leahy, who is a dumb bunny who finally gets wise; and you get Stillwell, who is a damn good guy, but who thought Chiang Kai-shek ought to have been an American; and you get Madame Longworth de Chambrun, in the middle of things in Paris . . . and they were all of them ham-ignorant of what ought to have been lammed into them at high school.

Corriere della Liguria: Ricardo M. degli Uberti's article "Why Pound Liked Italy" was originally published in Italian in *Corriere* (14 April 1956) and in translation in Pound's *Women of Trachis.*

246. TLS–1.

On stationery imprinted: Studio A, Kensington Gardens Studios, 29 Notting Hill Gate, London, W. 11.

July 29th 1956.

Dear Ezra.   I will willingly prepare the three essays about yourself which you want Peter Owen to use. But tell me which they are.

I spent one evening with I.A. Richards the other night. He gave me a very promising account of efforts to be of use to you – indeed, to get you out, going on at Harvard. Do be a little diplomatic with this fellow at Harvard [Richards was then at Harvard University] offering to help you. It would be such fun to have you at large again! And this can only be done by an American, and one not hated by the Authorities.

Have had a big Retrospective Show Picture Exhibition at the Tate ["Wyndham Lewis and Vorticism," July–August], with your portrait prominent, and greatly admired.

Give me new[s] of yourself.

Blessings.

W.L.

247. TLS–2. [St. Elizabeths Hospital. Washington, D.C.]. On air letter form.

2 Ag/ [August 1956]

    BANZAI.

        The three nobl whoops are the one in Tambi's Tomb of Tom/ where you stole the show from the frumps in the birthday card to Possum on his 60th. The one in Peter's Posies, dedicated to my 65th. and the one in some brit/ B.Bug. C. [BBC?] paper labled ROCKDRILL, whence the title on my last attempt to drill something into the pliocine occiput of the b.bloody pupLick.

///

Wrote Agnes [Bedford] yester, re/ a bit of wishful thinking as to how to drill some W.L. into the WOPlic.

Wildt's aspiring grandson [Vanni Scheiwiller] does not admire his carnal grampop save from sense of fambly duty, he finds him "troppo leccato"/ or mebbe it is spelt with one c.

He has done a IConografia EZ [*Iconografia italiana,* 1955], with all the orful wopresentations he cd/ lay hands on.

A[gnes].B[edford]. will assure you that he did a nice job on La Martinelli [1956].

        I mean the quality of production will be O.K. IF I can bloodily git him to PROduce.

There is still the old [pro]ject/ mentioned ten years or so ago/ re/ a VORT room in the bleedink Tate.

I dunno as foreign crit/ will assist. Shall speak to Amaral when he gets here. Universidad Mexico still supposed to be on brink of Cantares Pisanos, in a DAMN lively trans/
Brazil Educ. Ministero SAID it wd/ be proud to issue selection/ but a govt/ FELL three days later, Dunno if it dragged the KULCH/ dept with it.

Krautland is receptive FAR beyond the stodge of the Britains. IF I cd/ git wop vol, I cd/ I think get echo is [in?] Mexico and purzoombly north of the Yalps. One of the livliest young is Bo Setterlind up in Stockholm.

At last the bloody TRAX is in proofs in London [Pound's *Women of Trachis*]/ three years lag.

Do yu git any orstralian paperz?
Did yu kno my grandson [Walter de Rachewiltz] some years ago caused stir at Tate, by pausing before yr/ representation and saying firmly

ECCO IL NONNO   !

Of course he knows me only by iconography, yrs/ and Gaudiers but still ....

Have you ANY idea WHAT dear Archie [MacLeish] wants to appeal to?
(speakink of Haaarvud .....
and remembering Mr James (H.). quote: "And how my dear old friend
.... eh ..... HOWellZ   !!!!!
can ...etc.

Couple of weeks ago/ Querschnitt [German: cross section]. Rep/ of White
Citizens Councils / next day two kikessae
milking Ford Floundation and inviting me to participate
in activity which they openly boasted as "subversive". next day:
prex Geo. Washington Carver Foundation/ with signed letters from numerous, letters signed by all and sun/ wet. including [Natalie] Barney.
The dear fellow ⟨G. W. C. prex⟩ said he had been offered $5000 to take
Eleanor's [Roosevelt] name OFF his stationary, but that for fund-raising
purposes it was better to keep it on.

Mencken weakened his laughter by using it on minor objects. ALL the
authorities here do NOT love each other. And praps the dirty demmys
will not expulse Ike. Tho the proposal to putt an educated, in fact a civilized man on the ticket as veep to Ike may seem dangerous/ after 20 years
scum, the idea of a gent may strike you as perilous. Stassen on TV is considerably better than impression prevalent among the respectable before
he blasted. AND, of course, one shd/ not cantar vittoria prematurely ("to
Mr and Mrs L.Binyon, twins ..." end qt

Did I say old Rex [Lampman] sent on a lot of french mug's gazoons
re/ ART / all strugglin to pass off internal cliché by stunting. Not one
damn iota of either emotion or perception in the b/gg lot of 'em. AND
the furniture trade, ormolu k.t.l. [Greek: et cetera.]

Who krauts you? and what has been krauted?
                    slooty a tooty [saluti a tutti]/
⟨Brit⟩ Who Zoo at last got the
straight statement re/ Rome [broad]casts.

                    yrs   EZ

three nobl whoops: Lewis's essays, "Early London Environment" in *T. S. Eliot,*
    A Symposium, eds. March and Tambimuttu; "Ezra Pound" in *Ezra Pound:*
    A Collection of Essays, ed. Peter Russell; "The Rock Drill" in *The New States-*
    man and Nation (1951).
Cantares Pisanos: Los Cantares de Pisa, trans. José Vásquez Amaral (1956).

HOWellZ: This remark by Henry James about William Dean Howells is cited in
   Canto 104, p. 742.

G. W. C. prex: The Carver Research Foundation of Tuskegee Institute has never
   had a president, but its director at this time was Dr. R. W. Brown.

Who Zoo: Pound's entry in *Who's Who, 1956* included for the first time the statement: "Continued to speak on Rome Radio after Pearl Harbour on condition
   that he never be asked to say anything contrary to his conscience or contrary
   to his duties as an American citizen; a condition observed by the Italian Government."

248. TLS–1.

On stationery imprinted:
Studio A, Kensington Gardens Studios, 29 Notting Hill Gate, London,
W. 11.

Aug. 5th 1956.

Dear Ezz.   Am awaiting your reply to my little note of a few days ago.
Meanwhile Agnes [Bedford] has shown me your little note re an Quaderno.
My answer to that is Yes. You should have a good sale for it as a result
of Tate Exhibition.

   Wish that you would write to the publisher Peter Owen suggesting that he do a book of Bridson's Gilgamesh. I would write a preface.
Wish to support Bridson because of his independent services to Art.

   You mentioned Observer. Here is its latest.

Yours Ever.

old VORT

re an Quaderno: Pound wanted Vanni Scheiwiller to publish a book that would
   reproduce some of Lewis's paintings.

249. TL–1. [St. Elizabeths Hospital. Washington, D.C.]. On air letter form.

9 Ag/ [August 1956] caro COlegaaa.

LA Yankowska [Stephane de Yankowska] has sent on Tate effulgence. I doubt if Vanni [Scheiwiller] can do anything as impressive.

BUT as prelim/ why not send copies of that KittyLug to some wops. I suggest the following.

Carlo Scarfoglio, ⟨4⟩ via Largo Ponchielli, Roma
Sig/a O.R.Agresti, 36 Via Ciro Menotti, Roma
Fr/ Monotti, 9 Lungotevere Michaelangelo, Roma.
Diego Valeri, Palazzo Ducale, Venezia.
M.T. Dazzi, Biblioteca Querini-Stampalia, Venezia
Mary de Rachewiltz, Schloss Brunnenburg-Tirolo, Merano.
Vanni Scheiwiller, 6 via Melzi d' Eril, Milano
Vittorio Vettori, Lungarno Mediceo ⟨19⟩, Pisa.
Bo Setterlind, Lasarettsgränden, Strângnâs, Sweden.
Noel Stock, 436 Nepean Rd. East Brighton S.6
Melbourne, Australia.

YU have NO idea how iggurunt the wops are of EVERYthing outside woptalia/
knowing that nobody will pay ANY attention to them/ and that the foreign press wd/ lie like puke IF they did anything good soc/ pol/ or arty/ etc.

they PREfrain from waste motion / and remain Kleinstadt.
It wd/ be USEFUL to have 'em TOLD that W.L. is not mere airy phantaSSy, of yr/ anon/ crspdt.

I think Linati may have reviewed a W.L. vol/ once 20 years ago/ but he has been dead for some time. AND they dont like art except their owne etc.

dear Stef [de Yankowska] has underlined one new idea, p. 17. that Os S/1 [Osbert Sitwell] used to "dine regularly"
whether this indicates a lightening of the pressure ?????
Who Zoo, ten years late has printed at least one item which Faber Wilenski had not insisted on.
AND the B.B.C. included 2 pages of Benton canter [Cantos 88–89?] ⟨broadcast Lug 10 & 12⟩, tho dont spec they will PRINT it.

I will send on the Slobserver [*Observer*] clip to Mary [de Rachewiltz], who at least declines to take interest in the Frogcademician [T.S. Eliot] and the Ox Doc. J[ean]. C[octeau].

but will hold the Tate-ulaire for local properGander in whope Mr Rothenstein will accede to idea of distributing a few copies to the outer peRRy-Ferries.

I note alzo yr/ CLOSE friendship with Mr. Hulme#/ in fact news percolates, and accuracy declines.
#(wiff the h between the l an the m̲
possibly Mr Joyce and x̄ and y mȳght alzo figger.

Mrs Maj. Pease has writ/ to Hem/ who has sense enuf of humour to forward her outbreak. all ad/Maj[orem], D[ei]. g[loriam].

O.K. will mention Brid[son]'s Gilgam[esh]/ to Owen when I write /
slooty to tooty [saluti a tutti]

Tate effulgence: The catalog for the Tate Gallery's exhibition, "Wyndham Lewis
   and Vorticism." Lewis's introduction to the catalog is reprinted in Michel and
   Fox, eds., *Wyndham Lewis on Art,* pp. 451–53.
Who Zoo: See note to Letter 247.

250. TL–2. [St. Elizabeths Hospital. Washington, D.C.]. On air letter form.

W.L.

5 or 6 Oc[tober]/[1956] Having got to p. 92 [Lewis's last novel, *The Red Priest*], I wonder do yu remember yr/ first cheery invitation, to provide yu with "something nasty for BLAST". I think verbat/ it must have been: give me s.n. for B., pardon abbrev/ something nasty for Blast.
        One of the brighter y[oung]. m[en]. suggested last month that brit/ educ/ produces snobs, american idem, slobs. I spose Chatel will be using that. A chiel taakin' notes.
    phrase drug in re/ the observed scenes. Merely feeling how damned american the more active side of yu is. ⟨NOT in connection with the wise crack⟩ Might not have thought of it/ nacherly in them days the ex (as from yankShauung seen) otic wd/ have been more readily present to the somewhat, tho vurry faintly and opposedly) Jamesian views.

Wonder was there ANY english in the livliness or if Orage (with a french spelling) was the ONLY englander cent pour.

Violet [Hunt] said his real [name] was "Horridge" from Liverpool.

Hem[ingway] that I "was the ONLY man who ever got out (of the dismal Isle) alive."

Shd/ we add that the Possum [T.S.Eliot] went and died there ??

Wotz the betting that the Abbey will assemble him with the rest ov 'um?

all of which is frivolity in idleness. Until I git to end of yr/ clerical monstrosity [*The Red Priest*], I shd/ forbear serious theology. Can the old Wilenski firm [Faber and Faber] be doing something useful in announcing reprint of Plotinus? [*Enneads,* 1956]

I ought to keep QUIET (Q U I E T) until they actually do make that questionable step.

Wonder shd/ hist[oire]/ morale contemp[oraine] in the U.S? drag in the damn christers, who seem so participant in non-being, and NOTHING but bloody kikery visible as an element in the soc/ scene.

One never actually MEETS anyone who interrupts the normal activities of Sunday. but I spose they must be there. dozens of 'em drug off the ward on that day.

As to its being LATER than yu think / C[hâtel]. sd/ yester he had been talking to a lady who has one of the THREE (three and NO more) liquor stores in Wash/ D.C. that aren't owned by chewsz. She cant get credit, has to pay cash. Mebbe this is an advantage in the long run/ except that when the kikes go bust it will be kike lenders who take over. C/ said no one whom he had mentioned the item to seemd to find it news. i.e. lot of 'em knew it as familiar fact.

NEX day / Oke HAY, my old alarm-COCK. vurry readable. In some spots too damn MUCH style. alzo the very DIDaktik a bit bare in others BUT they need damn well to be TOLD. Oke hay, the VORT is a tellin' 'em.

the parson's history ⟨wot he takes for history not his personal life⟩ is as phoney as it nacherly wd/ be where Toynbee is took fer real. In this de-filed cuntynunk the profreezers are still using Toqueville [Tocqueville] to obfuscate.

PARENthesis/ did I say yr/ 2 page preface to your Picture show ["Wynd-ham Lewis and Vorticism"], one of the best statements yu hv/ ever made. I dunno whether yu note convergence (from two quite distinct angles) on agreement of 1913 or whenever. At any rate there was a convergence not merely a connection. Not sure you had, or have previously so clearly defined what I converged TOWARD.

or whether yu much supposed I was thinking at all. (this in ref/ my, (first in 30 years,) ref to wot I like in a pixchoor, pref/ Martinelli booklet [*La Martinelli*].)

purty nigh antipodal Fritz [Van der Pyle], re/ Vlaminck: "Large brute sweating paint."

later QUEERY/ your personae git vurry real

am wondering whether the England of Woodlouse & Co has

got to people saying what they feel but wouldn't SAY, with such

velocity, dispatch etc. to expedite the movement of the story. mebbe two wars have shukk 'em up.

Of course IF yu butt into religion/ various brands of bugwash used to get hold of temple lands and rents is main clue to spread of idiocy under xtn lable. Havent yet checked on Del M/[ar] that half the lands and slaves belonged to temples. Julian [the Apostate] tried to do something about it. "main clue" mebbe better say to Byzantine theolog/ ructions.

next note/ an BLIme, ef yr / old and often troublesome ally aint finished reading a novel. THAT don't 'appen often in these dize.

Ef yu aint had the Sq $/ series lemme know, and IF yu wanna READ it. alzo did I mention Peter Guillart "Lost Kingdom" [Peter Goullart's *Forgotten Kingdom*] Murray pubd/ it last year. bloke knows the score.

rest of yr/ kulchurl life can probably be left to yr/ own impulses and tropisms.

Four blokes have signed an interesting declaration which I hope to post yu in a week or so. nawthin personal.

with whom THE hell does one exchange an interesting word or intelligent in London at this time?

Jeanne Foster heard from after 17 years. sent on kodak shot of Quinn, Brancus[i] and Satie.

Woodlouse & Co: This may refer to P. G. Wodehouse. Pound knew that Wodehouse had broadcast on German radio during World War II without being charged with treason, and he compared Wodehouse's case with his own.

251. TLS–1. [St. Elizabeths Hospital. Washington, D.C.]. On air letter form.

7 Dec[ember]/[1956] W.L.   az ariSTOL [Aristotle] sez, an nevery buddy elsz wiff a grain of horse sense: kids shdn't muck round with philosophy / meaning general statements while too young to know bee from buzzard.

whether we shd/ now flavour posterity with show of coherence and convergence is up to you.

Have always held re/ vortex, dominant cell in somatic devilupment, convergence in atom structure etc.

IF a few can agree they can bust the massed slush of the sonvav assembled.

Think yr/ pref/ note to yr/ Tate Show ["Wyndham Lewis and Vorticism"] is important /
whether yu have bothered to read my foreword to Martinelli I dont know. Anyhow, mugging along with Plotinus, clear distinction between

EIDOS , form, shape   εἶδος
and Eikon, likeness.   εἰκών

use of greek, classic educ. etc. opposite pole from Swinburnian swish, and the formal 18th century classicism.

distinction in meanings of words,
and OMission of unnecessary words.

easy enough to sink into cliches re/ Plato's ideas etc.
however, shapes there before you can think
and the similitudes imitated.

    basta.

      saluti   EZ

az ariSTOL sez: See Canto 74, p. 441:
               as says Aristotle
  philosophy is not for young men
  their *Katholou* can not be sufficiently derived from
    their *hekasta*. . . .
mugging along with Plotinus: Pound may be drawing this distinction from the Eighth Tractate, "On the Intellectual Beauty," of *The Enneads.*

252. TLS–2. [St. Elizabeths Hospital. Washington, D.C.]. On air letter form.

W.L.   3 Feb' 57.   But for the PEculiar circs/ the yattering of banderlog wd/ be of no import and no interest. BUT "Facts Forum" [a radio program] in noticing the disease of modern awt listed all movements save the VORT/ AND as the listed movements were precisely those criticized in BLAST of holy memOry, and as by chance the main VORTS opposed pinkismo from the beginning the coINcidence shd/ be USED. Bridson recorded some Venison. Dunnoted at the time save to some 2000 brits/ below the Cambridge tea level and bloomsbuggery [Bloomsbury] pewkerei.

I cd/ use some kudos along that line. whether you need bother or not I dont know.

Possibly you dont recall the two russkies who turned up at Reb. Art. Cent. [in 1914] they may only have talked with me/ but they went away SAD "bbb uu bbbut you are INDIVIDUALISTS!!.

Ez : Wotterhell yu eggspekk? AND we did not fall for the fabian dessication /

disagreements in the fambly needn't crop up. Orage pointed to 'em in attempt to segregate me.

Still think yu'd have saved time if yu had plugged for a milder philosophy, BUT it might hv/ taken bump out of style where bump was needed, and HOW.

Kasp[er]/ has used expediency, and may have done some good, as the attempt to implicate grampaw in civic disorder don't seem to have got beyond the most stinking pinkerei. And "LOOK's" remark that J[ohn]. K[asper]. hadn't been in the news or wasn't news AFTER..etc. "Look" dated 19 th inst. visible yester on the 2nd.) rather deflated by three LARGE front page stinks in Jew York Herald.

AND there is no doubt that the young man has got several sanities printed in rotocalco.

12 inches, guinea an inch alzo even the putrid Meyerblatt [Eugene Meyer, publisher of *The Washington Post*], had a letter from some buzzard I never heerd tell on, quoting Mr Adams, the KOrekt J[ohn].A[dams]. and stating that IF cong/ etc. EVERY (buggaring) member ⟨gent/ whom we may for convenience call "Cantleman" told me he had been "violated by 86 government employes".⟩ of that (decayed) organization shd/ be held responsible for proper control (OV the $).

this is better than I had putt it, or that I had seen elsz where.

Am sending release of 2nd/ [Thomas Hart] Benton award by

schlow post. Shd/ of course have started this on a plain sheet of pipper not on a air-le'r.

Mebbe for auld lang tryin' yu better come across with something fer Edge [journal edited by Noel Stock]. Must by now be at least ten useful y[oung].m[en]. in the rump of angry-saxonry (includin the oirish).

The Soc. Guillaume Budé, 95 Bd. Raspail, started in 1917 to keep greek texts printed with froglation [French translation]. The LAST citadel of frog decency. I dunno if you can use it. F. Masai on Plethon [*Plethon et Le Platonisme de Mistra,* 1956], notes that gods are gods cause they got more hilaritas than the animal electoral, and alzo that they COMMUNICATE more rapidly with each other.

All of which shows how RIGHT wuz Ez, to mention Mr Plethon Gemisto in the Sidg. Canters [Sigismundo Malatesta Cantos, 8–11] when he wuz less in the pubk/ eye.

The fun of next 50 years is in greek not in latin. and the Fatcan [Vatican] trying to keep it under wraps.

Will Agnes [Bedford] read you the sq.$ vols if I have Dave [Gordon] send 'em.

I dunno why this hasn't been done, save that I can't think of EVERYthing. Like leaving the brit. WhoZoo without clear statement fer ten years.

Wd/ yu favour 50 pages of eggstrakks from the USEFUL statements by W.L.

There is an offset press interrupted by tank corps etc. but mebbe when one knows if Kasp[er] is in or out of jail it cd/ be moBIlized. OR, I think a special number of EDGE cd/ be used fer that porpoise. Again it waited fer gramp to GIT the idea.

W.L. constructor, vs/ the constricters. I think yu cd/ trust Stock to make it. something more lively than the egregious Kenner who is establishing his academic position (usefully but not in skirmishing line)

Bloke named Ralph (no connection wiff OTHER ⟨or others⟩) Reid even dug some BLAST out of Mr James (the late H.)

Mark Twain 2nd. cousin sez yr/ portrait of Carlyle is in S. Louis, it had been reePorted in N.Y.

"Am[erican] Mercury" alzo mentioning Fed. Reserve, ⟨Am. Merc⟩ running on baptist millyums apparently, with Xtianity as business asset. Wish yu cd/ remember what putt yu onto "CONstantinople our star." [See Letter 236]. You thought it was central, but I cant remember wot elsz.

ALZO IF we cd/
agree on tactics you COULD or you cd/ tell Agnes [Bedford] to TELL
some of yr/ acolytes to CONCENTRATE fire on partic. points. note pp/
in Benton release. ⟨sent by slow post⟩ WHY do we pay taxes? Need a
nation pay rent on its own credit?

Sovereignity inheres in the POWER (no matter about the right) to
issue money.

Doc. Wms. [W. C. Williams] complaining of MY obskewrity compliments
Mr Zweck or me on having found someone who can express it clearly..
hell we need a few more Voltaires.
best to the gals [Mrs. Lewis and Agnes Bedford]. yrz EZ.

⟨EP⟩

Bridson recorded some Venison: "Alfred Venison, the Poet of Titchfield Street,"
was Pound's pseudonym when he wrote political poetry for the *New English
Weekly.* D. G. Bridson recorded a series of three "Ezra Pound: Readings and
Recollections" for the B.B.C. for broadcast on 2, 11, and 17 July 1959.

attempt to segregate me: In a detailed note on Lewis's *Rude Assignment,* Pound
enlarges on this statement: "FOR the Wreck-ord (re/ p 52) I recall Yeats
re/ WL/ 'PoWWnd'z evIL genius' / both he and Orage trying to separate or
save EZ/ FORD never (let me say NEVER) made any such etc/ and, of
course, no such KIND of machination could have entered his occiput. Orage
argued on point of philosophic coherence/ and our opposite directions at the
time. Fact that mind better be ALIVE than dead, didn't convince him." See
Rude Assignment, ed. Forshay, p. 271.

"LOOK's" remark: Arthur Gordon, "Intruder in the South," *Look* 21 (19 February 1957): 27–31. I do not find any such remark that John Kasper's propaganda against segregation and the Supreme Court was not in the news after a
certain date. The article included a picture of Ezra Pound with the caption,
"Ezra Pound, the insane American poet, is Kasper's idol." The *New York
Herald Tribune* for 30 January 1957 carried a front-page story headed, "Segre-
gationist Kasper is Ezra Pound's Disciple."

hilaritas: This quality or virtue is crucial to Pound in *Thrones,* as in Canto 98,
p. 690:
"By Hilaritas", said Gemisto, "by hilaritas: gods;
and by speed in communication.

portrait of Carlyle: Pound refers to one of Lewis's portraits through a further
reference to Whistler's *Portrait of Carlyle.* The Lewis portrait may be his *Portrait of T. S. Eliot, I* (a study for his *Portrait of T. S. Eliot, II*), which was
bought by an American in 1938 and is now in Eliot House, Harvard University.
After the Tate Gallery bought the Pound portrait in 1939, it was hung next to
Whistler's *Portrait of Carlyle.*

Benton Award: An award given by a group Pound supported called the Defend-
ers of the American Constitution.

Mr Zweck: Pound had written to Williams about one of his fellow inmates in
"Zweck 2," a ward in St. Elizabeths.

Afterword

The last words are Ezra Pound's. After Lewis died on 7 March 1957, Pound launched numerous plans to reprint Lewis's books and began work on a Lewis memorial issue of *Edge*. He volunteered to write prefaces for any of Lewis's books that could be reprinted, with all royalties going to Mrs. Anne Wyndham Lewis, and wrote to A. V. Moore (5 September 1957) about plans to edit an anthology of Lewis's best prose: "which is NOT the philosophic meandering but the DELINEATION of people." But Pound's plans to memorialize Lewis, like his hopes ever since 1916 to write a book about Lewis's art, were never realized. His last statement on Lewis was written but not used for a preface to W. K. Rose's edition of *The Letters of Wyndham Lewis* (1963). The reference to "Vare" near the end of this preface is to the Italian diplomat Daniele Varé, who wrote in the conclusion to his memoirs *The Two Imposters* (1949): "Empires rise and fall in an epic cycle. . . . But ideals do not die."

> to the letters of one's most exciting contemporary
> > during the decades from 1908 to 28 or thereafter

It is a nuisance to have outlived one's intelligence, especially when one is called on for so simple a request as that for a brief introduction to some of his remnants,
> and when a diminishing number of survivors recall the excitements of a past era:
> > "Give me something nasty, for BLAST", or
"Co ..come and see me, eh, eh, I'll give you an address when I get one. (This after mature reflection re/ inconvenient correlations re/ several.

From the volcanic, as in comparison with Mr. Joyce's prudence,
exuberance of Tarr, russian and Scandinavian influx, in
contrast to the jesuitical insertion of gallic neatness,
Cantleman (Little Review suppressed for Cantleman, I think before
the first assault on Ulysses,
and for the terrible first chapter on Lady Fredigonde [in *The Apes of God*],
and then on thru America I presume, Self Condemned, one remembers

305

somewhere a bull dog, as a sample of beauty as defined St Thomas' Aqui[nas]
in his Summa "si perfecta representat rem," if it perfectly represent
the thing quamvis turpem?
not that one thought of W. L. as neoThomist.

There are plenty [o]f students capable of tracing the course of W.L's prose
from the first edtn, Tarr to the more careful delineations of Rotton Hill
but they will not get the successive stimulae of the appearance of W.L's
vols, before the pubk was ready for the contained shocks,

        his readiness to tackle unwelcome subject matter, whether
of the continent or of england.

Portrait of wife at Tate gal/ [Froanna] ample evidence that one was right in
discerning capacity in 1912. my function that of alarm clock
no taste for obit, account of
        rechewing the demonstrated and accepted.
H[enry].J[ames]. intolerable nostalgia he can rouse for something lost.
    an order, a decorum.
    W.L. the intolerable necessity that something come
to an end, that the hill is rotting, etc.
    James fixing it for fond memory, all too fond, fond memory,
a decorum has survived, as Vare predicted

an awful chaos has supervened, in the horror films.

in his Summa: Summa Theologiae, I, question 39, article 8: "An image is said
    to be beautiful if it perfectly represents the object, however ugly the object
    itself may be." In the "Scylla and Charybdis" chapter of *Ulysses,* Stephen
    Dedalus refers to St. Thomas as the "bulldog of Aquin."

Selected Bibliography
(Including Works Cited in the Notes and Significant Source Materials)

Works by Ezra Pound

ABC of Economics. London: Faber and Faber, 1933; 2d ed., Tunbridge Wells: Peter Russell/The Pound Press, 1953.

Active Anthology. Ed. Ezra Pound. London: Faber and Faber, 1933.

"Affirmations . . . II. Vorticism." *New Age* 16 (14 January 1915): 277–78.

"After Election." *New Review* I (January/February 1931): 53–55.

"An Anachronism at Chinon." *The Little Review* 4 (June 1917): 14–21.

Antheil and the Treatise on Harmony. Paris: Three Mountains Press, 1924.

"Augment of the Novel." In *New Directions in Prose and Poetry 1941.* Norfolk, Connecticut: New Directions, 1941.

"Aux étuves de Weisbaden [sic], A. D. 1451." *The Little Review* 4 (July 1917): 12–16.

Los Cantares de Pisa. Trans. José Vásquez Amaral. Mexico: Imprenta Universitaria, 1956.

The Cantos. New York: New Directions. Rev. ed., third printing, 1972. London: Faber and Faber, 1975.

"Canto 85." *Hudson Review* 7 (Winter 1955): 487–501.

Carta da Visita. Rome: Edizioni di Lettere D'Oggi, 1942.

Collected Early Poems of Ezra Pound. Ed. Michael King. New York: New Directions, 1976. London: Faber and Faber, 1933.

"Credit and the Fine Arts. . . . A Practical Application." *New Age* (30 March 1922): 284–85.

"The Curse." *Apple* (*of Beauty and Discord*) I (20 January 1920): 22, 24.

"Demarcations." *British Union Quarterly* 1 (January/April 1937): 35–40.

Dikter. Trans. Lars Forssell. Stockholm: A. Bonniers Förlag, 1953.

A Draft of XVI Cantos. Paris: Three Mountains Press, 1925.

A Draft of XXX Cantos. Paris: Hours Press, 1930. London: Faber and Faber, 1933.

"Edward Wadsworth, Vorticist: An Authorised Appreciation." *The Egoist* 1 (15 August 1914): 306–7.

Ezra Pound and Music: The Complete Criticism. Ed. R. Murray Schafer. New York: New Directions, 1977. London: Faber and Faber, 1978.

Ezra Pound and the Visual Arts. Ed. Harriet Zinnes. New York: New Directions, 1980.

The Fifth Decad of Cantos. London: Faber & Faber, 1937.

"Ford Madox (Hueffer) Ford; Obit." *Nineteenth Century and After* 126 (August 1939): 178–81.

Gaudier-Brzeska: A Memoir. London: John Lane, 1916; New York: New Directions, 1970.

"Gold Brokers." *Action* 163 (8 April 1939): 12.

Guide to Kulchur. London: Faber & Faber, 1938; New York: New Directions, 1968.

"Homage à la langue d'Oc." *The Little Review* 5 (May 1918): 19–31.

Homage to Sextus Propertius. London: Faber and Faber, 1934.

"L'Homme Moyen Sensuel." *The Little Review* 4 (September 1917): 8–16.

How to Read. London: Desmond Harmsworth, 1931.

"Imaginary Letters IV (Walter Villerant to Mrs. Bland Burn)." *The Little Review* 4 (September 1917): 20–22.

"Imaginary Letters V (Walter Villerant to Mrs. Bland Burn)." *The Little Review* 4 (October 1917): 14–17.

"Imaginary Letters VI (Walter Villerant to Mrs. Bland Burn)." *The Little Review* 4 (November 1917): 39–40.

"Imaginary Letters (W. Villerant to the ex-Mrs. Burn)." *The Little Review* 5 (May 1918): 52–55.

"Mr. Villerant's Morning Outburst (Four Letters)." *The Little Review* 7 (November 1918): 7–12.

Impact: Essays on Ignorance and the Decline of American Civilization. Ed. Noel Stock. Chicago: Henry Regnery Company, 1960.

Instigations. New York: Boni and Liveright, 1920.

Introductory Text Book. [Rapallo, Italy, 1939]. Privately printed in London by Bonner and Company.

Jefferson and/or Mussolini. London: Stanley Nott, 1935.

"Jodindranath Mawhwor's Occupation." *The Little Review* 4 (May 1917): 12–18.

Lustra. London: Elkin Mathews, 1916.

"Marconi's Violins." In *Ezra Pound and Music.* Ed. R. Murray Schafer, pp. 392–93.

". . . Mr. Chris Hollis in Need of Guide!" *Action* 182 (19 August 1939): 11.

'Noh' or Accomplishment. London: Macmillan, 1916 [i.e., 1917].

"Obstructivity." *Apple* (*of Beauty and Discord*) I (July? 1920): 168, 170, 172.

Pavannes and Divisions. New York: Alfred A. Knopf, 1918.

Personae: Collected Shorter Poems. New York: New Directions, 1949. Faber and Faber, 1952.

Personae of Ezra Pound. London: Elkin Mathews, 1909.

The Pisan Cantos. New York: New Directions, 1948. Faber and Faber, 1949.

Profile. Ed. Ezra Pound. Milan: Giovanni Scheiwiller, 1932.

Section: Rock-Drill, 85–95 de los Cantares. New York: New Directions, 1956; London: Faber and Faber, 1957.

Selected Letters of Ezra Pound. Ed. D. D. Paige. New York: New Directions, 1971. London: Faber and Faber, 1971.

Selected Prose 1909–65. Ed. William Cookson. New York: New Directions, 1973. London: Faber and Faber, 1973.

"A Social Creditor Serves Notice." *Fascist Quarterly* 4 (October 1936): 492–99.

"Studies in Contemporary Mentality . . . XV.—A Nice Paper." *New Age* 22 (13 Decemebr 1917): 129–30.

Three Letters of Ezra Pound. Ed. Bryant Knox. Master of Arts thesis, Simon Fraser University, 1978.

What Is Money For? London: Greater Britain Publications, 1939.

"Wyndham Lewis." *The Egoist* 1 (15 June 1914): 233–34.

Pound's Translations

Cathay. London: Elkin Mathews, 1915.

Confucian Analects. New York: Square $ Series, 1951; London: Peter Owen, 1956.

Confucius: The Unwobbling Pivot & The Great Digest. Pharos [Norfolk, Connecticut: New Directions], 1947.

Gourmont, Remy de. *The Natural Philosophy Of Love.* New York: Boni and Liveright, 1922.

Guido Cavalcanti Rime. Genoa: Edizion: Marsano, 1932.

Sophokles. *Women of Trachis.* London: Neville Spearman, 1956. New York: New Directions, 1957. London: Faber and Faber, 1969.

Works by Wyndham Lewis

America and Cosmic Man. London: Nicholson & Watson, 1948.

America, I Presume. New York: Howell, Soskin & Co., 1940.

The Apes of God. London: The Arthur Press, 1930. New York: Robert M. McBride, 1932.

"Archie." Olin Library, Cornell University.

The Art of Being Ruled. London: Chatto & Windus, 1926. New York: Harper & Brothers, 1926.

BLAST, nos. 1 & 2 (June 1914, July 1915). Ed. Wyndham Lewis.

Blasting and Bombardiering: Autobiography (1914–26). London: Eyre & Spottiswoode, 1937.

"The Bull-gun." Olin Library, Cornell University.

"The Burden of Dullness." Olin Library, Cornell University.

The Caliph's Design: Architects! Where Is Your Vortex? London: The Egoist Ltd., 1919.

"Cantleman's Spring-Mate." *The Little Review* 4 (October 1917): 8–14.

The Childermass. London: Chatto & Windus, 1928.

"The Code of a Herdsman." *The Little Review* 4 (July 1917): 3–7.

Collected Poems and Plays. Ed. Alan Munton. Manchester: Carcanet New Press, 1977.

"The Cosmic Uniform of Peace." *The Sewanee Review* 54 (Autumn 1945): 507–31.

Count Your Dead: They Are Alive! or, A New War in the Making. London: Lovat Dickson Limited, 1937.

"The Do-Nothing Mode. An Autobiographical Fragment." *Agenda* 7–8 (Autumn/ Winter: 1969): 216–21.

The Doom of Youth. London: Chatto & Windus, 1932.

"Early London Environment." In *T. S. Eliot, A Symposium.* Eds. Richard March and Tambimuttu. London: Editions Poetry London, 1948.

Enemy of the Stars (with *Physics of the Not-Self*). London: Desmond Harmsworth, 1932.

"Ezra: The Portrait of a Personality." *Quarterly Review of Literature* 5 (December 1949): 136–44.

Ezra Pound: Un Saggio E Tre Disegni. Trans. Mary de Rachewiltz. Milan: All' Insegna del Pesce d'Oro, 1958.

"Ezra Pound." In *Ezra Pound: A Collection of Essays.* Ed. Peter Russell. London: Peter Nevill Limited, 1950.

Fifteen Drawings. London: Ovid Press, 1920.

Hitler. London: Chatto & Windus, 1931.

The Hitler Cult. London: Dent, 1939.

"Hitlerism—Man and Doctrine: Creditcrankery Rampant." *Time and Tide* 12 (14 February 1931): 182, 184–85.

The Human Age. Book Two: *Monstre Gai.* Book Three: *Malign Fiesta.* London: Methuen & Co., 1955. [Book One: *The Childermass.*]

The Ideal Giant. The Little Review 6 (May 1918): 1–18.

"Imaginary Letters I (Six Letters of William Bland to His Wife)." *The Little Review* 4 (May 1917): 19–23.

"Imaginary Letters II (Six Letters of William Bland to His Wife)." *The Little Review* 4 (June 1917): 22–26.

"Imaginary Letters (William Bland Burn to His Wife)." *The Little Review* 4 (March 1918): 23–30.

"Imaginary Letters (William Bland Burn to His Wife)." *The Little Review* 4 (April 1918): 50–54.

"Inferior Religions." *The Little Review* 4 (September 1917): 3–8.

"Introduction to Peter Russell's Reading of the Cantos (Poetry Society, 1948)." Olin Library, Cornell University.

"Joint." Olin Library, Cornell University; Excerpts in *Agenda* 7–8 (Autumn– Winter 1969–70): 197–215.

"Kill John Bull with Art." *The Outlook* 34 (18 July 1934): 74.

" 'Left Wings' and the C3 Mind." *British Union Quarterly* 1 (January/April 1937): 22–34.

Left Wings Over Europe; or, How to Make a War About Nothing. London: Jonathan Cape, 1936.

The Letters of Wyndham Lewis. Ed. W. K. Rose. Norfolk, Connecticut: New Directions, 1963. London: Methuen, 1963.

The Lion and the Fox: The Rôle of the Hero in the Plays of Shakespeare. London: Grant Richards, 1927. New York: Harper & Brothers, 1927.

"The Man of the World." Olin Library, Cornell University.

Men Without Art. London: Cassell, 1934.

The Mysterious Mr. Bull. London: Robert Hale Limited, 1938.

One-Way Song. London: Faber and Faber, 1933; 2d ed., London: Methuen, 1960.

"Perspectives on Lawrence." *Hudson Review* 8 (Winter 1956): 596–608.

"The Politics of Artistic Expression." *Artwork* 1 (May–August 1925): 223–26.

"Prevalent Design I. Nature and the Monster of Design." *The Athenaeum* no. 4673 (21 November 1919): 1230–31.

"Prevalent Design II. Painting." *The Athenaeum* no. 4676 (12 December 1919): 1343.

"Prevalent Design III. The Man Behind the Eyes." *The Athenaeum* no. 4678 (26 December 1919): 1464.

"Prevalent Design IV. The Bulldog Eye's Depredations." *The Athenaeum* no. 4681 (16 January 1920): 84–85.

The Red Priest. London: Methuen, 1963.

The Revenge for Love. London: Cassell, 1937; Chicago: Henry Regnery, 1952.

The Roaring Queen. London: Secker & Warburg, 1973.

"The Rock Drill." *The New Statesman and Nation* 41 (7 April 1951): 398.

Rotting Hill. London: Methuen, 1951.

Rude Assignment: A Narrative of My Career Up-to-Date. London: Hutchinson, 1950. Ed. Toby Forshay. Santa Barbara: Black Sparrow Press, 1984.

Self Condemned. London: Methuen, 1954.

Snooty Baronet. London: Cassell, 1932.

"A Soldier of Humor. Part I." *The Little Review* 4 (December 1917): 32–46; "Part II," *The Little Review* 4 (January 1918): 35–51.

Tarr. New York: Alfred A. Knopf, 1918; London: The Egoist Ltd., 1918.

Time and Western Man. London: Chatto & Windus, 1927.

Timon of Athens. London: Cube Press, 1913.

The Tyro, nos. 1 & 2 (1921, 1922). Ed. Wyndham Lewis.

Unlucky for Pringle: Unpublished and Other Stories by Wyndham Lewis. Eds. C. J. Fox and Robert T. Chapman. London: Vision Press, 1973.

"War Notes." *BLAST* no. 2 (July 1915): 9–16.

The Wild Body, A Soldier of Humour, and Other Stories. London: Chatto & Windus, 1927.

The Writer and the Absolute. London: Methuen, 1952.

Wyndam Lewis and Vorticism. London: Tate Gallery, 1956.

Wyndham Lewis: Paintings and Drawings. Ed. Walter Michel. Berkeley and Los Angeles: University of California Press, 1971.

Wyndham Lewis on Art. Eds. Walter Michel and C. J. Fox. New York: Funk & Wagnalls, 1969.

"A Young Soldier." *The Egoist* 3 (March 1916): 46.

General Works

Adams, Brooks. *Law of Civilization and Decay.* New York: Macmillan, 1893.

Aldington, Richard. *Lawrence of Arabia: A Biographical Enquiry.* Chicago: Henry Regnery, 1955.

Alpert, Barry S. "Ezra Pound, John Price, and the Exile." *Paideuma* 2 (Winter 1973): 427–48.

Andréadès, Andre M. "The Economic Life of the Byzantine Empire: Population, Agriculture, Industry, Commerce." In *Byzantium, An Introduction to East Roman Civilization.* Eds. Norman Baynes and H. St. L. B. Moss.

Apollinaire, Guillaume. *Les Peintres Cubistes: Meditations Esthétiques*. Paris: Figuière, 1913.

―――. "Aesthetic Meditations, I." Trans. Mrs. Charles Knoblauch. (Excerpt from *Les Peintres Cubistes*.) *The Little Review* 8 (Spring 1922): 7–19.

Barbusse, Henri. *Le Feu: Journal d'une Escouade*. Paris: Flammarion, 1916.

Baynes, Norman, and H. St. L. B. Moss, eds. *Byzantium: An Introduction to East Roman Civilization*. Oxford: Clarendon, 1948.

Binyon, Laurence. *The Flight of the Dragon: An Essay in the Theory and Practice of Art in China and Japan*. London: John Murray, 1911.

BLAST 3. Ed. Seamus Cooney. Santa Barbara: Black Sparrow Press, 1984.

Bonaparte, Napoléon. *Voix de Napoléon*. Ed. P. L. Couchoud. Geneva and Paris: Éditions du Milieu du Monde, 1949.

Breton, André. *Anthologie de L'Humour Noir*. Paris: Éditions du Sagittaire, 1950.

Bridson, D. G. "An Interview with Ezra Pound." *New Directions in Prose and Poetry* 17 (1961): 176–77.

Bridson, D. G. *The Quest of Gilgamesh*. London: Rampant Lions Press, 1956.

Brown, Ashley, Thomas Laster, and Hugh Kenner, eds. "Wyndham Lewis Number." *Shenandoah* 4 (Summer/Autumn): 3–16.

Brown, John. *Panorama de la littérature contemporaine aux États-Unis*. Paris: Gallimard, 1952.

Buchan, John. *Oliver Cromwell*. Boston: Houghton Mifflin, 1934.

Burnet, John. *Early Greek Philosophy*. New York: Macmillan, 1957.

Butchart, Montgomery, ed. *Money: Selected Passages Presenting the Concepts of Money in the English Tradition, 1640–1935*. London: Stanley Nott, 1935.

Chambrun, Clara Longworth, Comtesse de Chambrun. *The Making of Nicholas Longworth, Annals of an American Family*. New York: R. Long & R. R. Smith, 1933.

Cork, Richard. *Vorticism and Abstract Art in the First Machine Age*. 2 vols. Berkeley and Los Angeles: University of California Press, 1976.

Dangerfield, George. *The Strange Death of Liberal England*. New York: Capricorn Books, 1961.

DeAngulo, Jaime. "Indians in Overalls." *Hudson Review* 3 (Autumn 1950): 327–77.

Drey, O. Raymond. "War Pictures by Mr. Wyndham Lewis." *Westminster Gazette* (24 February 1919): 2.

Domvile, Sir Barry. *From Admiral to Cabin Boy*. London: Boswell Publishing Co., 1947.

Dunning, John. *Tune into Yesterday. The Ultimate Encyclopedia of Old-Time Radio*. Englewood Cliffs, N.J.: Prentice-Hall, 1976.

Eliot, T. S. *After Strange Gods*. New York: Harcourt Brace, 1934. London: Faber and Faber, 1934.

―――. "Eeldrop and Appleplex, I." *The Little Review* 4 (May 1917): 7–11.

―――. "Eeldrop and Appleplex, II." *The Little Review* 4 (September 1917): 16–19.

―――. *On Poetry and Poets*. New York: Farrar, Straus and Cudahy, 1957. London: Faber and Faber, 1957.

Ellmann, Richard. *Eminent Domain*. New York: Oxford University Press, 1967.

Emery, Clark. *Ideas into Action: A Study of Pound's Cantos.* Coral Gables, Florida: University of Miami Press, 1958.

Fenollosa, Ernest. *The Chinese Written Character.* In Ezra Pound, *Instigations.* New York: Boni and Liveright, 1920.

Fjelde, Rolf. "Time, Space and Wyndham Lewis." *The Western Review* 15 (Spring 1951): 201–2.

Ford, Ford Madox. *The English Novel: From the Earliest Days to the Death of Conrad.* Philadelphia & London: J. P. Lippincott, 1929.

Frobenius, Leo. *Kulturgeschichte Afrikas.* Zurich: Phaidon-Verlag, 1933.

Fuchs, Werner, ed. *Poland's Policy of Expansion as Revealed by Polish Testimony.* Berlin: Deutscher Ostmarken, 1932.

Gallup, Donald. *Ezra Pound: A Bibliography.* Charlottesville: University Press of Virginia, 1983.

Gaudier-Brzeska, Henri. "Vortex." *BLAST,* no. 2 (1915): 33–34.

Goldring, Douglas. *The Last Pre-Raphaelite: A Record of the Life and Writings of Ford Madox Ford.* London: MacDonald & Co., 1948.

———. *South Lodge: Reminiscences of Violet Hunt, Ford Madox Ford, and the English Review Circle, 1943.* London: Constable & Co., 1943.

Gordon, Arthur. "Intruder in the South." *Look* 21 (19 February 1957): 27–31.

Goullart, Peter. *Forgotten Kingdom.* London: John Murray, 1955.

Graves, Robert and Alan Hodge. *The Long Week-end: A Social History of Great Britain, 1918–39.* London: Faber and Faber, 1940. New York: Norton, 1963.

Hemingway, Ernest. *A Moveable Feast.* New York: Charles Scribner's Sons, 1964.

Heymann, C. David. *Ezra Pound: The Last Rower.* New York: Viking Press, 1976. London: Faber and Faber, 1976.

Hoffman, Frederick J., Charles Allen, and Carolyn F. Ulrich. *The Little Magazine: A History and a Bibliography.* Princeton: Princeton University Press, 1947.

Homberger, Eric, ed. *Ezra Pound: The Critical Heritage.* London and Boston: Routledge & Kegan Paul, 1972.

Infeld, Louis, and Albert Einstein. *The Evolution of Physics: The Growth of Ideas from Early Concepts to Relativity and Quanta.* New York: Simon and Schuster, 1938.

James, Henry. *Selected Fiction.* Ed. Leon Edel. New York: E. P. Dutton, 1953.

Kappel, Andrew J. "What Ezra Pound Says We Owe to Edward VIII, Duke of Windsor." *The Journal of Modern Literature* 9 (May 1982): 313–15.

Keats, John. *Selected Letters of John Keats.* Ed. Robert Pack. New York: New American Library, 1974.

Kenner, Hugh. *The Pound Era.* Berkeley and Los Angeles: University of California Press, 1971. London: Faber and Faber, 1971.

———. *Wyndham Lewis.* Norfolk, Connecticut: New Directions, 1954.

Knox, Bryant, ed. *Three Letters of Ezra Pound.* Master of Arts thesis. Simon Fraser University, 1978.

Leahy, William D. *I Was There: The Personal Story of the Chief of Staff to Presidents Roosevelt and Truman.* New York: Whittlesey House, 1950.

Linati, Carlo. "Wyndham Lewis." *Pegaso: Rassegna di Lettere e Arti* Part 2 (1929): 437–48.

The Little Review. "Brancusi Number," 8 (Autumn 1921).

The Little Review. "Picabia Number," 8 (Spring 1922).

McLuhan, Marshall. "Lewis's Prose Style." In *Wyndham Lewis: A Revaluation.* Ed. Jeffrey Meyers. London: The Athlone Press, 1980.

Mangan, Sherry. "A Note: On the Somewhat Premature Apotheosis of T. S. Eliot." *Pagany* 1 (Spring 1930): 23–36.

Mariani, Paul. *William Carlos Williams: A New World Naked.* New York: Mc-Graw-Hill, 1981.

Marinetti, F. T. "Art and the State—VI. Italy." *The Listener* 16, no. 2 (14 October 1936): 730–32.

Martinelli, Sherri. *La Martinelli.* Intro. by Ezra Pound. Milan: Vanni Scheiwiller, 1956.

Masai, François. *Plethon et Le Platonisme de Mistra.* Paris: L'Association Guillaume Budé, 1956.

Meyers, Jeffrey. *The Enemy: A Biography of Wyndham Lewis.* London: Routledge & Kegan Paul, 1980.

Michel, Walter. *Wyndham Lewis: Paintings and Drawings.* Berkeley and Los Angeles: University of California Press, 1971.

Milhaud, Gaston. *Les Philosophes-Géométres de la Grec.* Paris: Alcan, 1900.

Mizener, Arthur. *The Saddest Story: A Biography of Ford Madox Ford.* New York and Cleveland: World Publishing, 1971.

Morrow, Bradford and Bernard Lafourcade. *A Bibliography of the Writings of Wyndham Lewis.* Santa Barbara, Calif.: Black Sparrow Press, 1978.

Mullins, Eustace. *This Difficult Individual, Ezra Pound.* New York: Fleet Publishing Corporation, 1961.

Nietzsche, Friedrich. *Joyful Wisdom.* Trans. Thomas Common. London: T. N. Foulies, 1910.

The Nursing Mirror: Pocket Encyclopaedia and Diary. London: Faber and Faber, 1936.

Olson, Charles. *Seletced Writings of Charles Olson.* Ed. Robert Creeley. New York: New Directions, 1951.

Picabia, Francis. *Jésus-Christ Rastaquouère.* Paris? 1920?

———. *Pensées sans Langage: Poème.* Paris: E. Figuière, 1919.

Plotinus. *Enneads.* 2d. ed. Trans. Stephen MacKenna. London: Faber and Faber, 1956.

Pound, Omar and A. Walton Litz. *Ezra Pound and Dorothy Shakespear: Their Letters 1909–1914.* New York: New Directions, 1984.

Pound, Omar and Philip Grover. *Wyndham Lewis: A Descriptive Bibliography.* Folkestone, Kent: Wm. Dawson, 1978.

Quinn, Sister M. Bernetta, O.S.F. "Ezra Pound and the Metamorphic Tradition." *The Western Review* 15 (Spring 1951): 169–81.

Rachewiltz, Mary de. *Discretions.* Boston: Little, Brown and Co., 1971. London: Faber and Faber, 1971.

Raine, Kathleen. "Il Miglior Fabbro." *The New Statesman and Nation,* 40 (25 November 1950): 510–12.

Read, Forrest, ed. *Pound/Joyce.* New York: New Directions, 1967. London: Faber and Faber, 1968.

————. '76: One World and The Cantos of Ezra Pound. Chapel Hill: University of North Carolina, 1981.

Reid, B. L. The Man from New York: John Quinn and His Friends. New York: Oxford, 1968.

Rothenstein, John. Brave Day, Hideous Night: Autobiography, 1939–1965. London: Hamish Hamilton, 1966.

Russell, Peter, ed. Ezra Pound: A Collection of Essays. London: Peter Nevill Limited, 1950; published in the United States by New Directions as An Examination of Ezra Pound: A Collection of Essays (Norfolk, CT., 1950).

Ruthven, K. K., ed. A Guide to Ezra Pound's Personae. Berkeley and Los Angeles: University of California Press, 1969.

Santayana, George. Dominations and Powers, 1951. New York: Charles Scribner's Sons, 1951.

————. The Letters of George Santayana. Ed. Daniel Cory. New York: Charles Scribner's Sons, 1955.

Schamberg, Morton L. "Philadelphia's First Exhibition of Advanced Modern Art, May 17th to June 15th, 1916."

Scheiwiller, Vanni, ed. Iconografia italiana di Ezra Pound. Milan: All'Insegna del Pesce d'Oro, 1955.

Seelye, Catherine, ed. Charles Olson and Ezra Pound: An Encounter at St. Elizabeths. New York: Viking Press, 1975.

Stock, Noel, ed. Ezra Pound: Perspectives. Chicago: Henry Regnery, 1965.

————. The Life of Ezra Pound. New York: Pantheon Books, 1970.

Stokes, Hugh. "Leaders of Modern Movements," The Ladies' Field (9 January 1915): 280–83.

Thompson, Denys. "The Robber Barons." Scrutiny 5 (June 1936): 2–12.

Uberti, Ricardo M. degli. "Why Pound Liked Italy." In Sophokles, Women of Trachis, trans. Ezra Pound. London: Neville Spearman, 1956.

Varé, Daniele. The Two Imposters. London: Murray, 1949.

Wagner, Geoffrey. "Wyndham Lewis and the Vorticist Aesthetic." The Journal of Aesthetics and Art Criticism 13 (September 1954): 1–17.

Wees, William C. Vorticism and the English Avant-Garde. Manchester: Manchester University Press, 1972.

Whistler, James McNeill. The Gentle Art of Making Enemies. New York: Dover Publications, 1967. (Originally published 1892.)

Williams, William Carlos. The Autobiography of William Carlos Williams. New York: Random House, 1951.

————. Selected Essays. New York: Random House, 1954.

————. The Selected Letters of William Carlos Williams. Ed. John C. Thirlwall. New York: McDowell, Obolensky, 1957.

————. "With Forced Fingers Rude." Four Pages (February 1948): 1–4.

Wistar, Owen. Philosophy 4: A Story of Harvard University. New York: Macmillan, 1903.

Woolf, Virginia. The Letters of Virginia Woolf, IV: 1929–31. Ed. Nigel Nicolson. London: The Hogarth Press, 1978.

Yeats, W. B. The Collected Poems. New York: Macmillan, 1960.

Zapponi, Niccolò. L'Italia di Ezra Pound. Rome: Bulzone Editore, 1976.

Glossarial Index

Letters are referred to by number and introductions by page number. Entries contain glosses only when needed to supplement annotations to the letters.

à Beckett, Captain Pat, 42–43
Abercrombie, Lascelles (1881–1938, English poet, critic, and professor), 155, 162
Abyssinia, 160
Académie Française, 201, 202n
Accademia Musicale Chigiana, 216
Action: For King and People (a journal of the British Union of Fascists, 1936–40), 221
Adam, 192, 241
Adamic, Louis (1899–1951, American popular writer), 227
Adams, Brooks (1848–1927, American historian), 202, 220
Adams, John (U.S. President, 1797–1801), 236, 252, p. vii
Adams, Mrs., 1n
Adelphi (periodical), 115
Adelphi Press, 72n
Adler, Mortimer (University of Chicago professor, 1930–52; assoc. editor of "The Great Books of the Western World" series), 217
After Strange Gods (Eliot), 238n
Agassiz, Louis (1807–73, Swiss-born American naturalist), 221–22
Agresti, Olivia Rossetti (Italian social commentator and Pound's friend; daughter of pre-Raphaelite W. M. Rossetti), 249
Aldington, Richard (1892–1962, English Imagist poet and novelist), 243, 245
Alexander the Great (356–323 B.C.), 221
Alfonso XIII (King of Spain, 1886–1930; refused to abdicate after Republican election victories in 1931, but forced to leave Spain and died in exile), 160
Alpert, Barry S., 138n
Alvarado, J. M. A., 219
Amaral, José Vásquez (translated *The Pisan Cantos* into Spanish), 246
American Mercury (periodical), 252
American Society for Aesthetics, 240
Anderson, Margaret (founder and editor of *The Little Review*, 1914–29), 232
Andréadès, Andre M., 236
Angold, J. P. (1909–43, poet and artist; killed in action with the Royal Air Force), 180
Antheil, George (1900–59, American avant-garde composer), 117, 133
Anthologie de l'humour noir (Breton), 208
Apollinaire, Guillaume (1880–1918, Parisian poet and art critic), 110, 208
Apple (Of Beauty and Discord) (periodical), 103
Aquila Press, 145n, 216
Aquinas, St. Thomas (1225?–74), 41n, 192n, p. 306
Arbuthnot, Matthew (1874–1967, photographer, signed the Vorticist Manifesto), 2
Areopagitica (Milton), 195
Aristotle (384–322 B.C.), 41n, 192n, 251
"Art and the State—VI. Italy" (Marinetti), 156n
Arthur Press, 145
Artwork (periodical), 125

172, 180–81, 186–88, 192, 195–98, 200–01, 203, 205–06, 209, 211, 215–18, 221, 236, 238, 241–42, 244, 247, 249–50, p. vii, p. ix, pp. xii–xv, p. 5, p. 122, p. 124, p. 143, p. 225, pp. 227–28

Ellis, Henry Havelock (1859–1939, English writer on the psychology and sociology of sex), 124

Eluard, Paul (1895–1952, French poet associated with the Dadaist and Surrealist movements), 184

Emery, Clark (author of *Ideas into Action: A Study of Pound's Cantos,* 1958), 236

Empedokles (Pre-Socratic philosopher), 238

"The End of a Perfect Day" ("A Perfect Day," words and music by Carrie Jacobs Bond; written in 1910 by an American, the song was an enormous success in both American and English music halls), 83, 85

Enemy: A Review of Art and Literature (ed. Lewis, 1927–29), 143, p. 122

The Enemy: A Biography of Wyndham Lewis (Meyers), 168n

The English Novel (Ford), 236

English Review (ed. Ford Madox Ford, 1908–10), 160n, 198, p. 3

The Enneads (Plotinus), 250, 251n

Epstein, Sir Jacob (1880–1959, pioneered the use of abstract and primitive forms in modern sculpture), 2, 66, 74, 195, 200

Equestrian Portrait of Philip IV (Velázquez), 171n

Etchells, Frederick (1886–1973, Vorticist painter), 56–57, 114, p. 4

Euclid (3rd Cent. B.C.), 221

European Jungle (Yeats-Brown), 180

Evans, Luther (Librarian of Congress at the time the Bollingen Foundation prize was given for *The Pisan Cantos*), 234, 236n

Evening Standard, 181

The Evolution of Physics (Infeld), 241

The Execution of Maximilian (Manet), 117n

Exile (ed. Ezra Pound, 1927–28), 138n, 236, p. 200

Ezra Pound: A Bibliography (Gallup), 38n, 142n, 165n

Ezra Pound: A Collection of Essays (Russell, ed.), 177n, 212n, 218n, 247n

Ezra Pound and Music (Schafer, ed.), 216n

"Ezra Pound and the Metamorphic Tradition" (Quinn), 219n

Ezra Pound and the Visual Arts (Zinnes, ed.), 103n, 108n, 117n, 133n, 151n, 156n

"Ezra Pound, John Price, and *The Exile*" (Alpert), 138n

Ezra Pound: The Critical Heritage (Homberger, ed.), 190n

Faber and Faber (publisher), 152, 156, 163, 172, 180–81, 188, 215n, 245, 249–50

Facts Forum (probably the NBC radio talk show *American Forum of the Air*), 252

Fascist Quarterly, 156, 163n

Feast, Rev. Willis, 230n

Fenollosa, Ernest (1853–1908, art critic and Orientalist), 221n

Ferdinand, King, 21

Ferrieri, Enzo (editor of *Il Convegno,* Milan), 109–10

Le Feu: Journal d'une Escouade (Barbusse), 81–82

Le Figaro (newspaper), 85

Firmage, George, 187n

Fitz Gerald, Desmond (1890–1947, Irish revolutionary politician), 217

Fitzgerald (*World Review*), 217

Fjelde, Rolf (founding editor of *Yale Poetry Review,* 1945–49), 219

Flannigan, Mr. (possibly a music hall character), 49

Fletcher, John (1579–1625), 192n

Flight of the Dragon (Binyon), 2n
Fontenelle, Bernard le Bovyer de, p. xii
Ford, Ford Madox (1873–1939), 50, 55, 111, 116, 180–81, 190, 198–99, 207, 218, 227, 236, 252n, p. xii, p. 3, pp. 65–66, p. 225
Ford Foundation, 247
Fordham University, 183
Forget-Me-Not (periodical), 98
Forgotten Kingdom (Goullart), 250
Forssell, Lars, 234, 236n
Foster, Mrs. Jeanne R. (friend and assistant of John Quinn), 250
Foster, Mrs., 1n
Four Pages (periodical), 195n, 196n, 198, p. xv
Fowler, Mrs., 1n
Fox, C. J., 86n, 108n, 211n
Francesca. See Piero della Francesca.
Frank, Joseph, 137
Frank, Waldo David (1889–1967, novelist and social critic), 137
Fraser, C. Lovat, 163
Frazer, Sir James (1854–1941, Scottish anthropologist and author of *The Golden Bough*), 124
French, Gloria, 229
French, Luke Ezra, 229
French, William, 229
Freud, Sigmund (1856–1939), 184, 224, p. xiv
Frobenius, Leo (1873–1938, German anthropologist, authority on prehistoric art and culture), 143n, 147, 184, 208–09
Fry, Roger (1866–1934, art critic and painter, promoter of French Post-Impressionism), 11n, 34, 50, 106n, p. 4
Fuchs (possibly Werner Fuchs, editor of *Poland's Policy of Expansion as Revealed by Polish Testimony*, 1932), 180
Furioso: A Magazine of Verse, 184n
Futurism, 156n, p. 5

Galdos. See Pérez Galdós.
Galileo Galilei (1564–1642), 184
Gallimard (publisher), 238
Gallup, Donald, 38n, 142n, 165n
Galsworthy, John (1867–1933, Edwardian novelist and dramatist), 180
Galton, Rev. Arthur (1852–1921), 38
Gaudier-Brzeska, Henri (1891–1915, French sculptor, one of the original Vorticists), 7, 38, 49n, 97, 99n, 183, 200, 207–08, 215, 221, 247, pp. xii–xiii, pp. 3–5, p. 41, p. 66
Gautier, Théophile (1811–72, French Romantic poet whose style in *Émaux et Camées* influenced Pound), 192
Gemistus Plethon (1355?–1450, Byzantine Neo-Platonist philosopher), 252
Gentile, Giovanni (1875–1944, Italian Idealist philosopher; Minister of Education in the Fascist government of Italy, 1922–24), 225
Gentle Art of Making Enemies (Whistler), 171n
George V (reigned 1910–36), 98n, 159
George VI (reigned 1936–52), 162, 200n
George Washington Carver Foundation, 247